D0948302

Rural Revolution in South China

Rural Revolution in South China

Peasants and the Making of History in Haifeng County, 1570-1930

Robert Marks

The University of Wisconsin Press

The University of Wisconsin Press
114 North Murray Street
Madison, Wisconsin 53715

The University of Wisconsin Press, Ltd.
1 Gower Street
London WC1E 6HA, England

First printing

Printed in the United States of America

For LC CIP information see the colophon

ISBN 0-299-09530-4

To Carrie and Rob

CONTENTS

MAPS AND TABLES

PREFACE

THIS STUDY arose because of my dissatisfaction with existing approaches to the study of China's rural revolution. Nearly all interpretations place its origins anywhere but in the rural society. The origins are sought in ideology, urban politics, Communist organization, fortuitous waves of peasant nationalism, or elite Communist policy and mobilization tactics. These seemed to me to be strange places to look for the causes and origins of rural revolution. Why not look to the rural areas themselves?

With one recent exception, studies of China's rural revolution have paid scant attention to the processes of change in rural society. The few that have included rural social structure in their analysis have relegated it to "background," along with the flora and fauna. This neglect is attributable in part to the conventional wisdom conveyed by the few existing studies of China's rural society and economy that there was no relationship whatsoever between rural socioeconomic relationships and conditions, and rural revolution. This is reinforced by definitions of the problem that place explaining Chinese Communist success at the forefront, rather than understanding the process of rural revolution.

The resulting conspiracy of silence is deafening in its message: no connection exists between rural revolution and rural social structure in China. This study challenges that view. It places the process of rural socioeconomic change squarely at the center of the inquiry into the origins of rural revolution.

The method chosen is that of a local study, focusing on Haifeng county in South China, the site of China's first rural soviet. As many China scholars now recognize, local studies allow the depth of study into the several layers of human experience and historical reality that phenomenon as complex as revolution demand—and that the diversity of China inhibits.

The criteria for defining "local" vary among social scientists studying China. Some have chosen to study political units smaller than the nation-state on the grounds that, in the words of one practitioner, the Qing dynastic "administrative system allowed considerable autonomy to the provinces," while G. William Skinner has divided China into nine regional socio-economic "macrosystems." As the reader will become aware, "Haifeng county" is just a shorthand term for what is as much a socioeconomic system as a political entity.

I chose Haifeng not because I had a particular theory about revolution to test, but because in the 1920s peasant attacks on landlords and the established political elite there paved the way for China's first rural soviet. In the four short months of that soviet's existence (November 1927–February 1928), peasants seized the land from their lords, redistributed it, and killed any lords who resisted the establishment of the new social order. The Haifeng Soviet was crushed in March 1928, not because of a lack of peasant support, but because of overwhelming military opposition. Haifeng county seemed to me to present a wonderful opportunity to examine not only the process of rural revolution, but also to learn something about the society out of which it emerged. Indeed, I was intrigued by the question of the origins and development of the society that the peasants of Haifeng were so intent on destroying. Why did they do it? What was it in that particular social order that the peasants found so abhorrent that it deserved nothing less than a sentence of death?

Since Haifeng was not known for a tradition of rebellion, the answers could not be sought by looking for forerunners or for an environment that continually produced rebellion, as others have done. What could explain it? Simply put, I looked for answers that were historical—historical in the sense of the long-term view articulated by Fernard Braudel. Detailed attention to the contours of Haifeng's rural social history over these centuries of slow development makes it apparent that the revolutionary movement of the 1920s did not spring full-blown, Minerva-like, from the head of Communist organizers, but grew organically from rural soils.

Preface

While I am interested in explaining the radical 1920s, that is not the sole or even the primary purpose of this study. This is also an exploration into rural social history. As Mark Bloch once observed, "Just as the progress of a disease shows a doctor the secret life of a body, so to the historian the process of a great calamity yields valuable information about the nature of the society so stricken." If understanding rural institutions such as land tenure and marketing systems helps us explain what happened in the 1920s, so too does that "great calamity," to borrow Bloch's term, make the social history of Haifeng more accessible to us. What is interesting and historically significant is the connection between the two.

To ground the actions of Haifeng's peasants in the rural social order and in its historical development—to show the specific strands of historical continuity—is the purpose of this study. The broader social history of Haifeng county is provided not merely as background information to the revolutionary 1920s; neither is the soviet treated as just one episode in the ups and downs in the chronicle of a Chinese county—for that any county would have sufficed. With the revolutionary movement, Haifeng has its own compelling and unique history. So in this study I have listened to the resonance between the two—between the broader social history and the unique moment—to interpret the era that produced them both.

This is social history with a small *s*. It makes no attempt to chronicle all the details of rural life. Literacy, food consumption, types of housing and furniture, dress, childhood and childrearing, or women and the family—all of these and more—are eminently worthy of study on their own account, and together would provide a start of the history of society. Perhaps someday we will be ready to write that history. The focus here is more narrowly limited to social relations between rural producers and others in the society who wielded wealth and power. For it is knowledge of these social relations and the forms they took over extended periods of time that provides tools for understanding social and historical change in rural China.

Thanking the many people who touched my life while I was writing this book, in an acknowledgment page, is a painfully inadequate means of expressing my sincere gratitude for their encouragement, support, and tolerance. These brief remarks should not be taken as a gauge of the depth of my appreciation. My greatest intellectual debt is to Maurice Meisner, a friend, teacher, and colleague, who supervised the dissertation this book is based on, and who more than any other person gave me a sense of historical processes. Edward Friedman and James C. Scott have read and critiqued various drafts, and shared with me their insights into peasant societies and their wonderful feel for the human condition. Joseph Esherick, Elizabeth Perry, Angus McDonald, and an anonymous reader commented extensively on the penultimate draft. Gregory Woirol and Richard Archer brought a comparative perspective when reading the draft manuscript. Brother Henry Pang, a warm, generous, and open human being, shared with me his family's history and arranged for me to visit Haifeng. Meeting him and making a great friend was one of the joys of this project. The Committee of Concerned Asian Scholars constituted a supportive community of scholars with whom I could share ideas. Special thanks go to Carolyn Moser, my editor, whose comments and queries on nearly every page sharpened my prose and argument. Institutions also helped: the original doctoral research was supported by a Fulbright-Hayes Doctoral Research Fellowship; the Universities Service Centre provided a stimulating environment to work in Hong Kong; and support from the Randolf and Dora Haynes Foundation allowed me to use the summers of 1980 and 1982 for final writing. Finally, and most important, I want to thank my wife Carrie and son Rob for reminding me of the other important things in life. These wonderful people helped me avoid mistakes and questionable interpretations; those that remain are my own.

INTRODUCTION

TO UNDERSTAND revolutions, we need to understand social structures.[1] Analyses of the Chinese revolution, however, more often than not ignore structural questions and focus instead on the revolutionary elite or on the politics of revolution. History in these accounts becomes past politics. This is true not only of modern adherents of "organizational weapon" theories, but also of more sympathetic treatments of the Chinese revolution.[2] To focus on revolutionary ideas (Marxism or the thoughts of Mao), or on the practice of the Communist party, implicitly lends those elements primary place in explaining social movements and revolutions, ignoring the role of common people in the making of their own history.

This perspective is being challenged by an emerging body of work that sees revolutionary movements (and other less spectacular forms of collective action) arising out of the more common patterns of everyday life created by class and other social group relations.[3] This suggests shifting attention from elites to the common people—in China's case, from the Communist party to the peasants. The agenda for research then is set on questions of rural social structure and process, rather than on the intent of revolutionary elites. This is a healthy corrective. In fact, one recent study goes so far as to eschew all such "voluntarist" explanations of revolution and to deny that ideology or the conscious actions of revolutionaries in themselves have any causal relationship to revolution whatsoever.[4]

This is not true of the prevailing interpretations of the Haifeng "peasant movement" and Soviet of the 1920s, both of which are attributed to the political insight and organizational abilities of a young intellectual, Peng Pai. Curiously, this interpretation is shared by American social science and Chinese Marxist scholarship. Both conceive of a peasant movement beginning when Peng Pai goes into the villages to organize peasants. The only question seems to be how he had arrived at that rather novel idea. The question of prior structural changes in the rural society creating new peasant experiences and social organization is never broached. Instead, assumptions about peasants and the nature of rural society take the place of historical analysis.

Chinese accounts mostly assume that the Haifeng peasants were exploited (and probably always had been) by a class of landlords, whose origin and development is likewise assumed. Peasants needed only Communist organization and correct ideas to become revolutionary, and these were supplied by Peng Pai.[5] The major American authority, Roy Hofheinz, Jr., on the other hand, assumes that peasants were easily malleable and that Peng Pai, by virtue of his organizing genius, was able to exploit "cleavages" in the countryside and mobilize peasants in struggles in which they presumably had no interest.[6] A peasant movement in this version was purely and simply a creation of outside organizers: to Hofheinz, it was the *Chinese Communist* peasant movement, not the *peasants'* peasant movement. Both Chinese and American approaches are elitist ones that see the problem of peasant revolution from the top down. This is not surprising in American social science; it is a bit more disconcerting in supposedly Marxist analysis.

Conventional wisdom about the Haifeng peasant movement is firmly grounded within the tradition of scholarship which ignores peasants and the social structures which patterned peasant life, preferring instead to explain revolutionary movements in terms of leadership and organization. This is explainable in part because the sources for the study of leadership and organization are more accessible. Rectifying the top-down approach to understanding revolution hence is partly a methodological one of investigating peasant society and economy. That is not an easy task, because the archival sources in China are still closed,[7] and because the sources for the study of socioeconomic structures are not all that obvious in any event. Documents generated for other purposes must be "coaxed" in order to learn anything at all about rural society and economy.[8] Travelers down this path need to beware: the way has yet to be clearly marked, and it is still filled with stumbling blocks, some of which are known and others of which still lie hidden.

Not surprisingly, very little work has been done on China's rural society and economy. And that which exists is not much help in understanding the Chinese revolution in general or the Haifeng movement in particular. Rawski, for instance, surely is correct in observing that "the Chinese peasant remains largely an unreconstructed figure in the secondary literature, too ignorant to improve his lot, and too oppressed by poverty to have the means, even if he had the knowhow, to do so."[9] But from this irrational being, Rawski transforms the Chinese peasant into utilitarian man pursuing economic self-interest. Chen and Myers build on this conception by showing how individual peasants negotiated contracts—presumably the rules governing individual behavior—to protect and further their individual interests.[10] How interests arise and how they are related to group interaction in class and kin are never asked. These are important problems and will be raised here.

The message from both those who have studied the revolutionary movement and those who have looked into the rural economy and society is consistent: there is no connection whatsoever between rural socioeconomic structures and the revolutionary movement. Some have even devised statistical tests that show an insignificant correlation between isolated socioeconomic factors and what is called "Communist success."[11] The bankruptcy of such an approach that separates "factors" from their historical and social contexts in order to measure some ill-defined "Communist success" is only beginning to be shown.[12]

It is my hope that this study will contribute to a new approach that defines the problem of understanding revolution in terms of the society in which it occurs. Such an approach must first of all be *historical*. This is necessary in order to show the slow, almost imperceptible development of social and economic structures which alone make the more visible "headlines from the past" intelligible. Historical analysis, according to some, is divided into two great camps: those who see history primarily in terms of structure ("structuralist" explanations) and those who see history in terms of human intention ("voluntarist" explanations). Often the advocates sit on opposite sides of a fence tossing taunts and jibes at each other, demanding that everyone else choose one side or the other. If this problematic is adopted, fence-sitting is not an acceptable academic pastime.[13] But what these partisans do not realize is that the side they have chosen is merely one aspect of the contradictory nature of historical reality. The reality is not which side of the fence you are on, but the fence itself. Fernand Braudel makes this point much more elegantly. The point of historical study, according to Braudel, is understanding the relationship between structure and volition (between submerged and conspicuous history, in his words). He sees this relationship as one of fundamental contradiction, not to be decried or made the object of partisan academic warfare, but to be used as a "vital tool of knowledge and research."[14] I agree.

Braudel divides historical time into three layers "of overlapping histories, developing simultaneously": geographic time, or the history of man in his relationship to the environment; social time, or the history of social groups and structures; and individual time, or the history of events, those "surface disturbances, crests of foam that the tides of history carry on their strong backs."[15] This study concerns the latter two kinds of time and tries to understand how in rural Haifeng they are connected. We shall take the long-term view of the social and economic structures that patterned the lives of peasants in Haifeng county from the mid-seventeenth-century Ming-Qing disturbances to the peasant movement and soviet of the 1920s.

Where Braudel's work informs the historical orientation of this study, recent work by Charles Tilly and others on collective action suggests important ways to understand the connections between social structure and human action, or between structuralism and voluntarism, if you will. Tilly has provided a taxonomy of collective action theories classified according to four general lines of argument identified with nineteenth- and twentieth-century figures: John Stuart Mill, Emile Durkheim, Max Weber, and Karl Marx. Mill's utilitarian approach seeks the roots of collective action in the individual's pursuit of self-interest; the Durkheimian approach tends to explain collective action as individual responses to social disintegration; Weber and Weberians look at collective action as the outgrowth of a commitment to common beliefs that often have their origin and articulation in the vision of a charismatic leader; and Marxists characteristically see collective action arising from the commonalities of interest based on social class.[16]

Analysts of revolution consciously or unconsciously draw upon these theoretical perspectives in order to define questions, order data, and make arguments. Those in the Durkheimian tradition focus research on social disequilibrium and the reintegrative efforts of elites; those in the Millian school concentrate on the determinants of individual decisions; Weberians look at the origins of belief systems and their routinization; and those in the Marxist tradition focus on questions of social class relationships and structures.[17]

Recent work that places rebellion and revolution within the context of social structure and the consequent patterns of group behavior has opened up new areas for investigation, suggested new lines of inquiry, and provided new perspectives. The results so far have been impressive. Not surprisingly, these analyses draw heavily on Marxist perspectives in understanding how collective action emerges from preexisting groups: primarily, but not exclusively, social classes that have historically defined interests and patterns of acting together. This study too is placed firmly within the Marxist tradition, with questions of class and class relations at the center of the inquiry. Hence I begin with an analysis of the historical origins of the rural class relations that dominated Haifeng for three centuries (Chapter 1–2) and of the exchange and social relations embedded in marketing structures (Chapters 3–4).

Attention to social structure should not be taken as structural determinism. There are those who argue, for instance, that certain forms of agrarian structures lead inexorably to equally certain forms of rural social movements. In this formulation, classes, individuals, political parties, and ideologies are swept along willy-nilly by the logic of the class structure chemistry.[18] But history is too rich and raggedy to be so neatly tied together. We are always surprised by this turn and that twist. The problem with structural determinism is that it sees structures as causes, leaving out an account through time of unique events and eliminating the role of people in the making of their own history.[19] History becomes "process *without* a subject."[20]

Here it will not. Robert Brenner has argued that while class structures may impose "strict limits and possibilities" on a society's long-term development, class structures posit only certain classes, not specific historical outcomes. According to Brenner, historical outcomes are dependent on the patterns of class development and relative class strength, influenced by internal solidarity, organization, and self-consciousness of the contending classes.[21] E. P. Thompson put it a bit differently when he argued that social class is something more than social structure: "By class I understand a historical phenomenon, uniting a number of disparate and seemingly disconnected events, both in the raw material and in consciousness. I emphasize that it is a *historical* phenomenon. I do not see class as a 'structure,' nor even as a 'category,' but as something which in fact happens (and can be shown to have happened) in human relationships."[22]

Experience, from this perspective, is important in the perception and articulation of class interest. Expressed in culturally derived terms, human experience provides the link between social structure and collective action. History becomes "process *with* a subject." E. P. Thompson and James C. Scott argue that for preindustrial societies, this experience is culturally expressed as the "moral economy" of the poor or of the peasant.[23] The concept of the "moral economy" refers to a class-based value system of popular beliefs about fair prices, just practices, and proper social norms that provided peasants with an impressive solidarity against outside threats to their subsistence. It is not that reference to the moral economy is a "voluntarist" explanation of why peasants took the actions they did, but why, *given* certain class relations, they might have. This puts the issue of peasant *mentalities* into a structural and historical context. This issue is raised first in Chapter 4, where the concept of moral economy of the peasant is introduced, and is then taken up in subsequent chapters.

What is most noticeable about the forms of social conflict in Haifeng is how dramatically they change from the nineteenth century to the twentieth. During the eighteenth and nineteenth centuries, factional feuds and rice riots were the characteristic forms of rural social conflict. But in the 1920s, Haifeng was ripped apart in class conflict. To the extent that forms of collective action are "intimately dependent on the structures of everyday life" (according to the Tillys), it follows that new forms of collective action should arise from "changes in the structure of everyday life and in the structure of power."[24] In Haifeng, what had changed and how?

In a word, imperialism. Surprisingly, however, the relationship between imperialism and rebellion and revolution is only dimly understood. This is partially because imperialism is located in a problematic that sees China's probable course of national development in the nineteenth and twentieth centuries as the central issue, rather than revolution, and because debate is framed in terms of the imperialist "impact" and China's "response."[25]

In literature on imperialism in China, the issue is not whether China was undeveloped. That is taken for granted by all sides. The debate, rather, is over its causes and which social systems or strategies were best suited for "development," "growth," or "modernization," as the process is variously called. One side in the debate, which can be loosely identified with modernization theory, has concluded that the impact of imperialism on China was on the whole beneficent. It furthered economic specialization and began to define China's "comparative advantage" in the modern system of nation-states. Whatever problems China faced on the road to modernization, according to this perspective, were internal ones that prevented further borrowing from the West, whether in the realm of culture, political infrastructure, or technology. This is seen as a "failure" to respond to the West, and its causes are located in various areas, from the state and elite politics to an economic "high level equilibrium trap." The rational response to imperialism, if any was needed, from this perspective, was reform; revolution was an irrational and unnecessary response to the imperialist challenge.

The usual radical critique of modernization theory concludes that the impact of imperialism was not beneficent. Economic specialization for the world market, in this view, was leading, not to China's "comparative advantage," but to perpetual underdevelopment. As the imperialist presence increased, China's integration into the capitalist system led to dependence and chronic underdevelopment. From this perspective, China did not "fail" to respond, but responded in wholly expected ways. Moreover, the rational response to imperialism was not to lock China into dependent underdevelopment, but to devise a new strategy for development. This strategy required seizing state power, and was then accomplished through the Maoist tactic of People's War.

In this debate on imperialism, revolution is understood as a strategy of development that was either rational or irrational, depending on the theoretical framework in which it is placed. Here the difficulty becomes apparent: both modernization theory and its radical critique allow only those explanations of revolution that are completely voluntaristic.

The analysis to be put forward here challenges this approach to understanding imperialism. From the perspective of the problematic that locates social class relations as the central issue in understanding rural revolution, the significant questions to ask about imperialism are not whether it furthered or hindered China's development, but how imperialism affected rural class relations. Did imperialism strengthen certain classes to the disadvantage of others? Did the periodic crises of international capital affect rural class relations? Did imperialism create new social classes? These questions are addressed in Chapter 5 in an attempt to understand the changing forms of rural social conflict in Haifeng county.

Introduction

The 1911 Revolution also is important for understanding rural social conflict and patterns of peasant revolt in Haifeng. This may appear a rather banal observation, but the 1911 Revolution is seldom thought of in terms of peasant rebellion and revolution. Most studies focus on Sun Yat-sen and his co-conspirators, following them from Hawaii to London and periodically in forays into China, or on urban elites and urban socioeconomic processes, concluding that the 1911 Revolution was an urban revolution with little connection to the countryside. Like imperialism, the urban revolution is supposed to have had an "impact" on rural areas, which in turn reacted in various ways.[26]

The urban biases of these studies result in two obstacles to a fuller understanding of revolution. First, these views from the city perpetuate the "urban reformist elite's" conception of the 1911 Revolution as their own, reinforcing the myth that no other revolution was occurring or was possible. But one of the most interesting features of the 1911 Revolution, as is argued in Chapter 6, is that there was a "revolution in the revolution," to borrow Regis DeBray's term, in which people in the countryside put forward their own goals for the revolution that explicitly challenged those emanating from the city. In the end, of course, neither would prevail, but that does not obviate the point. Second, the urban biases of these studies minimize the importance of social structures that transcend the cities for understanding the dynamic of revolution. For if any structural phenomenon affected the outcome of the 1911 Revolution, and the subsequent power structure in Guangdong province, it was the division and antagonism between town and countryside. And yet it is just this structure that is missed by focusing on essentially urban movements and structures.

Structural analysis is an important part of historical explanation, but alone cannot explain why things turned out the way they did. Changes in China's position in the capitalist world economy, in rural class relations, and in systems of political power may account for part of the dramatic story of what happened in Haifeng county in the 1920s, but not all of it. It tells us who the players are; it doesn't give us the script. That peasant collective action in the 1920s took forms different from those of the nineteenth century is hardly surprising; but it must be explained. The reason, I suspect, is not merely because of structural change, but because new interests and forms of organization arose that directed the actions of peasants in new ways. The question is not *whether* new interests and organizations arose, but *how*.

The conventional wisdom, at least as far as Haifeng is concerned, is that outside leaders—in particular, Peng Pai and the Chinese Communist Party—provided the organizational skills, and to a lesser degree articulated interests through the Party's ideology. This is supposed to explain both the origins of peasant action and the relationship between peasants and their Communist leaders. This perspective sees a "peasant movement" created *ex nihilo* by outside organizers who manipulated peasants as pawns in a larger political chess game. As objects of history-making elites, peasants seen in this way cannot have had a hand in the making of their own history. Chapter 7 shows that this interpretation simply does not stand up to close scrutiny, and must be replaced by a perspective that relates peasant collective action to rural socioeconomic structure and to how peasants understood their interests, *before* any organizers arrive on the scene. It may be that outside leaders like Peng Pai had a role to play in articulating new interests for peasants, but this has to be explained from the peasants' perspective, not assumed as the organizational genius of an outsider.

This perspective has important consequences for understanding the relationship between peasants and their leaders. Work by Peter Worsley, and more recently by George Rudé and Carlo Ginzburg,[27] suggests an interactional approach to the creation and articulation of interest that sees peasants not as passive recipients of outside ideology and organization, but as active participants in a relationship in which the ideology and organization of the leaders are as much changed by peasants as vice versa. Readers of Chapter 8 may be surprised to find to what extent the peasants of Haifeng imposed their no-

Introduction

tions of organization on Peng Pai in a dramatic reversal of expected roles.

The Haifeng Soviet—that extraordinary moment in history when peasants and Communists in China for the first time carried out a land revolution, burning land deeds, distributing land, and killing or chasing away landlords—is spectacle that, like all spectacles, can captivate the observer. The soviet was the arena for intense passion on all sides. The defenders of the revolution tried to catch the ear of the progressive forces of the world, just as its enemies tried to enlist support for its suppression from abroad. The historian too can be captivated by the pleadings of the partisans and confuse their explanations or justifications for what happened with historical explanation. The participants may have believed they were launching the Chinese revolution on a new course, and later analysts may suppose that the Haifeng Soviet provides the key to unlock the secrets of the later and successful tactics of "People's War." As Chapter 9 suggests, we should be skeptical of these claims.

Certainly a local study places restrictions on the ability to generalize about the historical and social continuum known as China. Haifeng county was no more "typical" of China than was Wallachia of Europe or is Iowa of the United States. But that does not mean that a local study cannot raise and examine issues of historical interpretation which transcend geographic and temporal boundaries. Even if the inhabitants of Haifeng county were not typical of China, they were nonetheless "ordinary"—ordinary people who would have gone unnoticed by historians were it not for the quite extraordinary moment of the 1920s. What lends the Haifeng Soviet its special significance, then, is that it occurred among otherwise ordinary people who had an otherwise ordinary past. When we take this perspective, instead of one trying to fit the movement into the history of the Chinese Communist Party, or even into the process of China's twentieth-century revolution, we begin to realize how profound were the changes moving rural China, and how much a part of the making of modern China were the millions of largely illiterate rural people.

Rural Revolution in South China

CHAPTER 1

Late Ming Land Tenure Relations

RURAL Haifeng county by the early twentieth century looked much like the rest of rural China. The land was divided into numerous small plots surrounding villages often only a stone's throw away from each other. Peasant smallholders either owned their own land or rented it, and they and their families spent the days with their backs bent in the fields harrowing, fertilizing, planting, weeding, transplanting, tending, and harvesting. In Haifeng, where the climate was mild, usually three crops per year could be had from the same plot of land. Every three or four days the villagers could gather up some produce from their farms, and truck it into the nearby market town. They had to carry it on their backs or in a wheelbarrow, if they had one, because the main arteries consisted of paths trampled along the top of the narrow strips of land separating one field from the next. In the market town, peasants would sell some produce, pick up a bit of cash, and maybe buy some salt or oil needed for cooking. Whatever cash remained would be socked away to pay taxes. Depending on the season, some peasants also would tote rice and sometimes chicken or fish to pay the rent to landlords. This is what life was like for Haifeng peasants in the early twentieth century. It had been that way for their parents and grandparents. For all anybody could tell, it had probably always been that way. They were wrong.

Since China was—and still largely is—an agrarian society, it is often assumed that life for the rural inhabitants has been virtually unchanging throughout the centuries. The picture of a tradition-bound China, marred only by the periodic upheavals that characterized the "dynastic cycle," is the one most

3

commonly painted in standard histories. Rulers and dynasties might come and go, but life for the common people continued unaltered. Given this commonly accepted picture of a timeless China, it is easy to assume that the rural China of the twentieth century had existed more or less the same from time immemorial. It had not. Its particular social, economic, and cultural institutions had been created by people living their daily lives and fighting their numerous battles, large and small, against nature, each other, and outsiders, dating back to the last decades of the Ming dynasty (1368–1644). In order to understand the peasants of Haifeng—how institutions patterned their lives and how they in turn shaped these institutions—we need to take an overview of rural China during the Ming dynasty. Here we will discover the forces that continued to move and shake rural China well into the twentieth century.

Serfdom and the Ming Estate

The rural order of the Ming period, which itself was a continuation of earlier developments, was a manorial economy in ways comparable to that of feudal Europe. Landed estates were worked by various types of servile labor, ranging from serfs who were held like chattel slaves to tenants who owed rent and labor services to the lord. Free peasants led a precarious existence on the edge of servility. By contrast, in the agrarian landscape which took shape during the Qing dynasty, the large estates had disappeared. There was instead a class of freeholding peasants who tilled their own plots of land. This new rural order was not brought into being peacefully; it was accompanied by a considerable amount of violence when serfs and tenants rose up to throw off the yokes of their masters.

When Zhu Yuanzhang drove out the Mongols and proclaimed himself the first emperor of the new Ming dynasty in 1368, he gave landed estates to the new nobility he created.[1] Both nobility (*zhuangren*) and officials (*jinshen*) of the new state could legally hold serfs. The jinshen, or officials who had their names listed in the register of officials, often held as many as two thousand serfs, resulting in estates that were truly enormous. The estates of the nobility were even larger: one prince owned an estate with an annual income of 150,000 piculs of rice, another estate comprised 70 to 80 percent of the land around Changsha by the seventeenth century, and a Shandong estate was over 40,000 *mou*, or about 65,000 acres. While we do not know the percentage of all arable taken up by the estates, it is quite certain that the enserfment of free peasants intensified throughout the dynasty as commoners as well as nobility and officials came to hold serfs.[2]

Serfs held by nobility and commoners were known by a variety of terms. Serfs held by nobility were known as *nupu*, *nongpu*, and *dianpu*. Others were called *zhuangpu*, *dipu*, and *huodian*, all of which belonged to the legal category of *shipu*, or those of hereditary servile status. Regional variants were also widespread. Within Guangdong province, for example, there were several local equivalents of the term "serf." One traveler in Guangdong observed that "serfs [*nupu*] are called 'lesser little brother' [*dicai*]. In Huizhou prefecture [where Haifeng county was] they are called 'dependents' [*laizi*] because they are dependent on the lord." Another writer noted that in Guangdong "the sons of serfs are called 'lesser family born' [*jiashengcai*]. . . . In Xinhui county serfs are called 'planters' [*zhongcai*]. . . . In Xiangshan county, tenant households [*dianhu*] who perform labor services are called *renqing* [an untranslatable term]."[3]

But this plethora of names should not be too disturbing. In medieval Europe terms for essentially the same phenomena had also varied enormously from region to region, or even from village to village. For Europe, the variety is explicable because of the fragmented nature of political power. For a centralized state such as China, more uniformity might have been expected. During the seventeenth century in Russia, for example, serfdom attained a considerable degree of homogeneity with the promulgation of a legal code institutionalizing serfdom on a nationwide scale. In Ming China, however, the central state never recognized the legal right of persons other than the relatively few princes and meritorious officials to own serfs. It simply was not in the interest of the Chinese state to encourage the growth of estates—and thus independent power-bases—by extending the franchise to hold serfs to commoners. Thus in China as in Europe, the number of local names for essentially the same thing varied greatly.[4]

Commoner lords often held serfs who were called "adopted sons" (*yizi*) in order to avoid the legal restrictions against holding serfs. As a Ming work on the conduct of family affairs cited by Mark Elvin noted: "The laws have provisions for making people enter official households to be serfs (as punishment for a crime), but how can the families of scholars and ordinary persons (legally) own serfs? For this reason serfs are called 'adopted sons' and female serfs are called 'adopted daughters-in-law.'"[5] Increasingly during the Ming, commoners also came to hold serfs through the practice of "commendation" (*touxian* or *toukao*), in which freeholding peasants entered into relations of dependency with a powerful household. Many of these powerful lords, of course, were privileged nobility or officials who were exempt from certain taxes and corvée labor demands. Peasants seeking protection against excessive taxation or labor demands thus sought to commend themselves and their families to these houses. But wealthy commoners too avoided these demands and thus also accepted commended peasants, as the Ming legal code suggests: "Those who accept commended families, except officials and nobility, will be punished." While early Ming emperors apparently enforced this law with considerable vigor, by the late Ming it was widely ignored.[6]

Freeholding peasants entered relations of dependency with a lord for a variety of reasons, such as inability to pay taxes or repay a personal debt, the need for housing, the location of ancestral gravelands on a lord's land, or marriage to a member of a hereditary tenant family. So many peasants had commended themselves by the late sixteenth and early seventeenth centuries that, according to an old saw quoted by one observer, "the lands of the rich lie end to end while the poor do not have enough land in which to stick an awl."[7] As peasants commended their lands, the tax base quite naturally shrank, increasing the tax burden on the remaining commoner landlords and freeholding peasants. Portuguese friars traveling in Guangdong province during the late sixteenth century were

6

told by "one Jacsui" that "there were seventy men in his household, and that he did not pay more taxes than for seven. Another told us there were about sixty in his, and that he only paid taxes for four."[8] Hence the official Ming history (compiled in the early Qing) recorded that "from the Hongwu reign [1368–99] to the Hongzhi reign [1488–1506], registered lands [for taxes] decreased by one half. This was especially so in Huguang [Hunan and Hubei], Henan, and Guangdong provinces."[9]

The lords, for their part, needed servile labor for social as well as economic reasons. When a peasant family entered into bonds of servitude, the family head often agreed not only to till the land but also to provide the lord with "wailing" services at funerals and labor at weddings, both socially necessary for any upstanding (or upstart) lord. The lord provided the commended peasant family with the means of production such as land, seed, and draft animals, besides food, lodging, and sometimes clothing. In return, the commended peasant agreed orally—initially at least—to become a hereditary tenant family on the lord's land. Others accepted servile status for a fixed period of time. As Peter Mundy, an English soldier of fortune, observed in 1637 of the region north of Aomen (Macao), "The poorer sort of Chineses [*sic*] [are seen] selling their Children to pay their Debtts or Maynetaine themselves . . . but with this conditions, as letting them to hire or bind them [as] servants For 30, 40, 50 yeare, and after that to bee Freed. Some sell them outrightt withoutt any Condition att all."[10]

Still others accepted servile status when taking a bondswoman for a wife. In return for a wife, one late-Ming peasant agreed to "look after and protect the gravelands, till the land, watch the fields and dikes, diligently serve, always come when beckoned, and never dare to run away."[11] Fu Yiling found many such bonds of servitude arising from marriage. But we should not assume that a man accepted servile status solely out of love for a woman. A better explanation is suggested by one contract which records that a peasant who was next to starvation agreed to work for the lord for twenty-two years in return for a wife. The taking of a lord's bondswoman for a

7

wife, it seems, was one way a destitute man could obtain a means of subsistence.

Bonds of servitude became contractual usually only after a peasant already had commended the family to hereditary servile status. If afterwards the family wanted to erect a new dwelling, for example, it had first to secure the lord's approval. A contract was then drawn up which stipulated that the family and its descendants would become hereditary tenants. The same practice prevailed when tenants needed burial grounds for their parents. Contractual bonds of servitude also arose if the tenant transgressed the customs of the estate, especially those which guaranteed the lord a labor force. When a runaway was captured, he or she had to sign a contract guaranteeing not to do it again. Similarly, if the lord discovered that a tenant had worked for wages or shares on another lord's land, the tenant agreed, as one contract phrased it, "to no longer, as was done before, hire yourself out to another. If this happens again, you will be punished by the lord." When a new lord acquired the land, again the tenants often had to sign a document affirming their hereditary servile status. The male tenants and serfs, however, could not sell themselves or their wives and children, and unlike slaves in some societies, they could not purchase their freedom.[12]

Lords also imposed other restrictions on their tenants. Tenants lacked the freedom to marry; to do so cost them two ounces of silver. They were not allowed to wear silk or satin or to wear the "big red hats" reserved for the wealthy. Tenants' lodgings and gravemarkers could not exceed a certain height, presumably lower than the lords'. The tenants' sons and daughters could not use the personal names of the lord or his ancestors; this "avoidance of names" (*bihui*) was strictly enforced. If a tenant struck a lord, he or she was beaten. But if a lord killed a tenant, no punishment was forthcoming if the lord could show that the deceased had "disobeyed orders."[13]

Nonetheless, not all tenants in hereditary servile status were kept in continuous economic dependence on the lord. Some even purchased land. Lords who treated their serfs and tenants somewhat better than did their neighbors may also have acted as a constraint on too strict enforcement of the bonds of servitude, for it was not unknown for runaways to commend themselves to another lord, who then offered them protection. And the lords knew the reasons for the willingness of peasants to flee, as one Ming family quoted by Mark Elvin discovered: "Once a family attains relatively comfortable circumstances it is necessary to keep male and female serfs. They rely on us for their upkeep, and we rely on them for their labour. Since they have their labour power, how should it be that they could not rely on others. To say that but for us they would have no means to survive is quite erroneous."[14]

Although an increasing number of peasants during the sixteenth century went in search of a lord-protector to whom to commend themselves and their families—perhaps at the cost of hereditary servile status—at the same time the lords of the land needed an expanding labor force to work their estates. For despite a general shortage of money, a market for grain was steadily growing. The price of rice rose steadily (except for two decades) from the early sixteenth to the mid-seventeenth century, providing an incentive for lords to produce grain for the market on their estates. In 1560 for example, an estate of 400,000 mou (over 65,000 acres) in Shandong province began to sell large amounts of grain in the market. Other estates also increased the amount of grain and other agricultural products marketed from the mid-sixteenth century on. Production on the estates could be increased because of a large and ready supply of labor. But the labor on these estates was not solely, or even predominantly, free labor. Neither was it supplied by free tenants. Rather, it was servile labor of varying types and degrees.[15]

Like European feudal estates, the Ming estate was composed of two main components: lands held in villeinage, or the plots of land tilled by peasant families, and the lord's home farm, or demesne. Although commended peasants tilled their own plots of land like tenants, both of whom owed rent and some types of labor services to the lord, Ming lords were not "merely" landlords: lords also held demesne arable worked by serf labor under their personal management. It was reported

9

that on the estate of the relative of a Ming official, for example, "her hundred serfs, young and old, male and female, would all come to report upon what they had been doing. . . . Her lands supported cattle by the hundreds, her streams bred fish and turtles by the picul, and her gardeners tended fruit, melons, mustard and vegetables by the tens of acres." The personal management of serf labor by the lords clearly refers to labor on the demesne: one lord "would supervise ploughing, sowing, cutting down undergrowth, dike-building, and the repair of irrigation ditches. . . . A program of work was laid out for each of the serfs he organized." The author of an early-seventeenth-century work on agriculture likewise mentioned that he allocated the serfs' duties.[16]

The demesne of the late Ming estate was in all probability compact, composed of fields, fish ponds, mulberry bushes, and garden crops clustered around the lord's manor. The manor itself was a complex which included the lord's residence, granaries, winnowing and threshing floors, and spinning and weaving facilities. The most important other estate properties not on the manor included water-powered mills and irrigation works. The lord of an estate near the city of Guangzhou, for example, implied that the demesne fields had to be sufficiently compact and close to the manor to be worked by gangs of serf and hired labor which he personally supervised.[17]

Wang Zhen's *Treatise on Agriculture (Nong shu)* provides a fairly good picture of the estate as it existed during the early Ming, and possibly much later as well. Wang described several kinds of fields, in some cases indicating the types of labor used on them. For *bu tian*, or gardens producing vegetables, fruit, and mulberry bushes, hired labor was employed. Wang also described *wei tian*, or enclosed fields, which were fields of several thousand mou enclosed by a fairly high and thick hard-packed mud wall surrounding the isolated manor of the lord. The *wei tian* and similarly laid out *jia tian*, or fields enclosed by bamboo-reinforced mud walls, undoubtedly constituted the larger part of the demesne. These fields, tilled by ox-drawn ploughs which could cover one hundred mou per day, were then weeded by teams of "husband-men" (*nongjia*), who

10

worked to the rhythm of a "weeding drum" (*haogu*) beaten by a "field headman" (*tian jiazhang*).[18]

The demesne of the Ming lord was worked by a specialized labor force composed of hired laborers (*gugong ren*) and serfs (*nupu*). Despite the two different names, there seems to have been little difference between them. On the Pang estate in Nanhai county in Guangdong during the late 1500s, the lord, Pang Shangpeng, often spoke of hired laborers and serfs in the same breath: "Hired laborers [*gugong ren*] and serfs [*tongpu*]: . . . . You must always give them food and drink, see whether they are hungry or cold, and give them leisure time."[19]

The lord of the Pang estate made general labor assignments on the basis of the serfs' ability to do different types of work. In his *Family Instructions*, Pang advised his heirs: "Thoroughly investigate how many male and female serfs there are, how many are fit for farming, how many are suitable to do the marketing, and how much food and clothing they need each year. Test each one's ability to work to see that they are suited for the task." The lord was equally conscientious in supervising the daily operation of the demesne. Pang Shangpeng wrote that "every night the serfs are to be directed what to do on the morrow and told when the task is to be completed. Their nightly reports should be checked to see if they were diligent or indolent. If you allow them to become lax and do not impede this tendency, our family's affairs will soon come to an end." On the other hand, Pang instructed his heirs to make sure the serfs were adequately fed, clothed, and housed, at least as far as prevailing standards for serfs went. Quoting a Tang dynasty poet, Pang told his heirs that "like you, this [serf] is another person's son. Treat him well." Pang felt that to get serfs to labor diligently, one must first know what pleased them; they would "then be loyal and faithful."[20]

The affairs of the Pang estate were under the careful management of the lord. Each year Pang Shangpeng took a census of the serf population and calculated the amount and types of crops to be grown. Annual planning on this scale obviously demanded that the lord have first-hand knowledge of the per capita consumption of grain, the yield of crops, and the amount

11

that could be marketed. It also suggests that there were more serfs on the manor than Pang could keep track of casually. The lord clearly took an active role in production as well. As Pang told his family: "The planting must be done under your supervision. Manage the rice harvest. Be extremely careful in calculating the taxes and corvée labor quota." The Pang lord may have participated in some types of manual labor, as the following warning suggests: "If you are afraid of labor and detest affairs, you must then rely on others for your eyes and ears. If you cannot distinguish beans from wheat, others will think you are stupid. If things are done like this, everything will become topsy-turvy."[21]

However much Pang Shangpeng may have wished otherwise, the entire estate was not under his personal supervision: Pang owned lands held in villeinage tilled by economically independent tenants. Pang was not entirely happy with this state of affairs, strongly implying that it was far more profitable to manage demesne production personally than to seek tenants: "When the fields lie scattered far and wide, they cannot be worked efficiently. You must then look for people and contract them as tenants. Investigation shows that the measure of strength is decided in favor of the old peasants." Pang thus laid considerable emphasis on keeping the estate as compact as possible. As he instructed his family, "Houses, buildings, fields, and ponds must not be broken up and sold."[22]

Even though demesne production may have been highly profitable, as Pang strongly suggested and as seems highly likely given the general rise in the price of rice, by all indications villeins did not perform agricultural labor for the lord on the demesne. Nevertheless, tenants such as those on the Pang estate did owe some types of labor services to the lord and were considered of servile status. Li Han, a Ming author, wrote in his *Treatise on Governance*: "Those who tenant fields and return rent for land, who are not the same as hired laborers, are commonly called tenants. They *therefore* perform labor services and pay rent. If the lord calls, even the wife must serve. The tenant does not dare to not comply."[23]

12

Others who entered servile status by the practice of commendation also were liable to perform labor services for the
lord. A bond of servitude dated 1623, for example, reads as
follows: "Zhangji, of Gangkou estate, being destitute, com-
mends himself to Zeng Laoye [address follows]. Zhangji enters
this estate by taking our Tianshou as his wife. He has willingly
asked that this contract be established. He will look after and
guard the gravelands, till the land, keep up the terraces, diligently serve, always come when beckoned, and never dare to
run away. . . . He will not dare to secretly sell the land which
he tills."[24] Other bonds of servitude indicate that commended
peasants were "to watch the tree nurseries," be night watch-
men, guard the lord's home and gardens, shoulder sedan chairs,
pole boats, clear the roads of grass, build houses, bury the
dead, and even "play music." These services varied, of course,
but whatever the demands on the peasants, they had "always
to obey, never to resist." Some bonds of servitude stipulated
the punishments for disobedience: ten strokes for not being
present to perform labor, twenty strokes for not replacing broken porcelain. Some even had to perform labor services for
several families. But most of the commended peasants' time
was spent on their separate parcels of land.[25]

Tenants and commended peasants had higher status than
serfs, but all were servile to varying degrees. Servility was
attached to the person of the serf, who could be bought and
sold; for tenants, servility was a condition of tenancy. Although
the state did not consider tenants to be of hereditary servile
status, as it did serfs, custom nevertheless dictated conditions
under which tenants were servile. Signing a contract of servility
obviously conferred servility, as did performing daily labor
service or receiving food and shelter from a lord. But even
without contractual bondage, tenants who simply tilled a lord's
fields, lived on a lord's land, and were interred on a lord's
estate were considered by customary law to be servile to that
lord. In short, the state did not have to institutionalize serfdom
in the legal code for servility to be a fact of life for tenants as
well. While the degree of servility differed for serfs and tenants

13

depending on how many of these conditions were met, both had "always to obey, never to resist" the demands of the lord.[26] In sum, servility in late Ming China covered a wide variety of social relations and human experiences ranging on a continuum from the nearly free to those held as chattel. On the one end were those whose servile status was a condition of tenancy. Tenants who owed certain types of labor service to a lord simply as a condition of tenancy were probably personally free to leave the lord and land, although evidence either way is lacking. On the other extreme were the legally owned serfs, who could be bought and sold without land by their lords. And somewhere in between lay the commended peasants, who had signed contracts of bondage.

The picture of the late Ming rural society and economy that emerges here differs from that painted in recent literature on the subject. Rawski argues that the existence of contracts of tenancy during the Ming shows that a free and equal relationship prevailed between lord and peasant.[27] The countryside presumably was covered with peasants bargaining with landlords for mutually beneficial terms of tenure. This is misleading. Rental contracts cannot be divorced from the political, social, and economic structures that made lords "more equal" than peasants. Even if written contracts were silent on the matter, tenancy carried with it conditions of servility. In addition, the lord exercised a considerable degee of control over production. This was particularly evident on lands held in demesne. As the Pang estate near Guangzhou demonstrates, lords were actively involved in all aspects of agricultural production, from the selection of seed to the harvest. The lord also provided those who worked the demesne—commonly called "serfs" (nongpu, nupu, tongpu)—with food, clothing, and lodging, and controlled even their personal lives. Even on lands tilled by tenants, lords had some control by supplying the peasant family with the means of production such as seed, tools, fertilizer, and housing. The peasant family supplied labor power. To be sure, there were economically independent peasant families, but if they were tenants, they still were servile. Tenants owed certain forms of service and deference to the lord simply as a

14

condition of tenancy. The ten to twenty days per year spent working for the lord could not then be allocated to the peasants' farms. Tenants surely were more economically free than the serfs who worked the demesne, but nonetheless were personally servile to, and to varying degrees economically dependent on, the lord.

In the *Pang Family Instructions*, Pang Shangpeng hinted that the willingness of lords to participate actively in the productive process began to wane in the late Ming period. The *Instructions* are replete with warnings that the position of the Pang family would deteriorate, socially as well as economically, if the estate were not personally managed by the lord. One can only assume that Pang saw other estates decline as lords withdrew from a supervisory role. The greatest danger to the estate, according to Pang, was the attraction of the city of Guangzhou. Under the section in the *Instructions* on "Prohibitions," Pang warned his family: "For several generations we have lived in the countryside. Everyone here has a definite station in life. My heirs must not move. After three years in the provincial capital, you will not know anything of agriculture or sericulture. After ten years, you will not know your lineage. Those who have made a habit of chasing after luxury or loafing about seldom have ability. Those who are above the common level have said from experience: There are ten-fold advantages to living in the countryside. Only to avoid bandits should you go temporarily to the city."[28]

Peasant Uprisings

The fear and existence of "bandits" reveal tensions in land tenure relations that would contribute to the fall of the Ming dynasty. Bonds of servitude, restrictions on personal movement, and the social stigma of servility existed for serfs and tenants alike throughout the Ming. But at the same time, serfs and tenants had acquired a certain degree of economic independence. Rural markets presented tenants with an opportunity to sell some of their produce, and serfs who went to market for their lords had the opportunity to mingle with the more economically independent tenants. As Fu Yiling argues, with

15

emerging commercial relations in the cities and periodic markets in the countryside, serfs and tenants began to demand the right to make their own production decisions.[29] The bonds of servitude became increasingly intolerable and finally were destroyed in the massive uprisings of serfs and tenants in South China that heralded the end of the Ming dynasty.

In the late Ming and early Qing period serfs and tenants in South China began to demand the freedom to leave the land, the freedom to choose the types of crops planted on the land they tilled, and the abolition of the bonds of servitude. Although peasant uprisings, such as the 1448 rising led by Deng Maoqi in Fujian, had punctuated the entire Ming period, those at the end of the Ming aimed specifically at overthrowing serfdom and the forms of bondage characteristic even of the relationship between lord and tenant. The demands of the serfs and tenants were expressed in a radical agrarian egalitarianism as trenchant and thoroughgoing as has arisen in any society. Peasants wanted "liberty," expressed as *tui-yue*, or the rescinding of the contractual bonds of servitude. They sought "equality," articulated as the demand for the abolition of the distinctions between "lord and serf" (*zhu pu*), "high and low" (*gui jian*), and "poor and rich" (*pin fu*). Slapping lords on the face, some righteously declared: "I will make people equal. How dare you call me serf! From now on, things will be different."[30]

The uprisings were especially prevalent throughout the Yangzi River valley, along the southeast coast, and as far inland as Sichuan. In Jiangnan, uprisings were described by a contemporary as follows: "In the 1644 and 1645 disturbances, there were some very crafty ones among the serfs who called for breaking the bonds of servitude because the dynasty had been overthrown. . . . When one called, a thousand responded. They went to the lords' homes, compelling them to hand over the contractual bonds. The lords respectfully complied. Shortly afterwards, the houses in which some lords had been tied were burned down." In Shanghai county, "serfs killed the lord, his father and sons, and immediately burned the houses down. All of the great houses [*da hu*] in the surrounding villages were

16

pillaged and burned down. There was a serf named Gu Liu who led others into the city to the homes of the lords demanding the bonds of servitude. These families were brutally beaten . . . and the contracts all burned."[31] In many of these mass actions, serfs occupied the lords' ancestral temples, took the position of honor, and forced the lords to kneel before them. Serfs in the Pearl River delta region south of Guangzhou also rose up *en masse*, forming armies and occupying areas for considerable periods of time. According to one report, "in February of 1646, the 'Association of Bandits' [*she zei*], composed mainly of serfs, rose up. The organization which led the uprising was also known as the 'Serf Bandits' [*pu zei*]. . . . [Throughout the delta region, serfs] for several years killed or chased away their lords and seized the land and houses; the most extreme took wives and children as prisoners and defiled their ancestral graves."[32]

Disturbances raged throughout China in the early 1640s— serfs and tenants rising in the Yangzi and Pearl River deltas, pirates raiding along the southeast coast, and the peasant armies of Li Zicheng and Zhang Xianzhong marching across the north and northwest. While they did not all have the same causes or goals, the cumulative effect was to bring down the Ming dynasty.[33] And with it came serfdom.

Serfdom did not disappear, as Mark Elvin has argued;[34] it was destroyed. The social and economic order that would arise in its place was only dimly visible, but its main outlines could be seen. Peasants wanted personal freedom and economic independence, and they fought for it. Lords who had not already been attracted to the cities were driven off the land, leaving large tracts in the hands of peasants. Some peasants may not even have participated in the struggle with lords, yet when the lord fled, peasants were left with the land anyway. And sometimes, if an area was invaded by outsiders, both lords and peasants fled, leaving the land to go to waste. What would happen when squatters moved in was anyone's guess. What would happen if lords returned, supported by a new dynasty, to reestablish their claims to land and to control production?

The answers to these questions would decide the fate of China's rural social and economic system. The answers were not to be dictated from above by the new emperors, but were to come from places like Haifeng county. Here, in a rural backwater about a hundred miles up the coast from Guangzhou, peasants and lords hotly contested the issue of whose claims to the land would prevail.

CHAPTER 2

Peasants, Lords, and the State
Qing Land Tenure Relations

H AIFENG county was engulfed by the disturbances that marked the end of Ming and early years of Manchu rule. Social violence and struggle was endemic in rural Haifeng, as it was in most of China, and it intensified as the weakened Ming proved incapable of maintaining order. While the authorities may have perceived events in Haifeng as symptomatic of general disorder, those who were causing disorder simply were trying to fashion a *new* order in which the main issue was control of the land. Peasants won important victories, and it was from this position of strength that the new land tenure system was put together. This settlement then underlay and channeled the subsequent flow of rural history.

Physical and Political Environment
Physically, Haifeng has little to recommend itself. A good part of the county is weathered mountains and stony hills; even by the twentieth century, only about 30 percent of its 2,000 square miles was tilled. In the late sixteenth and early seventeenth centuries, the only land being tilled lay along the few shallow rivers flowing the short distance from the hills to the sea, and along the coast just inland from the salt flats. Brackish swamps also decreased the easily tilled area, but when drained these could be planted with salt-resistant strains of rice.

Despite these limitations, Haifeng is not inhospitable to agriculture—indeed, archeological finds indicate that rice had been planted and harvested as early as 1500 B.C. Located just south of the Tropic of Cancer, Haifeng has a semitropical cli-

19

Map 1. Late imperial China

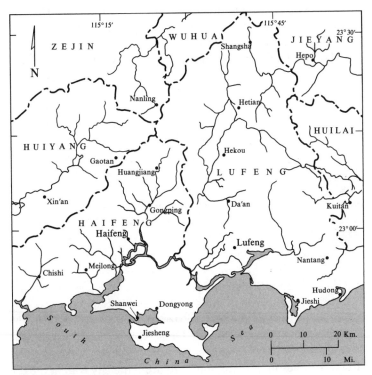

Map 2. Haifeng and Lufeng counties

mate. Frost is so rare that it was recorded in the *Local History* under "strange events," along with the sightings of comets. Humidity is high year round, but rain is generally confined to the May–September monsoon season, when about three-fourths of the annual rain falls. While the rivers are short and shallow, thereby limiting the possibilities for irrigation, rainfall is plentiful and concentrated in the growing season. By the nineteenth century, three harvests could be obtained annually, and even in the sixteenth century, double cropping was common.

By the turn of the seventeenth century, about when our story begins, there were perhaps 70,000 people living in Haifeng, mostly in the countryside, but also in the handful of small market towns that were emerging. For administrative purposes, the county was divided into seven districts (in 1730 the eastern three were consolidated into a new county, Lufeng), each of which in turn was composed of several subdistricts, or *li*. The subdistricts were the units for assessing and collecting taxes and corvée labor duties, the county magistrate's most important local administrative duties. The taxable populace was divided into thirty of these subdistricts, each of which in turn comprised 280 households (*hu*). One-tenth of these households were liable for labor service each year, for such things as constructing government buildings, repairing the city wall or moat, garrisoning the various postal stations, or providing messenger service, thereby spreading out the burden on any single household on a decennial rotation.[1]

Taxes were levied both on the land and on adult males (*ding*). Haifeng's land tax quota was just over 6,000 piculs of rice (*shi*), which was apparently due in two payments, the bulk of it being paid after the fall harvest. For most of the sixteenth century, the tax was paid in kind, but during the second half of the century it was converted into a silver money payment at a rate determined by the magistrate. Unlike the land tax, the ding tax had always been levied in money, and Haifeng's quota to the central government was 842 ounces of silver (*liang*), payable by about 9,500 ding at the rate of 88 copper cash annually.[2]

Although the number of adult male ding and household hu liable for tax and labor service were roughly the same, the figures do not represent a reliable census of adult males or households in Haifeng. For one thing, the figures were quotas levied on the liable population, and with changes in population, it is not inconceivable that someone would be responsible for a certain percentage of the ding tax, for example. But more important, as noted in Chapter 1, tax evasion was widespread. Powerful individuals hid both land and liable adult males from the tax rolls. And as peasants or other small landholders found it increasingly difficult during the second half of the sixteenth century to pay the land and ding taxes, levied and collected in silver, they commended themselves and their lands to those lords who could avoid the full burden of taxation.

Direct evidence for the practice of commendation in Haifeng county is lacking—but it was undoubtedly occurring, as the gross disparity between our best estimated population figures and the official tax figures indicates. Nevertheless, commendation was not the peasants' only response to the burdens of taxation. Tax resistance too was possible, and here, the documentation for Haifeng county is more complete. Indeed, it is doubtful if the land and ding tax quotas for Haifeng were ever met. In the second half of the sixteenth century this was because of stiff resistance put up by significant numbers of rural inhabitants.

Tax and Rent Resistance

In the years after 1552, when the collection of the land tax in Haifeng was converted from kind into silver, peasants tilling the more marginal lands further inland simply refused to pay any tax at all, even the more modest 88 copper cash ding tax levy. "The land skirting the hills has all been occupied by bandits," several of the local gentry complained in 1573, "so that for the last thirty years it has been said there that the people did not know there was a dynasty." Earlier attempts in the 1560s to collect the delinquent taxes, reportedly amounting to one-third of the county's quota, were repulsed, as the authorities alleged that "vagabonds, as a pretext for pillaging,

23

called far and wide for tax revolt." The response was apparently great; from the authorities' point of view, the result was that "nine of ten subdistricts have become waste, nine of ten lives lost, and in two districts, the people have fled, leaving only 10 to 20 percent."[3]

This was more than just a tax revolt: it was a struggle for control of the land. The charge levied against the peasants was that they had "forcibly occupied land" (*zhan tian*) on which they paid neither tax nor rent. The peasants knew the stakes involved, and their struggle to keep their land was intense. Local troops were unable to regain control of the rebel lands, so in 1573 some local lords took matters into their own hands and directed an appeal for help to the provincial governor, without going through the local magistrate, the proper channel. When a major campaign was mounted in early 1574, government troops soon claimed victory: over 10,000 "bandits and their leaders" were killed in the fighting or executed later. Lords then laid claim to the land.

We can only speculate on why the lords of Haifeng were so intent on gaining control of these lands. Most probably the reasons were related to the land tax. Haifeng county had been among the first in China to commute land taxes from payment in kind to payment in silver. Although the details of how this worked in Haifeng are not available, it is clear that after 1552 Haifeng's tax system was part of the general reform that has come to be known as the "single-whip" method of taxation.[4] Because the land tax had to be paid in silver, lords sold the rice they had collected in rent in order to pay the tax. As long as rice prices held steady or increased, this would not have presented taxpayers with any special problems. But from the 1560s to the 1570s, rice prices in many parts of China fell.[5] For those lords who did not own great amounts of land, price fluctuations considerably affected their ability to pay the tax. Caught in such a "cash flow" problem, these lords may have tried to solve it by seizing peasant lands they previously did not control, forcing peasants tilling the land to become their tenants, with servility accompanying tenancy.

24

Another possible reason for the attack on peasant lands in the 1570s may have been related to overseas trade. Ocean-going ships frequented the Haifeng coast, and it is very likely that wealthy Haifeng lords participated in the growing trade with Japan.[6] All along the southeast coast, wealthy persons were investing in ventures headed for Japan. But if this trade held the promise of great wealth, it also was very risky. Pirates overtook ships on the high seas and sometimes raided coastal villages that had profited from the trade. Besides, there was always the danger of bad weather and a shipwreck. Had the very wealthy lords of Haifeng invested in a trading mission to Japan that met with some disaster? If so, they too would have been in need of cash to cover their losses. Under these circumstances, peasants who paid neither rent nor taxes might have found themselves in a very precarious position indeed, pressed hard by those powerful persons who needed both. Thus, it is entirely possible that declining rice prices in the 1570s, combined with losses in overseas trade, is what prompted the lords of Haifeng to assert control over lands they designated "bandit land."

Whatever the case may have been, the lords and authorities of Haifeng may have been overzealous in their pursuit of bandit lands and taxes. The death and destruction accompanying the assertion of lordship meant that the land remained sparsely settled for the next two decades. "In Guishan, Yongan, Heyuan, and Haifeng counties," a 1596 prefectural report observed, "land is abundant and people few, causing vagrants from neighboring prefectures and provinces to come and till the land."[7] But when this land reclamation began in the 1590s, it was under the control of lords. By now the principle had been firmly established that the land was not there just for the taking—the presumption was that any tillers of the land were the tenants of and servile to some lord. In the late Ming, peasants could not simply move and freely take up land for cultivation elsewhere. The government had a standard procedure for registering new arrivals, indicating where they came from, where they now lived, and, significantly, on whose land they had taken tenancy. In fact, local authorities in Haifeng assigned

25

immigrants to a lord who was then responsible, along with the circuit chief, for their behavior. Thus when immigrants began reclaiming wasteland in Haifeng they did so not with squatters' rights, but as tenants. Lords offered very good terms in order to attract tenants onto their lands and, according to one report, "generously provisioned" them with food, seed, and tools. Relations with the native peasantry were friendly, as the new arrivals settled among them and intermarried. But relations with the lords did not remain so cordial, and the immigrants soon became embroiled in disputes over rent. As soon as the lords had attracted sufficient tillers of their land, they began raising the rent, even though the terms had been set when tenancy was first taken. This precipitated litigation of all kinds, but the suits were dismissed, prompting "some pretty fierce people who liked to cause trouble" simply to refuse to pay rent. Entire villages of both immigrants and natives thereby became "bandit" villages.[8]

Peasant Rebels and Their Organization

The bandit villages, located for the most part in the valleys in the northern part of Haifeng county, were not simply a conglomeration of discrete communities, but rather, constituted a social and political order quite unlike that of their enemies to the south. Although not under a unified military command, at least as far as can be ascertained, the villages together resembled a Spartan society of military men and farmers. The armed forces of the villages, ranging in size from several hundred to several thousand, were commanded by "generalissimos" (*zong*), some of whom were called the "fulfilling generalissimo" (*man zong*), the "rear generalissimo" (*wei zong*), and the "heavenly generalissimo" (*tian zong*). When a general was killed in battle, a ceremony held in his honor included the selection of a new leader. The mounted bands commanded by the "generalissimos" periodically swooped down from their base areas to attack market towns and county seats, both in Haifeng and in neighboring counties as well. Sometimes occupying a town for a few days, they would then return home with the booty taken from the wealthy.[9]

26

The rebel strongholds were composed of both fighters and their supporters. The valleys were farmed by runaway serfs, or vagabonds (*wang laizhe*, literally "those who flee from dependency," *laizhe*, or "dependent," meaning serf). These runaways, according to one contemporary source, "come from far and wide." But most came from the nearby agricultural districts, where bondage was the norm. The reasons for flight to these rebel villages were numerous. The natural environment had made life hard enough for peasants without having to contend with the rigors of lordship. Because Haifeng hugged a narrow coastal strip between the monsoon-bringing ocean to the south and rugged mountains to the north, it continued to be plagued with malaria even after land reclamation projects of the late fourteenth century began to drain the swamps and marshes that bred the anopheles mosquito. Besides being beset with malaria, the area was periodically struck by autumn typhoons. The typhoon of July 1637, for example, tossed ships inland, destroyed homes and buildings, and inundated the rice fields. Dearth often followed a destructive typhoon, but famine could occur at other times as well. The great famine of 1597 had left innumerable people dead of starvation; the famine of 1618 apparently was not so immediately destructive. But natural disasters hit the poor harder than the rich, especially if in addition they had to pay rent to a lord from the harvest they managed to glean in this precarious environment. Many just ran away.[10]

When runaways arrived in the rebel villages, they were organized into the *san ban*, or "off-duty militia" system. Groups of ten, known as a *cao*, each with its own headman, formed the backbone of the san ban militia. The role of the militia was to protect the villages when the regular forces were away. But its members' main duty was farming. The villages practiced a form of communal life in which loot taken in raids and food produced by the san ban reportedly were distributed equally. With the egalitarianism creating a strong sense of solidarity (fraternity, one might say), observed the contemporary Qu Dazhun, "the masses readily follow the rule of their leaders."[11]

27

Whatever may have prompted these bands to take the offensive against their enemies, or whatever broader goals they may have entertained, simply is not known, but in 1632 nothing less than civil war broke out in Haifeng county. Perhaps the authorities had begun to apply some military pressure, or perhaps the generalissimos wanted to enlarge the area under their control, but that summer the rebels fell upon the market towns of Da-an, Gongping, and Donghai (later Lufeng city), reportedly killing hundreds. By 1640, the rebels had become much more selective in their targets, preferring instead to kidnap and kill local gentry and their families. During these unsettled years, disturbances spread as local tenants and other servile persons in the rural districts of Yangan and Jinxi not under rebel control also rose up. According to the Haifeng *Local History*, "upright lords collected only twenty to thirty percent of the usual amount of rent": it was a time when "gentry and commoner alike endured great suffering."[12]

In the years around 1644, when the last Ming emperor in Beijing had capitulated, Haifeng city and surrounding market towns were occupied at various times by a bewildering array of forces, including not only the rebel bands but also Ming loyalist forces and pirates. In fact, pirates engaged in illicit coastal and overseas trade cooperated quite closely with the local rebels. The most important pirates aiding the peasants were the Su brothers, Cheng and Li. The Su forces were formidable, and after Su Cheng died in 1649, his brother took over leadership of the pirates. Qu Dazhun estimated that "he had a thousand ships and led tens of thousands of people. . . . His control extended for three hundred miles along the coast." "A thousand ships" may have been an exaggeration, but it is known that a flotilla of over seventy ships once occupied a Haifeng harbor. While it is probable that peasants joined Su's forces during his mainland raids, much of his support came from the "boat people" (*dan jia* or *Tanka*). Many of these people, classified as "mean" and "servile" by the Ming and later Qing legal codes, were fishermen who also transported salt for the government monopoly. The salt operations in Haifeng were among the largest in Guangdong, and many of the boat people participated in a flourishing illicit salt trade. In fact, the Su brothers were the leading figures in the salt-smuggling operations along the southeast coast. According to one estimate, they reaped "an annual profit of a hundred thousand ounces of silver from the fish and salt trade."[13]

Su Li could perhaps best be described as a "social pirate," following Hobsbawm's characterization of the "social bandit." Of all the necessities of life, salt was the one commodity which had to be purchased. But the salt tax, a major source of revenue for the Ming state, was also a major irritant to the people. Even if pirates could make large profits selling smuggled salt below the state price, everyone was better off. Su had close ties with coastal inhabitants: the boat people, salt field workers, and peasants evidently recognized that their struggles were related. He also did not hesitate to help in their struggles. He was, after all, an experienced general and leader of thousands of people. After Su had spent a decade leading attacks against the mainland, for example, the conquering Qing forces found it easier to make him part of their army than to fight him. But in the early 1660s, the Manchus forcibly relocated coastal inhabitants several miles inland in response to the continued attacks by Ming loyalists, dug trenches, raised fences, and posted guards to prevent any contact between the coastal population and the pirates. Fishermen, peasants, and salt workers, according to Qu Dazhun, "all lost their means of livelihood and became bandits." Su Li once again sided with the dispossessed and led his forces in revolt.[14]

Although Su Li and his forces had turned against the new Qing state, he did not belong to the Ming loyalist forces occupying several areas in eastern Guangdong and southern Fujian. Many of the so-called peasant armies in the Chaozhou area were in fact Ming loyalist armies. In Jieyang county, to the east of Haifeng, former Ming officials and nobility established a government in exile headed by a Ming pretender. There is no evidence to even remotely suggest that Su's forces or those of the runaway serfs in the mountains were in any way connected with these Ming loyalists. Furthermore, since

Su Li had been badgered by Ming forces, there is little reason to think that he felt any loyalty to them.[15]

The peasant uprisings were also accompanied by uprisings of thousands of tin and iron miners who worked the mountains about twenty-five miles east of Haifeng city. Permission to open the mines had been granted in the mid-sixteenth century on the condition of supplying the military with weapons and tools. "But," complained the Haifeng *Local History*, "they were really operated for profit." The mining and smelting operations were quite extensive. According to one traveler who observed other mines about the same time, "around each smelting ground live three hundred families, over two hundred overseers, three hundred miners, and two hundred furnace stokers." Engaging in trade initially with Japanese "pirates" and later with merchants from neighboring counties, the miners were a constant irritation for the Ming authorities and continued to be so for the Qing as well. Whatever their goals and demands may have been, the rebellious miners proved to be a sufficient threat to the new Qing state that the mines were closed down in 1665 "in order to cut off the source of the rebellion."[16]

The late Ming and early Qing peasant uprisings in Haifeng and elsewhere along the southeast coast were part of a wider insurrection which also included pirates and miners. The most surprising feature of these uprisings, though, is not that they occurred simultaneously, but that such close ties existed between them. The miners supplied weapons for the bands of runaways, while the pirates provided leadership and direction uniting these social classes into a common force. The pirates denounced the authorities as "extremely oppressive," an epithet which servile peasants could easily understand. Attacking the state forces with astonishing swiftness from Fujian to Guangzhou, the pirate forces provided peasants in widely separated areas with knowledge of conditions in other regions, cultivating a sense of participation in a wider insurrection. At the same time, they exposed the weaknesses of the state, thus encouraging those who wished, to take their fate into their own hands. Furthermore, the impact of the fall of the Ming house on the willingness of serfs and other peasants to challenge their lords should not be underestimated. When serfs farther north in the Jiangnan area of the Yangzi delta learned that the dynasty had fallen (*ding ge*), thousands rose up.[17]

The serf and tenant uprisings in the Yangzi River delta region and other areas were easily suppressed by the forces of order, but those along the southeast coast were much more difficult to control. At least part of the reason for the difference must be attributed to the leadership provided by the pirates. The peasants along the southeast coast were not isolated, as those further north had been, but rather acted in concert with other social groups. The Yangzi River delta region had become a national center of trade and commerce by the late Ming, but evidence does not indicate that merchants there provided leadership for the peasant uprisings. The difference undoubtedly lies in the nature of trade in the two areas. In the Jiangnan area, merchants were legitimate; those along the southeast coast had a long tradition of opposition to the state. They had been labeled "pirates" by a state interested in maintaining its monopoly over iron and salt; the pirates engaged in coastal smuggling were those most active in their opposition to the Ming state. The Su brothers, with their large flotilla and huge profits, were not the largest or most important of these armed smuggling bands. Others, such as Wu Ping, Zeng Yiben, Lin Daogan, and Lin Feng, had larger fleets. Many pirate recruits undoubtedly were serfs and tenants determined to escape the hardships of life on the mainland. Many of course fled to the mountains, but countless others fled to the seas. And in both cases, a well-armed and militarily organized force was augmented by runaways who were not too far removed from their experiences on the land and under the lord.[18]

The uprisings along the southeast coast thus were large-scale and broad-based, including peasants, miners, and pirates. But whatever promises the historical moment may have held for the establishment of a new social order based on an alliance between a peasantry expressing a radical egalitarianism and pirates opposing state restrictions on their trading activities, those chances rapidly faded as invading Manchu armies swept into North China in 1644 and into the south in the next year.

The Qing State and Rural Social Relations

After the Manchu forces had occupied Beijing (Peking) in 1644 and subsequently captured Nanjing (Nanking) the following year, the new rulers were confronted with a host of related problems beyond the immediate task of suppressing the remaining Ming loyalist forces scattered in the south: continued peasant uprisings south of the Yangzi, hugh tracts of land laid waste by the wars, and declining sources of state revenue. The Manchus realized that the peasant uprisings could not be ended by purely military means, nor could wastelands be brought back into production as long as peasants were not free to migrate. In a series of imperial edicts issued over a period of seventy-five years, the Manchu rulers codified what peasants had already accomplished in fact: the Manchus acknowledged the personal freedom of serfs and tenants. In addition, the new state extended incentives to the peasants to bring wasteland back into production without the fear that their land would be claimed by returning lords and themselves once again reduced to servility. By these measures the Manchus hoped to create a stable tax base for the state, end peasant disturbances, and bring land into cultivation.

As soon as the Qing forces occupied Nanjing, the new state incorporated into its own legal code the Ming law forbidding commendation. But unlike the Ming rulers, the Qing strictly enforced the code in order to allow peasants to migrate to the wastelands. In a 1650 edict anouncing the land reclamation policy, the regents for the Shunzhi emperor proclaimed: "Local officials are to attract immigrants. It does not matter whether they are natives or not, all are to be entered into the local registers. They are to reclaim untitled wastelands. You are to give them an officially sealed certificate guaranteeing them permanent rights to the land." The Manchu rulers soon learned that with the threat of bondage, peasants did not migrate to the huge tracts of wasteland in Hobei (Hepei), Hunan, Anhui, and Yunnan. Therefore, in 1660, the Shunzhi emperor forbade "selling tenants with the land and compelling them to perform labor services." And in 1681, the Kangxi emperor, responding to a memorial from the governor of Anhui, who felt that wasteland was not being reclaimed fast enough, ordered all lords to "allow their tenants to do as they please."[19]

With the Qing state enforcing these edicts, the great migrations of the late seventeenth and early eighteenth centuries began. The land reclamation policy of the Qing state was two-pronged and in both cases succeeded in consolidating what was to become a large class of freeholding peasants. First, ex-serfs, former tenants, and landless peasants who reclaimed untitled wasteland were given squatters' rights to till the land in perpetuity. Second, on lands to which ownership could be proved, the Qing state gave the owners incentives to bring the land back into production. But in both cases, the state—not the lord—provided seed, draft animals, tools, and "capital," and granted a ten-year tax remission to those who reclaimed wasteland.[20] A further obstacle to migration and land reclamation was removed in the 1720s when the Yongzheng emperor allowed integration of the labor service tax with the land tax, thereby freeing landless peasants from state-imposed ties to their native places.

Another move designed to augment the tax base also had an impact on rural social relations: the Qing state swept away the special tax privileges of the old Ming officials. During the Ming, the lands and serfs held by officials and nobility were for all practical purposes exempt from taxation. The Qing legal code abolished these exemptions: "Officials down to first-degree licentiate [*shengyuan*] are to be exempt only from the personal corvee labor tax [*ding yao*]. The land tax [*ding yin*] must be paid." Everyone—officials, landlords, and peasants alike—was expected to pay the land tax. Under the Ming this tax in one prefecture in Jiangsu province had been set at 5,000 silver *liang*, but the half levied on officials had been commuted, doubling the burden on the commoners. The Qing adopted the same assessment, but because it was more equitably distributed, the tax burden on the commoners was cut in half.[21]

The new tax laws resulted in a rash of land sales and a precipitous fall in land prices, at least where the law was rigorously applied. If the tax was not paid within two months of the due date, the ex–Ming officials were taken to court and either fined or imprisoned. As soon as it became apparent that they would have to pay taxes on the amount of land owned, many lords sold large portions of their land just to meet taxes. In four prefectures of Jiangsu province, 2,171 former officials and 11,346 officials of the *shengyuan* and *xunzhe* rank were indicted in a famous 1661 tax case. The result was something like a sheriff's auction. One official who owned 400 mou, for example, was forced to sell half of his land to pay the tax.[22]

The subsequent fall in land prices panicked the Jiangnan landowners. Some of the land placed on the auction block was purchased by peasant immigrants at very low prices. "In recent days," according to one report, "the large lineages which collect several score or hundreds of piculs in rent have been willing to cut the price and sell their land [to immigrants from Guangdong]. Some do not even care about gravelands, how long their ancestors have owned the land, or about their heirs. They are willing to turn everything upside down [*daojia*, a literary term meaning to invert lines of a poem]. . . . Some even give their surnames [to the immigrants]." In other cases, "calculating families" took the opportunity to buy up large tracts of land, ranging in size from 1,000 to 4,000 mou.[23]

It is nonetheless true that in some areas many lords, probably wealthy commoners who had taken commended peasants, had already begun to loosen the ties of servitude during the late Ming in order to allow peasants more time to increase agricultural production. When the Qing state began to enforce the regulations against commendation, these lords adopted a more paternalistic attitude in order to ensure payment of rent. Such a paternalist stance, according to one 1650 report from Zhejiang province, began to make headway after the fall of the Ming: "The landlord is responsible for providing seed, fertilizer, plows, and tools. The tenant [*dianhu*] is responsible for planting and harvesting. In times of flood or drought, the landlord provides food and the tenant supplies labor (repair dikes, dig wells, etc.). At the autumn harvest, rice and wheat are divided equally. The tenant gives a feast for the landlord, and the landlord gives a feast for the tenant (he can invite one guest)."[24]

Another former Ming lord likewise formulated three policies which, he told his readers, would have to be followed because of the new circumstances imposed by the Qing state. First, "when a tenant without capital tills your land, lend him two *dou* [pecks] of seed per mou. At the autumn harvest, collect the rent but do not add interest. In times of drought or flood, energetically help the tenant, and in normal times you will be repaid." Second, "when you have something to be done and call upon the tenant, pay him for his labor. If a tenant family raises pigs, sheep, chickens, or geese, and plants vegetables or fruit, buy these things at a fair price if your family needs them." And third, "if a tenant family conscientiously carries out good deeds (being filial, loyal, trustworthy, upright, etc.), you should give them wine and food on special occasions for their labors. If they fight [with the lord?], try to settle it by exhortation. Only as a last resort take away their land." Without the legal and extralegal means used under the Ming to extract rent and labor services, lords were compelled to adopt other methods to ensure the payment of rent. As one historian of the serf uprisings remarked, "By the Kangzi reign (1662–1723), the rich no longer dared to keep serfs."[25]

Regardless of the desires and policies of the Qing state, land was not speedily reclaimed in Haifeng county. During the decades of chaos in Haifeng in the mid-seventeenth century, lords in many areas had increased their hold over the peasants on lands they firmly controlled. As was the case with most of China, Haifeng had been a battleground upon which several very different armed forces competed. Ming loyalists battled the Chinese allies of the Manchus, while pirates, bandits, and freebooters of all kinds alternately fought and allied with any or all. And the villagers more often than not were the victims of all of them. Walls went up around the wealthier villages and towns, while defenseless villages were abandoned, the inhabitants either joining the rebels or seeking the protection of the walled communities. Local strongmen emerged who ruled little kingdoms from their little castles. They were the effective state power, for the Ming had fallen and the Qing had yet to establish its control. As the price of protection, these local lords could demand loyalty and any other material reward they could extract from the peasants short of causing them to run off. But run where? The outside world was now a very dangerous place filled with all kinds of marauders. Although Haifeng's population was probably declining, the uncertainty of the world ensured the lords of a demand for their protection.

The power of these local lords remained unchallenged until the 1660s. Then, under the direction of the new magistrate, Ruan Shipeng, a campaign was mounted to break their power, and the Qing state made its presence felt. Ruan Shipeng had been only a runner-up in the competition for the *juren*, or first level, in the prestigious metropolitan examinations. But he was from Jiangnan, an area reknowned for its scholars and where the competition was therefore very stiff. The Manchus were still having difficulty attracting qualified Chinese administrators to serve them, and if a second-rate scholar was all they could find for a malaria-infested backwater, he would have to do. Besides, Ruan probably saw his duty there simply as a step on a ladder to better positions abandoned by others—provided he performed as expected.[26]

Since he was from Jiangnan, a stronghold of Ming loyalists and of continued passive resistance to Manchu rule, Ruan may have felt that his loyalty to the Manchus and the new Qing state was for that reason somehow questioned, especially since the Manchu princes ruling as joint regents for the boy emperor Kangzi had expressed their contempt and hatred for Jiangnan by indicting over 13,000 ex–Ming officials in Jiangnan on tax evasion charges in the 1661 tax case. Regardless of his personal feelings on the case, Ruan knew that he would be expected to be equally uncompromising in Haifeng. And in 1665 he went after the local strongmen. He leveled charges against them for building walled villages, for issuing warrants on their own account, and for other practices such as cornering the rice market. To further ensure that their control over the local inhabitants would be broken, Ruan issued a general proclamation prohibiting the exercise of such private rulership and usurpation of state prerogatives.[27]

Magistrate Ruan also implemented a 1650 imperial edict ordering the reestablishment of the *baojia* registers. These registers had been one of the few direct links between the rural populace and the state, serving as the basis for militia service and sometimes taxes, but had fallen into disuse during the Ming. Their reconstitution by county magistrates like Ruan was clearly an attempt by the Qing to reestablish direct state control over the populace. And to prompt voluntary compliance, the 1650 edict had stipulated that those registered in the baojia rolls were to receive "an officially sealed certificate guaranteeing permanent rights to the land." Peasants under the thumb of local strongmen then had strong incentive to strike out on their own. And they did. In little more than a decade, from 1669 to 1680, over 400,000 mou of land was reclaimed, amounting to about 44 percent of all taxed land in Haifeng. During the early decades of the Qing dynasty, then, previously landless and poor peasants and other tenants came into direct possession of a considerable amount of land.[28]

If peasants had emerged from the Ming-Qing transition in a stronger position, landlords had been weakened. Political, demographic, and economic factors account for the declining power of the lords. The Manchu rulers were sparing no quarter in their efforts to drive a wedge between lords and peasants in order to extract revenue from a more pliant peasantry, and in Haifeng Magistrate Ruan was having considerable success on that score. The population of Haifeng had decreased as peasants fled the fighting of the 1640s, and those who returned were encouraged to settle new lands. This relative scarcity of labor power and abundance of land put the lords in a weakened position to begin with; and when the Qing state closed the southeast coast to all trade and moved everybody inland, whatever hopes lords may have entertained about increasing production once again were dashed. Even if they collected rent, lords could do nothing with it except store it. They simply had no incentive, even if they had the power to back them up (which they didn't), to seek higher rents from peasants.

Under these conditions, peasants demanded, and received, very favorable terms of tenure. What then developed quite independently throughout south and southeast China were land tenure systems which came to be known collectively as permanent tenure. The terms of permanent tenancy generally stipulated that the peasant who provided all the means of production would agree to pay the rent, while the lord agreed never to raise the rent, expel the tenant, or in any other way change the terms of tenancy. The rent was fixed in perpetuity at a certain amount of grain, sometimes as little as one-eighth of the normal yield from one harvest. Under the conditions of the time, the terms of tenancy were actually quite favorable to the peasant.

One form of permanent tenancy in Haifeng and other areas of Guangdong was related to the land reclamation projects of the late seventeenth and early eighteenth centuries. Besides the wasteland that had been given outright to· peasants, the state also encouraged bringing previously productive land back into production. The vast land reclamation projects in Yunnan and the provinces of central China had attracted many peasants, leaving Guangdong landowners with land but with no one to till it. In order to attract "energetic and ambitious peasants" to cultivate the land, landowners offered relatively favorable terms of tenancy.[29] Permanent tenure, including all the features discussed above, could be purchased by a peasant for a one-time payment of silver to the landowner. This form of land tenure was known as "manure investment" (*fen zhi*), while other forms of permanent tenure were known as the "patronage" (*zuo ge*) system and the "greater and lesser purchase" (*da xiao mai*).

All of these tenure systems developed in Haifeng county, where the different names indicate slightly different origins. The "manure investment" system probably prevailed on those lands registered in the tax roles but laid waste during the late Ming and early Qing and, recognizing the contribution of the peasant to production, especially the tenant's agreement to keep the land productive by using fertilizer, was incorporated into the name of the contract.

The "patronage" system, on the other hand, covered those lands which were never registered in the tax rolls and thus probably were newly reclaimed wasteland. Because the fee for reporting new land was sometimes prohibitive to any but the fairly well-to-do, migrants could seldom pay the fee. When a lord sought to reclaim wasteland, it was often hidden, or "black," land, the title for which did not have the officials' red stamp and hence was not taxed. Writing in the twentieth century, Chen Han-seng gave the following account of the patronage system:

> In Hwei-yang [Huiyang] and the neighboring district of
> Hai-feng [Haifeng] . . . there is the Tso-ko [*zuo ge*] system.
> . . . A Tso-ko is simply a descendent of a rich merchant or
> powerful official who was able to protect the small
> landowner against heavy taxation by having the power to
> defy government authorities. As a price for protection, the
> small landowner used to offer him a certain amount of
> grain every year, which in the course of time has come to
> be considered as a regular rent. That is, after a time, the
> Tso-ko took up the responsibility for the payment of land
> tax, and what had been a fee for protection now became a
> rent for the use of the land. The [original] landowner may
> sell his land, and the Tso-ko may independently sell his
> right to this particular rent.[30]

The "greater and lesser purchase" system in Haifeng combined certain features of the manure investment and patronage systems.[31] Like the distinction made in Fujian and other provinces between the subsoil (*tiandi*) rights and topsoil (*tianmian*) rights, rights to the land in the "greater and lesser" purchase system were split between the "great purchase" landownership rights to rent held by the lord and the "lesser purchase" rights of permanent tenure held by the peasant.[32] Like the manure investment system, the greater and lesser purchase system in Haifeng originated during the late-seventeenth- and early-eighteenth-century land reclamation projects. But unlike the manure investment system, permanent tenancy was purchased not with money but with the peasant's labor. The peasant who brought a lord's wasteland back into production with the fertilizer, seed, and tools provided by the lord was given the rights

39

of the "lesser purchase." As long as the peasant family held the lesser purchase, it was ensured the rights of tenancy.

Permanent tenure was not very favorable if the peasant was permanently tied to it. Thus, besides the actual terms of tenancy, it was very important for peasants to acquire the rights to sell or alienate the tenancy; otherwise, their position might have been little better than that of a serf. But the significance of permanent tenure goes far beyond the concessions innumerable peasants were able to wring from their lords at a time when political and economic forces over which they had no control had placed them in a relatively favorable bargaining position. Most important, the rights of permanent tenure greatly affected the way in which large landownership developed during the Qing dynasty. Conditions would not always be so unfavorable to large landownership as they were in the early Qing period. But it was not somehow preordained that such landownership would take the form of landlord control of innumerable plots of land leased out to individual peasant families. The lords could have organized and managed large-scale agricultural production on their own account using hired laborers. Indeed, the question of which would predominate—large-scale production or peasant smallholdings—was still open in the Ming when lords held lands both as demesne and in villeinage. The winning of permanent tenure in the early Qing effectively settled the question: smallholding would predominate. By tenaciously clinging to these newly won rights throughout the Qing, peasants ensured that large-scale agriculture controlled by lords would not develop when conditions more favorable to landownership emerged. Unless these peasant rights were destroyed, large landownership would take the form of landlordism developing on the basis of peasant smallholdings.

The State, Lords, and Peasants

The various forms of permanent tenure which arose in the wake of the seventeenth-century uprisings represented major gains for a new class of economically independent peasants. Peasants supplied all their own means of production and were free to allocate the labor power of the family in the best way they saw fit. With economic decision-making firmly placed in the hands of the peasant family, local specialization of agricultural production proceeded apace as peasants were freer to market the produce at their disposal. After the destruction of servile obligations, rural markets increased both in number and frequency. In Haifeng, the number of periodic markets jumped from eight in 1588 to eighteen in 1688—a century punctuated by the devastation and depopulation of war. Another indication of increasing production and productivity was the decreasing incidence of famine. The longest hiatus between famine in eastern Guangdong occurred between 1779 and 1833, or the period just following the vast land reclamation projects.[33]

There were also cases of freeholding peasants becoming quite wealthy and of some even becoming small landlords. By the nineteenth century, for example, it was not unknown for peasants who held manure investment fields on permanent tenure to become wealthy enough to sublet their lands to other tenants. Others became better off by planting commercial crops such as cotton, indigo, tobacco, and sugar cane. While there is evidence of large-scale commercial farming—sugar plantations in Yunnan employing several hundred workers, and fruit orchards in Henan of over 1,000 mou—there is, according to Li Wenzhi, no evidence to indicate that peasants became landlords by virtue of the wealth accumulated by planting commercial crops. These peasants were more interested in agricultural production; instead of renting surplus land which the family could not till with its own labor power they preferred to hire agricultural laborers.[34]

Prior to the eighteenth century, these economic and social gains of the peasantry were not guaranteed by the state. From 1644 to 1727, the Qing rulers confined themselves to enforcing the Ming restrictions against commendation, forbidding the sale of tenants with the land, and prohibiting the lords' demands for labor services. During the early Qing, the social and legal status of the peasants thus did not correspond to their economic position. In Hunan, for example, it was said that "tenants are like serfs. If the occasion arises, they must perform labor services, and dare not avoid working." And in Jiangsu,

41

"peasants who till others' fields perform labor services like slaves." Landlords in many areas continued to enforce these demands by arrogating to themselves the right of corporal punishment.[35]

This was not merely an affront to human dignity; it was also a challenge to the state's claim to a monopoly on the means of violence. Tenants had the right to bring suit against their lords in such cases, and large numbers did so as the Board of Punishments was flooded with hundreds of tenants' complaints. Finally in 1727 a new code was adopted abolishing the lord's right to inflict corporal punishment on a tenant. The specific case on which the Board of Punishments and the Yong-zheng emperor ruled was a petition from the governor of An-hui: "A member of the gentry [*shenjin*] privately punished a tenant by beating him with a wooden staff and taking his wife." The governor asked that the practice be outlawed. The emperor agreed and ruled that "landlord punishment of a tenant is unlawful." The Board of Punishments drew up new regulations which stipulated eighty strokes to a landlord found guilty of beating a tenant. The edict also stated that tenants were no longer liable to perform labor services for the lord, thereby removing one of the ostensible causes for the beatings.[36]

The freeing of all serfs and tenants from servile status did not occur immediately with the issuance of the emperor's 1727 manumission edict. Social relations which had emerged during the Ming died slowly in some areas. This was especially true of those areas where servile status was customary rather than contractual. Nevertheless, such peasants still held in customary servile status had knowledge of the emperor's rulings, as an 1826 decision by the Board of Punishments demonstrates. The case concerned two families, the Li and the Zhou. Sometime during the Ming, the Zhou had settled near the Li village. The Li provided them with seed to till 16 mou in return for rent and interest. But the Li also expected the Zhou to play music, carry sedan chairs, and perform other types of labor whenever the Li had a marriage, funeral, or other celebration. The Li considered the Zhou to be servile, even though that status had never been contractualized, and continued to treat them as

42

such well into the Qing dynasty. Although the Zhou knew of the Yongzheng emperor's manumission edicts, they had been afraid to press for their rights. But in 1821, when a member of the Li family demanded that a Zhou carry water, the Zhou finally refused and severely beat some members of the Li family. The Board of Punishments ruled that the Zhou were not culpable. The board found that if the tenant family merely tilled the lord's fields, lived on the lord's land, and was buried there, they were neither liable to perform any types of labor for the lord nor to be considered of servile status.[37]

Although the Yongzheng emperor was advised to limit even further the rights and powers of landlords by placing severe restrictions on the amount of land that could be owned, the landed class had not been swept away by the mid-seventeenth-century risings and would not be even after the issuance of the emperor's 1727 edict. The edict did not abolish tenancy, landlords, or rent, but simply the right of lords to use violence to extract the rent. This same edict prohibiting lords from beating tenants also stipulated that tenants who defaulted in rent payments were to receive eighty strokes. When the Qing state destroyed personal bondage and servile obligations as a means by which lords could extract rent, it agreed to use its power to enforce rent collection. As the governor of Yunnan interpreted the edict: "It is forbidden for lords to insult tenant families. It is forbidden to administer corporal punishment to a tenant family." But, he went on, "tenants are likewise forbidden to resist paying rent. When collecting rent, lords are forbidden to use the large measure. Apart from rent, lords are fobidden to take money, pigs, sheep, chicken, wine, or other such things from the tenant."[38]

If tenants defaulted in rent payments, they were still liable to be punished. But it was the state that decided the case and meted out the punishment; in short, the state was to have a monopoly on the means of violence. Nevertheless, there were cases during the next decade where the punishment of eighty strokes given to a lord was commuted to a fine. A bit later still, the Board of Punishments decided that if a lord beat a peasant because of rent default, the lord was to be exempt from punishment. As the Qing jurist Wu Tan was to write in the mid-eighteenth century, "Although a tenant family is not the same as a serf, there is nonetheless a difference between lord and tenant, tenants still being different from ordinary people."[39]

Regardless of the obligation of the Qing state to uphold the interests of the landed class in some areas, the goal of the early Qing rulers had been to expand the tax base by creating a large and stable class of freeholding peasants. The Kangxi emperor, for example, commenting on the fact that many peasants in the Ming dynasty had fled the countryside, said that "this was because local powers [*difang shihao*] had taken the people's land." The Qing jurist Zhao Zhu similarly remarked that in breaking up the Ming estates and prohibiting the practice of commendation, "it can be seen that the lives of the common people are thus tied to the fortunes of our dynasty." Another jurist wrote: "With land comes taxation, but that is the common people's joy." And the early Qing emperors were remarkably successful in attaining their goal. Freeholding peasants were predominant in much of North China, Central China, and in Yunnan. In many Guangdong prefectures it was observed in the eighteenth century that "all families are freeholders [*zigengnong*]; no land is leased," or that even where tenancy existed "there are not many poor or rich families."[40]

Furthermore, even in those areas of Guangdong, Fujian, Guangxi, and Jiangxi where tenancy existed, the form which it took—permanent tenure—was not much different from outright ownership. By the mid-eighteenth century, landlords in Shunde county in Guangdong, for example, one of the areas in the Pearl River delta which had seen tens of thousands of serfs rise in rebellion at the end of the Ming, "only know how much rent they are supposed to receive, but do not know the location of their fields." Whether they got their rent is another question. By the eighteenth century, permanent tenure had come to include the right of the tenant to bequeath, sublet, pawn, and sell the rights of permanent tenancy to others. Regardless of the fact that the tenant paid a small amount of rent, the rights of inheritance and alienation were virtually those of

44

juridicial ownership. As a common saying went, "Long tenancy becomes ownership."[41]

The significance of the rise of a freeholding peasantry (including those peasants holding permanent tenure) for the subsequent course of Chinese history cannot be underestimated. This fact conditioned the growth of marketing systems, created a new set of peasant attitudes toward the state and merchants, and determined the forms of land tenure. In short, a new class structure had emerged, quite different from that of Ming times, that created new patterns of rural life, configurations of collective action and violence, and forms of consciousness. These consequences will be taken up in greater detail in the following chapters.

CHAPTER 3

A New Pattern to Rural Life
Marketing Systems and Rural
Social Organization

THE new relations of production that arose in the wake of the late Ming and early Qing peasant uprisings were those characteristic of a smallholding peasant economy. These were accompanied by two other simultaneous changes in the structure of rural society, both of which followed from the emergence of the economically autonomous peasant family. On the one hand, the peasant family had to provide for itself the wherewithal to eat. Subsistence concerns then came to weigh very heavily in the peasant family's economic decision-making, giving rise to values and attitudes James C. Scott has called "the moral economy of the peasant." On the other hand, marketing opportunities also weighed in cropping choices and resulted in the development of marketing *systems* that reshaped the social and economic patterns of peasant life. Both led to forms of rural collective action and violence that peasant organizers in the twentieth century would interpret as peasant "localism" or "anarchism," blurring class lines and mitigating class conflict. The moral economy will be discussed in the next chapter; here the relationships between marketing systems, social structure, and rural collective action will be examined.

Marketing and Regional Agricultural Specialization
Markets existed during Ming times, but they were not as numerous or well-organized as they were to become in Qing times. Although Ming serfs and tenants had done some marketing for themselves, the larger share was for the lord. On

the Pang manor near Guangzhou, for instance, serfs had been categorized according to those who were "suitable" for farming, and those who were "suitable" to do the marketing. Not surprisingly, one of the grievances of tenants was having to market the lord's produce.[1] In short, the lord and his residence had been a major force structuring the economic and social life of peasants. From the seventeenth century on, however, as peasants became independent producers marketing for themselves, the marketing system became a major force structuring their lives. This system in turn linked the villages of Haifeng to broader regional and national markets.

Haifeng was about equidistant from two regional trading centers—Guangzhou, the provincial capital, about 150 miles down the coast and up the Pearl River; and Chaozhou, 100 miles up the coast on the Han River. From Haifeng, goods could be transported easily and cheaply by water to both of these major metropolitan areas. Haifeng's port of Shanwei overlooked a good natural harbor with a channel three meters deep, and at places more than five. While the steamships which began plying the coast in the late 1800s could not anchor too close to the waterfront, oceangoing junks had no such trouble. Indeed, since Ming times, these seaworthy vessels had been seen to "sail in and anchor in the harbor, benefitting neighboring villages," and ships from the Haifeng engaged in the lucrative late-sixteenth- and early-seventeenth-century trade with Japan.[2]

With such an extensive water transport system, peasants in Guangdong began to specialize in fruits, sugar cane, tobacco, and indigo, and by the mid-nineteenth century Guangzhou relied upon Guangxi for rice. Whereas Xie Zhaozhe had described early-seventeenth-century Guangdong as an area where "products are bountiful and the population sparse; there are many fields and rice is cheap," a nineteenth-century official reported that "Guangdong is the richest province in China and is universally acclaimed for its wealth. . . . Sugar and silk are transported to the north and west. It cannot be said that the profit attained is not vast. But the people are poor and dependent because the production of rice is insufficient."[3]

47

A New Pattern to Rural Life

The demands of the expanding city of Guangzhou for foodstuffs had sparked bureaucratic clashes between the governors of Guangdong and Guangxi at least as early as 1718, when people in Guangxi demanded that rice merchants not be allowed to export rice to Guangzhou. Less than a decade later, the governor of Guangxi, in a memorial protesting the extensive purchases of rice by Guangzhou merchants, attributed the rice shortage to the fact that a considerable portion of Guangdong's good farmland had been devoted to commercial crops. By 1880 internal levies on rice became so high that it was cheaper for Guangzhou rice merchants to import rice from Southeast Asia. Clearly, the degree of agricultural specialization in Guangdong had proceeded to such an extent that antagonism developed between the needs of the great coastal city of Guangzhou and the interior regions of Guangxi and Guangdong.[4]

But specialized agricultural production initially was based less on the demands of national or even regional markets than on local differences in geography and soil fertility. The development of rural standard markets was characteristically more related to local factors than to the iron (even if invisible) hand of the "market." Before the twentieth century, peasants exchanging products in the local market town dominated rural commerce; long distance trade was but a small percentage of the total. Even the percentage of crops generally thought of as market crops—bamboo, hemp, peanuts, sugar cane—actually sold in the market varied greatly in different areas of Guangdong. The percentage of peanuts sold in the market in 1933, for example, ranged from 77 percent in Jieyang county, northeast of Haifeng, to 3 percent in Nanyong county. The only product grown solely for the market in 1933 was sugar cane. During the eighteenth and nineteenth centuries, it is quite clear that the only crops peasants produced for sale in the market were nonfood crops such as indigo, sugar cane, mulberry leaves, cotton, tobacco, incense, and other industrial raw materials.[5]

Even with the human and property losses caused by the uprisings and wars of the Ming-Qing transition and the severe disruption of the economy occasioned by the forcible relocation of the population several miles inland in the 1660s, Haifeng's economy recovered during the late seventeenth and early eighteenth centuries. New villages rapidly covered the rural landscape as land was reclaimed. Peasants began to produce sugar, peanuts, indigo, hemp, and other raw materials on their newly acquired land, and new market towns arose, facilitating rural exchange and local agricultural specialization (see Table 1).

By the mid-eighteenth century, agricultural production in Haifeng had become specialized on the basis of local differences in soil types and irrigation possibilities. At this time, according to the Haifeng *Local History*, "in the areas around Haifeng city the four classes of people all live together. The streets in the market are as interlocked as dog's teeth and are very busy. There is no new land available for tilling. Shi-tang district [to the north and east of the city] is an agricultural district which specializes in beans, sweet potatoes, sugar cane, tea, and indigo. The foodstuffs are insufficient. . . . Yang-an district [to the south and west of the city] is extremely fertile, the annual harvest being double that of other areas. . . . It is said that when Yang-an has a good harvest, Haifeng is sufficient in grain."[6]

With a year-round growing season (winters, though cool, were warm enough for vegetables or wheat), plenty of rainfall, and irrigation ditches to control the water level during crucial stages, peasants in many parts of Haifeng could get two and sometimes three annual rice harvests on one plot. There were two different methods of double-cropping in Haifeng county

Table 1: Market Town Expansion in Haifeng and Lufeng Counties

Year	Market towns	Same	New	Defunct
1558	8			
1688	18	5	13	1
1750	26	12	14	2
1908	44	16	28	12

Sources: *Guangzhou fuzhi* (1558); *Huizhou fuzhi* (1688), ch. 4:10b–11a; *Haifeng xianzhi* (1750), ch. 2:9b; *Lufeng xianzhi* (1746), ch. 2:10a; *Guangdong yu ditu shuo* (Guangzhou, 1908), pp. 175, 180.

during Qing times. One method, relying solely on Champa, an early-ripening variety of rice originally imported from Southeast Asia, was simply the planting of two crops in succession. The other method was more complicated and utilized both Champa and the higher-yielding *geng*, or ordinary rice. The late-ripening geng was planted first in the early spring after the Qing-Ming Festival. In the early summer, Champa was transplanted between the rows of geng, and was thus called "dweller" rice. The geng was harvested first, as its stalks were taller than the newly planted Champa; the Champa was harvested in early November. After harvesting two crops of rice, the peasant family could either allow the land to lie fallow until spring planting, or, depending on family resources, could purchase extra fertilizer to plant other crops such as vegetables or wheat. The number, variety, and local variation of rice types in China was truly astounding. In Haifeng alone during Qing times, twenty different types of rice were grown, each with its own characteristics; some were suitable for planting in dry upland fields, while other varieties were planted in the brackish mud flats along the sea.[7]

While rice production was clearly predominant in Haifeng, it is perhaps best to see the local agricultural economy not exclusively in terms of rice production, with all other crops subordinate to it, but rather as an ecological system in which there were mutually reinforcing relations between all crops; in other words, as an agricultural ecology. Two broad areas of production formed the agricultural ecology of nineteenth-century Haifeng (see Map 3). On the sandy and drier high ground, some peasants planted primarily sweet potatoes and peanuts, while in the lower-lying irrigated fields, others planted rice and sugar cane. The two zones were mutually reinforcing. In general, the sweet potatoes and rice provided the means of sustenance, while the peanuts and sugar cane were sold in the local market. Peanuts were more important for their by-products than as food: they were pressed for lighting and cooking oil, and the husks left over from pressing proved to be an excellent fertilizer for sugar cane.

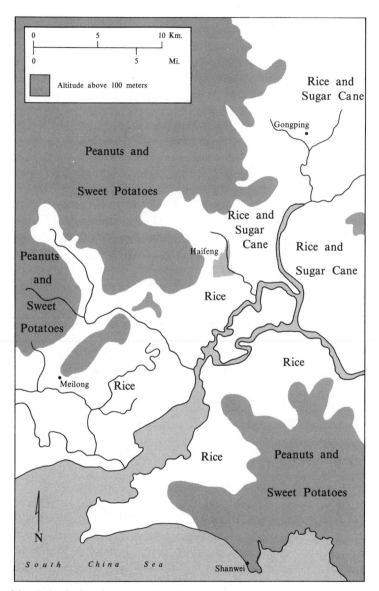

Map 3. Agricultural ecology of Haifeng

Various types of handicraft production developed on the basis of Haifeng's agricultural ecology. For example, peanut-pressing huts and sugar-cracking huts were necessary for converting those crops into usable form. Shops for pressing peanuts and cracking sugar usually did not employ full-time workers, but rather, were cooperative ventures of the producers. As Li Diaoyuan noted of late-seventeenth-century peasants who planted sugar cane, "Ten tillers share a bullock, each having use of the bullock for one day. . . . The bullock are all water buffalo. In the spring they are used to plow the fields, while in the winter they turn the grindstone for pressing sugar cane."[8] Peanut and sugar processing also led to the raising of pigs, for they could be fed on the bran from peanut pressing as well as on a rice-wine mash made from some of the cruder forms of sugar.

Several of Haifeng's large fishing villages doubled as markets for interior regions and as salt-producing areas. Where rural markets inland had craftsmen who specialized in making and repairing agricultural implements, the coastal markets handled the fishing and salt industries—boat building, net making and repairing, fish curing, and making salt pans. Several coastal markets had populations of several thousands: Jiesheng, for example, had a population estimated at 10,000 in the 1890s. Areas which specialized in salt production also supported large towns: Dongyong had a population of 5,000, nearly all of whom worked in the salt fields.[9]

Trade between neighboring areas in the major rural markets of Haifeng in the eighteenth and nineteenth centuries was predominately in the form of foodstuffs and other agricultural products, allowing some areas a degree of specialization (see Map 3). Complete specialization and production for the market did not occur, however, because of the tremendous risks involved in relying exclusively on the market for foodstuffs. Drought or flood which affected even local production could spell economic ruin or starvation for peasants who became too dependent on an imperfect market to supply their needs. Without reasonable assurances that grains would be available in local markets, peasants would not grow nonfood crops, even if the land was better suited for some cash crop which would yield a higher income. Had these risks not existed, there certainly would have been greater specialization and trade.

While trade within a marketing system or between neighboring markets dominated rural exchange, Haifeng in the early nineteenth century also exported a number of products which entered the national and perhaps international markets through its port of Shanwei. Wood and wood products accounted for the largest proportion of goods exported. With many mountainous and wooded areas in the eastern and northern sections of the county, there was a large supply of virgin pine as well as bamboo. Some of the wood was used in the coastal boat-building industry, but by far the largest amount fed the expanding construction industries in urban centers such as Guangzhou, Hong Kong, and Shantou (Swatow). Small amounts of yellow and white sugars, rice, fruits, wine, peanuts, and cloth were also exported, in addition to larger amounts of fish and shrimp from the coastal areas. Imported goods included tobaccos, clothing made from foreign cloth (including some woolens), and copper utensils.[10]

Unfortunately, the amount of goods imported and exported is unknown; only the gross amount of duty collected is available. By about 1850, Shanwei, the main port of Haifeng, was already relatively large, at least in comparison with other non-treaty ports. Annually, 2,800 taels (liang) of duty were collected at Shanwei, compared with 800 taels at Shantou, 1,400 taels at Huangpu (Whampoa, the port of Guangzhou), and 29,600 taels at Aomen (Macao). The duty collected at all three stations in Haifeng and Lufeng counties totaled 4,100 taels. In short, there was over five times as much trade through Haifeng in the mid-nineteenth century as through Shantou, a much more important port in the twentieth century.[11] Haifeng was not the backwater it had been.

Although statistical evidence is not available for the second half of the nineteenth century or for the early twentieth century, there are indications that Shanwei grew rather rapidly during that period. By 1911, missionaries described Shanwei as a busy port: "The town of Swabue [Shanwei] has grown very much lately and as a port it is very prosperous. Looking down upon it from a neighboring hill, one sees many new white-walled houses, some of them two-stories. . . . There is now a post-office in Swabue with an English-speaking postmaster, and sub-offices at several small towns in the neighborhood. . . . Hai-hong [Haifeng], a city some fifteen miles away, boasts a telegraph station and a newspaper."[12]

Market Towns

The local market town was the center for the economic, social, and religious life of peasants in the neighboring villages. Most market towns in eastern Guangdong did not hold markets every day, but rather at three-day intervals, since peasants generally had no need to market more than once ever three days. Neighboring markets usually had complementary schedules. This allowed itinerant peddlers to travel between towns, selling goods or services for which there was not a large enough demand in one market town to warrant a permanent shop. Market towns in Haifeng in the late nineteenth century ranged in size from estimated populations of 2,000 in Qingkang to 10,000 in Meilong, where the market was described as "bustling with business." The permanent shops typically included various types of food stores (meats, bean curd, rice), oil shops (for wick lamps), medicine shops, "paper" shops (usually selling the essentials for religious ceremonies, such as charms, incense, and candles), and very often an emporium which sold needles, thread, soap, matches, and the like. The market town also contained a number of craftsmen, such as carpenters and ironworkers who made and repaired agricultural implements, and service shops, such as barbers and scissors sharpeners.[13]

The sale of agricultural produce on market days usually did not take place within permanent structures, but rather, in such open places as temple yards, bridges, or yards near lineage halls. In eastern Guangdong there does not appear to have been a free "commons" or "marketplace" where peasants gathered to sell their goods. Agricultural goods were sold in special markets controlled by those who owned the land. The yam market near Haifeng city, for example, yielded an annual income of 500 yuan in the 1920s, although it is unclear whether this sum was collected on the goods sold or those selling the produce.

Peasants usually transported goods to market themselves, but if they were well enough off, they could hire others to carry their products. Except for the few shallow waterways on which boats were used, all transportation of goods in Haifeng was by human labor. As Mrs. Sutherland, the wife of a missionary, described transportation in Haifeng in the early twentieth century: "There are no wide roads in the district, and there is not a wheeled vehicle of any kind, not even a wheelbarrow. . . . All the carriage by road of goods is done by human labour, and many and long are the processions in single file are [sic] the burden-bearers. Even children have their little poles on the shoulder, with bundles slung from either end."[14]

Since market was held only once every three days, merchants had other activities to keep them busy on the "cold days." Grain merchants would go around to the villages collecting the grain contracted on market day. Others traveled to a neighboring market town to ply their wares. In some cases, the small merchant was also a peasant, such as Mr. Qiu, who lived in a small village in Haifeng. On market days, he managed his shop in the market town of Meilong, but, according to his son, "on ordinary days he would stay home and till the fields."[15]

Merchants who traveled between market towns making regular stops in larger cities provided peasants with news about the outside world. Gathering in the teahouse after the close of the market, they would relate news and stories which they had picked up in other places. One such merchant, who traveled throughout much of eastern Guangdong, brought his brother and neighbors who lived in rural Haifeng pictures of Kang Youwei (K'ang Yu-wei) and Liang Qichao (Liang Ch'i-ch'ao), and spoke in glowing terms of the 100 Days of Reform in 1898. On another occasion, this same merchant brought news of the 1900 Boxer uprisings around Beijing and condemned the subsequent Eight Power Intervention.[16]

Marketing Systems and Rural Social Organization: A Model

The rural market town with its ten to twenty surrounding villages of economically independent peasants formed a well-organized marketing system with its own structure and rhythm of life. The importance of marketing systems in structuring China's rural society was recognized by G. William Skinner, who focused his analysis on the process by which the "standard rural markets" increased on the rural landscape. Skinner stressed that "marketing structures inevitably shape local social structure and provide one of the crucial modes for integrating peasant communities into the social system which is the total society." Arguing that the standard marketing system, not the village, was the locus of the peasant community, Skinner suggested that the standard marketing area provided the framework for marriage arrangements, religious organizations, agnatic lineages, and secret societies, and that local political control was unlikely to be divorced from control over the market town itself.[17] This is a good starting point but, as will be pointed out below, needs to be refined in order to take into account social organizations based, not within a marketing system, but between systems.

Although Skinner did not go on to demonstrate his hypothesis, it was clearly shown in the surveys of parts of Jiangsu province conducted by Jiao Jiming in the 1920s and 1930s. Jiao's data for Jiangsu, more detailed than any available for Haifeng county or even Guangdong province, illustrates significant features of marketing systems that can be applied to other areas. For purposes here, then, Jiao's data will be used to construct a rough working model that will be helpful in understanding the relationship between marketing systems and rural social organization in Haifeng county.

Jiao was concerned primarily with demonstrating the close relationship between the boundaries of the marketing system and rural social organization—and social organization primarily meant religious organization. Religious organizations in Xunhua, the marketing system near Nanjing that he investigated, included single village altars devoted to local earth gods,

56

allied groups of four to eight villages, and a religious organization which encompassed nearly all the villages in the marketing system. Religious organizations in Xunhua, as in other parts of China, were concerned not merely with devotional activities but also with such other social functions as fairs and local defense. The annual festivals, for example, were also the time when the community made major decisions, such as whether to build a new bridge or school.[18]

The largest social group, the Song Gang Temple organization, coincided with the boundaries of the Xunhua marketing system (see Map 4). The Song Gang Temple organization did not arise spontaneously, but rather, in response to threats to the entire area posed by the Taiping armies when they occupied Nanjing in the 1850s. According to local oral tradition, "the forty-eight-village organization arose solely for self-defense. Originally the temple belonged to only one village, but during the reign of the Xianfeng emperor [1851–61], Nanjing was occupied by Hong Xiuchuan [Hung Hsiu-ch'uan, leader of the Taipings]. Neighboring villages were all threatened, buildings were razed, and the people fled. A local leader, Wang Yenzhang, relying on the peoples' strongly held religious beliefs, organized the peasants to help the Qing armies. Later battles with Hong's armies resulted in a string of victories. There were no local peasants who did not help. Mr. Wang's given name was Song, and peasants from near and far all called him Venerable Wang Song [Wang Song lao gong]. In commemoration of his work in organizing local self-defense, the temple in his village was renamed Song Gang Temple."[19]

Shortly afterwards, landlords from the villages in this organization held a festival to commemorate "Venerble Wang Song." Lasting for ten days, the festival became an annual fair where operas were performed and a mart was held for buying or exchanging agricultural tools. There was also a considerable amount of drunkenness. Local landowners and gentry organized the festival and conducted the religious ceremonies, while peasants contributed two copper cash as "incense-burning money." At the beginning of the festival, village leaders con-

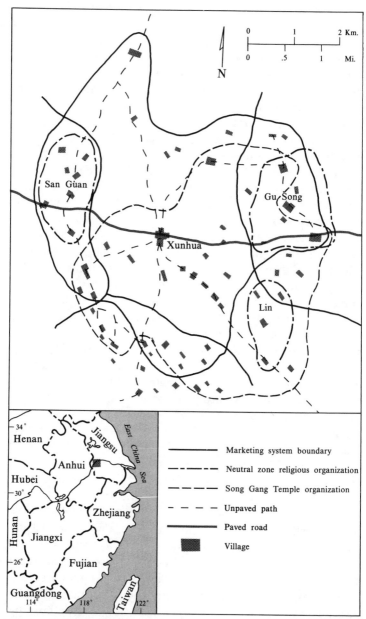

Map 4. Xunhua marketing system

ducted services at the village altar and then led a pilgrimage to the Song Gang Temple.

The correspondence between the organization of local self-defense by the landed class and the boundaries of the marketing system was not a phenomenon peculiar to the areas around the Taiping capital of Nanjing. It was also prevalent in provinces as diverse as Guangdong, Guangxi, Hunan, and Jiangsu. Local resistance to British forces in rural Guangdong during the Opium War, for example, arose in a similar process, revealing close association between the formation of self-defense organizations and market structure. Once established, these new forms of social organization did not disappear after the outside threat passed.[20] The military structures in Xunhua, for example, did not fade away after the Taipings were defeated, but rather, became incorporated into the social life of the inhabitants.

But it wasn't only the market towns and immediately surrounding villages that developed organizations for areawide social cooperation. The Xunhua marketing system had fifty-six villages in its sphere, but only half were completely dependent on Xunhua to supply their needs; the others were located in the interstices between Xunhua and one or two other market towns. Villagers in these areas, or "neutral zones" as Jiao called them, could market at two or more towns and hence were not dependent upon any single one. As the villages in these neutral zones multiplied, they formed systems themselves.

What is most interesting about these neutral zone villages was their propensity to establish religious or other social organizations well *before* attaining the status of an independent marketing system. Indeed, if the inhabitants of these neutral zone villages wanted to establish themselves as an independent marketing system—and there were certain economic and political incentives for doing so—it was clearly in their interest to organize themselves to achieve that status. According to Jiao's data for Xunhua, villagers in three of the neutral zones who had the option to trade at two market towns had founded religious organizations—the San Guan, Gu Song, and Lin Temple societies (see Map 4). With grain mills, general stores, teahouses, other permanent shops, and a number of schools established in the larger villages (Shangxia village had a population of 1,500), these neutral zone villages were clearly in the process of becoming marketing systems themselves, servicing some of the peasants' needs previously met only at Xunhua.

The core area of the marketing system—the market town plus the villages which traded solely at that town—thus was not the only socioeconomic and geographic base upon which local alignments of political, military, and religious power rested. Since a great deal of power was at stake, the growth of neutral-zone marketing systems often generated a considerable degree of social friction between the core area and the neutral zones on its periphery. Conflicts apparently did not occur while Jiao was investigating Xunhua. But in Haifeng and other parts of Guangdong province, intense social conflict occurred not only between the core and its neutral-zone periphery, but also between entire marketing systems.

Marketing Systems and Rural Social Conflict in Haifeng

As population increased during the eighteenth and nineteenth centuries and as the limits of land utilization began to be reached, rural conflict in Guangdong became widespread. Ho Ping-ti estimated that the population of Guangdong province increased from 16 million to 28 million between 1787 and 1850. Since there are no indications that Haifeng and Lufeng counties experienced any population loss due to war or famine during that period, it is reasonable to assume that the population there increased at the same rate, or from about 370,000 to 600,000 persons.[21] There are also strong indications that land in these counties had become very scarce by the last half of the nineteenth century. With population rising at the same time that the limits of land use were being reached, conflict over land and the produce of the land became endemic in Hailufeng (as Haifeng and Lufeng counties were collectively known) during the last half of the nineteenth and the early twentieth centuries. The conflict was not marked by landlord-peasant struggles, however, but by struggles between competing groups comprised of both lords and peasants. And these conflicts were intimately related to marketing system formation and elaboration.

Rather than view marketing systems as hexagons which fit flush with neighboring systems, as G. William Skinner did in his pioneering study, it is better to see them as they actually were—circular or somewhat irregularly shaped systems which not only overlapped in some areas but also left open spaces not belonging to any system. Overlapping areas contained settlements whose inhabitants attended two or more markets (the neutral zones), and open spaces often contained sources of water, wooded or hilly areas, or in some cases, ancestral gravelands. Conflict arose with the establishment of a new market by neutral-zone villagers (a new market, after all, decreased the social and political power of those controlling the old market), and also erupted over control of the important resources in the uninhabited open spaces.

Rural conflict often flared between competing lineages, the most important and powerful form of social oranization in southeast China. This form of struggle became particularly acute during the second half of the nineteenth century. Where more than one lineage lived within the same marketing system, the contest was to gain control over the land within the area. In some instances, the result was the elimination of other lineages from the marketing area. "On the plain that I have traversed, north of Swatow," Adele Fielde reported in 1894, "there was, a few years ago, a little village inhabited by a small and weak clan, surnamed Stone [Shi]. There were twelve neighboring villages, chiefly of the Plum [Tao] clan, and these all combined against the Stones, whom they far outnumbered. The Stones planted and watered their crops, and the Plums reaped the harvest. There were perpetual raids on the property of the Stones, and they, having no redress for their wrongs, were in danger of utter extinction. . . . [After continuous conflict] many of the Stones entered other clans, taking their names, some had gone into voluntary exile in distant cities, and others fled to foreign lands. . . . Now the clan Stone no longer exists, and the place of their habitation knows them no more."[22]

The cause of this particular struggle is not known, but in many instances religious issues created conflict between lineages. Where a strong lineage was unable to eliminate a weaker one, or the weaker lineage chose not to fight, the weaker group was often forced to pay for the protection of its ancestral gravelands. In Lufeng county, for example, a certain Lu lineage had an ancestral cemetery in the wooded hills separating them from the Zhuo lineage. An official reported that "it had been the custom for many years for the Lu to give gifts and money to the Zhuo when they performed their ancestral services. Because of a bad year [around 1880], the Lu did not have the money or the grain to give to the Zhuo, so the Zhuo plastered Lu gravestones with manure and knocked some over." Unable to obtain an official judgement against the Zhuo for reparations and feeling that their *feng-shui,* or the natural forces of "wind and water" which controlled good fortune, had been irreparably harmed, the Lu retaliated by kidnapping members of the Zhuo lineage, razing their houses, and desecrating their temples.[23]

With the rising demand for wood and wood products in the nineteenth century came a large number of conflicts over the control of woodlands. Prior to the nineteenth century, woodlands and other untilled areas classified as wasteland were subject to common rights, and villagers were free to cut wood and undergrowth for fuel. But by the late nineteenth and early twentieth centuries, Jamieson wrote, "certain villages have by custom appropriated to themselves the exclusive right of cutting the growth on waste lands in the neighborhood—a right which by reason of propinquity of situation and facility of access has a certain commercial value."[24] Struggles over woodlands often were expressed in terms of feng-shui when one lineage felt its good fortunes would decline if a particularly auspicious stand of trees was cut for lumber.

Another major source of friction between lineages was control over water for irrigation. Conflicting claims to water rights sparked feuds which continued on and off for decades, sometimes over the original issue and sometimes over other problems, even into the early years of the People's Republic. In the early 1870s, a conflict flared between two lineages in Puning county, just to the east of Haifeng, which soon expanded to include most of the villages and other lineages in the central part of the county. What originally sparked the fighting is not known, but it is clear that there were long-standing tensions in the area and that water rights became a central issue.[25]

When the fighting began, the local authorities could not stop it. According to William Ashmore, who visited the region in 1898, "the mandarins were weak and powerless. They often set at defiance [sic], and they and their soldiers would be driven in ignominious flight from the villages they came to reduce to order." With no other option, the magistrate let the conflict continue in the hope that both sides would be destroyed. Thus the fighting intensified: "There would not only be occasional pitched battles, but marauding parties would assail wayfarers and make it perilous, for months and even years, to be out of safe running distance. Roadways would be blocked, fields would be devastated; houses would be plundered and be left with doors and roofs battered down."[26]

Since the local authorities could not control the escalating conflict, a Qing general, Fang Yao, was called upon to restore order. General Fang may well have wanted dearly to use state forces in the feud, since he belonged to a large lineage living in Puning city that was involved in the fighting. General Fang thus did not merely restore order, but order advantageous to his own lineage. According to Ashmore, General Fang "effectually stamped out the feuds by stamping to death many of the men engaged in them. Before he got through with it he had burned some twenty towns and villages and cut off about four thousand heads. . . . Peace and order were restored." General Fang then awarded water rights, among other things, to the victors.[27]

Where a lineage or other social group did not have or could not gain control over the market town, it sometimes tried to extend its power by establishing a new market near the existing one. In an area just east of Lufeng, for instance, one lineage established a new market no more than a half-mile from a rival's market town. Kulp reported that "it is a market center that was deliberately created by the leaders of Phenix [sic] Village in 1904 in order to compete with 'Tan' Village, which contained a numerically stronger population." Although conflict did not break out while Kulp was there, these actions often precipitated armed struggle. In one area near Guangzhou, according to a Hong Kong news report, "the dispute arose over the question of the boundary between the new and old country markets. As a result of the fight, over 300 shops belonging to the Lam clan were razed to the ground with fire while 200 dwelling-houses of the Lo clan met the same fate."[28]

In many cases, one lineage was able to exercise complete dominance over the social and economic lives of the villages within the marketing system. The most powerful lineages in Haifeng not only controlled the market town itself, but also vast amounts of land in nearly every village in the marketing area. In the area around Meilong market town, the Lin lineage controlled the land of nearly every village that traded there. The Lin had come to Haifeng from Denghai county during the early Qing period and initially had engaged in commerce under the name of "Guifeng" (literally "Returning Prosperity"). By the early nineteenth century, the Meilong Lin had at least one member who had become an official of the senior licentiate rank. And by the early twentieth century, about three thousand adult members of the Lin lineage lived in the market town of Meilong, from which they oversaw the activities of the villages in the area. In Jiesheng market town in the southern part of Haifeng, the He lineage also held predominant power in that marketing system. By the 1920s, it was claimed that every He was a landlord. Like the Lin of Meilong, the He controlled the market town, had members who had become officials, and organized and controlled the local armed forces.[29]

In those instances where one lineage proved strong enough to force all others out of the marketing system, the area became inhabited by a single lineage. The standard marketing area thus provided the lineage with a material basis that was firmly embedded in the economic structure. Nanling market north of Haifeng, for example, an area inhabited solely by the Zhong lineage, was described by Zhong Yimou as "a bowl enveloped by mountains. It has one market town and several villages. The soil is fertile and the area is agriculturally rich. .... The several thousand members of the Zhong lineage who lived there formed a veritable kingdom. Under the control of large landlords and lineage heads, and relying on the fact that 'the mountains are high and the emperor distant,' they did not pay any taxes. For the past hundred years, the . . . Qing officials . . . could not but accommodate them."[30]

In most areas, new village settlements were established within the neutral zones between marketing systems by relatively weak lineages. Although it is not clear why smaller lineages would tend to settle in the interstices between marketing systems, a plausible explanation could be that these areas contained marginal lands not owned or controlled by the dominant lineage of the market town. In any case, these villages did not really "belong" to one marketing system, since peasants had the option to market at two or more. When the villages in these areas increased to six or seven, the inhabitants often banded together into religious and community organizations or fictive lineages (sometimes claiming common descent from the popular heroes of the Three Kingdoms period [A.D. 220]) or established other organizations to withstand the encroachments of stronger lineages. In a process similar to that discussed above for the Xunhua marketing system, seven villages inhabited by different families in a neutral zone in Haifeng established an association which provided a common temple for group religious services.[31]

With such a means of common identification and the solidarity that resulted, neutral zone villages often formed marketing systems themselves, though not as well-developed as existing systems. But these new markets cut substantially into the revenues of the older ones. Besides collecting considerable levies on the sale of produce, dominant lineages also owned many shops in the market town, and any shift of business to another area affected that income as well. The establishment of a new market, furthermore, reduced the human and natural resources for religious or military organizations, and had significant political consequences understood by all concerned.

Those who controlled the market therefore did not look upon such actions by the villagers with the least benign neglect.

Red Flags and Black Flags

Marketing system formation in Haifeng and Lufeng counties took a dynamic and potentially explosive form with the development of the Red Flag and Black Flag organizations. While the origin of these societies is somewhat obscure, they appeared initially in the period just following the Opium War. Xu Gengbi, a Lufeng official writing in 1878, believed that the Red and Black Flags grew out of mounting lineage struggles: "The midsection of Lufeng is inhabited by powerful lineages which have many members, while other lineages are very isolated. There is thus the difference between the strong and weak lineages. At first, only the strong fought among themselves, and there was always fighting and kidnapping. The weak lineages did not get involved in such things. But around the end of the Xianfeng reign [ca. 1860], village alliances sprang up among weak lineages in order to resist the strong. Thus arose the fights between the Red and Black Flags. There was much disorder, roads were blocked, and fields laid waste. . . . When fighting occurred, it often expanded as they linked up with other villages."[32]

The growth of the Flag societies in Haifeng and Lufeng counties occurred just as the number of markets was expanding. In the second half of the nineteenth century, when Flag conflict was endemic, markets rapidly increased from eighteen in 1877 to twenty-four just thirty years later. As villages spread in the neutral zones, villagers allied not only within religious or fictive lineage organizations, as they once had, but especially within the Flag societies. Flag membership did not require a common surname or worship at a common temple. In fact, the Flags were not limited to one locale, but expanded throughout the countryside.

The evidence indicates a pattern of Flag alignment in which weak lineages in neutral zone villages tended to unite under the Black Flag and to seek alliances with neutral zone villages on the flank of the more powerful neighbor who controlled the market town, while lineages controlling market towns allied with others under the Red Flag. By the late nineteenth century, the Flags had polarized Haifeng and Lufeng counties into two great camps—the Red Flags and the Black Flags. And since neighbors were enemies (or at least competitors for resources), the countryside had taken on the appearance of a giant checkerboard with neighboring marketing systems (or emerging systems) under opposing flags.

This direct connection between the Flags and marketing systems was confirmed in a rather remarkable fashion. In a December 1980 conversation in Haifeng, an old land reform cadre who had studied the Flags in the 1950s told a group I was with some of what he had learned. According to him, a county magistrate early in the Qing dynasty tried to govern Haifeng through the old technique of divide and rule. He got the idea for using Red and Black Flags from a wealthy landowner who raised red and black goldfish. When he put a red cloth over the pond, the red goldfish would come out; a black flag would bring out the black ones. The magistrate purportedly then divided Haifeng county into equal numbers of Red and Black Flag districts. But what is most significant is what this informant said about how the Flags were organized. Haifeng, he said, had marketing areas comprised of eighteen small villages and one large one (the market town). The magistrate designated neighboring marketing areas as alternately Red and then Black Flags. This story is probably more myth than anything else, especially since the magistrate who allegedly came up with this strategy is not to be found anywhere in the list of county magistrates in the Haifeng *Local History*. But we need not accept this explanation to recognize that the Red and Black Flags in fact had been based on the marketing systems, and that Haifeng had become polarized into two opposing camps.

Indeed, where conflicts over woodlands, water rights, or graveland locations had been limited to two lineages, the emergence of the Red and Black Flags provided the social network for calling together a force much larger than previously possible. A Flag society conflict which erupted in 1878 in the southern part of Lufeng county illustrates the relationship between marketing system formation and the Flag societies and indicates how the scope of the conflict expanded beyond the marketing system (see Map 5). The conflict started on the coastal plain, where the market towns of Jieshi and Hudong had arisen. Jieshi, on the west, was the largest marketing system, with eight villages in its inner ring and well over twenty in its outer orbit. Hudong, on the east, was a smaller system, with only eight villages firmly in its marketing area. In the neutral zone between the two marketing systems was a cluster of about ten villages that traded at both (see Map 6).

In the winter of 1878–79 there arose conflicting claims to a woodland located between the Hudong system and the ten neutral zone villages. The Red and Black Flag societies already existed, probably as a result of an earlier conflict. When a lineage belonging to one of the Flags cut down some trees in a stand claimed by members of the other Flag, the investigating official reported, other villages joined the squabble on the next day "because they belonged to the allied villages. . . . As soon as the call went out, the allies responded immediately, and before breakfast time a thousand people had gathered." Xu Gengbi claimed that "this fighting began on a small scale, and no one was even hurt. But when the allied villages joined the fighting, seven were killed and scores wounded."[33] The village alliances under the Red and Black Flag societies corresponded to the Hudong marketing system and the neutral zone villages, with villages from the Hudong marketing system inner circle entering the fray as Red Flags and their opponents in the neutral zone villages gathering under the Black Flag.

In the sixth district in eastern Haifeng a similar pattern emerged. Shagang market town posted the Red Flag, while the neighboring neutral zone area united under the Black Flag. In the mid-nineteenth century severe Flag fighting there had forced several families in the area to flee, and in 1902 a recrudescence of Flag conflict destroyed the market town of Nantu. In both cases, Red Flags were identified with the market town and immediately surrounding villages, while the Black Flags were neutral zones in the process of becoming marketing systems.[34]

Map 5. Flag conflict in Lufeng

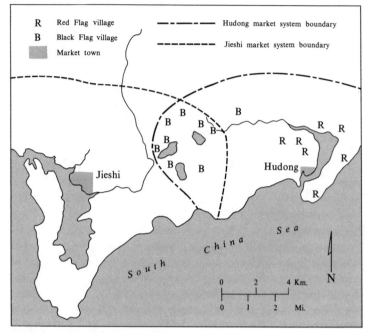

Map 6. Red and Black Flag villages

Much like lineage organizations, the Flags included both lords and peasants, although the lords provided the leadership while peasants were the actual combatants. The leader of the Black Flags in the area of Lufeng discussed above was a wealthy man with a purchased imperial degree who used his wealth and position to bribe officials to obtain favors for himself and his followers.[35] Flag leaders in areas not directly involved in a conflict could deliver peasant fighters—for a price. Peasants did not receive any remuneration except for food and lodging expenses, although loot was probably also a factor in their willingness to go.

The loyalty of peasants to their Flag was based primarily on the protection they could receive through their united strength against the enemy and through their leader's official connections against state demands for taxes. When the new county magistrate arrived in Lufeng, for example, he was not too surprised to find that even with a very low tax assessment, only 60 percent of the tax had ever been collected. But Xu Gengbi was much more surprised to learn that tax records had not been kept in the yamen office for decades and that the yamen staff had no idea what the tax assessments even were, or so they claimed. They had collected the tax without ever investigating who owned the land or how much was owned. Tax collection had simply been farmed out.[36]

Xu Gengbi, on the other hand, was an enterprising, aspiring, and perhaps incorruptible official bent on reform. He personally investigated land holdings and taxes in a few areas and, upon discovering that many landowners had paid only one-tenth of the assessed taxes, concluded that tax resistance aided the growth of the Flags: "Since the fighting began between the Red and Black Flag societies, the common people have taken tax resistance as a custom." Rather than wait for taxes to be brought to the yamen, Xu decided to induce payment by setting up tax collecting stations in the market towns and larger villages, thereby eliminating carriage fees from the amount collected. But when tax collectors went into the villages—more often than not under armed guard—villagers yelling and waving their flags at the village gate dared the officials

71

to enter. If they were brave (or foolish) enough to go in, Xu Gengbi quickly discovered, the villagers "seized officials, beat them, and gathered in great numbers to resist."[37]

This was localism at its best: the passionate defense against any outside threat, whether it was a neighbor competing for control of natural resources or the state collecting taxes. In a world in which it was commonly believed that wealth was more or less fixed, anything taken from the community by outsiders represented a permanent loss. But contrary to the zero-sum assumptions of the rural inhabitants, the economy did change (increasingly after trade began with the West), population did increase, and new marketing systems did form. The world was not static after all. The rural populace could not understand or explain these things, but they continually combatted the consequences of change. And, paradoxically, they fought it through social organizations whose very existence was not fixed but was intimately bound up with the marketing system, perhaps the most dynamic feature of the rural landscape.

All of these organizations—lineages, neutral zone societies, and the Flags—counted among their members both lord and peasant, rich and poor. These were vertical rather than horizontal cleavages in the countryside. Peasant loyalties were to the Flag or lineage, regardless of whether the wealthiest and most powerful controlled them. This was the dynamic of localism. The "other" was not the lord; it was other lineages, the enemy Flag, or the state, all competing for limited resources in a fragile world.

The social conflict between lineages and Flags in Haifeng and Lufeng counties in the nineteenth century was part of a broader phenomenon known to state authorities as *xiedou*, or endemic feud strife. As the valuable work by Harry Lamley shows, xiedou was prevalent along the southeast coast, including Fujian, Taiwan, and Guangdong provinces, and may have been present to greater or lesser degrees throughout China. Lamley describes xiedou as "deviant behavior" expressive of a "pathology of violence" among counter- or subcultures in rural China. These subcultures, Lamley argues, were communities that "subscribed to norms, customs, and practices in conflict with those upheld by the state and maintained by society in general."[38] What the norms of society in general may have been is not explicitly addressed, but presumably the deviant norms and customs of various social groups such as Flags or lineages led them into conflict with similar groups or the state.

The analysis here takes a very different approach, relating collective action and violence not to presumably deviant values or norms but to the actual patterns of life that created social groups and structured collective action and violence. This approach sees xiedou not as deviant or pathological behavior, but as arising from the very structure and operation of the society itself. Lineage and Flag conflict in Haifeng was not a pathological aberration but a natural part of the society in which it was embedded. Lamley hints at similar conclusions when he looks for environmental factors—population growth, migration, strong lineages, a history of violence, and commercialization—that might explain the prevalence of xiedou in southeast China. Unfortunately, he does not push this line of inquiry very far, falling back instead on the idea of subcultures with deviant values to explain the collective violence.

Environmental analysis as an approach to understanding patterns of rural collective action and violence has been put to use by Elizabeth Perry and has yielded impressive results.[39] In her analysis of Huaibei on the North China plain, Perry relates enduring traditions of rebellion to a precarious natural and social environment that led various groups to adopt different survival strategies. Those groups with fewer resources adopted what Perry calls a "predatory strategy," raiding wealthier neighbors, who in turn used "protective strategies" to ward off these outside threats. Depending on other conditions and circumstances, either survival strategy could evolve into a larger rebellion. Perry thus attributes rural violence in Huaibei to "environmental uncertainty . . . translated into action through the mediation of . . . class, clan, and settlement."[40] On the face of it, this sounds like an attractive explanation for the patterns

73

of collective action and violence in Haifeng as well. But a closer comparison reveals some interesting differences.

In general, Huaibei was a much poorer area than Haifeng, having lower agricultural productivity, population density, and commercial activity. With a low population density and poor transportation systems, Perry shows, "commercial life in Haui-pei was . . . quite undeveloped."[41] As we have seen, however, Haifeng's marketing and marketing systems expanded greatly in the late nineteenth century. Resources of all kinds just were more abundant in Haifeng. In Huaibei, not only did the natural and social environment create a precarious place for people to live; it did not change much over the decades. Perry therefore was able to show that the environment of Huaibei continuously produced and reproduced the same survival strategies, forms of collective action, and types of collective violence. As long as the environment did not change, neither did forms of collective violence. Predatory and protective strategies might spill over into rebellion, but rebellion on these bases could not easily be transformed into revolution. Perry shows that only in the 1940s when the Chinese Communist Party set about to change some of the environmental constraints on collective action did peasants begin to adopt revolutionary strategies designed to alter their social world.

By contrast, the social environment of Haifeng was not at all static. It was, rather, quite dynamic, and new forms of collective action and violence consequently emerged all the time. This was particularly because changes in the structure of the marketing system precipitated changes in the forms of rural collective action and violence in Haifeng. The forms of collective action and violence that emerged under the Flag societies differed in subtle but important ways from earlier and very similar lineage conflicts. As rural tension increased during the nineteenth century, the need of the leaders of rural social organizations for ever larger bases from which to recruit men and resources outstripped the boundaries of the local marketing area. While the Flags clearly were based on the dynamics of the marketing system, they transcended that base and provided the opportunity for peasants from different locales to meet and act together in a way never before possible. The Flags began to overcome the very localism that had spawned them, and this was to become an important factor in the 1920s, when peasants began to organize against lords. In Haifeng the tasks of organizers in unifying peasants into unions were to be greatly simplified by the Flags: instead of confronting dozens of diverse social organizations, they faced only two. Still, in the late nineteenth century, the lines of rural conflict remained vertical. As long as the Red and Black Flags integrated peasants and lords into strong organizations, rural conflict along horizontal class lines was precluded. This does not mean that the countryside was devoid of all but localistic and factional conflict. Indeed, strains in the social order were occasioned by the most fundamental of questions—those concerning the proper distribution of food.

CHAPTER 4

Markets and Morals
Peasants and the Question of Food

STARVING people stole some food," recorded Yu Buxiong in the Haifeng *Local History* under the entry for 24 April 1716. "Rabble-rousers agitated the mob," Yu continued, "and thousands clustered around the homes of the wealthy, several of which were then looted. But Magistrate Xu Xudan and Police Chief Li Dazhong arrested the leaders and executed a few people. That stopped the riot."[1]

As blunt as the repression was brutal, the county magistrate's portrayal showed the food riot matter-of-factly as a biological response to the elemental stimulus of the stomach: starving people simply stole some food. But how else could Mr. Yu—a representative of the imperial government—have described rioters other than as starving? As angry people perhaps? Or outraged people? These words would have implied that the people might have had other cause to steal food and loot the homes of the wealthy. So, to genteel society, they had to be just starving people. But in the popular mind, the people had certain rights (inalienable ones, if you will) that they had the legitimate right to defend, even if it meant causing an occasional disturbance in the Confucian order. In such cases the people could not act wrongly.[2] To be sure, the people's vision of the proper social order clashed with that of the higher orders on several issues, but it was especially in the matter of food provisioning that the difference was vividly exposed.

Food Riots

Food riots and the fear of riots were not uncommon during times of dearth or famine. Days like the twenty-fourth of April were on the minds of the authorities whenever harvest failure threatened to send the price of food soaring, and, as Table 2 illustrates, that was often. Peasants could not be absolutely certain that the summer monsoon would come, and if it did, whether it would be crop-nourishing or so severe as to cause widespread flooding. Both the typhoon of 1726 and the drought of 1749, for example, destroyed the crop, but at least the drought did not wash away houses.[3] Certainly, irrigation works somewhat mitigated the problem, but the environment remained unpredictable nonetheless. Even in good years, food supplies could run short, causing problems for the authorities: natural disasters just accentuated tendencies inherent in the social structure.

Although the great majority of the rural population were producers of food—the peasantry—they were nonetheless conscious of food prices. In the late spring or early summer, when the previous year's harvest had been consumed but the fall harvest was not yet in, they themselves had to purchase foodstuffs. Numerous entries in the Haifeng *Local History*, for ex-

Table 2: Harvest Failure and Rice Prices in Haifeng and Neighboring Areas, Selected Years, 1644–1883 (prices in copper cash per *dou*)

Year	Normal price	Famine price	Percentage of normal
1644	85	300	350
1649	85	450	530
1694	62	200	320
1697	62	500	895
1726	70	600	860
1747	140	300	215
1748	140	180	130
1770	150	300	200
1779	135	800	590
1834	355	400	110
1857	290	710	250
1858	290	1,000	350
1883	230	720	310

Source: Compiled from *Haifeng xianzhi* and *Huizhou fuzhi*.
NOTE: Famines also occurred in 1615, 1632, 1680, 1716, 1727, 1739, 1749, 1751, 1757, 1759, 1786, 1818, 1825, 1840, 1861, 1869–70, 1873, and 1879. There is, however, no data on rice prices for these years.

ample, began with the phrase: "In the spring, rice was expensive." Needless to say, the supply of rice and other foodstuffs was greatly affected by natural disaster, for shortages then might occur at any time of the year. Furthermore, rural China was not composed exclusively of peasants. In the cities and market towns, large numbers of urban poor gathered for day labor. Coolies, dockworkers, shopkeepers, potters, ironmongers, and the marginally employed all depended on the local market to supply their foodstuffs. When shortages arose, both urban and rural poor confronted the problem of obtaining food.

Divisions between the small town and countryside should not be exaggerated, especially in the matter of dearth. Although peasants certainly had some grain supplies, in "barren springs" they would be as much in need of grain as the urban poor.[4] If the urban poor had a stake in the market to supply their food needs, peasants clung to it as well. Furthermore, the market town was a strong link between urban and rural dwellers. Indeed, rural market towns—except those surrounded by walls— merged almost imperceptively into the countryside and were within easy walking distance of every rural inhabitant. In streets crowded with fortune- and story-tellers, and in teahouses animated with discussion of local and national events, the drudgery and monotony of rural life was periodically broken.

Food riots were of course triggered by a variety of factors, including soaring prices and scarcity, rice merchant malpractices, or widespread hunger, all of which aroused popular ire. These grievances, moreover, were placed within a framework of popular conceptions of what were fair prices and just practices. And these notions in turn presupposed a wider view of social norms and the proper actions the authorities should take when scarcity threatened. Any outrage to the moral assumptions of the people, just as much as actual hunger, was usually the cause for direct popular action.

The authorities' primary duty, from the point of view of the rural poor, was to ensure that the area under their jurisdiction had sufficient supplies of grain to provide for all inhabitants. For this purpose the government had, from a very early date, constructed "ever-normal" granaries throughout the countryside. In theory, these granaries would stablize grain prices and equalize supplies throughout the year. The county magistrates were to authorize the purchase of grain after the fall harvest when supplies were greatest to shore up the price, and were to sell grain in the spring and summer to prevent shortages and price-gouging. During the eighteenth century, the granaries seemed to function well enough. In the spring of 1770, for example, when heavy rains sent rice prices soaring, authorities in Haifeng county opened the granaries and sold grain at low prices. "The crowd was mollified," the magistrate later recorded in the *Local History.*[5]

The central authorities were so interested in rice prices that provincial officials routinely included them in their memorials, even when the topic was something quite different. When in 1714 the fifty-year-old Wang Wenxiong took up his new post as military commander for Huizhou prefecture (of which Haifeng was one of six counties), his first memorial included confirmation that he had arrived at his post, notes on the several old and new bandit cases he had to deal with, and a crop report: "Last year the fall harvest fell short, and rice prices rose to a range of 1 to 2 ounces of silver per picul." Although Wang's interest in rice prices was partly conditioned by his responsibility for provisioning his troops (and at the least cost possible), he was also obviously aware of the connection between rising rice prices and local disorder—disorder he would be called upon to repress if the local authorities, such as Magistrate Xu Xudan and Police Chief Li Dazhong in Haifeng county, could not handle it. But as we have seen, Xu and Li could indeed handle local riots. During Wang's tenure in office, he consistently reported excellent harvests and low rice prices for eastern Guangdong; when he left Huizhou in mid-1718 he could report that with a good harvest "everyone is well-off."[6]

Maintenance of the granaries was but one part of the authorities' duties. As described in *The Guide to Famine Preparedness* compiled in 1795, the people expected officials to take other actions as well in times of dearth. Besides opening the granaries, grain exports were to be prohibited, rice-wine making stopped, rice prices lowered, and taxes reduced. The authorities were also expected to exhort the wealthy to contribute rice, to set up soup kitchens, to donate relief funds, to provide public works such as road construction and bridge repair, and even to establish pawn shops. "During the famine," the author of the *Guide* observed, "the poor sell their clothing and tools in order to get food. The rich take advantage of their distress to buy these items at 10 percent of their worth. During such times, the government should appoint someone to buy these things so the poor do not take a great loss. After the harvest they can be sold back to the poor."[7]

Underlying official prescriptions for famine preparedness was the fear that the people would take action themselves if officials did not—a fear spelled out in *The Guide to Famine Preparedness*: "The poor and the rich live in different worlds. The rich exploit the poor and the poor hate the rich. The poor are always waiting for something to happen that will give them an excuse to act. As soon as there is famine, they will riot. First, they will steal rice. Next, they will steal from the rich. Finally, they will gather in great masses to plunder." The popular actions which the authorities could expect were clearly delineated, and they recognized a pattern to the targets and scale of operations of the rioters. In fact, the authorities knew that specific actions would elicit definite responses from the rural and urban poor. Thus from the authorities' perspective, famine relief was successful if, as they said, "the people were pacified" or "the crowd was mollified."[8]

Indeed, riots were not anarchic outbursts of undirected fury. Quite the contrary: crowds held very definite conceptions of what on their part were just and legitimate actions. The outright stealing of rice, for example, was not really all that common. Rather, the most prevalent "crime" during a famine was setting grain prices at a level popularly determined by the crowd. Only if the merchant or rich family refused to sell the grain at the price set by the crowd was it then taken without payment. "When there is a famine," warned *The Guide to Famine Preparedness*, "the people easily cause disturbances, such as forcing the sale of grain. If those who have grain refuse to sell it, everyone becomes what is called a 'guest at their table.'"[9]

But large quantities of grain were not taken. The rioting crowd usually requisitioned only about a pound per family, an extremely small amount. Far from being the embodiment of "disorder," these so-called mobs displayed a great deal of restraint and order. Generally, the people did not take direct action—or riot, in the words of the officials—unless the authorities and wealthy in the community did not fulfill their obligations. And then the crowd did not use force or violence unless their attempts to exercise what they considered to be their moral rights were opposed.

Rice riots were not altogether spontaneous affairs; literate persons sometimes wrote and distributed handbills calling upon the people to take direct action. The Imperial Board of Punishments, for example, heard a case in 1813, where, the justices wrote, "one Wang Zhankui, fearing that grain stores would not willingly sell grain during a bad year, wrote a handbill calling for the people to take the grain by force. The alarmed rustics responded by forming a terrifying crowd." The board decided: "This is an unlawful assembly, taking advantage of local dearth to form crowds, steal, and riot. Punishment: one degree less than the law on rowdies, one hundred strokes and three years' banishment." Interestingly, however, the board drew a distinction between leaders and followers. If "the poor did not recognize their crime," the board concluded, they were to be exempt from punishment. Even the state, then, recognized that the poor felt it legitimate to seize stocks of grain when hunger threatened the community.[10]

Natural disasters were not the only cause of famine. Even as shortages worsened and the urban and rural poor became hungrier, they had only to look at grain merchants carting away rice to be sold in the expanding metropolitan areas. Indeed, the authorities had long identified merchant practices as causing shortages, arguing: "The blame for the rise in the price of grain is not with the wealthy but with the merchants. Merchants hoard grain to force the price up."[11] Although the officials of the world's largest agrarian state certainly had their share of physiocratic bias, the people too had apprehensions about merchant behavior. The growth of large urban centers such as Guangzhou and the Chaozhou-Shantou region, the development of a rice market to supply their needs, and the consequent specialization of agricultural production had divided the "Two Guangs" (Guangdong and Guangxi) into two antagonistic camps, pitting the city's demands for grain against the moral assumptions of the rural poor. In the early eighteenth century, when Guangxi peasants pressured rice merchants to stop exporting rice to Guangzhou, for example, the governor of Guangdong demanded that the people holding up rice shipments be declared criminals and arrested. Less than a decade later, the governor of Guangxi again protested the extensive purchases of rice by Guangdong merchants. And by the nineteenth century, internal constraints on the export of rice from Guangxi to Guangzhou became so great that it was cheaper and easier for rice merchants to import rice from Southeast Asia.

Controlling grain exports was in fact a continuous policy in areas only marginally able to meet demands from their own area; in such areas grain exports, even in the best of years, could cause shortages. As Yu Buxiong observed of Haifeng county in 1750: "The grain from Yangan district can support the other three districts. It is said that when Yangan has a good harvest, Haifeng is sufficient in grain. Recently, however, grain from Yangan has not been sold only in the county market, as it should be. Merchants instead buy the grain and ship it to other counties in order to obtain a big profit. The army has now been ordered to suppress the trade, and local headmen have been ordered to make investigations. The masses will not stand for merchants getting fat off of agriculture!"[12]

In these situations, the authorities certainly had to take some actions to assure the people that grain would be available—and to stave off potential riots. As late as 1883, for example, Magistrate Xu Gengbi of Lufeng county fulfilled the people's expectations of proper official conduct by taking all the correct actions. The price of rice in that year had risen to about 720 copper cash per peck, or about 300 percent higher than normal. The magistrate felt that the shortages were caused not by a poor harvest but by large purchases of rice by merchants from Huizhou and Guangzhou. He slapped an embargo on exports, he said, "so that the grain can be used by the people here. . . . It is not that the rice produced here is insufficient for local use." Magistrate Xu also ordered wealthy families to sell their private stocks of grain: "Powerful families are permitted to have only a three-year supply of rice. If they have more than that, their rice will be sold at a low price and they will be punished."[13]

The people's conceptions of what officials had to do in times of dearth or famine therefore was conditioned at least in part by their experience with market forces. The market and the subsistence concerns of most peasants coexisted uneasily in the best of times, and the truce was broken whenever merchant practice appeared to threaten the peasant family subsistence. Even such commonplace institutions as the market day had been established and upheld in part in response to the expressed need of the people for protection against the unrestricted or unleashed forces of the market. Early in the Qing dynasty, the new Manchu rulers had forbade merchants from going into the countryside to buy up supplies of grain. The regents for the boy emperor Shunzhi discovered, however, "that in many places shopowners are suddenly disobeying the laws which forbid forestalling and engrossing. Seldom do they do as we wish. They rely on their power to coerce people into selling, and even trump up the charge that there are bandits around in order to frighten the people and cleverly corner the market." In the name of the emperor, the regents proclaimed: "Markets are to be regulated. Goods in the market are to be fairly priced."[14] The enforcement of a specific market day, therefore, was to prohibit grain from being brought and sold on any other day or in any place other than the market, thereby ensuring local inhabitants that grain would be available for their purchase.

The success of the rioting crowd in buying a pound of rice at a popularly determined price thus did not intrude only as a random disturbance of the Confucian order, but rather generally influenced the daily government and even some of the basic institutions of rural China. But while these actions cannot be described as political in any modern sense, neither were they apolitical, for they emerged from a broader conception of the proper functioning of the social order: the moral economy of the rural poor.[15]

These beliefs, more or less strongly held throughout the community, provided a standard against which official behavior was judged: when these norms were transgressed or violated, the people felt justified in acting to enforce traditional norms of conduct and behavior. If the rioting or price-setting crowd acted according to any consistent set of beliefs, it was perhaps a folk understanding of the paternalist model the authorities themselves held. There was, in effect, a shared universe of beliefs about the proper social order. But there was a crucial difference: the popularly informed conceptions clearly sanctioned and legitimized direct action by the people, which the authorities' model emphatically did not. If merchants or the wealthy in the community would not sell grain at a popularly determined price, anyone could become "a guest at their table."

But by the late eighteenth century, actual practice began to deviate substantially from the paternalist model. While the rice market was being regulated, a market developed in the rice export certificates that had been used as proof of local grain surpluses so that the merchants could ship the grain to other localities.[16] Perhaps more importantly, however, the granaries designed to ward off shortages had fallen into disuse and abuse. After a 1787 investigation of granaries in six counties in Zhejiang province showed each to be short by several tons of the amount stated in the ledger, the managers were given five years to replace the deficit. The problem was not limited to Zhejiang. Although there were "innumerable starving people" in Haifeng in 1786, authorities did not open the granaries or seek contributions from the wealthy. In 1794, the Qianlong emperor rather sarcastically remarked that "the provincial governors report each year that there is no deficit in the granaries. But when suddenly there is a bad year, I am told that it is no longer true. . . . I know that the granaries in each province cannot be full." He was of course right. The reason, according to reports

84

reaching the emperor, was that "degenerate officials commonly use their position to remove the grain or even to lend it out for interest."[17]

The situation became so serious that the next emperor, Jiaqing, felt obliged to restate the premises upon which the granaries—and social order—rested: "All affairs under heaven are based upon agriculture. If peasants experience hardship, then all will experience hardship. If this happens, it is the end of everything." But, cautioned the emperor, if peasants were guaranteed a livelihood and subsistence, "there will be no trouble anywhere under heaven." The emperor complained that the granaries were coming under the control of officials and landlords who used them as private funds for making loans to peasants: "The hardships of peasants are not to be found in bad years, but in good years," the Jiaqing emperor dourly remarked.[18]

By the late nineteenth century, officials faced with famine or grain shortages in Guangdong no longer opened public granaries. The last time officials in Haifeng dispersed food from the granaries was in 1833; two decades later there was no grain to distribute. Famine relief was now a fortuitous event, as officials came to rely on merchants and the market to supply grain, undoubtedly at a substantial profit. Nor did officials exercise the powers invested in them by higher authorities and expected of them by the people to ensure local supplies. But if the authorities wouldn't, the people would. In 1898, for example, it was reported from Bolo county, just east of Guangzhou, that with the price of rice dear, "vagrants prevented the export of rice and looted rice stores." In the spring of 1907, high prices again sparked direct action when people broke down and destroyed rice merchants' offices, robbed rice stores, and killed a rice merchant. Perhaps the most revealing statement of the nexus rural people saw between rice prices, the duties of the authorities, and the right of the people to take direct action to enforce their moral beliefs is contained in the confession of the leader of the 1907 riot: "The cause of this rebellion was that rice was very dear and scarce in that part and had been so for about a year. The authorities knew this the whole time and would not take any steps to make rice any cheaper. They knew well the laws and duties cast upon them in cases of this kind. They simply ignored the people and let them starve."[19]

Subsistence and Protection

The decreasing willingness and ability of the state to provide a modicum of subsistence guarantees to peasants by the late nineteenth century meant that other social relationships, such as lineage ties, patronage, and tenancy, became more important than they ever had been in the peasants' attempts to secure subsistence needs. Peasants, it is true, had not seen the state primarily as a provider, but as a taker. State claims on peasant production in the form of taxes and labor were the most regular and predictable state actions affecting peasants. On the other hand, eighteenth-century peasants may well have granted a bit of legitimacy to the claims put forward by the state. In edicts read in Haifeng market towns since 1674 under the institution known under the double entendre *xiang yue*, the "village lecture" or the "village contract," the emperors told those assembled: "If you realize that what the court worries over and concerns itself with day and night is nothing but the affairs of the people—that dikes are built when there is a flood, prayers are offered when there is a drought, and when locusts appear efforts are made to extirpate them; that you enjoy the benefits if fortunately calamities are thus warded off, and your taxes are exempted or you are given relief by your government if calamities ensue—do you have the heart to allow your taxes to remain unpaid, thus delaying the fulfillment of your government's needs?"[20]

When the Qing state was no longer present even in the matter of provisioning, the contract between people and state was easily nullified, and peasants sought to avoid paying taxes. Throughout Guangdong province, the rich and powerful could avoid taxation through outright bribery or by not registering land, and because of their connections, peasants sought their protection. Haifeng and Lufeng were not exceptions. In Lufeng county, for example, a new magistrate had complained in 1879 of a local landowner who bribed provincial officials and military officers in order to escape arrest and prosecution for tax evasion. Freeholding peasants who had been given title to waste land in order to bring it into production found themselves hard-pressed to pay the land tax or perform state labor services; it seemed advantageous to surrender a portion or the whole of their property to powerful families in exchange for protection against such demands.[21] Similar pressures during the late Ming had driven peasants to seek protection as well, resulting in the personal servitude of the peasant. In the nineteenth century, the results were quite different, for servility was now safely buried in the past. Peasant misfortune now would not lead to new forms of serfdom. What it would lead to will be discussed in more detail in the next chapter.

The development of new protection relationships was almost inevitable because of the very way in which the land tax was collected. Since the power of the Qing state did not reach into the countryside beyond the gates of the county seat, magistrates were dependent upon local landlords to collect taxes. Powerful families became tax-farmers for the magistrate, negotiating for the amount of tax to be collected from their area. Peasant freeholders paid a certain amount of tax to the powerful family in addition to an amount for a reduction in the rate, thus blurring the distinction between taxes and protection money against taxes. While powerful families could keep the difference between the quota and the amount actually collected, they were not predisposed to extract too much from peasants for fear that they would flee. During the nineteenth century, these payments took on more and more the characteristics of rent: the landlords paid the land tax, while what peasants considered to be tax was seen by the landlords as rent.[22]

Lineages also provided various types of protection and subsistence guarantees to their peasant members. Lineages owned a considerable amount of land in Guangdong, ranging between 30 and 40 percent of the arable. Lineage lands were collectively owned and had strict rules against alienation. Wealthy members also owned lands of their own not controlled by the lineage. But when these wealthy members died, they often bequeathed a portion of their private land to the lineage. The use of lineage land varied with the size of the lineage and the amount of land held. In smaller lineages, the income or rent from the land was usually just sufficient to cover annual expenses for ancestral worship and temple upkeep. In the five-hundred-member Kong lineage, for example, which owned 100 mou of land, the income from 65 mou was used to support the ancestral hall and related festivals. The income from the remaining land was distributed to members for marital, funerary, or educational purposes.[23]

The use of land in smaller lineages often rotated annually among members, who then bore ritual costs for that year. But the rotation was also designed to insure the subsistence of member families. The Liu lineage of Jiesheng village in Haifeng county was a small lineage rotating use of the land. But lineage regulations stipulated that "if a member suffers a hard year and it is not their turn to use the lineage land, the next in line will yield their turn." In larger lineages as well, the right of poorer members to use lineage lands for a contribution of a certain amount of grain to the treasury was commonly recognized. The large Wang lineage owned 4,000 mou which was let to members and outsiders alike. The income was used to support education, ancestral worship, road repair, and a local armed force. Lineage members regularly received funds for education, weddings, funerals, sickness, and backing in lawsuits and other civil conflicts.[24]

The landlord-tenant relationship in Haifeng also provided certain subsistence guarantees to peasants. Just as the rural poor had expected officials to take certain specific actions in time of dearth, so too did they expect their lord (when they had one) to respect certain rights guaranteed by the customary terms of tenancy. As was true in other rural areas, tenure systems in Haifeng were not all the same. Indeed, landlordism developed in at least two separate stages, each representing different social backgrounds for the lords, attitudes toward the land, and thus terms of tenancy. The oldest form of tenancy still existing in late-nineteenth- and early-twentieth-century

Haifeng was permanent tenure. As shown previously, various types of permanent tenure had been won from the old Ming lords by serfs and servile tenants in the late Ming and early Qing uprisings. Descendants of the Ming lords continued to hold land throughout the Qing period, but they were economically weakened by terms of permanent tenure favorable to peasants. Because the rent had been set during the early Qing, increases in productivity effectively reduced the rent to an extremely low point. And by the terms of tenancy, the rent was permanently set at that low level. But when a new kind of landowner emerged who collected larger rents, peasants were very interested in securing rights that would provide subsistence guarantees.

While the old Ming nobility was dying, a new class of landlords began to appear in the mid- to late eighteenth century. The new landlords came from merchant houses who saw land as a good investment because of the profit to be made from selling rice. Rice prices had declined steadily during the early Qing and had remained relatively low until about the 1730s, but began to climb steadily from the second half of the eighteenth century into the twentieth. Just as rising rice prices in Ming times had stimulated the lords' interest in producing for the market on their demesne, so too did rising prices in the Qing period spark an interest among merchants in the land and in marketing its produce. In 1740, for example, an official in the Yangzi valley remarked that "now that merchants have become rich, many are buying thousands of mou of land. Peasants till their land, and each year they collect several thousand piculs in rent." And in Hunan, it was observed in 1749 that "now, land is reverting to the wealthy. Fifty to sixty percent of the people who once owned land are now all tenants." Throughout China in the mid-eighteenth century, merchants began buying or even renting land to take advantage of rising prices not only for food grains but for other crops such as sugar, betel nuts, or hemp.[25]

Being a coastal county, Haifeng had easy access to cheap water transportation by which grain could be shipped west to Guangzhou and east to Chaozhou. And when Hong Kong and

89

Shantou were opened as treaty ports in the mid-nineteenth century, demand for grain continued to grow. The first complaints about grain exports from Haifeng had been raised in the mid-eighteenth century after merchant families had started purchasing land. The Lin of Meilong were merchants from Denghai county who began to acquire land in the mid-eighteenth century. The Peng family, which settled in Qiaodong, a suburb of Haifeng city, was also of merchant heritage and reportedly owned over a hundred shops in the city. During the late eighteenth and early nineteenth century, Peng Jingbao began purchasing land which by the early twentieth century netted the family an annual rent of over 1,000 piculs of rice collected from three hundred peasant families.[26]

But why rent the land out? Would it not have been more efficient and profitable for landlords to manage production themselves and pay wages to hired laborers rather than underwrite the subsistence of an entire peasant family? Where they could, merchants did just that, but the use of hired labor apparently occurred predominantly on new land just brought into production, land unencumbered by any previous claims of tenure. Merchants who purchased arable to take advantage of rising grain prices could not simply displace the peasant producers and bring in hired laborers even if they owned the land outright. For enshrined in the various types of tenure Haifeng peasants had won in the mid-seventeenth-century struggles—the manure investment, greater-lesser purchase, and subsoil-topsoil systems—were *inalienable* rights to the use of the land. These rights applied not only to petty proprietors but also to tenants. The only way merchants could acquire land and its produce for marketing purposes was to respect the peasants' hard-won rights. Because of the strength of peasant claims to the land, what developed to meet market demands for grain was not commercial farming but landlordism, with grain entering the market through rent.

Hence the landlords of merchant background had an attitude toward the land and its produce premised on the profitability of selling the grain. When purchasing land in Haifeng, according to one source, the buyer "carefully recorded the location of the purchased land, the rent to be received, and the time of the winter and summer payment. If the rent was in arrears, the landlord could change tenants as stipulated in the lease contract between landlord and peasant."[27] In addition, landlords were careful to draw up detailed contracts of tenancy which stipulated more than the name of the tiller and the amount of rent, as had been the case with permanent tenure.

But the new lords could not enforce terms of tenancy determined solely by the dictates of market profitability. On land held on permanent tenure, which accounted for the bulk of tenures, landlords could do little because rent was fixed at a light rate. The other form of rent payment during the nineteenth century was sharecropping, an arrangement providing the tenant with certain subsistence guarantees that likewise limited the amount of rent landlords could collect. Although the amount paid to the lord on a share basis would be substantial if the harvest was good, the peasant was never left without grain in a bad year, a common enough occurrence in Haifeng. Furthermore, the custom of farming on shares gave a tenant the right to a total or partial rent reduction whenever the harvest failed. Sharecropping did not provide strong incentives to increase production, but peasants thought so highly of the subsistence protections that they fought against landlord attempts to collect a fixed rent.[28]

By the late nineteenth century, however, fixed rents did begin to appear. As will be pointed out in Chapter 5, this development was associated with market opportunities. Fixed rent, about one-half the harvest of a good year, just as sharecropping was, could not be raised; but neither could it be reduced. Haifeng peasants complained about this "ironclad rent," which left them with very little if the harvest failed: "It doesn't matter whether there is drought or if it is a good or a bad year," they said, "tenants still have to pay the fixed rent and can't lower it even a little."[29]

Not all fixed rents were inflexible downward. Apparently community opinion in Haifeng was strong enough to force even lords who claimed to be collecting "ironclad rent" to consider a rent reduction of 10 to 20 percent in a bad year.

But the lord could either grant or deny the request. When lord and peasant could not agree on the amount of the reduction, according to one observer, "the subdistrict head sets a day for the lord to send an overseer to watch the harvest. The lord and the tenant then receive equal shares."[30] While fixed rents could thus be lowered, the lord-tenant relationship in this instance had subtly changed. What had been a right for peasants farming on shares had become a favor dispensed by the lord—the subsistence guarantee of a rent reduction.

If the landlord did not reduce rent in a bad year in accordance with customary rights, there were not many alternatives left to peasants. But they did feel justified in taking some actions. Observers noted tenants "drenching grain to increase the weight. Sand was also mixed with the grain. The most creative method was to mix empty rice husks with muddy, boiling water. When the husks had soaked up the mud, they looked exactly like ordinary unhusked rice. When the time came to pay the rent, 'mud rice' and good rice were mixed together. If the lord's house was outside the village, all the peasant families in the village . . . would substitute 'mud rice' for good rice."[31]

The paradox of tenancy in all of its forms in Haifeng was that it was simultaneously a system of oppression and exploitation, and one of protection and security. As rural conflict intensified during the late nineteenth century, landlords were not too inclined to violate the subsistence requirements of the peasantry. They may have attempted to fool peasants by using larger measures to collect rent or even straw baskets which expanded as grain was added, but peasants could see through these subterfuges. In fact, landlords could not openly attack peasants' subsistence guarantees because they needed loyal followers (for the Red and Black Flag societies) to defend their interests against the demands of the state or the depredations of others. As the struggle for the land increased, so too did the lords' needs for local support as well as the peasants' needs for protection and security. Unfortunate indeed was the freeholding peasant who did not have some means of protection in this world of strife and conflict.

By justifying their right to a portion of the harvest because of the protection they could offer peasants against the state, other powerful groups, or even agricultural failure, landlords quite naturally saw their relationship with peasants in the paternalist terms of benevolence, kind-heartedness, and goodness. The essence of this paternalism was the insistence upon mutual obligations, duties, responsibilities, and even rights between the lord and the individual peasant family.[32] In rural China, this was expressed as *ganqing,* or the mutual feelings of obligation between lord and peasant. Paternalism served to undermine solidarity among peasants by linking them as protected individuals to their immediate oppressor.

The question facing peasants was not so much one of accepting or rejecting the paternalist pretensions of their lords as one of making a realistic assessment of a world into which they were born and which they had little hope of changing. Accepting the lords' insistence on mutual obligations, peasants had the opportunity to transform paternalism into something quite different from that understood by their lords by fashioning it into a weapon of resistance based upon what they perceived to be their rights. Peasants may well have disagreed about what constituted a good lord, but they did implicitly agree on a minimum standard: a good lord respected their subsistence rights and acted according to a prevailing standard of decency that was understood by lord and peasant alike. They felt they had rights which the lord could ignore only at the risk of committing a specific act of injustice.

It is true that peasants often exhibited impressive solidarity and collective resistance, but those acts tended to be defensive attempts to restore the *status quo ante:* when a lord did not grant a rent reduction in a bad year, peasants felt justified in mixing sand and mud with the rice. What landlords saw as expressions of benevolence, peasants understood as rights. By developing a sense of moral worth and by asserting rights, peasants evinced a sense of solidarity that could be used as a weapon of resistance even within the paternalistically defined tenancy relations. Morally based claims of right, however, could not easily be transformed into an offensive weapon with which to attack paternalism. Peasants did take collective action, but only against specific lords or merchants. This was the very nature of paternalism, for both parties were locked in a continuous struggle which vacillated between the poles of protection and coercion.

The question of food had conditioned popular attitudes not only toward merchants but perhaps more importantly—in the world's largest agrarian bureaucracy—toward state officials and landlords. Peasants (and other rural poor) judged the actions of these people within a moral framework of what were considered fair prices and just practices governing the proper distribution of foodstuffs. If violated, these morally based claims of rights backed a community consensus favoring direct action, whether in the form of price-setting, tax evasion, or rent dodging. To a world that might have been structured had market forces freely operated, the people opposed their own vision of the proper human order. This vision was not one in which officials, merchants, and landlords did not exist, but one in which they simply respected community notions of fairness and justice. The curious thing is that neither merchants nor landlords openly disputed this vision by justifying prices or terms of tenancy on the basis of the operation of market forces and the price mechanism, even though they benefitted by the grain market and would have gained more if all obstacles— including the objections articulated in the moral economy of the peasants—had been destroyed. Even though merchants and landlords were greatly influenced by market forces, they adopted the basic assumptions of human rights that the people imposed on them from below—assumptions inherently opposed to the market. The attack on the traditional moral economy in Haifeng hence would not come from indigenous market forces.

Just as the early years of the European Industrial Revolution had seen a clash between irreconcilable views of the social order—between a vision based on fair prices, just practices, and mutuality, and one grounded in the operation of the free market—so too had a similar battle begun in rural China during the eighteenth and nineteenth centuries between the moral assumptions of the rural populace and the demands of urban markets. The difference was that in China, the indigenous market forces were not strong enough to overcome an economy that operated on different principles. In the end, it was to be the irruption of the capitalist world market into Haifeng which would disrupt the traditional moral economy.

CHAPTER 5

New Forces and Old Enemies
Imperialism and Rural Social Structure

P EASANT collective action in the eighteenth and nineteenth centuries had led to a considerable amount of rural social violence in Haifeng, but these disruptions could hardly be described as class conflict. Most of the conflict for which we have documentation occurred between lineages or the Red and Black Flags, vertically aligned social groupings, or between state and society, as in the food riots. Furthermore, since these forms of collective violence were systemic, it is difficult to see how rural class conflict could have emerged in Haifeng. And yet it did.

The key to understanding this development is to look for changes in rural social structure. As the work on collective action by Charles Tilly and others clearly demonstrates, changes in the form of collective action arise from changes in the structures that pattern people's lives. The difficulty, of course, is in documenting and demonstrating structural change. To do so here, we shall focus on how imperialism affected the rural social structure.

The Opium War of 1840–42 and the Arrow War of 1856 opened China to the West, and foreign merchants began trading up and down the China coast at specially designated "treaty ports"—five in 1842 and nine more in 1860—while Catholic and Protestant missionaries began seeking converts. Buying, selling, and even proselytizing were not new to China; neither was dealing with foreigners unique. What made mid-nineteenth-century relations with the West significant was that China was thereafter subject to the economic and political forces being forged by an expansive European capitalism on a world-wide scale. Like indigenous demographic and economic forces, imperialism too was a force which affected Chinese society, but only through the patterns of social relations described in earlier chapters. And in the process, the rural social structure was altered.

Missionaries

Missionaries were among the first foreigners to take advantage of the terms of the 1860 Treaty of Peking to penetrate the Chinese countryside. When they did so, they encountered a complex society with its own patterns of life and rules of behavior. To exist in that world, missionaries had to adapt to it, and some—the Catholics—even adopted the dress of Chinese scholars. Rural China molded them and defined their importance and position more than the other way around. They were outsiders, but outsiders with a difference: they had power. In the factionalized Haifeng countryside, that mattered. Where some rural inhabitants turned to Flags and lineages for protection, others now turned to missionaries.

Missionaries reached Haifeng in 1871. For the first decade, Catholicism spread slowly: the first convert was Cai Shunling, a fifty-three-year-old graduate of the first military degree, a not especially high or honored rank.[1] Within a few years, nearly all members of the small Cai lineage in Cai Cuo Wei village converted, and Cai Shunling became a man of local importance. Apparently the first time Cai used his special relation with the Catholic church, and through it his relation with the French consul-general in Guangzhou, was in 1875, when a lineage member asked his help in avoiding certain onerous governmental labor services which would have taken him away from home for some time. Traveling to Hong Kong to seek the aid of the Catholic bishop, Cai returned three months later to find that the provincial government had, at the church's request, resolved the matter to his satisfaction.

Cai Shunling's sphere of influence rapidly expanded, and people as far away as Shanwei, twelve miles to the south, knew of him. At least Yang Mouqi and Chen Dingjiang did. Yang and Chen lived near Shanwei, where Chen operated a small shop. Apparently Yang and Chen had a business arrangement whereby Yang supplied Chen with salt from nearby salt flats. But Chen's business was probably a fence for salt smuggled past the revenue agent, for one day Yang's salt was confiscated and his son was imprisoned. Yang trekked to Cai Cuo Wei, where he sought the aid of Cai Shunling. Shortly afterwards the Haifeng magistrate received an order from Guanghzhou directing the release of Yang's salt and son. Yang and Chen converted.

Yang Mouqi's luck did not hold very long, however, even with the protection of the church. In 1881 Yang was again arrested, this time for smuggling opium. Opium sales had been legalized since the 1860 treaty with France and Britain (which also allowed missionaries into China), but it was then subject to state taxation. Yang Mouqi made a good living smuggling salt and opium, and probably other contraband as well, for he had built a considerable estate which was divided among his four sons after he died. When he was arrested, Yang again sought the help of the church, but this time to no avail. Yang spent four years in prison in Guangzhou, was released in 1885 because of illness, and died shortly after returning home.

The magistrate of Lufeng, Xu Gengbi, was particularly incensed at what he considered this foreign meddling in purely domestic affairs. And he was determined not to let missionaries or the French consul interfere with his duties. But when squabbles over contributions to the village crop-watching society or other neighborhood affrays reached his attention, Xu often found that one of the disputants was a convert who relied on the power of the French consul to secure a favorable judgement in Xu's court. Xu found himself involved in adjudicating local disputes which could attain international significance, depending on how they were handled, and answering local accusations that he discriminated against church members.

Although sincere converts undoubtedly felt they could not get a fair hearing because they had become Christians, others converted to Christianity precisely to tip the balance in their favor. For example, after Zhuang Lianxi and two clansmen were accused of murder in an 1858 fight with a neighbor over rent, they retreated to their mountain village, joined the church, and staved off the authorities for twenty years. When Xu Gengbi became magistrate and used various subterfuges to arrest two of the Zhuang, the Catholic priest tried to intervene and secure their release. On other occasions, Xu wrote his superiors in Guangzhou explaining in advance actions he knew would draw the attention of the French consul and asking for their support when pressure was applied.[2]

Catholics were not the only ones to send missionaries to Haifeng; the Presbyterian Church of England did so too. Converts also approached the Presbyterians for help in local disputes, such as one over the use of a rice-drying floor, but these missionaries consistently declined, preferring to show in other ways how God provided for his flock. In the 1870s they built a hospital in Shantou, the treaty port 80 miles up the coast, and at the turn of the century constructed a sixty-bed hospital in Shanwei staffed by two English doctors who made rounds through the county as well. A boarding school for thirty boys was opened in 1907, and, according to the Reverend David Sutherland, the congregation was strong in Shanwei.[3]

Sugar Cane and Putter-Outers

Shanwei, Haifeng's major port, sat alongside the sea lane serviced after 1867 by the steamers of Jardine, Matheson and Company, or "Jardines," as the firm was called. William Jardine had made a fortune smuggling opium into China during the 1830s, and after the Opium War the profits allowed his firm to trade in other commodities at the treaty ports; after another war fought intermittently from 1856 to 1859, the opium traffic was legalized. Along with Butterfield Swire and Company, another British firm, and Russell and Company, an American group, Jardines shared domination of China's coastal and Yangzi River trade routes. With the advent of the steamship in the 1860s, however, competition between these firms became so intense that freight rates dropped sharply, not only destroying much of the Chinese junk traffic, but also prompting the foreign steamship companies to divide up the China trade. Removing its steamers from the Yangzi and leaving that field for

Butterfield and Russell, Jardines was free to develop the southern coastal routes.[4]

With the South China trade routes under its control, Jardines began hauling commodities such as raw cotton, tobacco, and raw sugar up and down the coast. Cotton and sugar assumed increased importance in the firm's operations after it entered directly into their manufacture. Under the *guan tu shang ban* (government ownership, merchant management) system, Jardines formed companies under official supervision and Chinese merchant management to weave textiles and refine sugar. (Indeed, no other course of action was possible before the 1895 Treaty of Shimonoseki, by which the imperialists wrested from China the right to open factories on Chinese soil.) In 1869 Jardines established a sugar refinery near Guangzhou under nominal Chinese ownership, but in a rare case of documented Chinese Luddism, attacks by local handicraft sugar pressers caused the refinery to close down. Thus in 1877, Jardines established the China Sugar Refining Company in Hong Kong (acquired by Britain in 1842 as war booty) and in 1878 built a branch refinery in Shantou. Butterfield Swire soon followed suit (having reentered the South China trade) by establishing the Taikoo Sugar Refining Company in Hong Kong and Shantou in 1882 and 1906, respectively. The refineries were large-scale enterprises: Jardines' Hong Kong operation had a daily capacity for refining 4,000 piculs (about half a million pounds), while the Taikoo refinery had a daily capacity of 12,000 piculs.[5]

Until 1907, nearly all of the sugar refined in these modern factories was purchased from peasant producers in Guangdong in the form of raw sugars. The total value of raw and refined sugars exported from China rose from 407,000 ounces of silver in 1868 to a high of 3,860,000 ounces in 1887. The total dropped to 2,723,000 ounces of silver in 1889, but began to increase once more until the turn of the century, when the value again reached 3 million ounces of silver. The increase in sugar exports came primarily from Guangdong and Fujian provinces, the major sugar-producing areas near treaty ports. In 1890 the Maritime Customs reported from Shantou, for example, that "this year was quite profitable for those families who plant sugar cane, as the price exceeds last year's. . . . It is said that the land planted in sugar cane will be double this year's. . . . The raw sugar exported next year should be 30 percent greater than this year."[6]

While most of the provincial increase in sugar exports came from Shantou, for decades raw sugar had been shipped out of Haifeng county on junks that plied the coastal trade routes. With the rise in demand, those shipments increased. And in the early 1890s, a solid link was forged between Haifeng county and the Hong Kong and Shantou refineries when Jardines established a steamship company for the Shantou–Hong Kong route, stopping along the way at Shanwei, the port of Haifeng. Although the amount of raw sugar exported from Haifeng is not known, it undoubtedly was considerable, since the Taikoo Sugar Refining Company also established a steamship line that called at Haifeng's port.[7]

Shanwei was about fifteen miles south of the main sugar cane growing areas east and north of Haifeng city. For three or four miles along the main postal route running east from Haifeng city, or along the Main North Road to Gongping, a dingy market town north of Haifeng, wealthier villagers sometimes planted sugar cane. Closer to the city rice was planted all the time because the cost of transporting night soil from Haifeng was relatively low; but at a certain point—maybe near Loshan on the East Road or Qinghu on the North Road, villages required to stable horses for the post—it became too expensive to use night soil. Other fertilizers could be used, especially crushed peanut shells from local sources or bean cake fertilizer imported from North China and Manchuria, but since this was fairly expensive, those few who could afford it often planted sugar cane, which especially thrived with the fertilizer. Besides, the carry-over to the next planting cycle fertilized either rice, peanuts, or sweet potatoes, depending on the rotation system being used. Sugar cane could be planted and harvested every year and a half with annual applications of the fertilizer.

Agricultural inputs necessary for growing cane also varied with the type planted. The "green" cane was grown largely

101

for local consumption, often just as cane stalks. Green cane could be grown on lands unsuitable for rice and required little in the way of labor or fertilizer to grow. The "bamboo" or "red" sugar cane that was grown for refining in the local sugar huts, on the other hand, required better land and larger amounts of water and fertilizer. In fact, the fertilizer for one mou of land planted in sugar cane was in many cases nearly twice the amount of rent for that parcel, and in the 1870s and 1880s, it was getting more expensive.[8]

Freshly cut sugar cane was not a marketable commodity: further expense was needed to transform it into raw sugar. Unless within hours sugar cane was crushed to get the juice used to make raw sugar, the cane rapidly lost its sugar content.The shorter the time between cutting and crushing, the greater the amount of recoverable sugar. So without access to a crushing and refining operation, the sugar cane would become worthless—except perhaps to children given a stalk to chew on. Chinese sugar refining was a small-scale handicraft operation, relying on stone rollers and animal power, a process which had remained unchanged for centuries. During the November–February harvesting season, the juice from the crushed cane was boiled to crystalize into various grades of raw sugar, ranging from a small amount of white sugar to increasingly darker and coarser raw sugar and molasses. While the white sugar was either sold locally or exported as it was, and the crude molasses was sold for local peasant consumption, the greatest portion of the darker raw sugar was packed in straw mattings weighing 150–200 pounds for export to the imperialists' modern refineries. Even a small-scale crushing and refining operation required considerable amounts of capital to buy or rent three bullock to turn the millstone, and to hire a sugar master, a bullock driver, fire tenders, and cane strippers. Some wealthy peasants carried on these operations by themselves, while other peasants formed cooperatives. But for most peasants, merchants played a key role.[9]

Even wealthy peasants sold their cane to merchants, who then assumed responsibility for refining. In 1750, for example, a peasant named Chen Daheng living in western Guangdong rented several plots of land, purchased fertilizer, and hired laborers to plant sugar cane. But because he did not have a large enough sugar hut for processing the cane, he contracted to sell the standing cane to Hu Dazhen, a merchant who "specialized in the sugar business." Hu apparently was something more than just a merchant, since he either owned or had access to a large sugar-processing hut and went in search of supplies to run it at full capacity during the sugar refining season. After concluding a private agreement with Chen Daheng on 2 April 1751, according to a report in the Board of Punishments, Hu Dazhen "traveled together with Chen Daheng by boat to Chenshikang market. Daheng announced that he had sugar to sell, whereupon Hu Dahzen agreed to purchase 50,000 jin [about 66,000 pounds] from Chen Daheng at a price of 3.5 silver taels per 10,000 jin [or 17.5 taels total]. It was agreed that Hu Dazhen would pay 200 copper cash down that day, and ten days later [12 April] pay the amount in full. On 14 April the sugar cane would be released." Why the agreement was announced in the market is unclear. It may have been to stage an auction in order to avoid charges that agricultural produce was not being sold openly in the market. Or it may have been that announcing it in a public place would make the oral agreement binding.

But the contract was not fulfilled. On the appointed day, merchant Hu brought the balance of the payment to Chen's home. Chen's father, for unstated but suspicious reasons, had taken away the steelyard for weighing money. Chen did not have another and told Hu Dazhen to come again two days later, or the day previously agreed upon to release the sugar. By the time Hu returned, the price of sugar had increased, and farmer Chen, desiring a greater profit, had sold his sugar to another. The merchant was so incensed, according to the Board of Punishments records, that he "caused a big ruckus, started a fight, and brought about a death." Who was killed is unclear. But what is clear is that Chen Daheng felt sufficiently independent of his guaranteed buyer to renege on the contract. He had capitalized his venture independently, and apparently felt he was free to dispose of his sugar any way he pleased, even to the extent of breaking a contract. He probably died because of it.[10]

When the market for Guangdong sugars expanded in the late nineteenth century, groups of sugar merchants (now called "sugar houses," or *tang hu*) began to advance peasants "sugar capital" (*tang ben*) to plant sugar cane. In the winter the merchants returned to set up sugar refining operations. What developed was a classic putting-out system to meet the demands of a national market, with merchants gaining some control of the production process.

The steamship and trading activities of Jardine, Matheson and Company were instrumental in forging that national market. Plying the Manchuria–Hong Kong route, Jardines' steamers carried sugars northward, returning with raw cotton and the soybean cake fertilizer which was then used for sugar planting. In order to secure freight for their lines, both Jardines and Butterfield depended on compradores. Because Chinese merchants could operate more cheaply than Western firms, which had agencies only at treaty ports, both the distribution of imported goods and the collection of goods for export came to be concentrated in the hands of Chinese merchants. The Western firms hired Chinese merchants as compradores to supervise their shipping, banking, and insurance interests, paying them on a commission basis. The Chinese compradore thus acted as a liaison between the Chinese market and the shipping company.[11]

When sugar merchants from Shantou and Fujian established merchants' guilds (*hui guan*) in the fast-growing city of Shanghai, the putting-out system expanded even faster. Shanghai had been emerging as the national trade center for commodities such as tea and silk; during the 1870s it became the financial center for the sugar market as well. With their ears tuned to the rising demands of the Shanghai market, the Shanghai merchants sold sugars to buyers for future delivery. In order to ensure that the supplies would be forthcoming, and to protect their own interests, the Shanghai merchants advanced money to their partners in Guangdong and Fujian, who in turn advanced money to peasant producers. Since local fertilizer or imported soybean cake fertilizer was needed to produce sugar cane, sugar merchants provided peasants with the fertilizer itself or with loans to buy it. One investigation, for example, showed that "sugar cane is the most important garden crop in Guangdong. Most peasants borrow money from city merchants and sell their produce to the merchant or usurer in repayment for the principal. . . . In one village where twenty-four peasants grew sugar cane, thirteen borrowed from merchants and eleven borrowed from other usurers." The 1901 Maritime Customs Report for Shantou also observed that sugar cane was grown on "small holdings, cultivated on 'rule of the thumb' methods by the peasant proprietors, often under advances from the exporting merchants." The agricultural putting-out system was a lending–quality control function exercised by merchants responsive to the demands of the market for particular kinds of sugar.[12]

The Jardine, Matheson and Butterfield Swire companies could easily link their compradore system to the existing putting-out system in order to purchase raw sugars for their Hong Kong and Shantou refineries. Shantou sugar merchants in Shanghai probably had already developed a working relationship with the shipping companies by soliciting cargo for them. It is known, for example, that a considerable amount of sugar had been shipped by steamer in the 1860s. And sugar merchants had already learned how to guarantee various grades of sugar from peasant producers through the putting-out system. Hence when Jardines and Butterfield built their large, modern sugar refineries at Hong Kong and Shantou, Chinese sugar merchants had larger and more dependable buyers.[13]

The Local Consequences of World Markets

The sizable purchases of raw sugar to keep these refineries operating had important consequences for Haifeng's social and economic systems. As the British-induced demand rose, the agricultural putting-out system enabled peasants who were otherwise too poor, to grow sugar cane. Merchants advanced them either the fertilizer or the money to buy it, and in return secured the crop for their sugar-cracking huts. Merchant advances and peasant indebtedness thus formed the link between sugar cane–producing peasants and the vagaries of the world market. As long as demand held, peasants profited.

How much money was pumped into the economy is not precisely known, but it is clear that the countryside prospered. Between 1874 and 1908, thirteen new market towns sprung up, bringing the total in Haifeng to twenty-four. Gongping, located in the midst of the cane-growing districts, boomed; it became a daily market, and seven new periodic markets popped up in the surrounding countryside. New markets also emerged all over Haifeng, changing marketing system boundaries and patterns of daily life for large numbers of peasants. Since the marketing system was basic to rural social and economic life, the widespread and rapid increase in market towns caused by the sugar boom placed the social fabric of Haifeng under severe strain.

During the sugar boom of the 1880s and '90s, rural social conflict between the Red and Black Flags had reached its peak.[14] It is likely that peasants in the neutral zones between market towns had been the most anxious to grow sugar cane. After all, access to outside sources of wealth would have enabled these peasants to lessen their dependence on the lineages controlling the market towns. As the number of new markets increased, so too did the level of violence. In short, the linkage of Haifeng's rural society and economy to the world market exasperated social dynamics that had long existed. Had the market for sugar cane continued to grow, what would have happened is anyone's guess.

But in 1907 the sugar market crashed. The capitalist world entered one of its periodic panics, this one triggered by some questionable banking maneuvers in New York by J. P. Morgan. In the new physics of the universe of international finance, random movements in New York sent waves all the way to Shanghai and from there into the villages of Haifeng.

Commodity markets were notoriously unstable, and sugar was no exception. Beginning in the late nineteenth and early twentieth centuries, world production of sugar cane and refined sugar rose rapidly as new areas were brought into production.

With Taiwan under Japanese control after 1895, a large part of that island's agricultural production had been forcibly converted to sugar cane; with Java under Dutch control, and Cuba and the Philippines under U.S. control, sugar production in those areas also rose significantly; in Europe, the extraction of sugar from beets increased supplies. Moreover, all of these areas refined sugar in modern plants by a process eminently more efficient than the ancient methods used by Chinese peasants. With all this new production of sugar, world supply peaked in the period 1900–1905, at which time prices began to decline, and to fall precipitously after 1905.

Jardines and Butterfield Swire purchases of Guangdong raw sugar reflected the general conditions of the world market: their buying increased until 1900, remained fairly steady for the next few years, and then rapidly declined after 1907 to almost nothing. Jardines and Butterfield Swire found that locally produced raw sugars had a downward price limit, after which time peasants switched back to rice or some other crop. Relying on these higher priced sugars, they found it impossible to compete with cheaper Japanese and Javanese sugars. The chairman of Jardines thus explained the company's 1905 losses to stockholders: "In former years it has been possible, when local conditions were averse, to find an outlet for our sugars in the more distant markets, such as India, Australia, etc., but I regret to say that during this last year, this was not the case and these markets were able to obtain supplies at prices with which we could not compete."[15] By 1907, the competition was severe enough to force the British companies to reduce output in the Hong Kong refineries temporarily and to close those at Shantou altogether. Rather than attempt to compete by obtaining raw sugars from Guangdong at a lower price (which they could not have done in any case since, unlike the Dutch or Japanese, they did not exercise direct control over sugar cane production through the exploitation of wage-labor), Jardines simply stopped buying sugar in Guangdong, turning instead to Java and the Philippines. These areas accounted for nearly all of its raw sugar stocks by 1908.

Faced with declining prices, Guangdong peasants switched land back to rice, vegetables, or peanuts. By 1911, according to the Shantou Maritime Customs Report, "little sugar is exported . . . because of deficient planting methods and little fertilizer." And by 1920, only one-tenth of the arable planted in sugar cane during the previous decades was still producing sugar. While some sugar cane was still grown and refined for local use, even that was coming under attack by cheaper imported sugars refined by Jardines and Butterfield Swire, the peasants' one-time buyers.[16]

Land Tenure Changes

While the loss of a market caused individual peasants to readjust their cropping patterns, the crash of the world sugar market sent reverberations throughout Haifeng. Some peasants reverted to cropping patterns prevailing in the 1880s, but the sugar market crash radically altered rural class relations. Sugar production for the world market had been possible in the first place only because of the loans advanced to peasants by merchants. With the crash, the peasants who had been brought into contact with the world market were economically weakened; some were destroyed.

Merchants and peasants alike suffered after the 1907 crash, but peasants no doubt bore the brunt of the downturn. The putter-outers had borrowed from larger merchants in Shanghai to advance money to peasants, who in turn borrowed from the putter-outer to produce what was now a worthless sugar crop. There was certainly pressure all along the line from Shanghai to the peasant in Haifeng to clear the debt. Depending on individual circumstances, peasants had either to sell or mortgage their land, or to seek loans from other sources if they owned no land, in order to repay the putter-outers. Where marketing opportunities earlier may have allowed peasants to become less dependent on local lords, the crash meant that these peasants now had to seek loans, land, and other favors once again from the lords of Haifeng. And lords could now bargain for terms more favorable to them from peasants who were in no position to argue too strenuously.

It was not just that those whose fortunes crashed with the sugar market were affected, for the ensuing bidding and competition for land affected relations between lords and tenants on a far wider scale. Reliable statistics for the number of tenants in Haifeng are not available, but there surely was an increase following the crash. In the early 1920s, Peng Pai estimated that over the two decades from 1900 to 1920, peasant freeholders had declined in some villages by 80 percent. If his estimate that by 1920 about 80 percent of Haifeng's peasants rented all or part of their land is even remotely accurate, then it would seem conservative to estimate that the tenancy rate two decades earlier would have been about half that, or 40 percent.[17]

But the rate of tenancy by itself is not all that significant. Not all tenants had the same terms; indeed, some were more like petty proprietors than tenants. In Haifeng, three systems of tenure can be discerned: permanent tenure, contractual leases running four to five years, and oral agreements renewed annually. The oldest form was permanent tenure, known in Haifeng as "manure investment" (*mai fen*), the "greater and lesser purchase" (*da xiao mai*), or "patronage" (*zuo ge*). Permanent tenure prevailed on lands in production since the late seventeenth and early eighteenth centuries, when lords had to seek tillers to reclaim lands laid waste during the seventeenth-century disturbances and therefore gave peasants advantageous terms and rights. As one Haifeng observer wrote, "The special features included a large amount of land, light rate of rent, freedom to choose crops, and the right to sublet. Except for collecting rent twice a year, the landlord had absolutely no right to take back land."[18] Under permanent tenure, lords sometimes did not even know where their land was located. Holders of land on permanent tenure simply had rights rivaling those of juridicial ownership. Moreover, the systems of permanent tenure in some cases were part and parcel of the lineage organization. In Haifeng, the rights of tenants holding permanent tenure from their lineage were engraved in stone in lineage temples. Near Shantou, Fielde found in 1888 that "much land is held on inalienable leases, given by an ancient proprietor to the family of a clansman. For such leases the annual rent is usually one or two baskets of paddy [about one-half the rate for other tenancies] for each mow."[19]

Contractual leases probably emerged when market opportunities arose. The first to seek contractually fixed obligations would have been those enterprising peasants seeking to increase their income by applying fertilizer, otherwise improving the land, and planting cash crops such as sugar cane. They needed a guarantee that the fertilized land would not then be let to someone else, and therefore sought four- to five-year leases, depending on the crop rotation system they used. In periods of general agricultural expansion, such as the late nineteenth century, peasants considered contractual leases and fixed rents advantageous, since the fruits of increased inputs would be theirs to keep.

Changes in land tenure arrangements occasioned by the sugar boom and bust are difficult to document precisely, but the broad outlines of what happened are clear enough. The predominant form of land tenure prior to the expansion of the sugar market had been permanent tenure; contractualized leases with fixed rents accompanied the commercialization of agriculture. After the 1907 sugar market crash, both of these forms gave way to a new form, the *koutou*, or oral, tenancy.[20] When the land was to be let, the peasant merely agreed orally that the rent would be paid on time. Because the koutou tenancy was based on the yearly performance of the peasant, according to early twentieth-century investigations, peasants never knew if they would have the land the next year or if the rent would be raised and a new tenant sought. Peasants holding koutou tenancies did not apply fertilizer or make improvements in the land for fear the lord would then have reason to raise the rent.[21]

The direction of change clearly was from the relatively secure to increasingly insecure arrangements. Where permanent tenure in the nineteenth century, according to one source, comprised the "absolute majority" of tenancies and it was said that "the rights of tenants are superior to those of landlords,"[22] by the 1920s most peasants held land on one-year koutou tenancies and could find themselves landless from one harvest to the next. In short, the securities and other guarantees of the older forms of land tenure relationships that had embodied significant aspects of the moral economy of the peasant had been destroyed. As mediated through the rural social structure, the forces of the capitalist world market had stripped peasants of their traditionally defined rights of tenure, placing their security on the land in the hands of the landlords who might or might not raise their rents and evict them. Unfortunately, the full story of these changes in land tenure in Haifeng will never be known. During the Haifeng Soviet's "land revolution" in late 1927 and early 1928, peasants burned 58,000 landlord rent books and 450,000 land deeds, destroying our documentation.

With the insecurity of the koutou tenancy, peasants came to favor sharecropping arrangements for paying rent. In the period of expansion, fixed rents were to the peasants' advantage; after 1907 they were not. Landlords, on the other hand, wanted to retain fixed rent: their income was guaranteed, and besides, the lords had no responsibility for the upkeep of the land or even for answering the tax-collector's inquiries—all that fell on the peasant's shoulders. Sharecropping, favored by tenants in a period of economic contraction, was troublesome for a lord. To prevent cheating, the lord or his agent would have to personally supervise the harvest. To be sure, there were elaborate means for ensuring an equal division of the harvest— the peasant had the right of drawing the dividing line across the field, and the lord then had the right to choose which half he wanted—but all this required more attention than the lord may have been willing to give.[23] These were the issues that exploded in Haifeng in the 1920s.

Inflation

Besides the crash of the sugar market, other economic factors eroded the bargaining power of the peasantry over terms of tenancy. First, a rapid inflation was sending the price of daily necessities and other manufactured goods climbing faster than the price of agricultural commodities. The depression in the countryside, contrary to what one might expect, was not accompanied by declining prices for manufactured goods or other daily necessities not produced in the countryside. Quite the contrary: the first decade of the twentieth century saw the intensification of an inflation in the price of manufactured goods that had begun in the 1880s. And the inflation was particularly great in the period after 1905, just when the sugar market had crashed and handicraft spinning was rapidly declining. Rice prices climbed about 10 percent per year from 1880 to 1905, while the price of manufactured goods outpaced the grain prices. A certain amount of the inflation was caused by relative shortages of grain, but a large part was simply caused by fluctuations in China's bimetallic currency system, as silver depreciated rapidly relative to copper, dropping about 60 percent from 1880 to 1905. The main reason for the falling value of silver was that following the worldwide depression of 1877, most Western nations abandoned their silver-based currencies for the more stable gold standard. Because the wholesale grain market operated on silver, retailers had to raise prices to their copper cash–paying customers just because of the weakened position of silver in the world market.[24]

The inflation intensified from 1905 to the eve of the 1911 Revolution because copper cash in turn became worthless. The depreciation of the copper cash can be attributed almost exclusively to the establishment of modern mints, the first of which was built in Guangzhou in 1901. In fineness and workmanship, the newly struck copper coins, at face value worth 10 copper cash, were exceedingly difficult to counterfeit or debase and thus were far superior to the old copper cash. Quite expectedly, Gresham's law took hold, and the old copper coins became devalued. Although 20 million new copper coins had been minted by 1911, they did not replace the old copper cash as the medium of exchange in the countryside. On the contrary, the new coins circulated less freely because they were highly prized, while the old copper cash became worthless. In short, bad money drove out the good.[25]

Even small merchants were caught in the growing crisis squeezing the countryside. The son of a small merchant in the Haifeng countryside reported that in the decade from 1895 to 1905, "village life was good and products bountiful. However, the family wealth lasted only as long as my grandfather was alive and the village environment remained the same. When he died [1906] and the business passed to my father, conditions gradually changed. It became more difficult to do business as exchange rates between town and countryside became unfavorable and expenses increased."[26] How many small merchants went out of business is not known, but conditions certainly were not good for them. When or if the Haifeng countryside began to recover from the depression also is unknown. But the rural economy never regained the vitality it had had during the sugar boom.

Handicraft Spinning and Weaving

The crash of the sugar market was severe enough, but the impact was greatly magnified because sugar growing and refining had been related to other economic activities as well, particularly handicraft spinning and weaving of textiles.

In addition to male family members, women also worked in sideline production, for the most part spinning yarn and weaving cloth. Kulp observed in an area northeast of Haifeng that a "general division of labor between men and women is to be found in Phenix [sic] Village. The men attend to business matters and do most of the field work; the women carry on the home industries. Practically all the village wives, rich or poor, engage in the spinning and weaving of flax into cloth for their own use. The whir of the spinning wheel . . . and the click of the loom are heard in every part of the village."[27]

For centuries nearly all yarn and cloth produced in the peasant home in South China had been made from hemp. Most peasant households possessing both a spinning wheel and a small wooden loom either grew their own or gathered wild hemp to make cloth. "But," observed Li Diaoyuan of late-seventeenth or early-eighteenth-century conditions, "it is not sold in the market. The average woman with the help of her children weaves one bolt [about sixteen yards] by the end of the year. It is used to clothe her husband and that is all."[28] As late as the late nineteenth century, nearly all cloth in Haifeng was woven from yarns spun from hemp for use in the home. Varying qualities were produced, ranging from a very coarse

113

and loosely woven fabric to a finer and more closely woven *tujing*, or homespun. Relying upon locally grown hemp, spinning and weaving were an integrated process carried on in the peasant home solely to meet family needs.[29]

With the rise of the sugar trade in the latter decades of the nineteenth century, a new material, raw cotton, became available for spinning. A Jardine, Matheson and Company report noted that "the Chinese peasant worked his own loom. The Fu[j]ian farmer traded his sugar for northern cotton which he then carded, spun and wove into a heavy durable material; after harvest time the entire peasant family was engaged in producing homespun."[30] And both sugar and cotton were carried on Jardines' steamers. In 1888, Jamieson observed similar conditions in eastern Guangdong: "Clothing is usually woven in the house, from the fibre of the grass-cloth plant (Boehmeria nivea) which grows here, or from cotton imported from Hankow."[31] Those who produced the best and most durable homespun, made partially from imported cotton, hence tended to be those peasant families most closely associated with the sugar trade.

The introduction of raw cotton into handicraft textile production did not precipitate major structural change in the home industry—both hemp and cotton could be spun on the same wheel—but the introduction of machine-made cotton yarns from Japan and England at the turn of the century did. Japanese and English yarns were cheaper and stronger than yarns homespun from hemp or cotton. Homespun yarns continued to be used in weaving, but only for the weft: foreign yarns were used for the warp to give the cloth strength and better quality.

Japanese yarns and Chinese homespun were both spun from cotton grown in North China. Before 1888, China was even importing raw cotton from India, the demand was so great. But with the rapid growth of the mechanized Japanese spinning industry in the decade following 1888, China became a net exporter of raw cotton. An 1889 customs report observed that "the heavy export of raw cotton may, by raising the price of the raw material, have created a larger demand for the manufactured yarn."[32] Thus in 1900, a spindle of the lowest-quality

Japanese yarn cost 16 yuan, whereas Chinese homespun of comparable grade cost three times as much.

The introduction of machine-made yarns restructured the handicraft textile industry. Cotton spinning died out, except in areas of North China that grew cotton, while handicraft production in Haifeng and surrounding areas shifted to weaving. Because few peasant households owned a loom, the importation of foreign yarns meant that peasants who could afford only the less expensive spinning wheels lost their livelihood. Many of these spinners shifted then to hand-weaving straw mats. Unlike homespun yarns, straw mats now could be sold: the straw hat was in vogue in the United States, and there was a better market for straw matting than for homespun. Initially, then, the importation of yarns did not necessarily spell economic disaster for those who spun because their raw material could be used for other purposes. But in 1904, the United States imposed restrictions on straw matting imports, and exports from Guangdong fell to 20 percent of the 1900 level.[33]

With the separation between spinning and weaving made possible by the introduction of foreign yarns, a putting-out system developed in many places. Cloth merchants bought the produce of weavers for sale in other markets, supplying yarn on credit in return for the delivery of a specific amount of cloth within a certain time. Like the merchants who had organized the sugar market, the cloth merchants had their ears tuned to market conditions and could act as quality control agents. With the emergence of putting-out, a substantial portion of control over the productive process had passed out of the hands of handicraft weavers and into the hands of merchants.[34]

The separation of spinning and weaving also meant that textile production could be spatially rearranged. Under the putting-out system, cloth merchants had to make periodic trips to the peasant home, or at least to the market, in order to collect the finished cloth. But why could the weaving not be done at a central location? This is precisely what happened in Haifeng, as looms were gathered under one roof in Haifeng city. With this important development, the productive process, the organization of work, the ordering of supplies, and the marketing

115

of the finished product came under centralized control. Haifeng's first textile mill, the Nanfeng Textile Mill, in fact originally retained some of the characteristics of the putting-out system. Since it was built in 1918 just as World War I was ending, there was probably sufficient war-stimulated business to warrant bringing together women weavers who had been scattered throughout the villages. Women weavers worked on a modified piece-rate system: they purchased yarn from the mill, wove it on their own looms, and sold the finished cloth back to the mill. Money did not actually change hands every time a bolt of cloth was woven, but separate accounts were kept and the balance settled periodically. The advantage of this form of organization, at least from the point of view of the manager, lay in the closer supervision of the work process, control over the type of cloth to be woven, centralized distribution of yarns, and ease of collection of the finished product.[35]

Soon after the Nanfeng Textile Mill was established, technological changes in the types of looms used apparently necessitated a new form of work organization. Around 1920, an improved loom with a faster shuttle was introduced in the Shanghai area. While it could weave a wider bolt of cloth at a faster rate, it also required several women to operate it. Using similar or possibly even larger looms, the Nanfeng mill by 1925 came to employ 350 women. Because several women now operated a single loom, it became impossible to calculate an individual's contribution to the finished product on a piece-rate basis, and the putting-out system gave way to wage-labor. In less than a decade, women had been transformed from individuals who owned their own looms into wage laborers who no longer owned or controlled any of the means of production. By 1925, three textile mills and two stocking factories in Haifeng employed over 500 women. These workers were paid wages less than those earned by male agricultural workers.[36]

Of the five mills in existence in Haifeng by the 1920s, information is available on the ownership and capitalization of four. The largest, the Nanfeng Textile Mill, capitalized at 60,000 yuan, was owned by Chen Jiongming. A native of Haifeng, Chen was a leader of the 1911 Revolution in Guangdong, governor-general of Guangdong on and off for the next decade, and perhaps the most powerful military commander (or warlord) in Guangdong and southern Fujian. The second largest mill, the Minsheng Textile Mill, capitalized at 20,000 yuan, was owned by Chen Jiongming's stepbrother, Ma Yuhang. Ma was finance commissioner of Guangdong whenever Chen was in power. The largest stocking factory, located in Meilong and employing seventy women, was built for 20,000 yuan by Lin Wen, a member of the powerful Lin lineage of Meilong. As noted previously, the Lin lineage had belonged to the landed class from the mid-eighteenth century and owned nearly all the land around Meilong. Although the Lin mill was relatively small, at least by Shanghai standards, it does show that at least some members of the old landed class were able to make the transition to industrial capitalism. Lin wealth was still based on land ownership, but 20,000 yuan was nonetheless a major investment in a modern enterprise. Perhaps the most unexpected owner of a textile mill was Peng Pai, who had established the Pingmin (Common People's) Textile Mill. As we shall see, Peng was the most important peasant organizer in Guangdong, a Communist who was the son of a large Haifeng landlord, and leader of the Haifeng Soviet Government of 1927–28.[37]

None of the new capitalists were primarily cloth merchants, although it is certainly possible that they had engaged in textile trading. The capital to build and operate the new mills was generated not by trade but by other sources. Capital for the two largest mills owned by Chen Jiongming and Ma Yuhang (80 percent of the total) most probably came from the coffers of the provincial government, while the capital for the other mills came from rents extracted from the peasantry.[38]

All yarn for both the textile and stocking factories was imported from Hong Kong and Guangzhou: none was purchased from peasant producers in Haifeng. The output of these factories was not exported, however: the market for all five mills was within Haifeng. With an annual output of 600,000 yards of cotton cloth, the annual per capita consumption in Haifeng was thus about one and a half yards of cloth. Even if the wealthy—landlords, merchants, and government officials—consumed more than the per capita average, by far the greatest percentage of the cloth was purchased by peasants and urban poor. The inescapable conclusion is that *handicraft* spinning and weaving had been destroyed by competition from factory-made yarns and cloth. Haifeng's textile industry *per se* was not destroyed by competition from foreign yarns and cloth, only its handicraft form. In fact, textile production probably had increased. Haifeng city had an integrated textile industry ranging from the textile mills to calendaring and dyeing facilities. But this should not obscure the tremendous changes in the organization of the textile industry: modern factories employing wage labor replaced peasant families as textile producers.

Thus the period from 1880 to 1925 saw the gradual disappearance of peasant spinning and weaving from the villages of Haifeng county. Before 1880, peasant handicraft production had relied on local materials for spinning and weaving. With the growth of the sugar trade after 1880, Haifeng peasants were able to exchange sugar for raw cotton that was spun and woven on the same wheels and looms. The introduction of foreign machine-made yarns around 1900 marked a major change in the organization of handicraft textile production: weaving had become totally independent from spinning. In the decade 1901–1910, the consumption of handspun yarns in all of China dropped to 42 percent of the total, and decreased further thereafter.[39] For those who owned only a spinning wheel, the importation of foreign yarns meant ruin. Although handicraft spinning and weaving continued in some areas of China, in Haifeng the textile industry was transformed into factory production, destroying whatever may have remained of peasant handicraft production.

Imperialism had come in many guises to the peasants of Haifeng: it appeared as the Catholic missionary who used his influence to aid converts in their factional conflicts with neighbors or in their attempts to avoid taxation; it appeared as the merchant who first advanced loans to villagers so that they could plant sugar cane and then returned to buy the crop for export to Jardine, Matheson; it appeared as the entrepreneur who gathered several looms under one roof in Haifeng city to weave bolts of cloth from yarn spun in Japan or in foreign-owned mills in Shanghai; and it appeared as the small-town merchant raising prices because of the devaluation of the copper cash. In all cases the force of imperialism was mediated through existing social relationships. The impact of imperialism on Haifeng, if we must use the word *impact*, was not directly on peasants, or anyone else for that matter, but on social relationships.

In assessing the relationship between imperialism and the Haifeng peasant movement of the 1920s, Roy Hofheinz, Jr., has argued that Haifeng and Lufeng, "bypassed by the lively steamboat trade between Hong Kong and Swatow [Shantou]," "remained isolated from the spread of commerce or foreign influence alleged to generate modern peasant unrest."[40] As has been conclusively shown here, Haifeng was not bypassed by the steamboat trade, and most certainly was not isolated from foreign influence. If anything, precisely the opposite was the case. The real issue, then, is not *whether* imperialism had an impact on Haifeng, for that much now is incontrovertible, but rather how imperialism was related to patterns of peasant collective action.

Imperialism created conditions under which collective action along the vertical lines of lineage and Flag would be replaced by collective action along the horizontal lines of social class. Rural social relations in Haifeng underwent significant change under the impact of imperialist economic activities. Although peasants benefited initially from an expanding market for their produce, they reeled from the blows sustained by the crash of the sugar market and the subsequent changes in land tenure relations. Not only did the number of tenants increase, but more importantly, the terms of tenure shifted dramatically against the peasant. On the eve of the 1911 Revolution, larger numbers of peasants than ever before were insecure in their holding of land, and these peasants had to be willing (or able) to pay increased rents, or else face eviction in favor of tenants who would pay higher rents. Such conditions were necessary

119

for the emergence of class and class conflict in Haifeng, but they were not sufficient. To understand fully how class rather than lineage or Flag came to pattern collective action of both peasants and landlords, we must now consider the political and social changes arising in the wake of the 1911 Revolution.

CHAPTER 6

"A Matter for the Police and the Courts"
Peasants and the 1911 Revolution

THE Haifeng countryside was teeming with rural social organizations in the summer of 1911. Some, like lineages and the Red and Black Flags, we have already seen, largely because they had earlier attracted the attention of the authorities. But these were not the only ones around. Many just were not visible until the 1911 Revolution churned up the countryside, allowing us a glimpse at even more that had been hiding just beneath the surface. Crop-watching societies, bandits, Triads, and religious sects all floated into view as they took part, for various reasons, in the 1911 Revolution. The participation of these groups in what we now see as a revolutionary movement shows just how complicated the 1911 Revolution really was. Every now and again, a popular and more radical undercurrent surfaced, revealing a revolution within the revolution. Peasants' concepts of the revolutionary movement, based on their own experiences, were at variance with the urban leaders' visions of the revolution. These peasant ideas never were visible long enough for us to get a good look at them, but they were there, tipping us off to changes in the forms of collective action that were in the offing.

Crop-Watching Societies and Bandits

In the summer of 1911, the Guangdong countryside seemed to be in chaos, notwithstanding the number and types of social organizations spread throughout rural areas. Bandits, the threat of bandits, the report of bandits, and the fear of bandits per-

121

meated the villages and market towns. Telegrams reporting bandits flowed into Governor-General Zhang Mingqi, who felt an increase in banditry alone was dangerous enough, without also having to cope with the agitation of the "revolutionary faction," Sun Yat-sen's Chinese Revolutionary Alliance (*Tongmeng Hui*). And because rural inhabitants did not enjoy having imperial troops around, it was becoming more difficult to quell the disturbances caused by bandits. As one official put it, "Under the name of bandit suppression, the people are the ones really hurt." Villagers had to quarter and billet the troops, besides often having to pay extraordinary fees, none of which they liked. Sometimes, they found it easier to deal with the bandits.[1]

The censor Wan Suanzou that summer argued that the question of bandit suppression really was one of easing the disruptive economic and social pressures on villagers which caused some of them to turn to what he called "banditry." Indeed, the decade following the turn of the century had been a period of flux in peasant life: old economic and social patterns changed rapidly as new marketing systems developed, countless peasants were ruined when the sugar market crashed, inflation continued unabated, a new currency had been introduced, boatmen were thrown out of work with the coming of the steamship, the place of women and girls in the family became precarious as handicraft spinning and weaving declined, and small merchants were caught in a scissors crisis. Besides being subjected to tremendous economic pressures, the rural populace was also confronted with the bubonic plague, which had reached Guangdong in 1910 and spread throughout the province in 1911.

Most of these problems had not been caused by government policy and in fact were quite beyond the state's control. But Censor Wan suggested that the government abolish certain taxes, work out the currency problems, and authorize villages to form local militia units under gentry leadership. This was a policy Zeng Guofan had used a half century earlier in defeating the Taipings, and was a cornerstone of the Tongzhi Restoration. Wan noted that the gentry had left the villages to par-

122

ticipate in the various new organizations spawned by the recent New Policy reforms and argued that their return as militia leaders would provide a bulwark against banditry and rural disorder.[2]

According to the governor-general's report to the cabinet in Beijing, nearly all of Guangdong was infested with bandits. There were only a few places, he reported, such as Huizhou prefecture, which seemed unusually peaceful in the summer of 1911.[3] He should have been more circumspect. Huizhou prefecture was part of the East River region, an area ideal for banditry. Of the major rivers converging near Guangzhou to form the Pearl River, the East River was shallow and broken by rapids, rendering it nearly impossible to patrol much further than Shilong or Huizhou, only 30 miles upriver from Guangzhou. And unlike the West River, the East was not patrolled by foreign gunboats protecting their nationals' steamers. Furthermore, the rugged coastline of Huizhou, including Haifeng, Lufeng, Guishan, and Huilai counties, was dotted with small harbors, making it equally difficult to police. Along the coast and on the East River, salt smuggling, gun-running, piracy, and banditry flourished, as they had since the sixteenth century.

The countryside here was actually in a state of siege. In Haifeng, bandits were becoming bolder, descending from the mountains and raiding villages on the plains. Following a raid on Mafulong Village, just three miles north of Meilong, the villagers set up a defense perimeter, fenced the village with bamboo spikes, and organized nightly watches of guards armed with newly purchased muskets. The countryside was alive with rumors that bandits would attack at any time, and sightings of bands of armed strangers sent the village into panic. But more often than not these were just the villagers' armed patrols from the other side of the hill. After the attack on Mafulong Village, for example, the villagers not only patrolled the perimeter but sent guards to the hills overlooking the village. They never saw any bandits. But when in the dead of night they became hungry, the patrol itself often stole grain, sugar cane, or fish from neighboring villages. The victimized villagers of course would then report a bandit sighting, and within a day or two the news would spread to other villages, returning, one would assume, to Mafulong Village, which undoubtedly increased its guard against the new bandits.[4]

Haifeng county provided a good environment for bandits. Of the total land area, only about 30 percent was farmed, while mountains and hills ringed the farmland like a horseshoe. There were even mountain spurs which jutted down to within a few miles of Haifeng city. Bandits had been using those mountains for centuries; these were the same mountains that had hidden runaway serfs three hundred years earlier. Large-scale bandit attacks had been reported throughout the nineteenth century, especially at the time of the Red Turbans uprising near Guangzhou, while the last big scare had come in 1900 when local bandits tried to stage a rising in concert with those in neighboring Guishan county. Smaller raids, such as the one on Mafulong Village, were much more common.

Reformers

Whenever there was such an incident involving bandits, the *Haifeng Self-Governance News* would run the headline: THE EVILS OF UNEQUAL PROPERTY. What precisely the editor, Chen Jiongming, meant is not clear, but he was probably more incensed at the government's method of dealing with banditry than with its material causes. When in 1907 the Qing commander charged with suppressing banditry in the East River region simply arrested and executed anyone he could catch in areas where bandits had been reported, Chen organized a group to seek his impeachment.[5]

Chen Jiongming was the leader of a reform-minded group of young gentry in Haifeng. This group would play an important part in the 1911 Revolution, which in many ways was a logical extension of their reform activities. Chen himself was to lead the People's Armies in the 1911 Revolution in Guangdong, and afterwards become the governor-general of Guangdong for a short while. In the decade and a half following the 1911 Revolution, he was a major military and political force in Guangdong, alternately cooperating and fighting with Sun

Yat-sen and his various political parties. He is sometimes thought of as a reformist warlord.[6]

Chen came from an influential and prosperous merchant family, but the family fortune declined when the estate was divided and redivided after the deaths of his grandfather and father. In early adulthood, Chen operated a small farm with his stepbrother Ma Yuhang, selling geese and eggs to Hong Kong, but found government regulations and transportation an obstacle. In many ways, the imperial system did not seem to work well for him. Perhaps that accounts for his interest in reform.

In 1898, at the age of twenty, Chen received the imperial *xiucai* degree, shortly before the civil service examination system based on those degrees was abolished. He then attended a new school, the Guangdong College of Law and Administration (Guangdong fazheng xueyuan), in order to pursue a career in government. While attending the college, he came into contact with several young radicals who had been hired as teachers; these men introduced him to the revolutionary movement. When Chen returned to Haifeng in 1908, he gathered around him a small circle of like-minded men to discuss the issues of reform and revolution.[7]

Most of those who joined his circle were gentry and the sons of gentry. Like Chen, several held imperial degrees. One had studied in the United States under John Dewey. Judging from their birthplaces in Haifeng city or its suburbs, they were among the more important of the Haifeng gentry. But the lesser gentry in the market towns also supported the revolutionary movement. Members of the powerful Lin lineage of Meilong supported the Revolutionary Alliance and even used the tremendous social power of the lineage to enlist members. Qiu Guochen recalled that in the summer of 1910, when he was sixteen, "my father brought me to the Meilong district office and told me to join the Chinese Revolutionary Alliance. The most important person there was the fourth uncle of district chief Lin Zonghan. He ordered me to raise my hand and take an oath, fill out a form, and pay ten dollars. That was it. My father later told me: 'They wanted me to join, but I was too old. I felt it better that you join instead.' "[8]

This group was the small-town equivalent of what Joseph Esherick has called the "urban reformist elite."[9] In Hunan and Hubei, this was the urbanized gentry with interests in industrialization, and in educational and political reform, which came to dominate the revolutionary government after the 10 October coup that set off the 1911 Revolution. In Haifeng county, Chen Jiongming and his associates too had developed interests that took them away from the conservative gentry positions first articulated in the Tongzhi Restoration (1862–74) and reformulated again in 1911 in the plans of the censor Wan Suanzou for bandit suppression. Chen had provincial political ambitions, floated plans for railway development, ran a modern newspaper, and advocated industrial development controlled by Chinese, not foreigners. In fact, after 1911 Chen and his group were responsible for whatever industrialization occurred in Haifeng. In all of these respects, the Haifeng group closely resembled the "urban reformist elite" of Hunan and Hubei.

In one respect, however, they differed: they were in a small town, not the provincial capital. This does not mean that Guangdong province did not have its equivalent of the urban reformist elite. As the work by Edward Rhoads makes clear,[10] the urban reformist elite, or what he terms the "New Gentry," played a role in reform and revolution in Guangdong similar to that they played in Hunan. But the existence of a small-town equivalent of the urban reformist elite is significant. First, it shows how far into Chinese society the forces creating the reformist elite had penetrated. But perhaps most importantly, it shows the extent to which this group in Guangdong had become a social class with interests that linked the elite of the small towns with that of the metropolitan areas. This helps us to understand why the revolutionary movement in Guangdong was not limited to urban political and military maneuvers, as it was in Hunan and Hubei, and why the revolutionary movement unraveled along lines that were at once defined by cleavages between town and countryside, and between social classes.

As other studies have pointed out, the line between reform and revolution was a thin one in the years preceding the 1911 Revolution. Chen and his group started out in reformist politics, only to form a secret cell of the Chinese Revolutionary Alliance in Haifeng sometime in 1910. Even as Chen began revolutionary activity, he kept up his image as a reformer. It was not even known in Haifeng until after the abortive 27 April 1911 uprising in Guangzhou, in which Chen participated, that he had anything to do with the "revolutionary faction." From 1909 until that time, Chen was the acknowledged leader of reform in Haifeng.

In 1909, Chen ran for the Guangdong Provincial Assembly and was elected in the June balloting. He clearly had wanted to be elected, for in April 1909 he had established the *Haifeng Self-Governance News* to promote his candidacy. Chen was editor-in-chief, and the other editors and contributors were all members of the reformist gentry group. The program Chen promoted in the Provincial Assembly, probably mirroring that published in the *News*, called for local self-government, prohibition of gambling and opium smoking, and the construction of a railroad from Huizhou to Chaozhou, routed through Haifeng.[11]

Whatever Chen's minimum program may have been, by 1910 he and his followers had committed themselves to the revolutionary overthrow of the Qing state and the establishment of a republic. The imperialists had been humiliating China for over half a century, and the Qing had been unable or unwilling to resist the aggression. It was now up to patriots like Chen. He may have felt that the Provincial Assembly was a step toward a constitutional monarchy at the very least, but when the Qing state in late 1909 made it clear that the provincial assemblies were to have simply an advisory role (and their advice could be rejected), Chen turned, as others did, to the violent overthrow of the Manchus. While in Guangzhou, he had maintained close communication with his comrades in Haifeng, who then coordinated county revolutionary activity with that in the capital. They also participated in the planning and execution of revolutionary actions, such as the 1910 New

127

Army mutiny and the 27 April 1911 Guangzhou rising. Revolutionaries from Haifeng had formed the largest contingent
in that abortive rising, and one of the famous "72 martyrs"
was Chen Chao, a young peasant from Haifeng's Youbu Village.[12]

Triads

Chen Chao was probably unique, for relations between
revolutionaries and the populace were based more on loose
ties with what have come to be known as secret or popular
societies (*hui-tang*) such as the Triad Society. In fact, Triads
figured in nearly every uprising in Guangdong province planned
by Sun Yat-sen's various revolutionary organizations between
1895 and 1911. That these ties existed is not in question; what
is problematic, because of its significance for understanding
the 1911 Revolution, is the nature of that relationship. Nationalist historiography, seeing the 1911 Revolution as the direct result of the activities of Sun and his revolutionary groups,
portrays the Triads as mere mercenary forces who added nothing to the revolutionary movement besides their numbers. Work
by John Lust and Mary B. Rankin, on the other hand, challenges this interpretation and greatly enriches our understanding of the 1911 Revolution by showing how the participation
of popular societies like the Triads significantly affected the
1911 Revolution.[13]

Valuable as this recent work is, it does not delve deep enough
into rural society to understand the extent to which the rural
populace participated in the 1911 Revolution. Lust has peeled
away one layer of the puzzle, revealing just beneath the surface
of the historical record the secret or popular societies; here we
shall peel away another layer to see even more of rural society
and how the rural areas fit into the 1911 Revolution. But because the Triads did indeed play a pivotal role, we will look
at them first.

The Triad society is one of several different groups Western
historians usually call secret societies. To Jean Chesneaux, the
term "designates associations whose policies are characterized
by a particular kind of religious, political, and social dissent

from the established order."[14] The Triad society, according to its legend, originated in opposition to the Manchu rulers of the Qing dynasty and in loyalty to the defeated Ming; this dissent was summed up in their slogan "Oppose the Qing, Restore the Ming." Triad society antidynastic sentiment, conveyed to members by way of initiation ceremonies and ritual, later provided an important opening for cooperation with the republican revolutionaries.

The notion of a secret society conveys an image of considerable organizational cohesion based on initiation rites, common ritual, esoteric language, and secret signs. The Triad societies exhibited all of these features, but they were hardly a unified conspiratorial group. To the contrary, the Triads were loosely organized, largely autonomous groups that went by three different names. The organization, if one can even call it that, was more cellular than hierarchical; Triad lodges (as the local societies were called) even fought each other on occasion. Because the Triads constituted a loose confederation without central direction, Frederick Wakeman observes, the Qing state had extreme difficulty suppressing Triad activity, but the Triads also had some difficulty cooperating with each other for very long.[15] Triad societies may have been ubiquitous in Guangdong, but they were not unified.

Little is known of Triad societies before the nineteenth century; by then they were engaged in much more than antidynastic plots (if indeed they ever had been so involved). Triad societies arose and flourished along the trade routes between town and countryside, centering their activities in the market towns and running the salt smuggling and protection rackets. The Triads were so involved in illicit trade that Feiling Davis has suggested that they constituted an illegal petite bourgeoisie.[16] In the market towns the Triads recruited from among the displaced and dispossessed peasants, the coolies and day laborers, the village and small town rabble who gravitated toward the interstices between town and countryside, belonging to neither, contemptuous of both. As the pool of the displaced and marginal swelled throughout the nineteenth century, Triad

129

lodges proliferated. And increasingly they caught the attention of the authorities.

In Haifeng, the Triads first entered the historical record in early 1806. The details of what they did are missing, but it appears that two Triad lodges, one somewhere in Haifeng and the other on the Lufeng coast, made a deal with some pirates to aid in an attack on a village near Meilong. Before being driven from this village by a gentry-led local defense corps, the Triads managed to post a red banner displaying "a heterodox slogan." Just what the Triads were after or what the banner read can never be known, but this episode does have some interesting features. First, it shows that by the early nineteenth century Triads had been around Haifeng long enough to be sufficiently organized to have contacts with other lodges and with pirates. Second, the Lufeng Triads were centered in a major salt-producing area, indicating early Triad involvement in salt smuggling. And finally, their target was Meilong, the center of Lin lineage wealth and power; it is unlikely that that was coincidental.[17]

The period of greatest Triad activity in Haifeng coincided with the Red Turban uprising in Guangzhou in 1854–56. Since Wakeman has examined the Red Turban revolt and the role of the Triads there in considerable detail, there is no need to go into that topic here.[18] Suffice it to say that when Triads around Guangzhou were attacking and occupying county capitals, Triads in Haifeng and Lufeng were attacking towns and villages as well. One can imagine that in Haifeng, as in the Pearl River delta, Triad societies had proliferated as the Triad lodge officer known as "Grass Sandals" openly recruited among the dispossessed in the market towns. The Haifeng Triad forces became quite large, numbering as many as 3,000 men in some detachments. However, they were not just marauding armies on the march from town to town (although there certainly was quite a bit of that); entire villages joined with the Triads, whether by choice, convenience, or coercion is unclear. The imperial state was as incapable of dealing with the Triads in Guangdong as it was the Taipings further to the north, so in Haifeng as in the rest of China, the local gentry organized militia to defend their villages and drive the invaders out. By 1856, Haifeng gentry forces—in which the Meilong Lin played a major role—had driven the Triads out of Haifeng.[19] Triads in Haifeng were not wiped out in the repression which followed the uprisings, for by the twentieth century Sun Yat-sen and other members of the Revolutionary Alliance were making contacts with the Triads to enroll them in the campaigns to overthrow the Qing dynasty. They had little difficulty finding Triads in Haifeng. Triad lodges were all over the county, but they were especially active in the salt-producing areas along the coast; other Triad groups were known to be in the hills and mountains surrounding Haifeng. As Lust and Rankin have demonstrated, ties between revolutionaries and Triads at this time were extensive. Indeed, Lust sees these ties as indicative of a "relationship between . . . 'movements from below' and the modern republican movement."[20] That is just part of the story, for it is misleading to think of the Triads as the only such movement from below or even as one representing the broader rural populace.

To be sure, the Triads were one type of social movement, but they were by no means the only organized group in rural Haifeng capable of collective action. As valuable as the work by Lust and Rankin is in showing that the 1911 Revolution was far more than a series of elite political or military actions, they have only scratched the surface: popular participation in the 1911 Revolution reached far deeper into Chinese society than even the popular societies. These societies in effect were intermediaries between the republican revolutionary movement and the revolution in the countryside. The reason they were able to play that role is not because revolutionaries such as Chen Jiongming designated such a role or because the Triads actively sought it, but because they were structurally situated in rural society to play it.

Work by Winston Hsieh suggests a useful framework for understanding this structure by relating the types of rural social organizations to places in the marketing hierarchy, starting with the villages and progressing up to larger cities.[21] At the lowest level were the village and lineage-sponsored organizations such as the crop-watching societies. The Red and Black Flags belonged here as well, uniting peasants in the villages with their leaders in the market towns. Although no documents attest directly to their role in the 1911 Revolution, we can be sure the Flags were there, organizing and directing the activity of thousands of peasants. Their interests were in local protection, and no doubt they were as vigilant in the summer and fall of 1911 as they ever had been.

If the market town was the apex of the Flag societies, it was likewise the base of operations for the Triads. Hsieh has shown quite conclusively that this is where most Triad recruits came from and where their activities centered. The market town, then, was where Flag leaders and Triads rubbed elbows and had to contend with each other's power. It is not inconceivable, of course, that a Flag leader was also a Triad. The actual extent to which Triads and Flags ever cooperated is open to speculation; only during the 1854–56 disturbances do the official sources even hint at a connection.

Triads also were active up the marketing hierarchy in local cities such as Haifeng. Just as Triad and Flag leaders met in the smaller market towns, so in the larger towns Triad circles intersected with those of yet another group: Haifeng's urban reformist gentry. Chen Jiongming was known to have made Triad contacts, and Haifeng city would have been a logical place to have made them.

The Triad society, then, sat in the pivot between groups in the villages and in larger cities who had a history of opposition to the Qing state. In the summer of 1911, it will be recalled, Censor Wan Suanzou had formulated a plan to deal with the disorder in the countryside, represented in part by the Triads. Presumably Wan wanted to repeat the mid-century suppression of the Triads by calling for gentry to return to the countryside to form militia. The irony of this plan by now should be apparent. Even in rural places like Haifeng, the gentry no longer had the same interests as their grandfathers, having been transformed in the interim into the urban reformist elite. So, when gentry like Chen Jiongming returned to the countryside in 1911, it was not to form militia to protect the Qing

132

state but to raise People's Armies to bring it down. As news of the 10 October 1911 Wuchang uprising spread, Revolutionary Alliance leaders and Triad chieftains returned from hiding in Hong Kong, Macao, and Saigon to form these armies.

People's Armies

To the Qing authorities, the People's Armies that converged on them in Huizhou and Guangzhou in October and November 1911 seemed to materialize out of thin air. But the reason for this swift coalescence of these armies was that they comprised already existent social groups with a history of taking collective action, from the crop-watching societies to the Flags and Triads. With all of these social organizations involved (and more that we will see), it is clear that the People's Armies were not simply Triads or "armies of brigands." On the contrary, the People's Armies arose out of rural society. To be sure, Triads played a pivotal role because of their structural position between the reformist elite *cum* republican revolutionaries and peasants at lower levels. By occupation, of course, the members of the People's Armies could be seen as poor peasants, middling peasants, handicraftsmen, young intellectuals, teachers, and even some merchants and gentry. But this static slice should not be allowed to obscure the less visible but more important social organizations that mobilized these people into the People's Armies in the first place. In Haifeng, they gathered almost overnight. One contingent, led by Chen Yuebo, Chen Jiongming's relative, took Haifeng, and another, led by Zhong Hanqiao, another of Chen's group, engineered the coup that took Haifeng. A young student recalled that "one night our teacher led me and some other students to join the People's Army in the attack on Haifeng city. All along the road I saw the gay and colorful People's Army. At midnight we halted about two miles from the city and waited for news. By dawn we still had not moved out. After a while, we learned that the magistrate had fled in the night, and with that the People's Army occupied the city. In that easy revolution, not one shot was fired and no one was even injured."[22]

After seizing county seats, People's Armies converged for the attack on Huizhou (see Map 7), coordinated by Chen Jiongming, revolutionary leader of the East River region. Huizhou fell quite easily in early November following a three-day siege by the People's Armies command by Chen Jiongming and the Triad forces led by Wang Heshun and Guang Renfu. The gentry and merchants of Huizhou, who had unsuccessfully tried to pressure the Qing prefect to declare for the Republic, remained in control of a significant portion of the military forces available to the city. When the People's Army besieged Huizhou, these merchants and gentry staged a *coup d'etat* and announced their support for the republican cause. Thus rather than risk a costly battle, Qing military commanders such as Hong Tiaowu, and gentry militia commanders, joined the revolutionary forces, assuming leadership of the People's Armies. Under the new leadership, the ragtag members of the People's Armies received their first military training. But, according to Chen Jinglü, one of these new commanders, the army's composition made the task nearly impossible: "The People's Army was composed solely of peasants. They always wanted to return to work in the fields, and thus could not stay in camp long."[23]

The People's Armies were not content with seizing just county or prefectural capitals. Once organized, they began to march on other cities and eventually on to the provincial capital, Guangzhou, along the way joining with other like-minded groups. The People's Army in Haifeng initially wanted to join Chen Jiongming's forces in the Huizhou campaign, but learning that that city had already been captured, many decided to go straight to Guangzhou. Some began the overland march while others took steamers directly to the Guangzhou waterfront.

But to the forces of order—the merchants and gentry of Guangzhou—the People's Armies from rural areas like Haifeng converging on Guangzhou were disorder. Indeed, political developments in Guangzhou during October and November had been premised on the call for "order!" The Qing governor-general's attempt to steer a middle course between monarchy

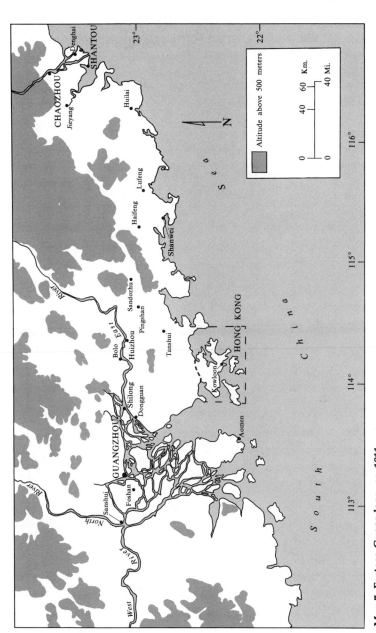

Map 7. Eastern Guangdong, ca. 1911

and republicanism by suggesting provincial autonomy (he would be governor) met with enthusiastic gentry approval and support, since it would provide for an orderly transfer of power. The governor-general's decision on 29 October to withhold finances and troops from the Qing court was taken by the residents of Guangzhou as a declaration of independence and greeted with street celebrations. Later that night, however, he announced that independence had not been declared and ordered the celebrations suppressed.[24]

The initiative then passed out of the hands of the gentry into those of the merchants. The merchants, who had been excluded from the negotiations (or conspiracy) with the governor-general, clamored for the preservation of order even as the People's Armies closed in on Guangzhou. If the People's Armies stood for radical republicanism, merchants hoisted the banner of orderly republicanism. Merchants demanded that the governor-general recognize the Republic as the only way to assure peace and order in Guangzhou—but their pleas fell on deaf ears. When Hu Hanmin, chief of the southern China bureau of the Revolutionary Alliance, delivered a letter to the merchants praising their efforts to effect a peaceful transmission of power but regretting that the governor-general's intransigence now meant that the takeover could not be bloodless, it became apparent that neither the gentry nor the merchants had been able to guarantee order. On 8 November, the merchants elected Hu Hanmin governor and invited the People's Armies into Guangzhou to restore order.

But the first months of republican rule under the joint stewardship of Hu Hanmin and Chen Jiongming (governor and vice-governor, respectively, of the new Provisional Military Government of Guangzhou) were anything but orderly. After the former governor-general fled in the dead of night and Guangdong joined the Republic, the People's Armies descended on Guangzhou; as many as 100,000 to 150,000 peasants, rural outcasts, vagabonds, and Triads occupied the city. These people were the real power in the revolution and in Guangzhou, but the forces of order knew it better than they themselves did. By late December, newspapers were filled with

136

reports that peasant troops had begun to take effective control of the city; they were enforcing their own laws, controlling prices, forcing rice shops to sell grain at a fair price, killing "Manchu spies," and sometimes looting. They were, in fact, carrying out those actions which they and their fathers had taken so many times before in the small market towns and county capitals. It was a form of organization and action with which they were familiar and comfortable. But now they were in the greatest of Guangdong cities—and the one which was the financial center for the entire province. For a while, the 1911 Revolution was to be the revenge of the countryside on the city.

But for the merchants and monied interests of Guangzhou, political disorder was causing financial chaos as well. The cost of maintaining the People's Armies—or of buying their quiescence—was draining the coffers of the fledgling government and precipitating monetary instability. Finding it impossible to carry on business as usual, merchants demanded that the new government restore financial stability and disband the People's Armies. They had, after all, provided funds to the republican government at the very outset to keep it from falling. Now they wanted order to pursue their economic interests.[25]

Initial attempts to control the People's Armies—in the eyes of the city, that riffraff from the countryside wreaking havoc in town—had proved ineffectual. With over a hundred thousand rustics disrupting a city merchants were trying to return to normalcy, Hu Hanmin thought instilling discipline into the troops would control the rowdies. Hu first appointed Liu Yongfu, an elderly military man with considerable experience with Triad forces, as commander of all People's Armies. Liu was soon removed and replaced by Huang Shizhong, a man Hu Hanmin felt could control the two rather independent-minded People's Army leaders, the Triad chiefs Wang Heshun and Guang Renfu. And to keep the problem of the People's Armies from getting any worse, Hu ordered any People's Armies not already in the capital to remain in the countryside. Their job, he said, was to secure peace and order in the countryside, prevent bandits from disrupting property relations, and allow people to go on with their lives.[26]

It was a curious command—to expect the forces that had arisen from the disorder of the countryside to restore it to an order conceived and articulated by other social groups. Clearly, it was an attempt to buy time for the city at the expense of the countryside. Who could really expect the People's Armies, composed of people Hu Hanmin himself described as "poor and landless peasants who had become bandits," to uphold law and order? And they didn't. Provincial merchants then proved no less vociferous than their urban counterparts in demanding order so that they could proceed with the business of making money. Telegrams from throughout the Guangdong hinterland flooded the new government with complaints about the pillaging of the People's Armies, or of those who claimed to be. At the call of provincial merchants, Chen Jiongming dispatched troops into the countryside, perhaps to gain experience for the showdown with the Triad chiefs Wang Heshun and Guang Renfu that was sure to come. The merchants heartily welcomed these disciplined soldiers, and in areas such as Baihai county, the troops "soon set to work and arrested nearly all of the disbanded soldiers and a lot of robbers too. The prisons are filled again, and all the new officials are busily engaged." The troops were restoring order and normality—full prisons and busy officials.[27]

The disbandment of the People's Armies occupying the capital had begun in January and continued into May, by which time 120,000 soldiers, most of whom "came from the agricultural classes," according to Hu Hanmin, had been dismissed. Some of them disbanded peacefully, but others did not. As head of the new "Pacification Bureau," Chen Jiongming presided over the daily execution of hundreds of people. The terror—or "pacification," in the language of counterrevolution—extended into the countryside, where mass executions were also reported. The strongest remnant of the People's Army, eight thousand men commanded by Wang Heshun, did not disband without a fierce four-day battle. The resistance of others then melted away. With the spring planting season fast arriving, many peasant-soldiers began trickling back to their homes. And language differences forced the Fulao-speaking soldiers from Haifeng to return home as well.[28]

The Revolution That Didn't Happen

Having fought for the revolution—indeed, having been the main force in the revolution—peasants from Haifeng and other places returned to the world they had left. They may well have wondered what they had been fighting for. That these armies—composed of peasants but led by others—had opted for taking cities and looting along the way reveals how far seizing the land was removed from the thoughts of their leaders. The closest the question of land and land use came to being raised by leaders of the revolution was the inscription of the character "jing" (for the ancient, mythological, and presumably equitable "well-field" system) on the flag of Chen Jiongming's army. What did the peasants who fought in the army believe they were getting? In many ways it was a lord protector in the person of Chen Jiongming. In Haifeng, according to Peng Pai, an unusually astute observer of such matters, "the peasants under Chen Jiongming's . . . regime ecstatically congratulated 'our commander' (Haifeng's affectionate nickname for Chen Jiongming). His good luck would spread to his fellow villagers! Better yet if he mounted the throne to become Emperor!"[29] But behind even this hope lay other expectations.

Peasants throughout Guangdong expected great things from the Republic. In Huiyang county just west of Haifeng, it was reported in February 1912, peasant "hatred toward the boy Emperor [Xuantong] is more on account of the poor crops, high rice prices, famine, floods and typhoons, for which he is generally held responsible, than for being a Manchu. A man of influence was asked if he did not want to be innoculated against the plague. He replied promptly: 'There won't be any plague under the Republic.' In certain places, instead of the ordinary sacrifices to the god of the earth, which were supposed to be necessary in order to ensure a good crop, the revolutionary flag has been used instead."[30]

To peasants who interpreted the revolution in religious symbols, it should not be too surprising that many of the trappings of the Republic had more fetishistic than rational meaning. Large numbers of peasants were excited on the eve of the 1911 Revolution, and many were ready to believe that a new world was in the offing. Mass hysteria had been reported by missionaries throughout the eastern Guangdong countryside; meetings "were marked with perplexing physical manifestations, crowds praying together, people trembling under conviction of sin, some writhing in agony, others falling prostrate to the ground."[31]

What peasants thought the revolution was accomplishing is difficult to ascertain with any precision. It seems reasonably clear that for many the revolutionary movement was inseparable from, and probably identical with, a religious movement which not only gave meaning and order to the events of the revolution, but also provided the framework within which goals were established and success evaluated. But whereas the goals of the leaders were specific and political, those supplied to peasants through their religious beliefs were much more general and spongy. It is thus not wise to try to impose too much order and clarity on folk beliefs that were not very precise to begin with.[32]

In Haifeng, the 1911 Revolution was accompanied by renewed and intensified activity of the Baling Hui, a folk religious sect that attracted widespread support in the rural areas to the west and south of Haifeng city. The Baling sect was a syncretic movement, drawing its name from a Buddhist adept and its basic beliefs from folk Daoist sources, especially those surrounding the cult of Lei Gong, Duke of Thunder. In popular mythology, Lei Gong belonged to the pantheon of gods on the Board of Thunder which controlled rainfall. Lei Zu (Thunder Ancestor), the chief deity, was assisted by Lei Gong, Dian Mu (Mother of Lightening), Feng Bo (Earl of Wind), and Yu Shi (Master of Rain). Although Lei Zu and Lei Gong were distinct deities, they were commonly taken as one and the same in popular belief. At the mythical installation of gods, according to Doré, Lei Gong was given "the supreme direction of the

Board of Thunder and the office of calling forth the clouds and meting out the rains for the furthering of all growth." Lei Gong was also charged with slaying the wicked and destroying the evildoer. To the common folk, the greatest sin was wasting grain. Doré observed that peasants "are very careful not to let grains of rice fall upon the flour [sic]; should this happen, the grains are scrupulously picked up lest they be trampled upon, for the crime of wasting or trampling on cereals may be punished by Lei [Gong] with his thunderbolt. It will be remembered that part of his office is the proper distribution of rain for the crops: therefore he punished those who waste the grain which he has brought to maturity."[33]

Since Lei Gong was charged with bringing the rains and making the crops grow, he was a particularly appropriate god for peasants. The Baling sect, based on this god, thus had its strongest appeal among peasants in the agriculturally rich Meilong district. During periods of drought when the harvest was threatened, rituals were conducted at Lei Gong's temple to bring the rains. Often conducted by Buddhist or Daoist monks, the ceremony was designed to eliminate any sources of pollution displeasing to Lei Gong.

The members of the Baling sect also perceived a relationship between the power of Lei Gong and human agents to affect the harvest, as indicated in a popular saying in rhymed couplet: "In heaven is Lei Gong, on earth is Guifeng." Guifeng was a reference to the Lin lineage of Meilong, which conducted its business under the name of "Guifeng." The meaning of the couplet is ambiguous. Did it mean that peasants felt equally powerless in the face of Lei Gong and the Lin? Both certainly affected the amount of the harvest remaining to the peasant. Lei Gong, after all, was supposed to punish those who wasted grain. Could the Lin as landlords have been seen as wasting the peasants' grain? Or did the verse imply that peasants believed they could exert influence over both Lei Gong and their landlords through magical charms and rituals? It is known, for example, that peasants employed a myriad of charms to placate and influence various deities. Did the practice extend to human forces as well? The couplet is tantalizingly suggestive, and the use of charms is not unknown in other societies. It may well have been that the couplet originally lauded the achievements of the Lin; later, because of the ambiguity of the couplet, it came to be interpreted quite differently. Whatever the case, it does reveal a rough sense of class on the part of the tenants of the Lin, who perceived their interests as somewhat different from the Guifeng Lin.

In the late nineteenth century, a number of the members of the Lin lineage converted to Catholicism, undoubtedly in order to obtain the help of the French consul in Guangzhou in their dealings in the magistrate's yamen. Both the Protestant missionaries in Haifeng and the magistrate of Lufeng county complained bitterly in the late nineteenth century about the Catholic converts' use of "temporal power" to win their cases in the "mandarin's court." Thus not entirely accidentally or even coincidentally, members of the most powerful landlord family in the Meilong area became Christians.[34]

Ever since missionaries had begun to win converts, there had been anti-Christian violence in Haifeng and Lufeng. Most commonly the violence was occasioned by the converts' refusal to participate in village and community affairs judged "pagan" by the church. In April of 1900, for example, the inhabitants of Dongjia village put on an opera to worship a local deity. When a convert refused a request for his customary contribution, he was surrounded and beaten by the villagers, who then took all the family belongings and seized his fields. Ostracized by the community, the Catholic moved from the village. In other cases, converts were attacked by members of their own lineage for refusing to contribute to the local crop-watching society.[35]

When members of the Lin lineage converted to Catholicism, they broke their ties with the local community and, like other converts, no doubt refused to contribute to the community religious expenses. The Baling sect then had greater appeal than ever before, especially among the peasants who were Lin tenants or who lived in the Meilong region. The Lin now were not only landlords: they were also Christians who refused to honor their community obligations.

The first recorded activities of the Baling sect—those peasants who had perceived a relationship between Lei Gong and the Guifeng Lin—were attacks upon missionaries and Chinese Christians. In 1906, Catholic missionaries reported that "in the past several years the anti-Christian Baling sect has become very strong in the rural areas around Meilong; but the city folk just looked the other way. There were constant conflicts between them and our followers." By 1907 the sect "lorded over" the rural areas: "They do not fear officials, do not obey the law, and have no propriety." Constantly harassed, Catholics secured the support of their Lin patrons to suppress the "heretical" Baling sect "once and for all." Suppress it they did, at least for four years.[36]

During the 1911 Revolution, a Baling leader named Guo Yi-en returned to Haifeng in November to revitalize the sect. Members of the sect in at least one village then seized the property of a Catholic, ostracized the family from the village, and refused to allow them to return. How often this occurred in other Haifeng villages during the critical month of November is not known. Clearly, those who were both Catholic and landlords had something to be concerned about, both in terms of religion and of property. Incidents in other villages showed that when members of the Baling sect attacked a family on religious grounds, the attack soon moved to property. The Lin of Meilong did not wait to find out whether this was to be their fate as well. Soon after he returned to Haifeng, Guo Yi-en was arrested and executed by the commander of the revolutionary troops in Haifeng.[37] This was to be expected. The Lin, after all, *were* the Revolutionary Alliance in Meilong.

The 1911 Revolution was not to be a rural revolution. It is true that much of the action of the 1911 Revolution in Guangdong took place in the countryside and that groups of peasants participated in the revolution. But in the end the revolutionary movement split apart—not surprising in view of the number and variety of social groups and classes within it—and peasants were left without much to show for their efforts. The movement did not come apart randomly, however, but along clearly identifiable lines.

The first cracks appeared at the top of the marketing hierarchy in Guangzhou, between the monied interests of the city and what seemed to them the rabble from the countryside. Then, in the small towns all over Guangdong province, merchants voiced complaints about the activities of the People's Armies. And finally, those in the market towns, like the Lin of Meilong, regarded the villages as the source of disorder because of the activities of groups like the Baling sect. To those who had led the revolution—those clearly associated with the urban reformist elite in each of these urban areas—the actions by people from the countryside, arising out of their own forms of organization and experience, were causing "disorder." Actions that earlier had been lauded as "revolutionary" now were seen as counterrevolutionary and had to be repressed.

The revolutionary movement initially split along lines defined by the divisions and antagonisms between town and countryside. The definition of "countryside" changed as one moved from the large cities to the market towns: all of Guangdong province was rural to those in Guangzhou, while to the Lin in Meilong, the countryside comprised their villages. But regardless of definition, to each urban area the threat to order came from the countryside. The division between town and countryside also can be seen in terms of social class. In the course of the revolution, the urban reformist elite—from the market towns all the way to Guangzhou—had become increasingly conscious of its interests and acted to enforce them. They wanted order, and the countryside was causing disorder. In this sense, the 1911 Revolution was an important experience in the making of a new landlord class. Any further disturbances in the countryside henceforth would be treated as "a matter for the police and the courts."[38] But to do so, of course, required police and courts.

New Landlords

If it is assumed that the urban reformist elite operated only in the center of power in Guangzhou, it would be tempting to conclude that they had been driven from power in 1913, opening the way for the seemingly endless line of militarist contenders for power that characterized the "warlord" era. But this will not do, for as we have seen, this class extended into the market towns of Haifeng as well. Here this group came to power in the 1911 Revolution—and stayed in power into the 1920s.

Those sons of the gentry who had first joined with Chen Jiongming in 1908 now filled the local political offices, and if there were not enough posts to go around, they created new ones. They became the county magistrates, not only in Haifeng and Lufeng, but in other eastern Guangdong counties too. They took up posts in the newly created educational system, and they controlled the newspapers. They even launched new industrial enterprises: nearly all of the textile and stocking factories in Haifeng were built by the old Revolutionary Alliance members. And they controlled the police. Zhong Jingtang, a charter member of the Haifeng revolutionary contingent and lieutenant of Chen Jiongming, now commanded an armed force of over two hundred soldiers stationed at Shanwei, while full-time police forces were organized in other towns as well. The new levers of power extended beyond Haifeng into the provincial government, where revolutionary Haifeng gentry now became provincial officials overseeing the Bureau of Roads, the Education Department, the Guangdong mint, and the Board of Revenue (at least whenever Chen Jiongming was in power). New power in Haifeng was everywhere; it was said that "military commanders outnumber dogs, and magistrates line the streets."[39]

These victors in the revolution gained the land. They didn't quite steal it, but they didn't necessarily buy it either. The financial difficulties of the provincial government just made it easier. Besides reimposing numerous sumptuary taxes on wine, sugar, fish, oysters, cloth, and pig and chicken butchering, among others, in order to meet severe government deficits (occasioned in part by payments to the People's Armies), Hu Hanmin made it clear that the land tax would be raised through implementation of Sun Yat-sen's ideal of the "equalization of land rights." Adopted from Henry George, Sun's proposal would have prevented land speculation or monopolization by

145

state confiscation of all future increases in land value not brought about by improvements. The state would then use the funds for industrialization. Every landowner was to be issued a new land deed by the government, at which time the landowner would assess the value of the land. Because the state reserved the right to purchase the land, owners presumably would not set too low a value; but neither would they make the assessment too high, since taxes were to be paid on the self-assessed value.[40]

Sun's good intentions, however, were never realized. In Haifeng at least, the "equalization of land values" precipitated a landgrab by the relatives and hangers-on of Chen Jiongming. After the seizure of Guangzhou, according to Peng Pai, "Chen Jiongming's lineage set up a 'commander's office' at the south gate of Haifeng city, with Chen's mother and sixth uncle Chen Kaiting, an opium addict, in charge." All transactions, including taxation and the equalization of land values, had to be processed through the commander's office. "Among the deeds and documents a good number were centuries old; they were hard to make out, of course, and the location and extent of the land was not exactly clear. But the Chens bought them up." Relatives and cronies of Chen Jiongming benefitted handsomely from the protection afforded by Chen's army. When Chen's mother and uncle set up the commander's office in Haifeng city after the 1911 Revolution, according to Peng Pai, "it goes without saying that it used political devices to extort a good deal of money. Though most of it went into foreign banks, part was used to purchase land in Haifeng or as usury capital."[41]

Lords who threw in their lot with the Chens and their friends prospered, while those who did not were squeezed out. These "newly arisen" or "newly prosperous" landlords (*xin xing dizhu*), many of whom peasants could easily identify by their new Western-style two-story villas, were those most rapacious in their demands on peasants. As one investigator put it, "Before the 1911 Revolution, lords were a bit more polite."[42]

Not all landowners in Haifeng, of course, were relatives or longtime friends and allies of Chen Jiongming. But those who

had not been squeezed or bought out by the Chens also benefitted by the changes wrought by the 1911 Revolution. Not
only had the military come under the direct control of landlords, but some even had their own strongmen for collecting
rent. Peng Pai observed that "to collect rent in the villages,
guards or police were always sent under arms. When the few
families of Yuanma Village could not pay up because of a bad
year, guards were sent to rake through the house: they seized
women's hair ornaments . . . six ragged items of children's
clothing, two pints of rice, and one peck of seed grain." To
add insult to injury, peasants were forced to pay "shoe leather
money" to the rent collectors. Other landlords, such as the Cai
lineage of Lujing village (Peng Pai's in-laws), had other more
draconian measures for collecting rent. The Cai held land in
over one hundred surrounding villages; to ensure that the rent
was paid, "every year they sent a few dozen henchmen, including a manager, to live in Rent Hall and prompt rent from
the peasants. Rent Hall also had tall ladders, ropes, chains,
whips, rods, and other instruments of torture. . . . Peasants
whose rent payments were overdue or incomplete, or whose
old debts were in arrears, were seized and confined in Rent
Hall. They were even hung up—this was called the 'monkey
hang.' A peasant would hang there until his family sold his
ox or son, or married off his wife, and redeemed him with the
money."[43]

Under the economic and political conditions prevailing in
the years following the sugar market crash and the 1911 Revolution, it should not be too surprising that the new landlords
began to alter the terms of tenure. Lords raised the rent on
lands held on permanent tenure, and if tenants resisted or
refused to pay the increase (after all, the terms of permanent
tenure stipulated that rent could not be raised), the lord sought
a court order forcing them off the land. And since peasants
knew they had about as much chance winning a case in the
magistrate's court "as a sand castle standing in the ocean," few
fought these increases. Lords also broke contracts with im-
punity. Although leases stipulated terms of four or five years,
lords would now raise the rent after a year or two. By such

measures, the Lin of Meilong tripled their rental income to 10,000 *shi* (about 500 tons) of rice in the decade after the 1911 Revolution. According to one source, "The rents were raised, and if [tenants] could not pay, the land was taken back and rented to someone else."[44]

Since the landlord held the only copy of the lease agreement, tenants in these instances did not have a leg to stand on. The oral, or *koutou*, tenancy, which became the dominant form of land tenure by the 1920s, was especially suitable to lords who wished to raise rents, change tenants, or otherwise alter the terms of tenure—there was no written contract, and the rights to the use of the land lasted just one year. This was a major change from nineteenth-century conditions, when peasants had secure tenancies.[45]

Accompanying changes in the terms of tenure, according to recent work on landownership in Haifeng, was a concentration of ownership. Guo Chengxiang attributes this concentration to the "newly arisen landlords" who squeezed out peasant smallholders and small landlords. His work confirms the findings here, and adds some specific statistics. He estimates that landlords comprised 2.68 percent of the population and owned 46.95 percent of the land. The total annual rent collected by landlords living in Haifeng city alone reached 100,000 shi; the really large landlords such as the Lin and the Cai cited above are not included in this figure. The villages from which the rent was collected were composed mainly of tenants. Dafusai village near Haifeng city had twenty-eight families, twenty-six of whom were tenants. The 400 mou of village land yielded 2,000 shi, of which peasants paid 1,090 shi in rent, a bit over 50 percent of output.[46]

Under the various types of tenure that had emerged during Qing times, as well as the sharecropping arrangement for paying rent, peasants had claimed the right to a rent reduction in bad years. With the emergence of fixed rents, peasants continued to claim this right, even though the contract said otherwise. But what peasants had regarded as customary rights, enshrined in oral tradition and inalienable even by contract, landlords now regarded as favors to be dispensed at their pleasure. When the crop failed, peasants had to go to the lord's home, get on their knees, and beg three times for a rent reduction. And even then, the lord could deny the request.[47]

Tenancy relations did not stand alone but were embedded in other social relationships, particularly the lineages and the Red and Black Flags. The lords of the land were lineage and Flag leaders; tenants were members of lineages and Flags. Peasants perhaps saw tenancy as an exchange relationship in which for the payment of rent they received something in return. Sometimes it was just the use of the land. But if they belonged to a lineage (40 percent of all land in Haifeng was lineage-owned) or to a Flag, they received in addition protection from all kinds of outside threats, ranging from armed incursions to taxes and even harvest failure. This may have been considered a fair exchange. But over time and for the reasons discussed above, the terms of exchange tipped against the tenant, either because the cost (i.e., the rent) increased, or the benefit (i.e., protection) decreased. Tenants could then easily see the exchange relationship—tenancy as well as the lineages or Flags—as unfair.

Lineage leaders had been obliged to rent land to members at customary rates, but they began to let land to outsiders, who could be charged a rent higher than could otherwise be obtained from lineage members. Poorer members then had to compete on the general market for land. Wealthy lineage members also began to refuse to make loans to peasant members without considerable collateral. Under these conditions, peasants in the villages began to turn to each other for mutual assistance, forming credit clubs, burial associations, and marketing groups. Daniel Kulp observed in 1919 that in Phenix village northeast of Haifeng county, these "associations arise out of the failure of the familist group to cope with the needs [of the poorer members], economic, protective, or recreational. Where the economic family fails, voluntary alignments of resources and capacities of a cooperative nature secure successful adjustments in special crises." Kulp felt that "as cooperation weakens and antagonisms grow, there will arise a strengthening of influence on non-kinship groups."[48]

This "disintegration," as Kulp called it, of traditional social organizations affected not only the lineages, but the Red and Black Flag societies of Haifeng as well. No longer did peasants see the Flags as protective of their interests; in fact, they had come to see the Flags quite differently, as the following song suggests: "Unjustly, the village leader sends us to death. We meet our maker, he collects eighty cents." Disillusionment with the Flags was sufficiently widespread to cause peasants to wonder why they fought each other. It was commonly believed that the factional strife had been created by the alien Manchus in order to prevent unity among the conquered Chinese: "They were a minority, so it was difficult for them to control us Han Chinese. Thus they created these two factions so the people would fight each other." Although this belief had no basis in fact, it nonetheless does indicate that Flag members had come to feel strongly that the Flags did not serve their interests: the Manchus had been overthrown, so why did the fighting continue except to enrich the Flag leaders? The peasant logic was impeccable.[49]

While lineage and Flag solidarity weakened, these social organizations did not just disappear. Lineages were not all the same, for instance, but varied in size and strength from a few hundred to tens of thousands. Furthermore, not all areas experienced the same extent or kind of socioeconomic change. Some places, in fact, were quite isolated from the commercial forces emanating from the coast. In the northernmost part of Lufeng, a sheltered valley over forty miles from the port of Shanwei, lineages remained strong, and lineage conflict continued as the dominant form of collective violence. But this is the only case that could be found, and it occurred in the most remote part of Lufeng county.[50] It is the exception that proves the rule—lineage (and Flag) solidarity throughout Haifeng waned in the decade after the 1911 Revolution.

As peasants began to cooperate in self-help organizations such as credit and burial associations, the dissolution of the traditional paternalist ties between wealthy and poorer members continued. This led at times to peasant actions that landowners saw as "cheating," such as when peasants mixed sand or water in with the rice that was paid as rent. Sometimes, if a whole village felt wronged, everyone pitched in and felt wholly justified in doing so, especially if the landlord used a larger or expanding basket the next time to collect the rent. In some areas of Haifeng, such as around Meilong, ties between landlords and peasants already were strained, as the experience of the Baling sect demonstrates.

Thus, in the decade after the 1911 Revolution, both landlords and peasants began to act more in terms of class than of lineage or Flag. The major difference was that under the leadership of the reformist gentry, the "newly arisen" landlords of Haifeng had taken the offensive. The results of the 1911 Revolution had tipped the balance of power decisively in favor of landlords, and they used that to their advantage. The reformist gentry used the police and the courts to maintain order, but under the surface simmered class grievances that would take very little to bring to a boil.

CHAPTER 7

The Politics of Backwardness
Intellectuals and Peasants

ONE day late in May 1922, a thirty-year-old peasant ladling fertilizer onto his fields in the Chishan district, just east of Haifeng city, looked up and saw a tall young man smartly dressed in a white, Western-style suit and hat. "Sir, have a smoke," the peasant said, adding suspiciously: "Have you come to collect taxes? We around here haven't put on an opera." Using words and phrases the peasant only partly understood, the young gentleman replied that he had come not to collect taxes but to make friends and talk with the villagers about their hardships. "Ah! Bitterness is our fate," the peasant said, adding that he couldn't stay and chat, and then hurried on his way. In a little while the gentleman came upon another peasant, this one younger and more intelligent looking. "Sir," the peasant asked the well-dressed man, as he would any stranger who came into the countryside, "what military outfit are you with? Do you have official business? What has brought you here?" The stranger claimed he was not a soldier or official but that he had come especially to make friends. The peasant laughed: "We're useless fellows here, not up to you fine people. Here, have some tea." Without lifting his head, he hurried off. The next day the stranger returned to the village, and a middle-aged peasant asked if he had come to collect debts. Again the gentleman denied it.[1]

Tax collector, official, soldier, debt-collector—these usually were the only well-dressed city folk to venture into the countryside. And like the young man, they too were treated respectfully—if they couldn't be avoided. When strangers came into the village, all the doors and windows closed, and the village became deserted. People from the city usually only meant trouble for the villagers, and yet here was this young gentleman who claimed he just wanted to be their friend. No one believed him.

The people from that Chishan village would not have seen the white-suited man again soon unless they happened to be carting produce to Haifeng city to sell. At a crossroads in the countryside where paths from villages in several districts met, this same young man was standing under a spreading banyon tree in front of the Longshan Temple, lecturing to peasants who had stopped there to rest and gossip. But now he had changed his clothes into ordinary peasant garb, and without a hat, his face was more visible. He was tall and had long, combed-back hair that revealed his angular features. His speech and mannerisms still betrayed his gentry upbringing, but he no longer used language totally foreign to peasants. He talked not about some new tax but about the "three packings" (the landlord practice of tightly packing rice into the containers used to collect rent), "gifts" to landlords, fixed rent, rent increases, and other things villagers understood.[2]

Every day for half a month the young man talked to groups of peasants. The numbers grew steadily from a few to dozens of peasants. Gradually they learned who he was. His name was Peng Hanyu, son of the Peng landlords who managed their lands under the "Minghe" company. He called himself Peng Pai, having taken his new name (a homonym of "roaring of the waves") a few years earlier while studying in Japan. One day when Peng was talking about various forms of landlord oppression such as the three packings and iron-clad rent, a forty-year-old peasant in the audience shot out: "What a load of shit! Talk about reducing rent! If you Minghe people would quit pressing us for back rent, I'd think you're all right."[3]

Soon a debate broke out; a young tenant of another lord retorted that what Peng Pai said made sense to him. Afterwards the young man, Zhang Ma-an, told Peng that people in his village argued well into the night about what he had been preaching during the day. Zhang added: "There are a lot of us who believe what you say." Anxious to meet these unseen allies, Peng invited Zhang to bring them to his home. That evening, Zhang arrived with four others, all of whom were under thirty. Over tea they talked about why Peng had trouble getting peasants to listen to him, and how they could help. They told him to speak more like a peasant and offered to show him around to the villages, provided he didn't criticize their gods.[4]

That was a rather extraordinary evening: the son of one of Haifeng's greatest landowning families had sat down to tea with five peasants, talked about rent reductions, and formed an organization to pursue those goals. By 1923 he would organize thousands into peasant unions pressing for rent reductions, and in 1927 would lead peasants in the most radical attack on the rural order until that time, foreshadowing in many ways the experiences across rural China in the revolution of the late 1940s. When Peng Pai met with Zhang Ma-an, it was the beginning of a long relationship with the peasants. Peng Pai soon becomes their conscious spokesman, articulating peasant grievances and demands. Peasants were ready to listen to what he had to say.

His family wasn't. They were aware of what he was doing but had a harder time than peasants in understanding him. In fact, they thought he had gone insane, called a doctor, and counseled him to remain in bed. Many peasants also thought he was crazy and became frightened when they saw him coming. After all, he was heir to one of the greatest fortunes in Haifeng, and here he was wearing old clothes, having tea with peasants, and talking about reducing rent. Why? Clearly, we need to know more about Peng Pai to understand how he had arrived at the heretical (if not insane) views that made a peasant leader out of a landowner's son.

Peng Pai

Peng Pai came from a wealthy family that inhabited a large walled compound in Haifeng's eastern suburbs. So large was the Peng lineage, it was said that "if you throw a stone into the air, it will come down on the head of a Peng."[5] Peng wealth rested on landownership. According to Peng Pai, "our family could be considered one of Haifeng's big landlords. It took in over a thousand shi of rice every year, and managed no fewer than 1,500 peasants—men, women, and children. There were not over thirty people in our family, so each one had about fifty peasants held like serfs."[6] Other family members put the total rent at 3,000 shi. Whatever the exact amount, it was truly enormous in an area where an acre was considered a "competence." Family wealth had been accumulated in the late eighteenth and early nineteenth centuries by Peng Pai's great-grandfather, Peng Jingbao. Jingbao was a merchant who "made his fortune only after the age of forty," as the family was proud of pointing out. Jingbao conducted his business under the name of "Jingji," while money generated in trade was invested in land and managed by his son under the business name of "Minghe," or Reknowned Harmony. By the turn of the twentieth century, the Peng family owned several thousand mou of land and over one hundred shops in Haifeng.[7] The Peng were not much different from the other landlord families now living in Haifeng city.

Peng Pai, the fourth of his father's seven sons—the second by his concubine—received a properly Confucian education, and as a child was described as mildly precocious. Peng's upbringing was traditional in other respects as well, for in 1912, when he had just turned sixteen, his parents married him to Cai Suping, the daughter of a wealthy family from Lujing village. She was described as an "attractive but old-fashioned and conservative country girl" who hobbled around on her "little feet" until Peng Pai reportedly unbound them. Their marriage would not remain traditional, however, for Cai would work closely with her husband in the peasant movement and emerge as a leader of the women's liberation and trade union movements.[8]

After the 1911 Revolution, Peng attended the new Haifeng Middle School established by the reformist gentry leaders of the revolution. The school graduated four classes of about fifty students, most of whom were sons of wealthy Haifeng families. New subjects taught at the Haifeng Middle School included history, geography, biology, science, English, music, handicrafts, and physical education. In 1916, owing to financial difficulties, Haifeng and Lufeng combined their county schools into a jointly operated school, the Lu-an Normal School, occupying the premises of the old school. Lu-an Normal School soon became infused with the student radicalism of the New Culture Movement sweeping China under the influence of journals such as the famed *New Youth Magazine*.[9]

Students' activism was directed more at the military rulers of Guangdong than against the Confucian tradition attacked by Chen Duxiu in the pages of *New Youth*. When General Long Jiguang captured Guangzhou from Chen Jiongming following the abortive "Second Revolution" of 1913, he appointed a minor officer, Liu Gancai, to suppress opposition to President Yuan Shikai in eastern Guangdong. For reasons that are unclear, Chen Jiongming's relative, Chen Yuebo, led the group vigorously supporting Liu's efforts. Chen Yuebo, it will be recalled, had led the People's Armies in the 1911 attack on Haifeng, and clearly belonged to the group of reformist gentry. It is somewhat puzzling, then, that he would cooperate with Chen Jiongming's enemy.

Undoubtedly realizing that Liu Gancai would suspect Haifeng, Chen Jiongming's native county, as a center of opposition to the new rulers, Chen and other Haifeng gentry often visited Liu's Chaozhou headquarters to curry his favor. They even planned to erect a statue of him in Haifeng to replace a shrine of the local military hero of the Southern Song dynasty, Wen Tianxian. When students of Lu-an Normal School learned of the plans for the statue, some protested to Chen Yuebo. Chen responded by reprimanding the principal and teachers for not maintaining stricter control over the students. Determined to continue their protest, Peng Pai and several other students established the Progressive Masses Society (*qun jin hui*) to submit memorials to Long Jiguang in Guangzhou and post handbills throughout Haifeng. But their action, seemingly innocent enough, attracted Liu Gancai's troops to the school to quell the disturbance, and to protect Liu's only likely claim to fame. Finding their petitions ignored and their protests suppressed, Peng Pai and several others sneaked into the sculptor's studio

156

one night and chiseled the nose off Liu's statue, forcing the gentry to dump the desecrated rock into the sea.[10]

Soon after this incident, Peng Pai decided to leave provincial Haifeng to further his studies in cosmopolitan Tokyo. For several decades Japan had been the primary medium through which Chinese intellectuals had learned about Western institutions and culture. During the first decades of the twentieth century, most leading intellectuals had studied in Japan; not the least important of these were Chen Duxiu and Li Dazhao, leaders of the New Culture Movement of the late teens and later founders of the Chinese Communist Party. For young Chinese intellectuals who yearned for the knowledge and methods which would prevent China from being carved up by imperialist powers (Japan included), Japan was an eminently suitable place to learn.

Peng Pai was not the only young intellectual at Lu-an Normal School who wanted to study in Japan. Peng's younger brother Ze and his schoolmates Li Guochen, Li Zhendao, and Lin Tieshi also decided to study in Japan. Although the Peng family was among the wealthiest in Haifeng, Peng Pai had to seek financial aid to go abroad. Control of family finances had fallen into the hands of Peng's opium-smoking step-brothers, who were unwilling to provide their half-brothers with the funds to study in Japan. Hence Peng Pai, his brother, and his schoolmates journeyed to Zhangzhou in Fujian province to seek the assistance of Haifeng's patron, Chen Jiongming. Chen was then encouraging local youths to study abroad, and by 1919 had helped eighty-three men and women to study in France, England, Japan, and the United States. With Chen's assistance and traveling money provided by his wife's dowry, Peng Pai left for Japan in 1917 with his younger brother and schoolmates.[11]

Radicalizing Experiences in Tokyo, 1917–1921

The five years Peng Pai and his fellow Haifeng intellectuals spent in Tokyo, 1917–21, were eventful ones for Chinese students. They felt the continuing repercussions of Japan's 1915 "Twenty-one Demands"; they saw the exposure of the secret

157

Russo-Japanese agreements to divide Chinese territory between those two powers; and they participated in the demonstrations in May 1918 commemorating "National Humiliation Day." But most important of all were the events and demonstrations culminating in the May Fourth Incident of 1919, a day which was to lend its name to an entire generation of Chinese intellectuals and political leaders. On that day, thousands of university students in Beijing demonstrated against China's treatment at the hands of the forces of democracy and freedom at the Versailles Peace Conference. But the significance of May Fourth lies not in the demonstration or even the arrest and injury of several students, one of whom died three days later, but in the ensuing demonstrations that spread throughout China, drawing students, merchants, and workers together in a massive anti-imperialist movement. It was out of these struggles that the Chinese Communist Party was born and Sun Yat-sen's Guomindang was rejuvenated.[12]

Chinese students abroad also held demonstrations. News of the May Fourth Incident appeared in the Japanese press on 6 May. Like Beijing students, those in Tokyo were already planning a 7 May National Humiliation Day demonstration. News of the May Fourth Incident strengthened their resolve to demonstrate, despite memories of the previous year's arrest and beating at Humiliation Day demonstrations and reports that their request to hold the demonstration at the Chinese legation had been denied. Unable to meet in the Chinese legation, the students marched in separate groups to the British, U.S., Russian, and French legations shouting, "Destroy militarism," "For the preservation of peace," "Remember National Humiliation Day," and "Return our Qingdao now." Harrassed by Japanese troops, police, and onlookers, the students fought back, with the result that over one hundred students were injured and thirty-five were arrested.[13]

Peng Pai was one of the organizers of the demonstration. After the incident, Peng sent a message back to the Haifeng Student Association written in his own blood: "Never forget National Humiliation." One student later recalled that Peng's letter, which was posted at Lu-an Normal School, made a deep impression on the minds of the nationalistic students. Peng then joined other Chinese students returning home to protest Japanese and Western treatment of China. In Haifeng, Peng helped organize the anti-Japanese boycott in Haifeng and in the port of Shanwei.[14]

Peng Pai had come to Tokyo a committed nationalist. The Progressive Masses Society in Haifeng had strong nationalist drives, and he had left Haifeng in the first place in search of solutions to China's problems. When he first arrived in Tokyo, he thought Christianity could cure China's ills. But the May Fourth Movement soon disillusioned him with anything Western, as it had most young Chinese intellectuals, and he began looking elsewhere. He began to find some answers in radical Japanese student circles.[15]

His introduction to Japanese student radicals came in the fall of 1919. After a summer of agitating in Haifeng, Peng returned to Tokyo and enrolled at Waseda University. Shortly afterwards, he joined the Builders' League (Kensetsusha Domei). The Builders' League had been formed in September 1919 at the suggestion of a Tokyo University group, the Shinjinkai (New Man Society). The Shinjinkai's modest goal, shared by the Builders, was "to form a group for the discussion of socialism, anarchism, and so forth." The Shinjinkai did not have a well-defined ideological position, but rather was informed more by a "mood" and "an amorphous rhetoric" which permeated the writings of Shinjinkai members. Shinjinkai imagery emphasized the "new," as indicated in its name, "brightness," which symbolized the "hope for the dawn of civilization," and "youth," whose conscience, one member emphasized, "is pure, whose intellect clean, whose spirit afire. The blood of youth is untainted, the ideals of youth are lofty. Has not the day come for youth to rise up as one?"[16]

The similarities between the ideological perspectives held by young Japanese students and those of Chinese intellectuals of the New Culture Movement are quite striking. Chen Duxiu's lead article in the first issue of *New Youth*, for example, likewise celebrated the qualities of youth: "Youth is like early spring, like the rising sun, like trees and grass in bud, like a newly sharpened blade." These qualities, Chen hoped, would enable youth to "disregard resolutely the old and rotten, regard them as enemies and as a flood of beasts." Chen advised the youth of China to "keep away from their neighborhood and refuse to be contaminated by their poisonous germs."[17] Like the Japanese youth in the Shinjinkai and Builders' League, the New Youth generation regarded the old as dark and obscurantist, while the new was bright and enlightening. With such intellectual affinities, it is not surprising that ties between Chinese students and Japanese leftists in Tokyo were close. In fact, Shinjinkai leaders hosted a delegation of May Fourth Movement leaders from Beijing University for a three-week speaking tour of Japan in the spring of 1920.[18]

But unlike young Chinese intellectuals, who were rather eclectic in their beliefs, the Shinjinkai and Builders' League members were strongly attracted to Russian Populism. Evincing a deep hatred for the evils of capitalist development, they frequently contrasted the beauty and balance of nature with the injustices apparent in capitalist society. Through the exertion of pure conviction and energy, they believed, they could "eradicate the system of materialistic competition which stands in the way of the spirit of love and peace, and . . . liberate mankind from this state of materialistic struggle." Like the Russian Populists, whom they consciously emulated (their journal was called *Narod*, Russian for "the people"), Shinjinkai members did not clearly analyze the question of who or what was to be the bearer of the new society. On the one hand, they condemned capitalism for destroying the inherent harmony and cooperation of human society. They thus deified the "people" as the repository and source of all that was honest, natural, and pure. But as intellectuals, they also believed that they had a special historical role to play: "They had only to shout out . . . and they would be answered, revolution would be theirs."[19]

Like the Russian Populists, the Japanese radicals released the tension between the belief that the people alone embody innate purity and goodness, and the contradictory belief that they knew how society had to change, by the call, "To the people!"

Intellectuals and Peasants

We know what it is we want:
We know what the people want
And we know what's to be done.
Yes, we know even more than the young
Russians of 50 years ago.
Yet, even so, not one of us clenches his fist,
and shouts V'NAROD![20]

And many of the Shinjinkai members went to the people—
not to the peasants like their Russian forebears, but to the urban
working class. It was left to the Builders at Waseda University—
those students who shared the same Weltanschauung as the
Shinjinkai—to go to the peasants. Perhaps out of a traditional
rivalry between their private school and Tokyo Imperial University, they followed a teacher's suggestion that since leadership of the labor movement had already been claimed by
Tokyo University's Shinjinkai, they should concentrate on the
peasantry. But the decision to go to the peasantry was not made
merely on the basis of academic narcissism: Japanese peasants
were already organizing themselves.[21]

Peng Pai was deeply influenced by his Japanese comrades
in the Builders' League. He participated in discussions of ideology, syndicalism, anarchism, the women's question, socialism (anarchism and Marxism), and society. He was particularly
impressed with the selfless attitude of the Builders, who flung
themselves into work with Japanese peasants. "I heard that
when they went into the villages," Peng wrote in a letter to a
friend, "they didn't sleep for days, and afterwards got dys-
entery."[22]

While it is not known whether Peng Pai actually participated in the rather extensive peasant organizing drives of the
Builders' League, he certainly knew of his comrades' activities
and the peasants' struggles. In fact, it may be more than co-
incidence that when Peng began organizing peasant unions in
Haifeng, the membership regulations closely resembled Japanese peasant union rules. Thus when Peng Pai went home
in 1921, he brought with him the Populist-inspired intellectual
predispositions of the Builders, knowledge of the Japanese
peasant movement, and a suitcase full of books on socialism.

161

When Peng returned to China, however, there is little in his actions or in his few writings to indicate that he was fully committed to organizing the peasantry as a necessary step toward the realization of socialism in China. For it was fully a year after his return before he broached the idea of organizing the peasantry. Instead, he plunged right away into student and county politics.

Radicalizing Haifeng, 1921–1922

During his four-year absence, Peng had maintained close ties with the student movement in Haifeng, returning home in the summers of 1918 and 1919 to organize student protests. Picking up where he left off, Peng quickly reestablished his ties with Haifeng student circles. Anxious to share what he had learned in Japan with his allies in Haifeng, Peng organized a study group to read and discuss the books he had brought back from Tokyo. The Society for the Study of Socialism, as Peng named the group, included students from the Haifeng Middle School and Lu-an Normal School. Others included Peng's Tokyo classmates as well as some progressive teachers.[23]

The Society for the Study of Socialism was not just a study group, but became a political force in Haifeng county as well. And when Peng returned to Haifeng in the summer of 1921, politics in Haifeng were rapidly changing. The patron of Haifeng's reformist gentry, Chen Jiongming, had marched his Guangdong Army from its Fujian sanctuary across Guangdong and into Guangzhou, driving out the Guangxi warlords who had ruled Guangdong since 1916. Allied for now with Sun Yat-sen, Chen established a new government in Guangzhou. Sun saw in Chen a military force that would push northward and unite all of China, driving out both warlords and imperialists. This issue would break up their alliance in 1923, for Chen was more interested in "Guangdong for the Guangdongese." This slogan meant above all else self-government.

Creating the institutions of self-government was Chen's major goal. He had little interest in leaving Guangdong on a "northern expedition" until at least this much had been accomplished. One of the failures of the 1911 Revolution, in Chen's view, was that it had not created new democratic institutions, a mistake he did not want to repeat. In February 1921 he outlined his reforms.[24] Self-government would begin with elections at the county level, moving from there in two directions: up to the provincial level, and down into the villages. The county would be the pivot, and Chen concentrated most of his efforts there. The voting qualifications would be possession of a house or dwelling in the county (whether this meant "ownership" is unclear) and continuous residence for two years. That was all. Elaborate regulations setting forth the proper procedures for the election of the county magistrate (*xian zhang*) and the county assembly (*xian hui*) were then published. The county residents would elect three nominees for magistrate, and the provincial head (who happened to be Chen) would select one of the three. The duty of the county magistrate and assembly was solely to promote education and commerce. The county government itself was not to get involved in business; it did not have the right to manage irrigation or communications, tax goods imported from other counties, or tax raw materials needed elsewhere.[25] This was a solid reformist gentry platform, and it had strong support in Haifeng.

What is perhaps most surprising about this is that it was not just a paper program produced to make someone look good. In Haifeng county, at least, it was carried out. What is not surprising is that it was controlled by the reformist gentry.

In the short period from August 1921 to May 1922 (the only period for which documentation exists), county residents elected the three nominees for magistrate and the members of the assembly. These officials, in turn, authorized the establishment of new schools, began to build roads and harbors, repaired bridges, began bus service in the county, and ran a newspaper, the *Lu-an Daily*, to report on these activities.[26]

Educational reform had always been an important aspect of reformist gentry programs in Haifeng. After the 1911 Revolution, this group had created new schools, and Chen Jiongming had maintained a personal interest in sending students

163

abroad to study, Peng Pai among them. Now, plans called for establishing several new schools, including schools for workers, for training teachers, and for introducing sericulture into Haifeng. Peng Pai and the members of the Society for the Study of Socialism knew that changes in the county government were afoot, and had as good a claim as anyone else to be involved in the education reforms. To make sure no one missed the point, Peng Pai wrote a handbill critiquing the usual educational setup as too often serving only the interests of the wealthy without attending to the needs of laborers and peasants. The handbill was passed out under the imprimatur of the "Society for Sympathy for Workers," which had as its goal the promotion of education for workers.[27] This was a goal that Chen Jiongming and the reformist gentry could live with. The handbill also served public notice that Peng Pai intended to be part of the reform movement.

The opportunity to join soon presented itself. In early August, the county education commissioner, Chen Bohua, resigned his post, leaving for Guangzhou to head up the provincial educational reform drive. Leaving little to chance, on 12 August the Haifeng Student Association petitioned the newly elected county assembly to appoint Peng Pai to the vacant position. At the same time, Peng left for Guangzhou, accompanied by two members of the Student Association, presumably to present their case personally to Chen Jiongming. Their efforts paid off. On 1 October it was formally announced that Peng Pai was the new education commissioner for Haifeng county.[28]

By that time, Peng Pai's general views on society and education had been well publicized in the pages of a new journal. Peng Pai had helped the Student Association launch this journal, *New Haifeng*, and their ideas and perspectives were clearly laid out in its pages. The young intellectuals who wrote for the journal, mostly members of Peng's Society for the Study of Socialism, were filled with the enthusiasm and desire for change which the New Culture Movement in general and *New Youth* magazine in particular promoted. To be "new" and "modern" was the overriding concern, and they had faith that history and progress were on their side. But the *New Haifeng* intellectuals realized that their struggle had only begun. As *New Haifeng's* statement of purpose stressed: "The opposite of New Haifeng is Old Haifeng. Old Haifeng exists both in the past and in the present. . . . The new is positive and progressive. . . . The old is negative and obscurantist. . . . It stinks, is evil, and supports the status quo. . . . The purpose of a New Haifeng is to expose the darkness of Old Haifeng, to clarify the turbid, to change the conservative to the progressive, to equalize classes, and to raise up the backward. New Haifeng is our morning bell: awake all who are sleeping!"[29]

Unlike many other young Chinese intellectuals who responded to Chen Duxiu's call in *New Youth* to be "cosmopolitan" and not "provincial," the young Haifeng intellectuals did not identify the forces of renewal as foreign or urban generated, but rather saw the process of regeneration starting in rural places like Haifeng. Many intellectuals had tried to resolve the contradiction between the continued existence of the "old and rotten" and their desire to build a new China by fleeing from the rural towns and villages to the more modern and exciting metropolitan areas, where the old and rotten were less visible; the young Haifeng intellectuals decided to remain in Haifeng and struggle with the forces of conservatism there. The call of *New Haifeng* was therefore for youth to struggle in the here and now: "Our lives in New Haifeng are necessarily based on struggle and creativity. At all times and in all places we must struggle; at all times and in all places we must be creative. . . . Seize the hour; endeavor to move forward; do not fear disorder; do not fear hardship. . . . This is our standard!"[30]

Ideologically, *New Haifeng* writers and supporters were a mixed bag of socialists, ranging from anarchists to those with some Marxist inclinations as well, such as Peng Pai and his close friend Zheng Zhiyun. This was pretty much the state of the student Left throughout China at that time. When Peng had traveled to Guangzhou to present his case for being appointed education commissioner to Chen Jiongming, he had also joined the Socialist Youth Corps (SYC) then being organized by Chen Duxiu. Chen Duxiu—noted New Culture leader, editor of *New Youth*, and one of the co-founders of the Chinese Communist Party (CCP)—was in Guangzhou to advise Chen Jiongming on educational reform. While he was there, he took the opportunity to organize the student Left. Chen was a committed Marxist by this time, having just debated anarchists in Shanghai and driven them out of the Socialist Youth Corps in the process. He may have tried to achieve a similar ideological purity in Guangzhou; but if he tried, he failed. Peng joined the SYC, but returned to Haifeng with anarchist and Marxist ideas still intact. To reinforce the point, when he became education commissioner, he hung two pictures on his office wall: one of Karl Marx and the other of Prince Kropotkin.[31]

His thought still was an amalgam of anarchist and Marxist ideas when he articulated his views on the nature of Chinese society and his hopes for the future in "To My Compatriots," a 1921 *New Haifeng* article that appeared while he was in Guangzhou. Here, Peng dealt with theoretical and philosophical issues, trying to sort out for himself and others how to find solutions to China's problems.[32] All of his later writings were to be primarily descriptive accounts of his relationship to peasants, an activist tendency only implicit in "To My Compatriots." It is the theoretical bent of this article that makes it so valuable for understanding Peng Pai's intellectual development.

Peng's analysis of Chinese society followed closely anarchist condemnations of law, government, and the state. The one point on which he disagreed with the anarchist position concerned the causes of exploitation and the means by which socialism would be attained. For anarchists, the state was the root of all evil—abolish it, and private property too would vanish. Peng Pai, on the other hand, argued that this "unfair social system" would not wither away with the destruction of the state, but only with the revolutionary overthrow of private property.

Quoting approvingly a classical maxim that "all things in the universe are one, recognition of ownership is deception," Peng hoped one day for people to once again exercise rational control over society. The means to achieve this end, which he called socialism, was "nothing but social revolution." But what was to be the dynamic force of this "social revolution"? And who or what was to be the agent for carrying it out? For a Marxist, these were questions of prime importance. And in Marxist fashion Peng argued that socialism would be realized by the proletariat.

But he understood the Chinese term for "proletariat" (*wuchan jieji*) in its literal sense as the "propertyless class" in general, and the peasantry in particular. His description of the system of private property and the position of the "proletariat" in it, for example, is explicitly a description of the relations between landlord and tenant: "If the sunlight, air, and land were not created by man, then sunlight should be free to enjoy, air free to breathe, and land free to use. Now, is it any exaggeration to say that it is therefore not natural for a small privileged class to own the fields, gardens, pathways between the fields, ancestral halls, and big houses, while the poor do not have enough land in which to stick a hoe? . . . The poor till the land but have no food, weave but have no clothing, and build houses but have nowhere to live. The rich . . . do not produce anything at all, but still have more than enough food, clothing, and shelter."

The overthrow of this system of private property, Peng believed, could come about only through social revolution, by which he meant a mass, and implicitly peasant, revolution: "All societies are activated by the people in them. Social revolutions—social movements—are the mass movements of the people of that society. A revolution cannot be brought about by individuals or small groups. To succeed, it must be a genuine social movement, a social revolution." The achievement of socialism thus presupposed the revolutionary activity and creativity of the people themselves: it could not be brought in from the outside or imposed from above, nor could a small party of professional revolutionaries substitute for the masses.

While Peng had identified the source of revolutionary creativity with the largely undifferentiated "people," he did not believe that socialism was a predetermined historical necessity which would simply arrive on the scene; it required the in-

167

tervention into history of consciously acting individuals. Indeed, the entire tone of "To My Compatriots" is characterized by an impatience with history and a feeling that only conscious revolutionary activity could give birth to socialism. Peng did not see a necessary historical dynamic by which law, government, and the state would wither away. They had to be destroyed. And even socialism was more a question of the fulfillment of a moral imperative which demanded that the "evil social system" be washed away than of the inexorable workings of historical laws of development.

But if socialism was to be the result of the revolutionary activity of the "people," and emphatically not of an individual or small group of people, what role did intellectuals such as himself have to play in the social revolution? Peng Pai did not yet have a very clear answer. He suspected only that intellectuals would "awaken" the innate but hidden revolutionary strivings of the people. His answer in 1921 was just to exhort radical intellectuals to engage in fervent activity: "We must quickly awaken; we must quickly unite. We must quickly move forward; we must realize the new society before our very eyes!"[33]

His position as education commissioner was the logical expression of his belief in the power of education to change society. And, as he clearly acknowledged, society certainly needed change. Peng was appalled by the human suffering he saw everywhere around him in Haifeng: "There have been many people, because of the hardships encountered in their lives, who have gone so far as to sell their wives and children, or to resort to infanticide. And you can see this repeatedly, even to the extent that some commit suicide. But why are the people in such dire straits? If you go to the root of the problem, they are all spawned in the evil and wickedness of the capitalist system."[34]

Because of his family's position in Haifeng, Peng may have felt more deeply the pain of the peasants' plight than intellectual commitment alone would have permitted. Of early Chinese Marxists, Peng Pai most closely resembled the Russian "conscience-stricken gentry." His family was one of the great-

168

est landlords in Haifeng, and he stood to inherit a considerable amount of land. But unlike other Chinese revolutionaries who had become physically (if not emotionally or intellectually) separated from their past by moving to the cities, Peng found himself still living with his landlord family after he had become committed to socialist goals. While the psychological burden of his landlordism was undoubtedly heavy to bear, it was somewhat lightened so long as he believed (or tried desperately to believe) that "education," "awakening," and his work as education commissioner were useful to the task of building for socialism.

As education commissioner, Peng removed old teachers and headmasters, replacing them with young intellectuals from the Society for the Study of Socialism. He created some village schools, revised the curriculum, and added *New Youth* to the list of required reading. During the school year, he attended classes and instructed students in political economy, introducing them to Marxism, anarchism, and the idea of land tenure relations.[35]

He encouraged students to investigate local social problems and to publish the results in *New Haifeng*. Several articles exposed local social evils, calling for struggle against "local despots." One contributor discussed the conditions of factory workers "who sweat for twelve hours day in and day out," while another held up the Soviet Union as an example of a new society. A concern for the position of women was evident in many articles on women's liberation (all written by men, including one by Peng's older brother, Hanyuan). Perhaps most interesting were the few articles based on local investigations, including "An Investigation of Living Conditions in Haifeng," and "The Social Movement and Haifeng's Villages."[36]

Peng Pai and the *New Haifeng* group no doubt thought their investigations would prompt the reformist gentry–dominated county government to correct the problems they had uncovered. They had reason for hope. Peng, after all, was county education commissioner. In addition, in November 1921, Chen Jiongming announced his choice for magistrate from among the three nominees elected earlier in August. One nominee had been his "Sixth Uncle" Chen Kaiting, but Chen selected Weng Guiqing instead. February 1922 was set for the inauguration of both Weng and the thirty-seat assembly. In the meantime, Weng called the assembly to order to select officers. The assemblymen chose a Mr. Huang as chairman and Peng Pai's older brother, Peng Hanyuan, as vice-chairman. On hand for the opening session on 2 February was Chen Jiongming. Chen had just arrived from Guangzhou, no doubt to witness the realization of his self-government reforms. Dutifully, the assembly gave Chen an official welcome, its first act.[37]

Then the assembly got down to business. As acting magistrate, Weng had already authorized the construction of new roads, the repair of bridges, and the creation of county bureaus of public works, education, finance, and public safety. All of these acts so far had been in keeping with Chen Jiongming's desire to have county governments promote education and commerce. The assembly took this charge one step further. On 8 February, while Chen was still in town to observe, Peng Hanyuan offered a motion that the city walls be removed in order to facilitate commerce. The assembly unanimously agreed and instructed Magistrate Weng to announce the decision. This he did on 24 February.

The decision to raze the city wall proved to be controversial, revealing some of the differences among Haifeng's reformist gentry. In fact, the controversy may have cost Peng Pai his job, dashing hopes of the *New Haifeng* group for reform. The details of what happened are not available, but this much is known. A group of gentry led by Chen Yuebo opposed the destruction of the city wall. We can only guess that the reason had to do with beliefs about city gods residing in city walls. This group supported commerce and ease of transportation, Chen assured the assembly, but didn't want the wall to go. He suggested that there was time before the new roads reached Haifeng, and so there was no harm in waiting for a while before tearing the wall down. Apparently not receiving satisfaction from the assembly, Chen led his group to ask the education commissioner, Peng Pai, for his opinion. The next day, 3 March, Peng gave his reply. We do not know what he said, but he left Haifeng for Guangzhou immediately after delivering his opinion. Whatever else his business may have been in Guangzhou, while he was there he attended the founding congress of the Guangdong Socialist Youth Corps. The SYC by now was under the strict guidance of the Chinese Communist Party, and one of the purposes of the SYC was to prepare members to join the CCP. Not all members of the SYC were Marxists, but Marxism, rather than anarchism, syndicalism, or reformist socialism, was the dominant ideological tendency. Evidently Peng Pai was becoming increasingly Marxist in his views, moving away from both his earlier anarchist beliefs and the social reformist approach of the Haifeng county government. How far he had moved away from the reformist gentry of Haifeng, and no doubt Chen Jiongming as well, was revealed on 19 March. From Guangzhou, Peng telegraphed his resignation as education commissioner to Haifeng county. Weng Guiqing immediately wired back that it was not accepted. Peng remained in Guangzhou until 27 April, and upon returning to Haifeng apparently engineered events so that his resignation would be accepted.[38]

No doubt still flushed with the excitement of the SYC conference, which had been attended by over three thousand people, Peng organized a May Day parade for Haifeng. Because of rain, the march was postponed until May Fourth, which was a good day in its own right. The parade was not very large, involving as it did only students and teachers, but it did disturb Peng's colleagues in the county government. Students inscribed "Bolshevize" on banners and stomped through the streets, while Peng recited a poem he had written for the occasion.[39] This demonstration had all kinds of repercussions in the county government.

The next day, the public security chief offered his resignation, which was refused. On the same day, Chen Yuebo's younger brother, Chen Bohua, returned to Haifeng, having resigned his provincial post. Peng later wrote that these two forced him out of his position, the elder brother telegraphing Chen Jiongming to accuse Peng of advocating "communism," while the younger brother attacked Peng in the pages of the *Lu-an Daily*, which he now edited. If so, they were successful, for on 9 May, Peng's resignation was accepted. The county finance commissioner too had resigned on the previous day; no doubt he had been implicated in the scandal as well.[40]

The split between Peng Pai and the reformist gentry widened in the following days and weeks. At issue was the meaning of socialism. To the reformist gentry leaders, socialism meant pretty much what they were doing through the county government: creating democratic institutions, improving the economic climate, and making education available to workers. To show its social consciousness, the *Lu-an Daily* had even given its workers May Day off. In short, their brand of socialism was social and economic reform controlled from the top. This is what socialism had meant to nearly all those who had participated in the 1911 Revolution in Guangdong,[41] and what it still meant.

But it is not what socialism meant to Peng Pai and the *New Haifeng* group. Their May Day banner proclaiming "Bolshevize" symbolized the differences. Peng had already said that socialism could be realized only by mass mobilization, by social revolution and class struggle from below. The problems confronting Haifeng county and China, he had argued, could not be solved in any other way. He clearly saw socialism coming by revolt from below. Apparently his stint as education commissioner had shown him the futility of trying to make progress through reform from above. The May Day march was his declaration of independence from the reformist gentry and their approach to socialism.

For a few weeks after his dismissal, he kept busy replying to the Red-baiting charges of the *Lu-an Daily*. Peng responded to the attacks through the *Chixin Weekly*, a broadsheet he and Li Zhendao had created for the purpose. In one article, entitled "Who Should Advocate Socialism?" Peng related how two acquaintances, one an editor of the *Lu-an Daily*, had questioned his credentials for propagating socialism. They pointed out what appeared to them the hypocrisy of talking about socialism while living a life of luxury, "living in a big house and eating white rice produced with the sweat and blood of peasants." The editor of *Lu-an Daily* said that if Peng was sincere, he would give his wealth away. Peng replied that since socialism was a universal goal, its advocates need not be restricted to any particular social strata. Besides, he added, "if I really used my wealth for social revolution, the editors of *Lu-an Daily* would accuse me of rebellion and call for my arrest." Peng clearly understood the differences between academic discussions of the merits of socialism and any actions taken to realize it.[42]

Peng was troubled by the thought that his wealth and education somehow might be obstacles to the realization of socialism. He had been talking about socialism and revolution since the previous September. But what had he actually done? Nothing, really. All of his work had been with intellectuals. And even there he had not had much success in winning over the reformist gentry who controlled the county government. He had always assumed that doing educational work would somehow "awaken" the people, and, *voila*, social revolution would happen. This was the same dilemma that Russian Populists had gotten themselves into: who or what was to be the agent of socialist revolution, and what was the intellectuals' relationship to it going to be? Now, after his experience as education commissioner, his resignation, and then the continuing debate with the *Lu-an Daily*, Peng decided. As his subsequent actions demonstrate, he had concluded that the agent of social revolution was China's peasantry, and it was the task of intellectuals to help organize them. He published these views in June 1922 in *Chixin Weekly* no. 6, the last to be issued.[43] It was his parting shot.

When he came home after this broadside had hit the streets, he found his sister blocking the doorway. She said she wouldn't let him in because his mother right that moment was inside crying her eyes out, sobbing that she would kill Peng. When he worked his way around her and into the house, he found his youngest brother reading the article to his mother. "I thought then," he wrote later, "that if peasants could read it, they would be extremely happy; but here was my mother crying like mad."[44] Then and there, he said, he decided to stop debating and start doing. Decked out in his white suit and hat, he strode off. He walked out of the courtyard, turned left, and continued along the Long River, past the Longshan Temple with its spreading banyon tree, and toward the villages not more than a mile from his house. This is how Peng Pai came to be talking with the peasants we met at the beginning of the chapter.

More than just two individuals crossed paths that day in the countryside. Peasants and intellectuals had had quite separate histories that had run their own courses and had their own rhythms. Peng Pai had been drawn to the countryside for reasons that had little to do with rural social history. He was in fact quite ignorant of what had been happening in the countryside, not just in the preceding decades, but even in recent years and months. He may have concluded that peasants were exploited and that they held the key to China's social revolution, but that in itself cannot explain why peasants were ready to listen to what he had to say. Young intellectuals in other places had reached similar conclusions, only to be rejected by the peasants. This is what happened to the Russian youth in the Populist-inspired "to the people movement" of the 1870s. Had Peng been around in the 1870s and had he gone into Haifeng's villages then, he too would have found a peasantry hostile to him and his ideas.

But in 1922, when he went into the villages, peasants were prepared to listen to him. They too had a history and experiences that confirmed what he was saying. They had lived it: Peng wasn't making it up. Peasants were ready to have someone articulate their grievances and demands, and Peng Pai was now prepared to be their spokesman.

Peng Pai and Peasants

While Peng Pai was growing up, peasants in Haifeng had begun to perceive and express a commonality of interest among themselves and opposed to landlords, as was shown in the last chapter. In the wake of the sugar market crash and the 1911 Revolution, new social relations were preparing the way for new types of collective action. But in 1922, there were still many obstacles to such action. Old divisions among peasants kept them suspicious of each other, and lineages and Flags still commanded their support. Tenancy was becoming an issue that would transcend these differences, but the countryside that Peng Pai stepped into in his white suit and hat by and large was a factionalized one. Here the forces that divided overshadowed, for the time being at least, the ties that bind. It took Peng Pai to articulate issues in such a way as to create a new type of social organization among peasants, clearing the way for collective action along class lines. But what is ironic is that the way in which peasants interpreted what Peng said and did gave rise to a form of peasant social organization that was quite different from that envisioned by Peng Pai.

The more Peng Pai went into the villages in May and June, the more the pressure increased on him to return to the fold. His closest friends refused to help, warning him: "Peasants lack cohesion. Not only are they incapable of organization, they are ignorant as well. It won't be easy to spread your ideas, just a waste of time."[45] Members of the reformist gentry group also tried to get him out of the villages by bribing him with an offer of a good position in Guangzhou.[46] But family pressure was the greatest. According to an unnamed source in Peng's draft biography, his eldest brother approached him about dividing the family property. If they couldn't get him to be quiet, at least they could divorce him from the rest of the family. Peng reportedly replied that "the family wealth was all stolen from the peasants and should be returned to them." When he then received his share of the property settlement, he tried to give the deeds to his tenants, but they refused to take them. So one day he called the tenants to his study and burned the deeds, saying "From now on you are free and don't have to pay rent."[47]

His landlord ties gone with the smoke of the burning deeds, Peng Pai persevered in his efforts. Once he had made contact with Zhang Ma-an and the other young peasants who helped him, he began to make progress. The peasants would introduce him in the villages in the evenings, and he then would lecture, embellishing his talks with magic shows and music from a wind-up Victrola. On 29 July 1922, Peng and his six peasant friends formed the Chishan Peasant Union, and within a few weeks increased the membership to thirty. The numbers continued to rise when Peng and the union began to prove that they could help peasants in their daily struggles.[48]

Most of these, of course, revolved around conflicts with other peasants, not with landlords. That was the way the countryside was. The first such case arose when the six-year-old child bride of a union member fell into a latrine and drowned. Thirty to forty members of her mother's lineage came to charge homicide, threatening in the time-honored way to seek revenge if they could not get proper restitution. Peng Pai called thirty union members together to confront the child's family. By writing the names of the family members down and suggesting they might go to jail if they did not quietly disperse, Peng Pai frightened them into departing. Lineage conflict over similar issues, of course, long had been quite common. Thus when union members came to the defense of the widower, they acted in a pattern which was quite familiar (and familial) to them. In fact, union members emphasized the brotherhood of the union to the deceased child's family, suggesting it was better than a real family: "You still don't know we have a Peasant Union, the poor man's union, organized and as close as brothers?"[49]

The union attracted other members, paradoxically, because of competition for land. When peasants fought for land, they now realized, landlords could raise the rent or evict tenants without fear that the land would lie fallow. Thus, upon joining the union, members pledged not to contest another member's land unless that member's consent and union approval had been given. Peng explained that "when a landlord raised the rent and evicted a member of our Union, no member whatsoever might farm the land in issue." In one case where the landlord raised the rent and evicted a union member, the union announced the formation of a "No Farming League." The landlord, afraid the fields would go to seed, felt obliged to return the land to the original tenant. The union let it be known that "if conflicts arose between any union members, they must report it to the Peasant Union first of all. . . . If instead a member reported to the gentry and officials, it made no difference who was in the right, we would announce his expulsion and use all our power to help the other member, his opponent." Soon peasants were reporting their troubles to the union's newly established Arbitration Department, and, according to Peng Pai, "business for the police and courts fell off."[50]

From July 1922—when a half-dozen young peasants had formed a union at Peng's suggestion—to November, membership increased to five hundred. Most of the members were from villages around Haifeng city in Chishan district, and the first union, the Chishan District Peasant Union, was established there. While Peng Pai's influence and good faith in returning the land may have been crucial for organizing peasants in his home district, peasants were soon organized in more than ten districts (see Map 8), with members joining at the rate of twenty per day. For example, led by the young peasant Ye Zixin, the tenants in the Meilong region, who had commonly been treated as "low class" by the powerful Lin lineage, formed a union in late 1922 or early 1923. The peasants here did it on their own without any contact with, or help from, Peng Pai and his union.[51]

Peng had done nearly all of his organizing without the help of any of Haifeng's young intellectuals. Except for support from his younger brother and from his wife and sympathy from his elder brother Hanyuan, he was pretty much on his own. His friends in the *New Haifeng* group thought he was wasting his time and declined to help. But as he made progress, some began to offer to help. The first was Lu Chuyong, whom Peng met on the street one day and told in detail of his activities. Lu, proprietor of a Western apothecary, was moved and decided to help. He offered to sell peasant union members medicine at a discount as an incentive to get some to join. This became the Peasant Clinic. Lu also offered his shop as the mailing address of the union. From that day on, Peng and Lu were out "from dawn to dusk," in Peng's words, organizing.[52]

Soon others joined. Among them were Zheng Zhiyun, Chen Xunyi, Lin Daowen, and Yang Wang, all members of the Hai-

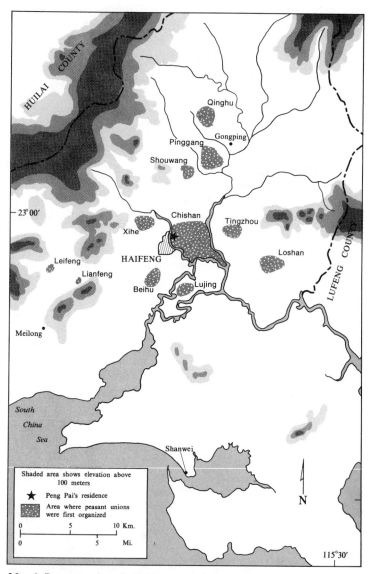

Map 8. Peasant unions in Haifeng county, November, 1922

feng Student Association who had joined Peng Pai in the Society for the Study of Socialism while Peng was education commissioner in 1921, and Li Laogong and Lin Wunong, who quit the School of Sericulture in Haifeng city to join the movement. With this growing number of intellectuals agitating in the countryside, unions emerged throughout rural Haifeng, spreading east toward the Lufeng border, north toward Gongping, west toward Meilong, and south toward Shanwei (see Table 3). According to Peng Pai's estimation, nearly twenty thousand households had joined district peasant unions by the end of 1922. On New Year's Day, 1923, representatives from the district unions met to inaugurate the Haifeng General Peasant Union.[53]

Although the union continued to grow during the first half of 1923 by organizing traditional forms of mutual-aid societies, such as a credit association and a burial society, as well as a school and clinic for peasants, traditional divisions within the peasantry hindered further expansion. One of the more serious obstacles to growth was the continuing conflict between members who belonged to the Red and Black Flag societies. Peng

Table 3: Peasant Union Membership by District, Late 1922

District (yue)	Households (hu)	Villages
Chishan	565	28
Shouwang	212	5
Yinxi	374	10
Xihe	230	6
Beihu	307	5
Loshan	295	10
Qinghu	156	4
Pinggang	245	11
Shouwang II	230	8
Tingzhou	73	3
Leifeng	30	1
Lianfeng	48	1
	2,765	92

Source: Li Zhendao, "Haifeng nongmin yundong ji qi lingdaozhe Peng Pai," in *Peng Pai yanjiu shiliao* (Guangzhou: Renmin chuban she, 1981), pp. 291–92.

observed that even where a union local had been established, "armed fights often broke out killing an awful number of people." Peng tried to alleviate the strife between union members by raising a different flag: "The flag of the Peasant Union combined four fields of red and black . . . to combine the brave fighting spirit of those days into making revolution; peasants' loyalties to Red or Black disappeared, and they all used a single peasant flag." Although this ploy may seem too slick to be believed, it should not be dismissed out of hand. As we have seen in the previous chapter, relations between gentry leaders and the peasantry in these societies had already been strained to the breaking point. In fact, there was a deep yearning among members of the opposing Flags to bury their differences. Popular belief, according to a local resident, blamed the alien Manchus for fomenting this dissent among the conquered Chinese: "They were a minority, so it was difficult for them to control us Han Chinese. Thus they created these two factions so the people would fight each other." The Manchus were gone now, and Flag members hoped to be reunited. When Peng Pai raised a new flag, he fulfilled a deep-seated wish among the peasant Flag members to stop the fighting. Their interests were more in uniting than in continuing to fight. Peasants were ready to break their ties with the Flags, and Peng Pai, through the Peasant Union, presented the opportunity.[54]

Peng Pai was in fact an astute observer of the importance of peasant traditions in building—or hindering—the development of peasant unity. When asked for their opinions on "the warlord-imperialists ruining the nation," for example, most peasants replied: "Until the true Son of Heaven appears on earth there won't be peace in the world. Once the true Son of Heaven appears, all guns will be silenced and he will immediately become Emperor." On the question of poverty, the majority said: "It's the will of Heaven," or "our *feng shui* [geomantic force of "wind and water"] is bad." These attitudes, Peng believed, reinforced peasant passivity in the face of landlord oppression, rendering it difficult for the Peasant Union to develop into anything more than a mutual-aid society. But Peng readily recognized that arguing would not shake peasant beliefs. When he first began going into the villages, he followed a young peasant's advice not "to oppose their gods." Rather than mount a direct attack on peasant beliefs, Peng Pai instead tried to infuse a new content into traditional cultural forms. He rewrote old peasant songs, making new references to "gentry oppression" and "landlord exploitation," or added a few lines here and there for the same purpose.[55] One of his first compositions was a song he wrote in part to overcome his loneliness caused by his alienation from the world he had just left, and separation from the one he had yet to join. He taught the song to children tending oxen:

> *Dong, ya, dong! Tenants curse the lord:*
> *"Lords eat polished rice, tenants work the fields till death!"*
> *The fields belong to everyone; he shouldn't get a share, you*
> *   shouldn't have to divide the harvest.*
> *If you work, you should eat; now you work but have no food.*[56]

The most important of all cultural forms was the opera. Peng felt that traditional opera fostered servile ideas among peasants, thereby futhering landlord dominance. If the content were changed, Peng hoped, the opera could become an important tool for agitation. The opera traditionally had been performed at New Year festivals, but in Haifeng this usually joyous time had become more closely identified with debt collection. Peasants in Haifeng had a saying which expressed their uneasiness about the coming of the New Year: "Don't be afraid if the monkey lantern walks the street; only be afraid when the door spirit appears." The "monkey lantern" was a decoration sold about a month before New Year's, while images of the "door spirit" appeared two or three days before New Year's Day. Thus when the door spirit appeared, debt collectors would too. As Shu Huai, a contemporary of Peng Pai, described a typical New Year's in Haifeng: "Merchants close accounts and figure out how to collect debts. The rich send their workers everywhere to collect rents and debts. And the poor? It's pitiful. While everyone else sees happiness in the New Year, for them it is simply a matter of life and death—they owe house rent, land rent, and money. When New Year's arrives, they can no longer avoid repaying their debts. Everything has to go to repay debts; they can't even think about a New Year celebration. . . . There is thus the common saying: The rich have New Year's, the poor have hardship."[57]

For the 1923 New Year, the Peasant Union put on a "Haifeng Peasant New Year's Celebration," replete with music, drums, lion dances, singing, and an opera. Six thousand members and three thousand nonmembers attended. Putting on an opera, of course, had been the duty of the local gentry, but for some time none had been held in Haifeng city. The celebration was, in fact, so unique that it was reported in a Hong Kong newspaper, the *Huazi Ribao*. In addition to speeches by Peng Pai and other union leaders, the newspaper reported, the "Propaganda Department performed a vernacular peasants' tragedy play entitled 'Two Pecks of Rent.' The scene where the poor peasant was bullied by the landlord was very moving, drawing loud applause from members of the audience, who were filled with both sorrow and anger by this scene."[58]

The 1923 Peasant New Year's Celebration was the first festive one in years for large numbers of Haifeng peasants. After the celebration, the Haifeng Peasant Union grew even faster. Two thousand people joined on the day of the opera; afterwards one hundred joined per day. Not only peasants, but boatmen, workers, small merchants, teachers, and students joined as well, representing a cross-section of Haifeng society (see Table 4). Furthermore, some Haifeng natives who had migrated to Hong Kong and Guangzhou also returned to help the movement. Some had been in Chen Jiongming's army, while others had been rickshaw pullers.[59]

The union set up a formal structure, linking the locals to the county union, formulated membership rules, handed out membership cards, and adopted a platform. Its goals, seventeen in all, included stopping landlords from raising rents or squeezing extra payments out of peasants, getting rent reductions in bad years (a traditional right), and halting peasant bickering and infighting. The peasant union program was a general protest against all kinds of social ills, ranging from inadequate public sanitation to banditry and war.[60]

Intellectuals and Peasants

Table 4: Composition of the Haifeng Peasant Union, 1923,
by Land Tenure and by Occupation

Land-tenure status	Percentage	(No. of families)
Freeholder	20	(2,400)
Semi-freeholder	30	(3,600)
Tenant	40	(4,800)
Hired laborer	10	(1,200)

Occupation	No. of people
Worker (salt-field worker, barber, dyer, etc.)	500+
Boatman	400+
Unemployed	300+
Ex-Christian peasant	50
Student	30+
Primary school teacher	10+
Shopkeeper	10
Small landlord/freeholder	10
Village gentry/gentry teacher	10
Chen Jiongming's bodyguard	3
Shaman	1

Source: Based on Peng Pai, "Haifeng nongmin yundong," in *Diyici guonei geming zhanzheng shiqi de nongmin yundong* (Beijing: Renmin chuban she, 1953), pp. 83–84.

Although rent reduction had been adopted as a goal, Peng felt it could be carried out only after five years of organizational experience—"it could not be done at the moment." But conflict with landlords over the issue of rent was not to be posed by the union: rather, the union was soon forced to come to the defense of the peasants' traditionally sanctioned rights of land tenure.[61]

In early 1923, a landlord named Zhu Mo, who lived in Haifeng city, informed his tenants fifteen miles away in a village near Gongping market that their rent for the coming year was to be raised. The peasants protested that their fields had been tilled for centuries on permanent tenure as "manure investment fields": the landlord clearly did not have the right to raise the rent or to reclaim the land unless the rent were years in arrears. How many times this lord had raised rents or otherwise altered the terms of permanent tenure without encoun-

183

tering resistance is not known. But now peasants were organized to fight back. Rather than pay the increase, the tenants asked the union for permission to quit the land. With the union so strong, Zhu knew he would have trouble finding other tenants unless they could be persuaded to renounce their rights to the land. Zhu then filed a spurious court suit accusing them of "tenant misappropriation of land," evidently hoping that the suit and the police sent to serve the summons would be sufficiently persuasive. At the hearing, peasants rallied by the union packed the Gongping District Office, so intimidating the official that he dismissed the case, scolding Zhu Mo for not producing any evidence to support his case.[62]

Zhu Mo turned then to the county government and the reformist gentry circle which controlled it. At a meeting called by Chen Yuebo, five hundred landlords heard Zhu Mo tell what had happened to him and call for the landlords to stand together. At Chen Yuebo's suggestion, the landlords formed an official-sounding organization, "The Society for Maintaining Grain Production," with Chen as chairman, the new county magistrate, Wang Zuoxin, as vice-chair, and Chen Jiongming's "Sixth Uncle," Chen Kaiting, as treasurer, to oppose the peasants. There was also some empty talk, according to one source, that landlords could do without tenants: they could "hire labor and manage the land themselves."[63] But the major order of business was to teach the peasants a lesson in the law. A new hearing was ordered, and to make sure that no peasants other than the accused attended court, the Society for Maintaining Grain Production hired thugs to stand at the gates of the city and beat up any peasant who tried to enter. (Maybe this was one reason Chen Yuebo had opposed tearing down the city walls.) Union representatives could not attend the trial, and Zhu Mo's hapless tenants were promptly thrown into jail.[64]

Peng Pai then called a mass meeting of the Peasant Union. Looking out over the six thousand peasants who responded to his call, he pointed out that the imprisonment was not merely the problem of those arrested, but rather, concerned all members of the union: "Our peasant friends are innocent! They are being held by the court unjustly,and the magistrate has broken the law. We have to be clear that this is not a personal matter; we have to see it as a matter for our peasant class; if they lose, all peasants lose; if they win, all peasants win." The crowd decided to send Peng Pai and twenty others to the magistrate's office to demand the release of the peasants. The peasants were soon freed, but not necessarily because of the union's show of force. During the meeting with the peasant delegation, the magistrate told Peng Pai: "Brother Peng, you are a good friend of mine; please withdraw the petitioning peasants first, and tomorrow I'll free the others." Peng coldly replied, "We can't talk of friendship today because I am here as a peasant representative."[65]

At the reception for the released peasants, Peng Pai spoke for the peasants: "For hundreds and thousands of years, peasants have been taking injustice and oppression from the landlords, gentry, and officials, never daring to make a sound. Today we were able to free six peasants from jail—whose power is this?" Most gleefully shouted that it was Peng's, some said it was the union's, while others replied that it was the peasants'. Peng answered in a manner that was to become characteristic of his leadership style, pointing out that he had little to do with the victory: "The power that won today's victory comes from the fact that the Peasant Union could show six or seven thousand peasants how to unite in one place and act together. We concentrated our power . . . so that the officials had to be afraid."[66]

That was Peng's perception; peasants saw it differently. Indeed, it was not peasants who were strengthened by the experience, but general folk beliefs and prophesies about how the world changes. Villagers were beginning to believe that there was something about Peng Pai that could not quite be expressed in everyday terms. He was the son of a great lord, and yet he helped peasants. Clearly, Peng Pai was special, but what kinds of categories did peasants have in their mental map of the world that could explain what Peng was doing? There weren't many. The categories that made sense to peasants were those derived from folk religious beliefs. Peng Pai soon was seen as "Prince Peng," and especially as "Peng the Bodhisatva" (*Peng pusa*).⁶⁷ A Bodhisattva, in Buddhist folk belief, was a person ready to enter Nirvana who instead elected to remain on earth to relieve the suffering of the poor. To peasants, this was a good description of Peng Pai.

It was also the beginning of a charismatic cult around Peng Pai. The use of the concept of charisma here follows that developed by Peter Worsley. In his work on the charismatic "cargo" cults of the South Pacific, Worsley developed an "interactionalist" model of charisma that differs somewhat from Max Weber's original concept. Worsley argues that charisma is not a quality of a certain person, as Weber had indicated, but rather is a type of social organization linking followers, who have "possibly utopian or at least diffuse and unrealized aspirations," with a leader who "articulates and consolidates their aspirations." The leader then "specifies and narrows these aspirations, converting them into both more concrete goals toward whose achievement collective action can be oriented and organized, and into beliefs which can be validated by reference to experience."⁶⁸ It is important to note that the charismatic leader does not articulate *any* ideas or beliefs, but those which are in close touch with the experiences and beliefs of the hearers.

The charismatic cult, then, is a form of social organization that leads to collective action. This is an important reformulation of the concept of charisma because it draws attention away from the person of the leader, toward the relationship between leader and followers, and toward the beliefs and interest of followers. It is also important in helping us understand how interests are formulated among newly emerging groups. The cult figure, in Worsley's interactionalist model, articulates the interests of the members of a diffuse group unsure of their commonalities of interest, creating in the process a new type of social organization where none had previously existed. The cult then facilitates collective action toward a common goal. In the specific case of Melanesia, Worsley shows how the cargo cults united previously factionalized islanders to deal with the common threat posed by the intrusion into their lives of European imperialists. As the cults brought people together in collective action, they gave way to modern nationalism and its institutional expressions. The charismatic cult in Melanesia, Worsley argues, was a transitional form of social organization leading to the creation of institutions that sustained collective action over longer periods of time. Something very similar was beginning to happen in Haifeng.

In a countryside with a long history of factional conflict between villages, lineages, and Flags, Peng Pai's voice sounded a note that helped the villagers overcome their differences and begin to act together for common goals. They listened, not because he had a special way about him, but because their experiences, occasioned by socioeconomic changes, had prepared them. The reason the social organization of peasants took the form of a charismatic cult had to do with the factionalism in the countryside and general folk religious beliefs about how change in the world occurs. Paradoxically, however, the cult was a new form of social organization that gave rise to class-based forms of collective action. Whether the cult was a transitional form that would make way for other more stable forms remained to be seen. It is to Peng's credit that he understood how peasants interpreted his words and actions, trying in the meantime to create the institutions through which peasants could pursue the goals that he had initially articulated. These were the peasant unions.

After the Zhu Mo affair, Peng Pai's fame spread throughout Haifeng, east into Lufeng county, and west into Huilai. Peasant unions sprang up all over. For May Day 1923, Peng wrote a proclamation telling the world about the peasant unions and ending with "Workers of the world, unite!" As the number of union locals increased after May Day, Peng reorganized the union into the Huizhou [Prefecture] Peasant Union, and when villages outside even that area founded unions, he renamed it the Guangdong Provincial Peasant Union. Requests for help were coming from all over, including one from Guangzhou asking him to take charge of peasant organizing there. As he was packing his bags to go, on the evening of 26 July, a typhoon struck. To deal with the emergency, Peng delayed his departure. Then on 5 August, a second and more severe typhoon hit.[69]

Peng Pai reported being kept awake by the wind, rain, and the "sound of houses collapsing." When he peered from his window, he could see great trees being uprooted, and when daylight broke, floodwaters were rising. Initial reports indicated thousands left homeless, thousands dead, and most of the rice crop ruined. And each passing day brought higher totals.[70]

Traditional peasant rights under these conditions included either a total rent reduction, or at least a greatly reduced rent, leaving peasants sufficient grain until the next harvest. The custom for centuries had been for peasants to ask the landlord to inspect the harvest and then be granted a rent reduction based on the extent of the damage. Thus in a bad year, peasants would not harvest the crop until the lord had inspected it. The situation in the autumn of 1923 was even more critical because the crop was ready for harvesting; any delay in landlord action would mean that whatever remained of the crop would rot. Because the Peasant Union had not decided on a unified policy in the aftermath of the disaster, most peasants followed custom by asking landlords to inspect the fields. Some lords respected peasant customary rights, but many did not, refusing even to inspect the fields. The peasants were desperate and outraged. According to Peng Pai, "Countless peasants were very angry. Some were for murder, some for riot."[71]

At a union meeting called to discuss what action to take, it was clear that most peasants wanted to refuse to pay any rent whatsoever. They had been grievously wronged, and they knew it. But the union leadership, itself divided over what course of action to take, settled upon a compromise of "thirty percent rent at most," which barely passed a vote of the peasant assembly. Given a choice, Peng would rather have waited until there was a bumper harvest to press for a rent reduction: "A peasant liberation movement or rent reduction movement occasioned by a bad harvest is not worth much," is how he put it to a friend.[72] But now, peasants had little choice. In the following days, union representatives rode throughout the countryside advising peasants of the decision. Some landlords accepted the traditionally sanctioned arrangement; others did not. An incident soon precipitated a showdown. Peng Pai described what happened:

> On 11 August, Lin Zhuocun [chief of local militia], who also managed some school property, went to Beihu village [a small one with about thirty families] to collect rent. Tenant Dai Ya-niu begged for a rent reduction on account of the disaster. Lin replied: "There is no rent reduction on school land; pay the whole amount." Ya-niu had no way to pay. Lin then hit him with a *dougai* stick. Ya-niu fled and Lin pursued. Villagers heard the ruckus and came to help. Sensing the danger, Lin galloped away cursing. . . . [On 12 August], Magistrate Wang Zuoxin sent twenty armed men, who surrounded Beihu. Villagers fear officials, so when they heard shots, they ran. Floodwaters had not yet receded; there was no place for women and children to hide, so they screamed and cried. Soldiers followed and seized them, raking through their houses. Finally, they demanded 30 yuan. They took Dai Ya-fu and three others off to jail.[73]

On 13 August, Peng met with Wang Zuoxin to try to secure the release of these peasants. This had worked once before in the Zhu Mo affair, but Wang was not moved. Therefore Peng told him the Peasant Union would hold a big rally the next day to protest the jailing. Wang warned Peng not to, but Peng went ahead anyway. In the meantime, the Peasant Union attended to the material needs of the jailed peasants. On the fourteenth, the day of the rally, Wang stationed thirty policemen at the gates of the city and another thirty around his offices. By 10:00 A.M. four thousand peasants had already arrived in the city, so the police were powerless to prevent the rally. By noon, twenty thousand peasants crowded the streets of Haifeng. After listening to several speakers and shouting "Long live the peasant union!" the crowd dispersed.

That evening, the chairman of the county assembly came to the Longshan Temple headquarters of the union looking for Peng's brother Hanyuan. Given their relationship in the as-

189

sembly, that was plausible. But Peng Pai later charged that this was a ruse to find out how many people were at the union headquarters so that the landlords could plan their strategy. According to Peng, Wang Zuoxin chaired a meeting that night of forty to fifty landlords, who discussed what action to take. Some called for crushing the Peasant Union once and for all. Peng Pai didn't believe the gentry would start a fight, so the union leaders took few precautions. They should have.

Early in the morning, Longshan Temple was surrounded by police and soldiers. The day before, Wang had wired for help to Zhong Jingtang in Shanwei, who commanded about two hundred troops. They were supposed to arrive in time to disperse the rally, but upon hearing that twenty thousand peasants were in the city, decided not to interfere. They had arrived in the evening, and now in the morning advanced on the union headquarters. Peng Pai and a few others escaped, but twenty-eight were arrested. Records were seized and 900 yuan and two horses confiscated. The union was closed up, and proclamations posted throughout the county banning the union. On 17 August, the peasant clinic was shut down, and Lu Chuyong too was arrested. Landlords then sent armed rent collectors to extract the rent. Those who resisted were thrown into jail.[74]

The consequences of this one repressive action in terms of human suffering were tremendous. Not surprisingly, Haifeng suffered the worst famine in living memory. The Reverend E.L. Allen, a missionary stationed in Haifeng, reported the following spring that "many families have already died of starvation: reckon 6000 will die unless supported for two months." A month later, Allen detailed the worsening conditions in one village: "The young men have gone abroad, the old people have died of starvation, and only women and children are left. I entered the village at the time of the evening meal: in house after house the people were without food, while the bowls and chopsticks were clean and dry as though they had not been used for days. . . . Then there are the children abandoned by their parents, old people dying by the way as they go out to beg, and children being offered for sale."[75]

What happened in Haifeng after Peng Pai walked into the countryside in 1922 is universally described as the beginning of the Haifeng peasant movement, or even of the broader Chinese peasant movement of the 1920s. Peng Pai used the term "peasant movement" (*nongmin yundong*), his contemporaries did as well, and so do recent Chinese and American histories. But how useful is the concept in helping to understand the events of 1922–23? Not very, I am afraid. The main reason is that it is an outsider's view of what was happening in the villages, carrying with it elitist assumptions about history and historical change.

There are several assumptions built into the concept of "peasant movement" that severely limit its usefulness. First, it implies that before the movement started, peasants and rural society were for all intents and purposes static and without any real history to speak of. Peasants, in this view, only become historically significant and active once someone else recognizes them. This is what happened when Peng Pai went into the villages: he assumed that what he was seeing for the first time was newly created. As has been shown clearly and forcefully here, however, this is not even close to the truth. In just the short period considered in this study, peasants from the late Ming on had played a significant role in shaping rural institutions and making their own history. Their history did not begin when Peng Pai walked into the countryside.

Another argument in favor of the concept of "peasant movement" is that what distinguishes the peasant movement from earlier periods is that it was directed toward a specific goal. This does not hold up under scrutiny either. Peasant collective action in Haifeng from the late Ming to the twentieth century had been directed toward specific goals, whether those goals were buying rice at a fair and reasonable price, protecting local resources, or realizing religious prophesies. Peasants had their own history, forms of organization, goals, and experiences in collective action long before what has been called the "peasant movement" began. Should these forms of collective action too be seen as "peasant movements" then? The concept of "peasant movement" usually excludes these as "spontaneous" forms of collective action, again on the assumption that a peasant movement is directed toward a "larger" goal. But where do these "larger" goals come from? By implication, not from peasants.

This leaves another possible meaning for "peasant movement": action by peasants that is not spontaneous but directed by others. This, I think, is the meaning of "peasant movement" as it is usually used in the literature. By definition, then, peasant movements begin only when outsiders provide goals and organization for peasants. It is no wonder that studies of "peasant movements" focus on the ideology and organization of outsiders, and often conclude that outsiders created peasant movements. This conclusion is true by definition. In the most reified form of this argument, the peasant movement is seen as something completely divorced from peasants, instead being conceived, organized, and imposed on peasants by outsiders. The most prominent example of this approach is in the study by Roy Hofheinz, Jr., *The Broken Wave: The Chinese Communist Peasant Movement, 1922–1928*: "Just as the idea of rural work preceded the practice in the Chinese Revolution, so the template of organization antedated the casting of the Chinese peasant movement. . . . [Chinese Communists] would march into the villages and present an astonished peasantry with their ultimate weapon—organization."[76] Thus begins the "peasant movement."

The picture I have drawn here is substantially different. Here the concept of "peasant movement" is discarded altogether, for it is based on assumptions that are demonstrably wrong and leads to conclusions about peasants that are equally questionable. Instead, what happened in Haifeng in 1922–23 is viewed in terms of the historical development of forms of peasant collective action. When peasants gathered four thousand strong in the Zhu Mo affair, or twenty thousand strong after the typhoon, they were drawing on tactics handed down from previous generations in order to protect what peasants considered to be their rights. In actions echoing those of their forefathers two centuries earlier—when, on 24 April 1716, "starving people stole some food" and rioted—peasants in 1923 tried to gain their ends through an expression of moral outrage and the threat of a riot. It was a faint echo, for the world had changed dramatically. Haifeng's landed class was not receptive to peasant appeals, not because some supposed element of advocacy had entered the landlord-tenant relationship,[77] but because landlords had military forces at their disposal. They could, and did, impose their will regardless of peasant wishes. Peasants too had changed. They were more united than ever before, due in part to their own efforts and in part to those of Peng Pai. By a long and emotional path, Peng had gone in search of peasants just when peasants began to search for new ways to understand the forces that buffeted their world. What he said made sense to them. Even though in their first contest of strength with landlords, peasants suffered a disastrous defeat, they had found a voice to articulate their grievances. This was important not only because it was the basis for the cult of Peng Pai, but also because Peng Pai had a provincial and even national audience to which to appeal peasant demands. And when this happened, Haifeng was no longer isolated but was part of a broader revolutionary movement.

CHAPTER 8

The Cult of Peng Pai
Social Class and Political Power

THE repression of the Haifeng peasants revealed how isolated and vulnerable they really were. Regardless of the growing strength of the Haifeng peasantry, peasant collective action in 1923 had been tradition-based and tradition-bound. Although exhibiting some modern elements, not the least of which was the leadership of Peng Pai and other radical intellectuals, peasants had neither the organizational nor social basis to withstand attacks from landlord forces. Prior to 1924, no organizational framework existed for uniting and directing urban and rural struggles toward a common goal. Like countless other uprisings and expressions of peasant discontent, this one too had been isolated from urban allies, rendering it simply a "matter for the police and the courts." But with the reorganization of the Guomindang (GMD) and the conclusion of the Guomindang-Communist Alliance in 1923, the organizational structure under which the worker and peasant struggles could be united had been forged. From 1924 on, urban forces would create new conditions under which peasants could act—but they would also impose certain restrictions.

Although the policy of cooperation between the Chinese Communist Party (CCP) and the Guomindang had been implemented during the summer and fall of 1923, Peng Pai did not request assistance from Sun Yat-sen and his Guomindang, which had established a base in Guangzhou, after the Haifeng Peasant Union had been ruthlessly disbanded. Rather, he looked to Sun's rival and patron of Haifeng's landed class, Chen Jiongming. Chen's relatives and cohorts had been instrumental in the repression in Haifeng, but Peng felt that he might be able to persuade Chen that it was in his political interest to support the peasant unions. Peng had had a long and friendly relationship with Chen, going back at least to 1917, when Chen had helped him go abroad to study. After traveling for over a week in August through rugged mountain terrain to reach Chen Jiongming at his stronghold in Laolong, a hundred miles north of Haifeng, Peng obtained Chen's support for the Haifeng Peasant Union.

Peng and other comrades who had escaped the repression then spent several weeks traveling with Chen, taking time to establish fictitious peasant unions in eastern Guangdong and publicizing large membership figures in order to impress him. By doing so, Peng Pai was able to convince Chen to send a telegram to the Haifeng magistrate, Wang Zuoxin, supporting the peasant union, ordering the release of union members arrested in the crackdown, and establishing a public court to decide rent reduction cases. "Because of the typhoon and flood," Chen's telegram read in part, "peasants have lost the harvest and have demanded a rent reduction. . . . Although customarily lords and tenants have divided the harvest, there are really many difficulties now with this practice." Chen ordered the establishment of a "Rent Arbitration Board" comprising two lords and two tenants and chaired by one "upright gentry."[1]

After Chen's telegram reached Haifeng, Peasant Union leaders were allowed to operate openly, and they began work on reestablishing the union. But on the day of the mass meeting called to celebrate the restoration of a union local in the market town of Jiesheng, Haifeng landlords and their rural militia once again forcibly disbanded the union. Chen Jiongming had betrayed Peng and his peasant followers. Although Chen undoubtedly wanted the support of Peng Pai and his Peasant Union, he could not afford to alienate his real base of support in Haifeng. Only after the second suppression of the Haifeng peasants did Peng Pai turn to Guangzhou and the reorganized Guomindang for support.

The Guomindang's Peasant Movement

The Guomindang had adopted a policy of protecting what it called the "worker and peasant movements" at its first congress in January 1924, but it was too weak to act upon it, for at the time Guomindang power hardly extended beyond the city walls of Guangzhou. While Sun Yat-sen's goal was to unify China and drive out the imperialists, his first step had to be to extend control over Guangdong. Guangdong was still ruled by a score of petty warlords who had camped there after the 1911 Revolution, milking the areas they controlled for revenues to maintain their armies and their power. Even in the areas under nominal Guomindang control near Guangzhou, warlord armies expropriated taxes as the price for their allegiance to Sun and the Guomindang. The financial situation was so chaotic, and Guomindang power so weak, that Liao Zhongkai graphically complained: "The taxes of the whole province are carved up like a melon, without a sliver left over for the government!"[2] The Guomindang itself was dependent upon the Guangxi and Yunnan warlord military forces, and could not even hope to gain control over revenue sources that had been farmed out to warlords or were controlled by the imperialists.

Since the Guomindang lacked a reliable military force, some of its members saw the establishment of peasant unions in the rural areas surrounding Guangzhou as one way to extend its power beyond the city. The first "Plan for the Peasant Movement," proposed by the Peasant Movement Committee in mid-1924, thus selected "those counties which are politically and militarily important to Guangzhou" as the focus for the organizational drive. These counties included Shunde and Xiangshan in the Pearl River delta, Dongguan on the East River approaches to Guangzhou, Foshan on the West River approach to Guangzhou, and Guangning on the militarily strategic West River border with Guangxi.[3] From the very beginning, then, the peasant movement sponsored under Guomindang auspices was to be responsive to urban needs and forces, important not in itself but for its usefulness to the Guomindang.

The Guomindang was not completely cavalier in its regard for peasants, for it gave them a central role in the National Revolution to unify China. Liao Zhongkai, second in stature only to Sun, explained the importance of peasants in the National Revolution: "Our party has historically taken on the mantle of the National Revolution. The responsibility is great, but how can we be successful? The most important force of the National Revolution is the people, the vast majority of whom are peasants. Thus the most important task is to get peasants to understand the National Revolution and to rally under the flag of the Party." Many Guomindang members believed this task would not be difficult. Liao clearly identified the peasantry as the primary bearer of Chinese nationalism and force of anti-imperialism. The fundamental struggle of the peasantry, Liao argued, was not with the landed class; rather, it was against the imperialists who had destroyed what he imagined to be the natural harmony and tranquility of the villages. Liao thus believed that peasants would fight imperialism and warlordism to protect their own interests: "The peasant movement is fundamentally a movement of international importance," he declared.[4]

To Liao Zhongkai and other leaders of the Guomindang such as Gan Naiguang, the peasantry expressed not a narrow class interest but rather China's national interest. But they did not argue that the National Revolution was a "whole people's revolution" without class struggle. Gan Naiguang, in fact, argued precisely the opposite. In an article written in the autumn of 1926 entitled "Who Is the Main Force of the National Revolution?" Gan criticized those who "suppose that the National Revolution is the whole people's revolution and do not find it necessary to discuss its class nature." While Gan agreed that imperialism was China's main enemy, he did not believe that class harmony was necessary for the completion of the National Revolution: in order to fight for their own interests, which Gan identified as the overthrow of the "warlord-bureaucrats," peasants would have to overthrow imperialism as well. Gan thus identified the peasantry both as the "class base of the Guomindang" and the "main force in the National Revolution."[5]

When Peng Pai arrived in Guangzhou in February 1924 after the second suppression of the Haifeng peasant unions, the Guomindang already had established a Peasant Department to carry out its peasant policies. With his experience in organizing peasants, Peng was the logical choice for secretary, the person below the largely ceremonial department head who would do the actual work. Peng proceeded to gather sufficient bureaucratic power to control the department, and is even said to have claimed that "whatever is not under my personal jurisdiction is not within the realm of this department."[6]

Actually, the Guomindang Peasant Department was almost exclusively the domain of members of the Chinese Communist Party. Under the terms of the GMD-CCP united front worked out by Sun Yat-sen and Chen Duxiu, members of the Communist party were to join the Guomindang as individuals. In this form, at least, the united front was not to be an alliance of two parties. In fact, the CCP was not even to form a clique within the Guomindang, and its members were to be subject to GMD party discipline. Under this arrangement, many Communists had joined the Guomindang. This included Peng Pai, who had become a CCP member.

Even if the national CCP did not form a clique within the Guomindang, its Guangdong district committee certainly did. At a late May 1924 meeting, twenty CCP members met in Guangzhou to form their district committee, elect an executive committee, and formulate policy for working in the Guomindang. Along with four others, Peng Pai was elected to the executive committee, being charged with the Worker and Peasant Committee. The Guangdong CCP also decided that all peasant organizing activity would be carried out under the Guomindang.[7] But Peng Pai made sure that CCP members controlled the GMD Peasant Department.

For most of 1924, Peng Pai was responsible for organizing the Peasant Department, although overall policy was set by the Peasant Movement Committee of the Guomindang. In order to implement its "Plan for the Peasant Movement," the Peasant Movement Committee established a Peasant Movement Training Institute for training "special deputies" to organize peasants in the strategically important counties around Guangzhou. When the institute opened on 3 July 1924 with thirty-eight students (twenty of whom were CCP members),

Peng Pai was the principal, organizer, and probably sole teacher. In sessions lasting over a month, Peng Pai lectured on ten subjects, including the theory of the peasant movement, the policy of the Guomindang peasant movement, Guangdong agricultural conditions and reform measures, the condition of the Guangdong peasantry, regulations for organizing peasant unions, history of the Guangdong peasant movement (probably based on Peng's Haifeng experiences), relationship of cooperatives to the peasant movement, the peasant movement in other countries, the relationship of peasants and workers to the Guomindang, and the Peasant Self-Defense Corps. After graduation ceremonies on 21 August, which also marked the beginning of the second class of the institute, all graduates received military training at the newly established Huangbu (Whampao) Military Academy.[8]

In all, six sessions of the Peasant Movement Training Institute were held, lasting until September 1926. Although Peng Pai headed only the first, he lectured in all six sessions. In addition, the experience of the Haifeng peasants as recorded in his "Report on the Haifeng Peasant Movement" was used as a model for the students. By the end of the sixth session, nearly eight hundred students from a dozen provinces—but mainly from Guangdong, Hunan, and Jiangxi—had been trained. About half of these graduates were peasants.[9] The peasants of Haifeng now had national significance. While most of the graduates returned to their hometowns to organize peasant unions along the lines of those in Haifeng, a number from each class were selected as "special deputies" to be sent on troubleshooting missions for the Peasant Department. Two-thirds of Peng Pai's first session became special deputies who organized the first unions in the strategically located counties around Guangzhou.

Even while the first session was in progress, Peng and his students began organizing. In late July 1924, two hundred peasants and two thousand others attended a mass meeting to begin organizing the Guangzhou Municipal Peasant Union. Besides the peasants, a contingent of rickshaw pullers attended, most of them Haifeng natives. The meeting was chaired by

Peng Pai, and both Liao Zhongkai and Sun Yat-sen delivered speeches. Shortly afterwards, a steering committee composed of Peng Pai, Tan Pingshan, and three institute students began organizing unions in Xiangshan county. When the county union was inaugurated in August, Sun Yat-sen lent his authority to the proceedings, while Liao Zhongkai delivered the inaugural address. Special deputies also organized peasant unions in Guangning, Dongguan, Panyu, and Hua counties, all of which had been cited by the Peasant Movement Committee for their strategic importance to the Guomindang.[10]

Haifeng county was not included in the Guomindang's strategic planning. It was not necessary to the defense or provisioning of the capital, and it was not located along any route that Sun Yat-sen's Northern Expedition was likely to take. As secretary of the Peasant Department, Peng Pai probably would have tried to bend Guomindang interest in the direction of Haifeng and help the peasants reorganize themselves. But in the meantime, Haifeng remained under the control of the landed class, with its close ties to Chen Jiongming's military might. Throughout 1924 and into 1925, Haifeng's villages were grim places to live, with the memory of the typhoon, repression, and famine lingering on.

The Eastern Expeditions

Things might have remained like that had it not been for a fortuitous—at least from the perspective of Haifeng's villages—convergence of circumstances in the capital. For in 1925, the Guomindang launched two military campaigns through eastern Guangdong (and hence Haifeng) aimed at breaking Chen Jiongming's control of that part of the province. And with the Guomindang came new allies for Haifeng peasants.

Short on money but long on ambition, the Guomindang had been tapping every possible source in Guangzhou to finance its revolution. This meant biting into the pocketbooks of merchants, who had never liked official squeeze from whatever quarter and had been organized since the 1911 Revolution to protect their interests. The Merchant Volunteer Corps was an increasingly militant (some called it fascist) organization led by Chen Lianbo, chief compradore of the British-owned Hong Kong and Shanghai Banking Corporation and president of the Chamber of Commerce. In May 1924 Chen had welded the Guangzhou Corps together with those of nearby towns into a force of ten thousand men to be armed with mausers he had just ordered from Germany.[11] Chen and his fellow merchants liked the various taxes imposed by the Guomindang authorities very little, and were more than mildly piqued when in August the Guomindang confiscated the newly arrived weapons.[11]

The merchants went on strike, demanding that the weapons be returned, taxes abolished, and city elections held. The strike lasted until early October, when Sun acceded to their wishes. In the meantime, Chen Jiongming's army began marching on Guangzhou, evidently hoping to take advantage of the Guomindang's weakness and help his ally Chen Lianbo, while the British in Hong Kong sent ominous notes about the "red menace" in Guangzhou, threatening to send a few gunboats if the Merchant Volunteer Corps were attacked. With its very existence threatened and without a reliable army of its own, the Guomindang authorized the arming of workers and peasants.[12]

During October Tenth National Day celebrations, contingents of the recently armed Merchant Volunteer Corps and the Peasant and Worker Self-Defense Army parading on the Bund clashed. Regardless of who fired the first shots (accusations crossed as much as bullets in the next days), compromise was out of the question—either the Guomindang or the Merchant Volunteer Corps would win control of the capital. Surprisingly, it was the Guomindang. They did it by bombarding the Western City, where the Corps had retreated, burning it down—either intentionally or accidentally with the shelling—and routing the remaining defenders.[13]

Chen Lianbo and other leaders of the Corps packed off to Shantou to join forces with Chen Jiongming, who had decided the time was inopportune for an attempt on Guangzhou, and shortly thereafter formed a "Guangdong Provincial Assembly" under his military protection.[14] An alliance with Guangzhou's bourgeoisie now concluded, Chen Jiongming felt sufficiently strong by February of 1925 to move against Guangzhou. But

201

a new Guomindang army, organized in the intervening months and officered by the politically educated graduates of the Huangbu Military Academy, counterattacked, smashed Chen's forces, and proceeded to unify Guangdong for the first time in a decade.

Marching through the eastern Guangdong countryside, the Guomindang army was preceded in some areas by peasant uprisings and was met with a spontaneous outpouring of affection. Unlike other armies which had ravaged the countryside, the new Guomindang army was an army with a difference. It was under strict orders to "express love for the common people," to obey the political teachings of the Huangbu Military Academy, to pay for supplies at a fair price, to pay for porter services, and to billet its troops in camps, not the people's houses. And when the army camped, meetings were held to discuss ways of winning peasant support. As one officer recorded in his diary, peasants thus "expressed their solidarity with the Party Army."[15]

While a number of the peasant uprisings may have been spontaneous, there was in fact a good deal of planning entrusted to the GMD's Peasant Department and its predominantly Communist members. A CCP Guangdong Regional Committee document reported that even before the Eastern Expedition began, "we called our comrades from the East River region to come to Guangzhou to discuss basic slogans. We instructed them to agitate for peasant organization, opposition to miscellaneous taxes imposed by Chen Jiongming, and assistance for the National Revolutionary Army. Cadre were told to inform peasants that with a victory, peasant unions will be able to put a halt to oppression, but that now we can only oppose miscellaneous taxes." Peasant Department propaganda teams accompanying the army and led by Peng Pai and Ruan Xiaoxian then easily set up peasant unions throughout the East River districts after the army passed through. In Huiyang county, just west of Haifeng, for instance, Ruan Xiaoxian and graduates of the Peasant Movement Training Institute organized unions in several villages.[16]

On the eve of the First Eastern Expedition, Peng sent a message to the underground network in Haifeng, led by his older brother, to prepare for an uprising when the Guomindang army approached. Indeed, the assistance of the peasants organized by Peng Pai in Haifeng was crucial for defeating Chen Jiongming and the Merchant Volunteer Corps. Besides the moral victory that could be won by taking Haifeng, Chen Jiongming's home town, Haifeng also occupied a strategic position on the land route from Guangzhou to Shantou. Mountain ranges extending from the coast deep into the interior of Guangdong were broken only by a pass on the western border of Haifeng. Chen Jiongming was equally aware of the strategic importance of this pass, having garrisoned it with a large force. When the Guomindang army of Huangbu cadets commanded by Jiang Jieshi (Chiang Kai-shek) was unable to take the pass and advance through Haifeng to Shantou, Peng Pai was given command of the attack on Haifeng. Accompanied by a group of peasants, Peng slipped over the mountain trails into Haifeng. Promising the expropriation of the land held by Chen and his followers, the equitable distribution of land owned by other large landlords, and a general reduction in rent for everyone, Peng gathered a small peasant army. Other peasants spread rumors that the attack on Haifeng had already started, caused disturbances, and cut telegraph wires. Confused, Chen's troops retreated further east, abandoning Haifeng. Without assistance from the Guomindang army, thousands of peasants then occupied Haifeng city, ecstatically welcoming Peng Pai.[17]

Peng Pai described the first few days after the victory as follows: "When we entered the . . . Meilong area, peasants gave our army an especially enthusiastic reception, raising either the White Star–Blue Field Guomindang flag or the Peasant Union flag. . . . They brought tea and water, continually shouting 'Long live the revolution!' When I arrived in Haifeng on 28 February, peasants asked me when the Peasant Union would be restored. Seven to eight thousand people, who had suffered three years' hardship under Chen Jiongming's oppression, welcomed me. On 1 March, over ten thousand came from Lufeng, Huiyang, and Huilai to the Peasant Union, and I was unable to get any rest. On 3 March, we called a 'Welcome the Army' celebration in Haifeng city attended by over thirty thousand. . . . In the midst of the wildly waving peasant flags and ecstatic shouting, Tan Pingshan, General Galen [the Soviet advisor], and General Xu Zhimo gave speeches to thunderous applause." The response was especially enthusiastic when General Xu told the celebrating peasants that 50 percent of Chen Jiongming's expropriated property would go to the Peasant Union, 30 percent to the labor unions, and 20 percent to the student unions.[18]

The new county government had to deal with the disaster that was still taking its toll. Thousands of Haifeng peasants had died of starvation in 1924, following the 1923 typhoon and landlord repression of the peasant unions. The 1924 harvest had not been good, and by the spring of 1925 rice shortages were apparent, prices were rising, and landlords and grain merchants were profiteering. The county government of Wang Zuoxin had authorized the repression, and landlord members of the county assembly now profited handsomely. To peasants, landlords had violated traditional peasant rights by collecting rent following a bad harvest, and then the county government had refused to do anything to make food available at a reasonable price. It was like a nightmare from the eighteenth or nineteenth century. Then, peasants more than once had rioted in order to prompt government or landlord compliance with the values in their moral economy. In 1924 they could not. The military force at the disposal of the government simply was too great; besides, landlords and officials had just proved that they refused to play by the traditional rules. Peasants and landlords no longer shared any ideas about the proper place of each in the universe. Now there were two separate moral universes, and peasant protest would not have elicited a favorable response from landlords. The new government, however, did not have to wait for peasant protest to know what its duties and responsibilities were in situations like the one confronting peasants in the spring of 1925.

With Peng Hanyuan now county magistrate, the first act of the county government was famine relief. The government prohibited the export of rice from Haifeng, investigated local stocks, ordered that hoarded stocks be sold at fair prices, bought rice from merchants at controlled prices, ordered those granaries with funds to purchase rice for distribution, and established a relief agency. Taxes were to be collected from the wealthy, but the poor were to be exempted. All of this was rather traditional. In addition, the new government dismantled the self-government institutions put in place by Chen Jiongming and the reformist gentry in 1921. The post of district leader (*yue zheng*), which had been used by landlords to deliver votes in the county elections, was abolished, along with any "self-government associations" that remained. Finally, the maintenance of peace and order was to be entrusted to the newly formed Peasant Self-Defense Corps. The new government had been installed by the Guomindang, and the Guomindang in Haifeng was controlled by Peng Pai.[19]

But the new government did not get very far in consolidating its rule before it was forced to retreat. In early June, allied warlord armies charged with protecting the rear during the Eastern Expedition revolted, and the Guomindang army withdrew from Shantou and eastern Guangdong to meet the new threat. As soon as the army pulled out, Chen Jiongming once again moved in his army from its Fujian sanctuary, reexerting his rule throughout the rural areas. Although Chen's armies met with little resistance as they moved through most east Guangdong counties, peasants in Haifeng were not ready to allow Chen Jiongming to reestablish the rule of his relatives and political cronies. They remembered only too well the repression that had met every attempt to organize peasant unions. But the dependence of peasants upon the protection of the Guomindang army proved disastrous for them.

Peng Pai was acutely aware of the danger of this dependence, and it was because of this that he had begun organizing the autonomous Peasant Self-Defense Corps. When Chen's troops moved on Haifeng in September, Peng advised peasants not to resist. He pointed out that in the four short months since the First Eastern Expedition, the training of the Self-Defense Corps was still incomplete, guns and ammunition were insufficient, and thus armed struggle was impossible. Disregarding Peng's advice, some peasants spontaneously resisted when Chen's troops entered Haifeng. A Hong Kong newspaper described the fighting that ensued: "Probably because modern firearms were not available, these peasant corps used pipes and javelins to attack. The only ones armed with rifles or pistols were the leaders of the different squads. Still their attacks were so severe that vanguards of [Chen's] army had to retreat. When reinforcements . . . arrived, the peasants were routed."[20]

To the peasants of Haifeng and eastern Guangdong, Chen Jiongming and his localistic slogans of "Guangdong for the Guangdongese" had become outmoded. But Chen was a dangerous anachronism all the same. Peasants knew what he meant to them—destruction of peasant unions, revenge, murder, pillage, and rape. And when Chen's troops took Haifeng, terror spread throughout the countryside. Peasant unions were disbanded, peasant leaders executed, and villages razed—all under the slogan "It is better to kill a thousand than to let one Communist escape." Altogether, over three hundred people were reported killed in Haifeng and Lufeng counties during the few short weeks Chen's army occupied Haifeng in the autumn of 1925.[21]

But once again, and for reasons quite extraneous to Haifeng, the Guomindang mounted a military campaign to unseat Chen Jiongming from eastern Guangdong. Where the first Guomindang excursion into Haifeng had been generated by urban class struggles in Guangzhou, the second was fired by the anti-imperialist sentiment sparked by the May Thirtieth Incident in Shanghai and deepened by the 23 June slaying of demonstrators in Guangzhou by British police guarding the foreign legation. In order to enforce the anti-British strike and boycott called to break imperialist power in South China, it was essential to close the port of Shantou, the only open entrepot for British goods. But Shantou was held by Chen Jiongming, who was openly courting foreign military aid by keeping the port open. The goal of the Guomindang's Second Eastern Expedition in October 1925 was to close Shantou to British trade.[22]

Like the First Eastern Expedition, the Second received considerable peasant assistance throughout the eastern coastal region. In addition to peasant help in scouting and portering, a large number of peasants decided to join the army. Swelled with new recruits including both men and women, the victorious army once again marched through Huiyang, Haifeng, and Lufeng, followed by a crowd of people with red handkerchiefs tied around their necks. But victory celebrations were not joyous: "In celebration of what is said to be a government victory at Hoilufung [Hailufeng]," reported the *South China Morning Post*, "a small detachment of troops paraded through the city last night followed by motor cars in which rode a number of more-or-less prominent officials. The affair had more the appearance of a funeral procession than that . . . following a victory."[23] With so many people killed in the reaction and fighting, it is not too surprising that the mood was somber.

Little Moscow

After the First Eastern Expedition, Peng Pai had drawn up an agenda for establishing political control of Haifeng. Besides resurrecting the peasant unions and pushing through an immediate 25 percent rent reduction, Peng also proposed sending organizers to neighboring counties, establishing a peasant military force, and bringing to trial all those labeled "reactionaries." Peng clearly envisioned radical changes in Haifeng. As he had told a cheering crowd in March: "We must proceed quickly to eradicate all vestiges of the old order."[24]

For the next two years, Peng Pai single-mindedly pursued that goal. But there is no reason to assume that peasants always saw goals the same way Peng did. As success followed success, the peasants' belief that there was something extraordinary about him seemed repeatedly confirmed. The future had never looked so promising. Only the golden ages of folk tales looked better; and who knew, maybe a new age was dawning. As Peng Pai rekindled age-old prophesies, a tension arose between what Peng thought he was doing and what peasants believed he was doing. Peng was well aware of these differences but believed that as peasants gained experience in mod-

207

ern organizations, their "superstitions" would wither away. The first order of business after the Eastern Expeditions, then, was to resurrect the peasant unions.

It was a task Peng Pai enjoyed immensely. Although Peng was by no means the only one doing the agitation, he certainly was the one person most widely known and respected. Besides chairing the various mass meetings in Haifeng, he energetically scoured the countryside doing propaganda work. A *Huazi Ribao* correspondent traveling with him reported that everywhere he went, Peng "advocated resisting the landlords. He always received a warm welcome from the peasants. At each meeting over ten thousand people came, many from extremely long distances. Thus in the Hailufeng–East River region, Peng has the reputation of being the toilers' leader. . . . Each day he walks ten miles, speaking everywhere. He fears no hardship and is continually enthusiastic. He has the ability to greatly move people, especially the people of the East River region. This correspondent can verify it, having seen Mr. Peng single-handedly arouse the peasants."[25] Despite a reputed stutter, Peng's oratory powers in fact were legend: it was said that he could speak better than a bird could sing.

By May of 1926, nearly 200,000 peasants had been organized into 660 village unions, accounting for nearly every adult peasant in the entire county and for fully one-third of peasant union membership in all of Guangdong province. While it is true that people friendly to the peasantry governed the county— at least for the time being—peasants exercised more power in Haifeng county than anywhere else.[26]

Besides reorganizing peasant unions, the formation of a peasant armed force was foremost on Peng's mind. He had paid scant attention to military training during the 1922–23 period, with the result that peasants had been crushed easily. When he became secretary of the Guomindang Peasant Department, military training became an integral part of his work and was institutionalized in the courses at the Peasant Movement Training Institute. And as noted earlier, he had organized and led the Peasant Army which joined in the class struggles in Guangzhou. Now, whenever a peasant union was formed, a Peasant Self-Defense Corps was organized along with it. In Haifeng, the corps had a strength of five hundred men and women in April 1925. Peasants received training at the Peasant Self-Defense Corps Military Training Institute from Li Laogong and Wu Zhenmin. Two classes lasting several months each were held, training about 150 peasants in each session. Most were young peasants, with leaders chosen from among those described as the "strongest, most class conscious, and honest peasants."[27]

Intensified by demands of revenge for the hundreds killed by Chen Jiongming's forces, the offensive in the rural class struggle passed to the peasantry as a rent reduction movement was carried out under the slogan "All Power to the Peasant Union." Disregarding the general 25 percent rent reduction sanctioned by the Guomindang and presumably supported by the CCP, peasants put forward their own program for a 40 percent rent reduction, demanding that landlords who resisted be jailed or executed. When another typhoon struck Haifeng in the late summer of 1926, destroying about half the crop, the peasants mandated another 40 percent rent reduction, for a total reduction of 64 percent within less than a year. The only thing left to demand was the land itself.[28]

This time, landlords were powerless to enforce their class interests as they had following the typhoon three years earlier. Indeed, landlordism in Haifeng had been submerged in the high tide of Haifeng peasant activity. Most large landlords had fled to Hong Kong or Xiamen following the defeat of Chen Jiongming's army. Many of the remaining small landlords were having difficulty making ends meet because of the 64 percent rent reduction and had petitioned the county government and Peasant Union for some land to till in order to make a living. But the Peasant Union ignored their appeals, while peasants seized and beat those who had complained. Furthermore, as land prices fell during 1926, peasants evidently began to purchase land from frightened and fleeing landlords. By late 1926, only 27 percent of the land in Haifeng was landlord-owned, a considerable decrease from earlier years, when landlords owned nearly 50 percent. While tenancy figures for this period do not exist, it is reasonable to assume that tenancy decreased also. Even those few peasants who were not union members began to demand rent reductions. In order to expand its membership and strengthen peasant solidarity, the Peasant Union printed "rent reduction cards" which read: "No rent reduction without this card; invalid if transferred to another." Just as peasants had once called fixed rents "ironclad rent," they now called the rent reduction card the "ironclad contract."[29]

When interviewing peasants in the 1950s for his history of the Haifeng peasant movement, Zhong Yimou was told that there had never been such a good year as 1926. There was no one to "prompt" the rent from peasants, no one to collect debts, and no one to force them to bow before landlords. It was somewhat like a permanent All Fools Day: landlords remaining in Haifeng "bowed their heads to the peasants and did not dare say a word." Where peasants had once been the butt of landlord jokes, where they had once been unceremoniously beaten and cursed for not bowing to a lord, the world was turned upside down: peasants now slapped landlords on the face, cursed them, and sent them scurrying for safety to the cities.[30]

After Jiang Jieshi's 20 March 1926 coup, county magistrates were replaced with persons hand-picked by the Right-Guomindang, but a CCP analysis of Haifeng claimed that the "center of political power was not the county government, but rather the Peasant Union. All political decisions required the approval of the union. The peasants had absolutely nothing to do with the county or district governments. . . . The payment of taxes also required the approval of the peasants to be implemented. . . . The Haifeng Peasant Union was not a 'shadow government'; it was the only government." During the early months of 1926, according to Zhong Yimou, "all the hatred of the oppression that had built up over the ages exploded like a volcano. . . . Peasants spontaneously rounded up all the landlords and gentry who had oppressed them, brought them bound to the Peasant Union, and demanded that they be punished. . . . Peng Pai did not merely accede to these violent actions, but actually gave license to them."[31]

The peasants were no longer satisfied with the two 40 percent rent reductions they had mandated, but by mid-1926 now vigorously demanded land. An anonymous Communist report criticizing the mistakes of the national Party leadership argued that "the Party center had very little to say about the land question at that time. But you could see that in Haifeng the land question was already on the agenda, and the Haifeng CCP knew it. . . . The peasants demanded the land, and as soon as we did propaganda work, peasants would get up and tell you to demand the land from the landlords. . . . The peasant movement just could not be stopped in its tracks. But several methods were tried to diffuse peasant radicalism: starting cooperatives, opening wasteland for cultivation, reforestation, building public roads, etc."[32]

It is always embarrassing for a Communist party to appear less radical than the masses, and in Haifeng it led to a growing split between the CCP cadre and the peasants. Peasants argued that because there was no Guomindang power in Haifeng, the land question could be resolved. Most CCP members were much more timid, recognizing that Haifeng was the only county in Guangdong—perhaps in all of China—which had advanced that far: "We should wait until other counties reach our stage and then press forward together."[33]

Although peasants sometimes expressed dissatisfaction with the leadership provided by the Chinese Communist Party, they really had few doubts that the CCP, not the Guomindang, better represented their interests. Peasants hesitated to join the Guomindang, which they derided as the "party of those who wear felt caps and socks." Indeed, where there were only twenty CP members in Haifeng in late 1925, by mid-1926 there were seven hundred, and by March 1927 about four thousand, representing one-half of the total CCP membership in Guangdong at the time.[34]

With nearly every person belonging to one organization or another, Haifeng became renowned throughout China as a model for the revolution. Observation groups arrived from counties throughout Guangdong to see what the revolution could accomplish in rural areas. Principal Mao Zedong even planned a fortnight investigation of Haifeng into the curriculum of the sixth session of the Peasant Movement Training Institute. When 318 institute students arrived at Haifeng's port of Shanwei in mid-August in time for the commemoration ceremonies of the 1923 rent resistance movement, thousands of representatives of the various mass organizations greeted them.[35] A correspondent for the Guangzhou *Young Vanguard* accompanying the institute students wrote glowing acounts of Haifeng under the headline "Little Moscow Correspondence."[36] Known thereafter as "Little Moscow," Haifeng certainly had the appearance to many in China of being the center of the Chinese revolution. Red flags and revolutionary slogans hung everywhere along streets renamed Lenin Way and Karl Marx Road. When the leftist Shanghai writers Li Jiming and Zhao Jingshen arrived in Haifeng to teach and to observe the revolution, they could hear in the streets choruses of the "Internationale," as well as a song composed by Peng Pai:

> *Green mountains, emerald water, beautiful hills and streams.*
> *Whose labor, whose efforts? The fruits of labor!*
> *Beautiful grain, fresh grain, elegant houses.*
> *Whose labor, whose efforts? The fruits of labor![37]*

The Rising Tide of Reaction

If Haifeng had become a model for the Chinese revolution, it held lessons for reactionary forces as well: for both it was the face of the future. Although workers and peasants made substantial gains during the Great Revolution of 1925–27 under the protection of the Guomindang and in a unified Guangdong, contradictions within the Guomindang became ever more apparent as the mass movement threatened property rights in both town and countryside. The Guomindang openly split into the Right-Guomindang, which had strong ties to urban capital and rural land, and the Left-Guomindang, which supported workers and peasants, but only insofar as they were necessary for attaining the proclaimed goal of the unification of China.

The goal of national unification, of course, was held by all factions in the Guomindang. But it was Dai Jitao, leading theo-

212

retician for the Guomindang and close to the rightists, whose writings on the National Revolution explicitly condemned social revolution as antithetical to the national goals. Dai was well versed in Marxism and had even attended the founding congress of the CCP. He was particularly drawn to the Leninist theory of imperialism, arguing that the class struggle had been superseded by a national struggle of the poor nations against the rich. And in this struggle, Dai contended, it was above all necessary for the exploited nation to have internal class harmony if it was to be able to fight imperialism. Dai believed that the choice facing China was quite clear: internal class harmony and victory, or social revolution and defeat. Within the prevailing Guomindang orthodoxy, social revolution was seen as clearly antithetical to the National Revolution, since it would sap the national strength in the face of imperialist aggression. For large numbers of Guomindang members, this meant that the radicalized workers and peasants would have to be crushed, or at least effectively controlled, if the National Revolution were to be successful.[38]

The conservative Shanghai *Guomindang Weekly* clearly understood what this meant for the Guomindang peasant movement. After citing the obligatory statistic that China was 80 percent peasant and even acknowledging that peasants were oppressed by warlords, officials, and evil gentry (sans landlords), the *Weekly* conceded that many peasants "have become very poor. The poor cannot support themselves and become bandits." The only legitimate goal of peasant unions, then, was to preserve rural order. But, argued the *Weekly*, by fanning the flames of class struggle, the CCP was rupturing the "mutual rapport" (*ganqing*) between lord and peasant. By disrupting traditional village harmony, the CCP and the peasant unions were sapping the national will for unification. The *Weekly's* solution was to disband the existing Communist-infested peasant unions and establish in their place "Agricultural Advancement Societies" controlled by landlords and the Guomindang.[39]

The unification of Guangdong and the preparations for completing the Northern Expedition paradoxically created favorable conditions for the reaction to develop in the countryside. Members of the CCP Guangdong Regional Committee were sensitive to the reasons why the Guomindang had supported workers and peasants in the first place and believed that with Guangdong unified, the Left-Guomindang would no longer protect peasants from attacks by the Right: "The Left-Guomindang has used the peasant movement to protect its own position. . . . Now that the Northern Expedition is beginning . . . the Left-Guomindang will no longer protect the peasant movement."[40]

Indeed, the Right-Guomindang had begun to attack the CCP and the peasant unions in the spring of 1925, soon after Sun Yat-sen died. Besides using the Guangzhou Mechanics Union to disrupt the urban labor movement, Zou Lu (a leader of the Right-Guomindang) claimed that he also helped the right-wing "Sunist" societies in eastern Guangdong attack and harass peasant unions. The Guomindang rightists claimed that the peasant unions and peasant militia which had been growing rapidly under Peng Pai's guidance were merely hideouts for "local rascals and bandits" whose "past crimes were overlooked and who could do anything they wanted." The rural militia (*mintuan* and *baoweituan*), those officially armed bands that supported landlord order, Zou Lu preached, "were the real organizations for self-protection in the countryside." Without providing details, Zou Lu later wrote in his memoirs that he also "secretly helped the rural militia to struggle against the CCP."[41]

As the July hour of the long-awaited Northern Expedition drew near and Guomindang cries for class harmony were echoed by Comintern murmurs of "restraint," attacks on peasant unions escalated from verbal denunciations of the unions as bandit hideouts to armed reprisals. Indeed, the rural militia were causing peasant unions considerable difficulties. Throughout the spring and summer of 1926, they attacked peasant unions and villages in Gaoyao, Guangning, Shunde, Zhongshan, Dongguan, Zengcheng, Sehui, and Hua counties. While most of these attacks aimed specifically at destroying peasant unions, with looting a secondary consideration, the rural militia also assassinated a number of the Provincial Peasant Union's special deputies.[42]

Peasants and Communists

The inability—or unwillingness—of the Guomindang government to curb militia attacks on peasant unions contributed to a widening gap between peasants and the political organizations which claimed to represent their interests. The Provincial Peasant Union's journal, *The Plow Weekly* (*Litou zhoubao*), carried a mid-September article entitled "How to Resolve the Conflict between the Peasant Army and the Rural Militia," written by the Rear Area Political Work Unity Committee, which called upon the Guomindang to recognize the serious consequences of losing peasant support through its inability to control the rural militia. "Every day for the last few months," wrote the committee, "we have read news accounts about the police destroying a peasant union or the police burning down villages or murdering peasants." Not only did this disrupt the revolutionary base area just as the Northern Expedition was beginning, but it also "causes the most revolutionary, heroic, and organized peasants to doubt and lose faith in the government." And this, the committee admonished the Guomindang, "is the gravest problem facing our party and government."[43]

Some members of the Guangdong branch of the Chinese Communist Party active in peasant organizing, most notably Peng Pai, had been aware of these problems for months, arguing that the time was right for the CCP to assume open leadership of the peasants. But not only did the CCP center not have a clear policy for leading the peasants (it was assumed that peasants, embodying petit bourgeois interests, were better formally represented by the Guomindang), it did not even have a formal peasant department in which to discuss these issues. In order to remedy this incredibly awkward position—awkward at least to those Guangdong Communists who had distinguished themselves as peasant leaders—the Peasant Committee of the Guangdong branch drew up a lengthy document entitled "Report on the Guangdong Peasant Movement," to

215

be presented to the Second Plenum of the Central Committee of the CCP scheduled to meet in July 1926 in Shanghai.

The Guangdong cadre argued that the basic problem was that by working only through the Guomindang, the peasant unions had been able to offer the peasantry exclusively political goals which did not meet the peasants' most pressing needs. "We have placed too much emphasis on political work over the past two years," the Guangdong CCP Peasant Committee suggested to the Party center, "and too little on economic aspects. . . . The result is that many people say the union is always doing something, but at the same time the peasant masses cannot think of how the union has benefitted them." But that was only the tip of the problem—they readily admitted that they had no idea what the economic needs of the peasants were: "We are in complete ignorance of the basic details of the peasants' situation."[44]

The inability of the peasant unions to win economic gains for peasants, and thus the failure of the CCP—through the GMD's Peasant Department—to provide leadership for the peasants and articulate their demands, was at the heart of a growing crisis. As Luo Qiyuan explained, "the result of several years of struggle—of really leading peasants in political and economic struggle—is that peasants in return have received only constant and increased oppression from local bullies and gentry." What did peasants see in the claims of the Guomindang to represent their interests? Nothing, suggested Luo: "Peasants have lost faith in the National Government and doubt the Guomindang." What was urgently needed, the Guangdong CCP Peasant Committee pressed upon their comrades at the center, was a systematic survey of rural conditions. In support of their proposed "rural investigation plan," the Peasant Committee argued that a socioeconomic analysis which examined land tenure relations, the differences between rich, poor, and tenant peasants, and the extent of the commercialization of agriculture, among other things, would provide the basic information upon which policies responsive to the needs of the peasants could be formulated.[45]

216

The Guangdong Peasant Committee was not in complete agreement on the question of whether or not the CCP should assume leadership of the peasantry: Luo Qiyuan felt that it should not, Peng Pai, that it should. Luo took the orthodox Leninist position on the role of the peasantry in the revolution. Generally speaking, Luo had argued, peasants were naturally conservative: "Reflective of their social status and economic position, they can never break with feudal localism, individualism, and familism." However, because China was a semicolonial country, peasants could play a revolutionary role in the bourgeois-democratic phase of the National Revolution.[46]

Peng Pai disagreed. The Communist party should formally lead the peasantry, as peasants were spontaneously looking to the Party for leadership. He argued in the "Report on the Guangdong Peasant Movement" that the CCP should not refuse to lead a peasantry already looking to it for guidance. His was an impassioned plea, if couched in somewhat unorthodox Marxist terms, for the CCP to recognize the revolutionary potential of the peasantry. Peng Pai recognized that the peasantry, as a class, might have difficulty attaining "revolutionary consciousness" because of its localism, belief in spirits and gods, and lineage ties. But, he argued to the Central Committee, objective conditions in the countryside were making it possible for "peasants themselves to break down and cast off their weaknesses." The CCP center was told that the hardships and bitterness experienced by peasants had already caused them to have "self-awareness": "After peasants have this self-awareness, they are receptive to revolutinary propaganda. Thus when we go into the villages, we can get them to form a peasant union in half an hour. . . . Now when people say to them, 'Get Organized!' they are receptive. The result is that they embrace revolutionary propaganda . . . and overcome their natural weaknesses."[47]

If the CCP Central Committee was not already aware of the rising tide of reaction and the consequences of the Northern Expedition for the peasant and worker organizations in Guangdong, the report prepared by their comrades made it crystal clear: the peasant unions (and the labor unions as well) would be crushed. "Since Guangdong is now unified and the National Government is preparing for the Northern Expedition, only the peasant movements in Hunan and Guangxi will be countenanced. Peasant support in Guangdong is no longer needed, and peasant unions obviously will not be tolerated."[48] This prediction proved to be correct—but only because the Central Committee disregarded the warning. As Zhang Guotao, a participant at the plenum, later wrote: "The Guangdong District Committee advocated that GMD-CCP cooperation not be allowed to obstruct the peasants' struggle, which should be developed regardless of anything to the higher stage of solving the land problem. They stressed the importance of land revolution, maintaining that within the Guomindang only those supporting land revolution should be considered leftists, and such leftists were very few. Such a view implied that the focus of the revolution had shifted from the issue of national revolution to the issue of land revolution."[49]

The Guangdong CCP and its peasant advocates came away from the plenum empty-handed. The Central Committee continued to uphold the basic line that the National Revolution and the Northern Expedition remained the central tasks of the Chinese revolution, and rejected the more radical (one suspects they might have been labeled heretical) proposals of their Guangdong cadre. The plenum did decide, however, to establish a peasant department on the Central Committee. Perhaps heeding the Guangdong branch's prediction that the Hunan peasant movement would now become important because of the exigencies of the Northern Expedition, the Central Committee selected a Hunanese, Mao Zedong, to head the new department.

And the plenum passed a resolution on "the peasant movement." But the principal points revealed how far removed the CCP center was from peasant activity in Guangdong. The CCP "demanded" that peasants pay no more than 50 percent of the harvest in rent and 30 percent annual interest on loans. The resolution also called for the freedom of assembly and organization for peasants and for a united rural front in which peasant unions should exclude only the largest landlords.[50] Peasant

218

movement leaders Peng Pai, Luo Qiyuan, and Ruan Xiaoxian were expected to bring this program back to the Guangdong peasants—peasants who in Haifeng were already demanding land—explaining that the "demands" were minimal so as not to jeopardize the successful completion of the National Revolution and Northern Expedition. Luo Qiyuan did accept Party discipline, defending the policy in the pages of the organ of the Guangdong Provincial Peasant Union, *The Plow Weekly*. Peng Pai did not.

The issue was joined over raising taxes and selling war bonds to support the Northern Expeditionary armies. In an article entitled "The Public Debt and the Peasants" in *The Plow Weekly*, Luo Qiyuan defended the taxation, arguing that new taxes were absolutely necessary to support the Revolutionary Army in the Northern Expedition. But he did not explain why it was necessary, in turn, for peasants to support the Northern Expedition. In a rather extraordinary request, Luo asked Peng Pai to read the article and offer his comments. In a biting and extremely sarcastic manner, Peng remarked that when the eastern Guangdong branch of the Peasant Union learned of the tax assessment on Guangdong, only three groups of people rejoiced: officials, gentry and local bullies, and Chen Jiongming's old cohorts. Peng Pai vehemently opposed the Northern Expedition, explaining that the measures necessary for its support—taxes and rural harmony—meant peasants would suffer: "On the one hand, we start the Northern Expedition, and on the other we lose the masses. . . . The revolutionary base of the government [Guangdong] has been thrown into the hands of rotten officials, gentry, landlords, and local bullies. What a fine state of affairs!"[51]

To be sure, many members of the CCP opposed the Northern Expedition, believing, like Peng, that it was necessary to break with the Guomindang in order to lead the mass movement. But opposition to Party policy was internal: before Peng Pai, no one had broken party discipline by publicly attacking CP policy. But then no other member of the CCP, with the possible exceptions of Deng Zhongxia and Zhang Guotao, leaders of the workers, had a base of mass support outside the formal structure of the Chinese Communist Party to which they could appeal. And during the last half of 1926, Peng Pai continued his attacks on the Party line in the pages of *The Plow Weekly*, as the adverse impact of CP policy upon peasants became apparent.

At its July 1926 plenum, the Central Committee of the CCP had ordered the Guangdong CCP to continue working through the Guomindang to curb attacks of the rural militia on the peasant unions, rather than offer open CP leadership, or what was worse yet, allow peasants to make alliances with bandits. Either one of these would have threatened the alliance with the Guomindang. The problems facing peasant unions were put on the agenda for the first "Enlarged Plenary Session" of the Guangdong Provincial Peasant Union, a mid-September gathering called by CCP members Luo Qiyuan and Ruan Xiaoxian in their positions as officers of the unions. Although the Enlarged Plenary Session was chaired by such Guomindang stalwarts as Gan Naiguang and Tan Yenkai, the articulation of the major problems and the wording of the resolutions came from CCP members. Rather than take a position which could be seen as too radical by Guomindang conservatives, the Peasant Union demanded in its resolutions on the "rural militia question" not that the militia be completely dismantled and replaced with the Peasant Self-Defense Army, but merely that its leaders be elected by a village assembly.[52]

The Peasant Union resolutions on the militia drew a *pro forma* response from the Guomindang government. Soon after the close of the Enlarged Plenary Session, the Peasant Department of the Guomindang called a three-day conference "to resolve the question of the conflict between the Peasant Self-Defense Army and the rural militia." Attended by representatives from the Guomindang center, the Guangdong Provincial Peasant Union, the GMD Guangdong Provincial Peasant Department, the Civilian, Worker and Peasant Bureau of the government, the GMD Central Peasant Department, and the political departments of the various Guomindang armies, the conference adopted with only slight modification the proposals of the Peasant Union, the most important of which called for the popular election of the militia chief, restriction of militia membership to fully employed local residents, prohibition of taxation by the militia, and publication of militia expenses and income.[53]

The resolutions of the Peasant Union and their adoption by various levels of the Guomindang bureaucracy and the government in the hopes of curbing militia excesses proved ineffectual. But then Lenin, after all, had warned Communists in *State and Revolution* not to try to seize control of state organs through elections, but to smash them. Hence the militia of Hua county once again attacked and burned villages for three consecutive days in early October, almost as if it was consciously challenging the September decisions of the government on controlling the militia; in mid-October the Zhongshan county rural militia beat up and harassed peasants as they returned from a worker-peasant unity meeting; on 29 October, four hundred peasants from Xigang Village in Shunde county marched to Guangzhou to petition the government for protection against the militia; and when villagers in Binnan county who were attacked by thirty bandits called upon the militia for help, the members of the militia proceeded to plunder the village worse than the bandits had.[54]

As attacks by the rural militia on the peasant unions and subsequent peasant arrests and deaths all mounted with the growing reaction in late 1926, Peng Pai became ever more explicit in his attacks on CCP and Guomindang policy. In the process, he was ever so slowly inching toward the conclusion that the large cities had become centers of reaction, while the countryside was the only place keeping the revolution alive. In a long article detailing the reaction in Hua county, where the rural militia had viciously attacked peasants, and explaining his role—one imposed by CCP policy of restoring and maintaining rural harmony in Guangdong during the Northern Expedition—as only a "peace negotiator," Peng revealed in painstaking detail the bankruptcy of that policy. To be sure, Peng Pai admitted, he was able to negotiate a settlement between peasant forces and the landlords' militia forces. But as soon as he left Hua county, the militia attacked the villagers even more savagely than before. How could rural harmony be imposed upon warring classes, Peng Pai wondered? The answer, of course, was that it could not and that any attempt to do so would simply end in defeat for the revolutionary forces. "We must realize," Peng warned, "that the struggle between revolutionary and counterrevolutionary forces . . . cannot just be halted. A peaceful settlement and the writing up of a few conditions on a piece of paper . . . will just be tossed away."[55]

Although many soldiers and army officers stood on the side of the peasant masses, as they had in Hua county, where they too were dismayed at their "neutral" role in the struggle, it had become clear to Peng Pai that the "Generalissimo" of the army did not. Unlike other Communists who kept their reservations or fears about Jiang Jieshi's revolutionary credentials to themselves or within the Party, Peng Pai now openly charged that "Jiang Jieshi . . . stands on the side of the counterrevolution, protects bandits and rural militia, and pitilessly sacrifices the people's interest in the name of the Northern Expedition." Reactionary forces had seized the cities and were now spreading into the countryside. Peng Pai had long been wary of the influence of urban events on the fortunes of the peasant unions, trying many times and in many ways to minimize the city's influence over the rural social organization. With state power now in counterrevolutionary hands, Peng felt that the revolution could be kept alive only in the countryside, and argued in *The Plow Weekly* that the revolution in Guangdong had taken a new form. To safeguard the revolution as a whole, it was above all necessary to eliminate counterrevolutionary forces from the countryside: "Thus the revolution has left the cities and has entered the countryside."[56]

Peng Pai once again had hit upon a fundamental issue affecting the course and outcome of a revolution—the relationship between town and country.[57] He had concluded that with the Northern Expedition and attendant political changes in Guangzhou, the countryside was more revolutionary than the city, and that to ensure the survival of the revolution, it had to break its ties to the city. He feared—correctly, as it was to turn out—that hanging onto the cities would spell disaster

222

for the revolution. But his belief that revolution in the countryside could be isolated from reaction in the cities was mistaken.

In Guangdong province at least, the ties between town and countryside were strong and could not easily be broken. Whether this was true of other areas of China is open for investigation, given the later success of Mao Zedong in Jiangxi and in Shanxi. Historically in Guangdong, strong economic ties linked the villages not only to the local market town, but through it, to the centers of political and economic power in Guangzhou and Shanghai. This had been one of the consequences of the late Ming–early Qing peasant uprisings and establishment of the small peasant economy. Even events in New York, as we saw in the case of sugar, reverberated all the way into the villages of Haifeng. The countryside hardly was immune from these broader economic forces emanating from the cities.

The 1911 Revolution had revealed another significant link between town and countryside—the urban reformist gentry. This new class linked individuals in market towns such as Meilong to those in Haifeng, Huizhou, and Guangzhou. In the course of the 1911 Revolution, this class had come to see its interests more clearly and acted to preserve its gains before the revolutionary movement from below got out of hand. Because of both of these factors, "rural" revolution in Guangdong province was inconceivable, for it would have enemies all the way from the market towns to Guangzhou. Besides, economic survival alone would necessitate ties to cities. This is why the alliance between workers in the city and peasants in the countryside was so vital for the success of the revolutionary movement. Once the workers of Guangzhou had been "disciplined," as they were in the summer and fall of 1926, it was only a matter of time before it was the peasants' turn. This is what Peng Pai feared. But Guangdong province was not neatly divided between town and countryside, and revolution could no more be isolated in the countryside than it could be kept alive there.

Peng Pai should have recognized this. After all, he was the one who had pointed to the connection between the landlords' militia attacks on peasants and the reaction in the cities. He saw an impending disaster for peasants and wanted his political party to do something about it. He had been disappointed.

The Cult of Peng Pai

Faced with a Party which had become quite conservative in its "leadership" of the peasantry, but nonetheless convinced that peasants would continue to struggle for their interests regardless of what the CP center in Shanghai said about restraining the mass movements, Peng Pai increasingly went directly to the peasantry over the head of the Party to present his proposals. If the Party would not articulate the demands of the peasantry, Peng Pai would take that task upon himself personally. But this seemed to Peng more like a cross he was forced to bear. In an extremely moving article entitled "Cry for the Wuhua Peasants!" Peng Pai's agony and the suffering of the peasantry merged as he took their burdens onto his own shoulders: "My peasant friends, for thousands of years with manure packed on your legs, cursed by others, cheated, demeaned, oppressed, enslaved, treated worse than cows and horses; when beaten, you don't dare weep, when one of you is killed, you don't dare cry out; holding unspoken in your hearts the agony of injustice, only in the dark of night do you tell your secrets to the spirits. . . . So listen, everyone, while I cry for the Wuhua peasants!"[58]

Lest it be imagined that Peng Pai was merely releasing pent-up frustrations on paper that would have no consequences, it should be remembered that for quite some time peasants had attributed very special qualities to Peng Pai, seeing him as the one person who could articulate their hopes and aspirations and deliver them from their sufferings. This had been most graphically illustrated in early 1926, when Peng Pai helped the peasants of Puning county in their struggles with an extremely powerful landlord lineage. The Puning struggle had had a long history, dating back at least to the 1870s, and continuing more or less unabated into the 1920s. Although the

Puning peasants had received the help of Peasant Union organizers after the Second Eastern Expedition, their combined forces were still too weak to win any concessions from the landlords—until Peng Pai arrived. As soon as the landlords learned of his imminent arrival, they came to terms with the peasants. The Puning peasants were not blind: they too knew that Peng Pai was coming and that after decades of struggle this was the only reason the landlords had negotiated with them. They clearly saw their victory in terms of Peng Pai: he was their strength, their spokesman, their savior. "When Peng Pai arrived in Puning, seven thousand peasants, men and women, young and old . . . came from miles away to welcome him. The crowd was very excited. Several peasant women held their children up to see him, shouting 'Look! The Eternal One [wansui] comes! Look! The Eternal One comes!' "[59]

Peng's goal of creating an independent, class-conscious peasantry had informed his organizing style. He had been aware for some time that peasants regarded him with an extraordinary degree of adoration that bordered on idolatry, and he believed that these religiously cast ideas hindered his organizing attempts. In Haifeng he was known as Prince Peng (Peng Gong) or Peng the Bodhisattva (Peng Pusa). Peng had never asked peasants not to call him "wansui" or "Pusa," preferring instead to hope that in the praxis of revolution, the peasants' religious beliefs would wither away as they acquired organizational skills and class consciousness. In fact, Peng often instructed peasant organizers "not to attack peasant beliefs in spirits or gods. To do so hinders our work." He explained that because peasants never had an opportunity for education, their minds were filled with simple religious beliefs which could not be shaken by argumentation. Those beliefs helped peasants explain and interpret events and would remain firmly entrenched until they learned how to use other concepts. Thus Peng told peasant movement cadre: "When we work in the villages, the first step is to gain the confidence of the peasants. . . . And you can't gain their trust if you attack their belief in gods. There are times when we must not only not insult their gods, but even worship along with them. This doesn't mean that we capitulate to religious superstition, but only that some concessions are necessary to even begin to do our work."[60]

Peng Pai furthermore was very much aware that these beliefs contributed to the peasants' dependence on outside leaders. He had placed great emphasis on the necessity for peasants to arm themselves, in the hope that they would then begin to believe in their own power. He also instructed cadre always to explain to peasants that all victories arose from the power of the peasant masses themselves, having nothing whatsoever to do with the leadership. As Peng explained: "After a victory, some comrades do not say that it was the peasants' victory, but instead boast of their own contributions. This causes peasants to doubt their own strength."[61]

These policies reflected the belief he had expressed five years earlier in the pages of *New Haifeng* before even organizing peasants: "Social revolution is not something one person or a small group can accomplish." Peng's policies had been successful, at least insofar as Haifeng peasants were now demanding the land, offical Party policies to the contrary notwithstanding. With the CCP refusing to give programatic form to the peasants' revolutionary goals, Peng Pai was forced, against his better judgment, to acknowledge and nurture what had been growing all around him since 1923: the charismatic cult of Peng Pai. "Let me cry for the peasants," he demanded. Like the leading player in a Shakespearean tragedy, Peng Pai felt himself forced to betray all of his work during the previous years, when he had tried to create an independent, class-conscious peasantry. He allowed the peasants to attribute to him all those extraordinary qualities enshrined in the folk understanding of "Pusa" and "wansui" merely in order to keep what he saw as the peasant movement—and thus the revolution—alive.

Peasants spontaneously made Peng Pai the center of a cult whether he liked it or not; he had no conscious hand in its making. Ultimately it was his actions, not his words, which provided sufficient confirmation to peasants of the general folk prophesy—he was a Pusa or wansui. Even his actions in establishing the peasant unions—modern social organizations replete with rational bureaucratic structures and rules—could be taken as confirmation of the prophesy. It may well have been that those organizations, given sufficient time to develop, could have ultimately fulfilled the peasants' deep-seated need for a political voice. But with the onset of the Northern Expedition and the beginning of the reaction, the peasantry became alienated not only from the Guomindang, but also from the Communist party, both of which refused to lead them and articulate their demand for land. Peng Pai became the only spokesman for all their hopes and aspirations: he became the Eternal One.

If ever an "independent kingdom" had appeared in the history of the Chinese Communist Party prior to Gao Gang in Manchuria in the 1950s (or perhaps Mao Zedong in Jiangxi in the early 1930s), Haifeng under Peng Pai was it. As a 1928 CCP report on the Haifeng movement obliquely observed, "All social movements were controlled by Party members—but they were not responsible to the Party center." The CCP center realized that the movement in Haifeng and in other areas of Guangdong was beyond its control, "but that mistake was quickly corrected," a CCP document later announced.[62] Presumably it had been corrected in March 1927 by sending Peng north to Wuhan, where the National Government had been relocated. Perhaps falling victim to Leninist beliefs in the power of a Communist party to control mass movements, the CCP undoubtedly tried to cool the demands of the peasants and preserve the united front with the Guomindang by removing Peng Pai from Guangdong. But Peng Pai had only been a vessel for the transmission and articulation of these demands; he was not their source. The absence of Peng Pai from Haifeng or Guangdong could not now conceal the revolutionary implications of the peasants' own activity.

The charismatic cult of Peng Pai, as was shown in the last chapter, was a form of social organization that allowed peasants to take collective action toward goals that had been articulated initially by Peng Pai. Peng Pai had not created those goals; he had merely articulated those of peasants. Nor had he created that particular form of organization, for it too had arisen from the peasants' own experiences. To be sure, Peng

227

Pai thought he had provided peasants with a new form of organization, the peasant unions, and had continued in that effort from 1924 to 1926 as head of the Guomindang Peasant Department. He expressed hope that peasant unions would provide the organizational form for peasants to pursue their goals, that peasant religious beliefs about him would wither away, and that peasants would form an independent class conscious of its own powers and goals. From 1923 through 1926, these two forms of social organization—the charismatic cult and the peasant unions—existed side by side in uncertain and unacknowledged relationship. Whether Peng Pai was right that the cult ultimately would give way to the more permanent institutions became a moot question in 1926 as the cult overtook the unions.

This was not the inevitable expression of peasant political power, and if Peter Worsley is right that charismatic cults become institutionalized in other forms of social organization, then in a way it represents a regression. But it is explicable. Because of the terms of the GMD-CCP united front, the CP refused to allow its members working in peasant unions to articulate peasant demands that would strain the alliance. Instead, it ordered its cadre to control the peasants. At the same time, the Guomindang was abandoning any pretense of representing peasant interests. Controlled by the right wing after Sun Yat-sen's death, the GMD leadership had sanctioned attacks on peasants and their unions, all in the name of preserving the class harmony presumed to be necessary to carry out the Northern Expedition. In effect, both of China's modern political parties removed themselves as spokesmen for peasant interests, blocking peasants from using the organizations they had provided to pursue their goals. That left peasants with only one alternative: the charismatic cult of Peng Pai.

By 1926, the cult was somewhat different from what it had been in 1923. Then, Peng Pai had articulated peasants' inchoate ideas into sharply defined goals. Peng had had a hand in the precise formulation of peasant demands—the reduction of rent, a halt to landlord abuses of power—and to that extent he had influenced the direction of peasant collective action.

But then those actions, along with the repressive responses of the local government and gentry, in turn became a part of the peasant experience. Peasants no longer had to reinvent the wheel. In 1926, peasants had a pretty good idea of what they wanted but found that the institutions formed to pursue those goals had instead become obstacles. At that point Peng Pai could no more control the activity of peasants than the Guomindang or the CCP could. He was a vessel for the transmission of their demands, and the cult was the social organization for achieving them. As peasants then acted to realize their goals—not only in Haifeng but in central China as well—the strains in the GMD-CCP alliance finally gave way, and the united front came apart.

CHAPTER 9

The Haifeng Soviet

THE mass movement of workers and peasants was rapidly creating the conditions for what Antonio Gramsci has called a "crisis of authority"—a historical condition in which social classes become detached from the political parties which had represented them, primarily because they become more revolutionary than their political representatives. By early 1927, both workers and peasants were transgressing the national goals proscribed for the National Revolution, pressing their own revolutionary goals. "When such crises occur," Gramsci wrote, "the immediate situation becomes delicate and dangerous, because the field is open for violent solutions, for the activities of unknown forces, represented by charismatic 'men of destiny.' "[1] As it turned out in China, it was to be Jiang Jieshi who was to try to turn his destiny into China's destiny.

Where Haifeng once had been a model for the rural revolutionary movement, by early 1927 the agriculturally rich and densely populated provinces of central China were progressing through the same identifiable stages as had Haifeng: strong peasant support for the revolutionary Guomindang army, rapid formation of peasant unions, the radicalization of the peasants under the slogan "All Power to the Peasant Union," and ultimately the raising of the demand for land. These parallel developments can be seen quite clearly in Mao Zedong's report on the Hunan peasant movement: "After the peasants had organized themselves, action ensued. The main targets of the peasants are local bullies, the evil gentry, and the lawless landlords. . . . The dignity and prestige of the landlords are dashed to the ground. With the fall of the authority of the landlords, the peasant association becomes the sole organ of authority, and the slogan 'All Power to the Peasant Association' had become a reality. Even trifling matters, such as quarrels between man and wife, have to be settled by the peasant association. Nothing can be settled in the absence of association representatives."[2]

And just as Peng Pai had understood earlier, Mao now learned that peasant collective action acquired a momentum of its own. But the difference in early 1927 was that it was now on a national scale with national consequences: "All revolutionary parties and all revolutionary comrades will stand before them to be tested, to be accepted or rejected by them. To march at their head and lead them? To follow in the rear, gesticulating at them and criticizing them? To face them as opponents? Every Chinese is free to choose among the three, but circumstances demand that a quick choice be made."[3] Mao was not merely committing Leninist heresy by demanding that the masses judge the revolutionary qualities of the Party; he was describing what in fact was happening. In Haifeng, the peasants judged the Guomindang reactionary, but the CCP refused to articulate their demands. Peng Pai had chosen "to march at their head and lead them," but had been criticized for not restraining them. Now Mao once again threw the gauntlet to the CCP center, and once again it fell to the ground. This was just a part of the "crisis of authority."

Just as peasant actions threatened property relations in the countryside—much to the displeasure of the CCP center, which was trying to keep the CCP-GMD alliance together—so too did workers threaten property rights in the cities. The working class of Guangzhou had shown its strength and resolve during the first half of the sixteen-month-long Hong Kong–Guangzhou Strike and Anti-British Boycott (June 1925–October 1926) when the Strike Committees assumed control over most municipal police and juridical functions. But in the summer of 1926, working-class unity in the "home of the revolution," as Guangdong was sometimes called, was shattered by rightists determined to dispel the threat to property posed by a united and revolutionary working class. While open repression of the left-wing labor unions in Guangzhou was not effected until January 1927,[4] the constant warring among union factions that had been instigated by GMD rightists noticibly weakened worker organizations. In fact, the Guangzhou working class became so enfeebled by the internecine struggle that the anti-imperialist strike and boycott ended in October 1926 with a wimper so soft it could not be heard above the din of the factional strife.

The working class of Shanghai was much more united in its organization and goals and, consequently, less susceptible to the divisive tactics used by the Right in Guangzhou to blunt the revolutionary edge. For that very reason, however, it was much more dangerous: Shanghai, the most modern of China's cities, was the home of China's capitalist and financier classes, as well as China's major entrepot for foreign capital. All of these classes were threatened by the workers of Shanghai.

As the Northern Expeditionary armies moved into Hunan in late 1926, and then down the Yangzi valley toward Shanghai in early 1927, strains within the Guomindang grew. Ever since Sun Yat-sen's death in 1925, there had been strategic differences between the leftist civilian leadership of the GMD and the more conservative officer corps of the army. As the army moved northward, the civilian leadership under Jiang Jieshi established a rival Central Committee of the GMD at Nanchang. At issue was how far the GMD leadership was willing to let the mass political organizations of workers and peasants go toward realizing their increasingly radical goals. Jiang was ready to dispense with mass politics, preferring instead to rely on the army to achieve the goal of unifying China. The mass organizations and the Communist party simply were too dangerous for Jiang, and on 12 April he led a bloody coup in Shanghai that destroyed the worker organizations there, touching off the White Terror throughout China.[5] The left-GMD members in Wuhan, on the other hand, were unable to decide what to do with the mass organizations and the demands being made by workers and peasants. To keep the masses involved in the campaign to unify China, the Left-GMD wanted to satisfy some of their demands, especially those of peasants for land, but not at the cost of alienating its military supporters, many of whom were from landlord families.

The forum where these issues were debated was the GMD Land Committee. During March and April 1927, the Left-GMD and CCP members who participated in these discussions were unable to resolve the issue of how to satisfy peasant demands for land without also making inroads on the property owned by military officers. In the end, the decisions were made for them. In May, the military officers who had supported the Left made overtures to Jiang Jieshi and turned on the Left-GMD, the mass movements of workers and peasants, and the Communists. When this happened, Angus McDonald has concluded, "the alliance of the radicals and the liberals—the hope of urban revolution in Hunan—was at an end."[6]

What had happened at the national level in the spring of 1927—the split between the radicals and their more liberal allies—bears striking parallels to what had happened in Haifeng county in 1922–23, when Peng Pai broke with Chen Jiongming and his reformist gentry group. Then, it will be recalled, the issue was whether China's "socialist" revolution would be controlled from above, as Chen and Haifeng's reformist elite wanted, or be ushered in by mass revolts from below, as Peng Pai wanted. McDonald argues that in the 1926–27 revolution as well, "the fundamental contradiction . . . was between those who hoped to keep power, wealth, and prestige monopolized within a narrow segment of the population (with themselves on top), and those who wanted to use the opportunity of the revolution to transform social relations in China and to bring the nation from semi-colonial subservience to modern independence and prosperity by expanding the polity to include the masses (with themselves on top)."[7] Just as Peng Pai and his former liberal allies in Haifeng had split over the issue of how active peasants were to be in the political process, so too throughout south and central China in late 1926 and early 1927, peasants forced elites to confront this issue and to take sides. When Jiang Jieshi launched the counterrevolution in April of 1927, the equivalent of Haifeng's reformist gentry throughout rural China still had the power and ability to move against the mass organizations and their leaders. This class then followed Jiang's lead in suppressing peasants and their organizations. Haifeng was able to escape this counterrevolutionary terror because its reformist gentry had already been confronted and driven out. In Haifeng, there was no social basis for the reactionary movement.

Nonetheless, armed reaction and White Terror spread through Guangdong just two days following Jiang's 12 April massacre of Shanghai workers. The commander of GMD forces in Guangdong, General Li Jishen, had just returned from an early April meeting near Shanghai, where plans for the coup had been laid. Upon returning to Guangdong, he unleashed the terror there: trade unions were raided, workers were arrested *en masse*, and Communists and labor leaders were executed.[8] In the countryside, a British missionary reported in late April, "one night all over the territory [GMD troops] seized and shot Communists, among them many ignorant peasants and workers and students, both boys and girls, who were merely pursuing the path on which they had been started by this same party. But the power let loose was not so easily brought within bounds again, and to it are due the misery and lawlessness rife in [Guangdong] province today."[9]

Haifeng escaped the immediate ravages of the White Terror. In mid-March, a GMD functionary, Su Minwang, arrived in Haifeng to make contact with any "faction" that would support the reaction when it began. Out of pure stupidity or plain ignorance, Su contacted Wu Zhenmin, Communist commander of the Haifeng Peasant Self-Defense Corps. The Haifeng Peasant Union then instructed Wu to feign support in order to receive advance warning. The union didn't have long to wait. Shortly after General Li's 15 April Guangzhou massacre, Wu received a telegram from the GMD advising him to prepare to "liquidate" the CCP and the peasant unions from Haifeng and other east Guangdong counties.[10]

A People's Government and Its Enemies: May 1927

Haifeng was an island in a sea of reaction, and leading Communists there were unsure what they could or should do

234

next; they were, as a CCP document attests, "totally in the dark concerning the policy and plans of the CCP Regional Committee." Furthermore, the Haifeng CCP leadership was leaderless, for in early 1927, Peng Pai had left Guangdong to join the Left-Guomindang in Wuhan. Peng was not to return to Haifeng until early November, after returning to Guangdong with troops which had staged the abortive 1 August Nanchang Uprising.[11]

Although the CCP-led Peasant Self-Defense Corps was the strongest military force in Haifeng, the Haifeng CCP branch was nonetheless unsure whether or not to seize political power, and if they did, whether to organize the government in the name of the CCP or the GMD. The prevailing Communist orthodoxy—and one with which Peng Pai had serious disagreement—was that at the present stage, the tasks of the revolution would be democratic and antifeudal, certainly not socialist. When the CCP Guangdong Regional Committee uprising plans dated 20 April finally reached Haifeng members, they were assured that the reaction was merely a struggle between the Right- and Left-Guomindang, between "democratic power and feudal power." Their task as Communists was to join with all other democratic forces in Guangdong for a 1 May uprising which would estabish a "People's Government" under the slogans "Support the Wuhan Government," "Oppose All Counterrevolutionaries," and "Support the Three People's Principles."[12]

But once again, the Haifeng cadre, now headed by Peng's older brother Hanyuan and long-time comrades Lin Daowen and Zheng Zhiyun, were caught in the dilemma caused by leading a movement which had already transgressed the safe bounds of the goals of the "National Revolution"; now only the most severe inroads on landlord property rights would gain the widespread support of the Haifeng peasantry. Taking political power was relatively easy. But what then? As Haifeng Communists later complained, "There were few slogans connected with peasant needs; only those calling for the formation of a county People's Government and the abolition of miscellaneous taxes had any slight relevance at all. But in Haifeng even these could not be considered demands because tax resistance was already widespread, and the slogan . . . of a 25 percent rent reduction—the resolution of the Guomindang Central Committee—was a joke in Haifeng. . . . The uprising would necessarily be a revolution. But afterwards, what could be achieved? There were no obvious answers."[13]

Nevertheless, preparations for the 1 May uprising proceeded. The Peasant Self-Defense Corps, under its new name of the Worker and Peasant Save-the-Party (that is, Left-Guomindang) Army, selected a vanguard "dare-to-die" corps of four hundred members and trained another one thousand peasants in the use of rifles. The remainder, armed with old fowling pieces or sharpened farm implements, defended the villages. Although peasants knew an uprising was certainly in the offing, all details remained secret, even the day of the uprising. The CP and Peasant Union cadre concentrated almost solely on military preparations, paying very little attention to mass agitation. Perhaps they had realized that the slogans chosen by the Regional Committee would have failed to stimulate peasants in any case. It is thus not too surprising that when the order for the uprising was passed down on 30 April, the seizure of political power had more the aura of a military coup than of a mass uprising. There was, in fact, very little fighting on the night of 30 April and in the dawn of 1 May: the police and salt inspectors were arrested and disarmed without putting up any resistance.[14]

During the ten days of its existence, the new "People's Government"—composed of representatives of the Communist party, the Left-Guomindang, and worker, peasant, and merchant organizations—did not raise the issue of seizing the land. The tasks of the uprising, as envisioned by the CCP Guangdong Regional Committee from its hideout in Hong Kong, were merely strategic—to prepare for the ultimate seizure of political power in Guangzhou following a province-wide revolt. But the plan was never realized: Communist commanders in Guangzhou did not lead their troops in revolt; peasants in other areas did not rise up; and the workers remained quiescent. Haifeng was isolated.[15]

As Haifeng Communists occupied themselves with figuring out how best to meet the Regional Committee's expectations, the peasants were left to fend for themselves. Without a program to follow, those peasants who acted during those "ten days of political power"—and they were few indeed, at least compared with Peasant Union membership—took matters into their own hands, killing landlords and "evil hegemons." CCP leaders such as Lin Daowen could only look on rather helplessly at the spontaneous actions of the peasants. "What pains me the most," Lin wrote in his diary, "is that there are worker and peasant brothers pillaging; I've heard that looting is the greatest in the suburbs." A few days later, Lin again observed that "during these days it is like there is *no* government. The masses are seeking revenge and are killing. I've heard that those killed in revenge already number over two hundred." Two days later, Lin painfully wrote that "the pillaging by worker and peasant brothers has worsened." But those who had led the Haifeng peasants since 1923 did not attempt to channel, or repress, these spontaneous peasant attacks on rural order.[16]

The peasants, for their part, were fast losing confidence in the ability of their longtime leaders to do anything right. The peasants' opinion of the CCP cadre, and especially of the Peasant Army, sank even lower after the one attempt to defend Haifeng from invading Guomindang armies ended in disaster on 9 May 1927. As GMD forces led by Liu Bingcui pressed closer to Haifeng, the leaders of the People's Government wanted to retreat to the safety of the hills, abandoning Haifeng—and the peasants—to Right-Guomindang and landlord rule. Rather than rely on the strength of the organized peasantry, the CCP leadership—Peng Hanyuan, Lin Daowen, Zheng Zhiyun, Yang Wang, Lin Tieshi, and Wu Zhenmin—decided to fight a frontal battle. Occupying a strategic pass on the route from Huizhou to Haifeng, three hundred full-time troops and some temporarily organized peasants armed with few guns, little ammunition, and one cannon, hoped to defeat the numerically stronger GMD army. After the cannon broke down, the Guomindang army had an easy march to Haifeng city, which it occupied at 3:00 P.M. on 9 May.[17]

237

Liu Bingcui had taken Haifeng city, but with his limited troop strength, that, along with Shanwei, was about all he could hold; establishing GMD rule in the countryside required the formation of local militia. Local armed forces controlled by landlords had disappeared from rural Haifeng as the power of the Peasant Union grew throughout 1926, and most larger landowners, especially those "newly arisen," or reformist gentry, landlords who had been closely aligned with Chen Jiongming, had fled to the safety of Shantou, Guangzhou, and Hong Kong. All that were left were the smaller landlords who did not even live in the market towns, but still resided in the villages. It was to these people that Liu Bingcui turned to form the Peace Preservation Corps and rural militia (*mintuan*) charged with restoring order in the countryside.

According to a source close to the Guomindang, Liu made Lai Junhua head of the Haifeng and Lufeng Peace Preservation Corps; but to the Communists, the most hated corps leader in Haifeng came to be Dai Kexiong. Dai was a small landowner in Yanqian, a village about three miles south of Gongping, who reportedly had graduated from the Huangbu Military Academy in Guangzhou. With his knowledge of military organization, Dai soon organized Peace Preservation Corps in most of Haifeng's market towns, while Guomindang regulars garrisoned the larger towns of Gongping and Shanwei.[18]

Presumably the corps were manned by locals; ruffians and small-time hoodlums from the market towns were likely candidates. Dai also had connections with an organized force, the Long Hair Party (*chang fa dang*), in Lufeng county. The Long Hair Party was an obscure religious sect with its own peculiar rituals, beliefs, and gods, but otherwise probably was much like the Baling sect that had been around Meilong. And like the Baling sect, the Long Hairs seemed to attract mainly peasants. For whatever reasons, the Long Hair Party was opposed to the Communists, and Dai used his connections to enroll some of them into the Peace Preservation Corps. The Long Hairs had few members in Haifeng, but in Lufeng and Huilai counties had a considerable following. It was from these areas, especially around the market town of Kuitan, that Dai sought his employees. Dai Kexiong was not the only landowner to organize armed forces; in the rural areas west of Haifeng city, landlords Lu Songru, Chen Yuwu, and Liang Bozuo sought and received outside aid from Cai Tengui, a strongman from just over the hills in Huiyang county.[19]

Within a very short time after the arrival of Liu Bingcui's troops, local landlords had either organized or hired their own military forces, and began to reestablish their rule. By June it was apparent that the landed class was in control. In addition to Liu Bingcui's troops, two or more divisions commanded by Chen Xuexun arrived from Shantou. Landlords and former officials returned from their urban havens and set up a new ruling body, the "Haifeng Reconstruction Committee," chaired by Chen Jiongming's old friend and comrade Zhong Xiunan. This committee, not surprisingly, was controlled by and for Haifeng's old reformist gentry group. To establish its presence in the countryside, the Reconstruction Committee sent troops to villages chosen at random to collect taxes and search for Communists. As local cadre reported, "The only task of the Guomindang troops was to mop up the villages; every village was searched, and any Peasant Union cadre found was arrested or executed." CCP members, no longer safe even in the villages, had to move daily to a different village, working at night and sleeping in stables during the day. Propaganda workers for the reorganized and GMD-controlled Peasant Union went into villages to collect union "dues" (that went to support the Peace Preservation Corps), and to inform peasants that they were still entitled to the GMD-guaranteed 25 percent rent reduction. The cruelty of this "rent reduction" was not lost on peasants, who knew that in reality it was a rent *increase*: during 1926 they had already mandated reductions totalling 64 percent, while many had paid no rent at all.[20]

As landlords pressed their advantage in the countryside, villagers resurrected traditional forms of resistance, like the crop- and bandit-watching societies so prevalent on the eve of the 1911 Revolution, to defend their families and villages. One woman later recalled: "The peasants were always careful about having guards. There were always three—two outside the village and one inside. After the uprising they paid special attention to sentries. The outer guard would report instantly, and the whole village would be roused. In an hour or two the women and children would all be gone to the hills. The Kuomintang [Guomindang] was afraid of the hills, not knowing how large a force might be hidden there. All the villages did this when Kuomintang movements were reported. The peasants tried to estimate the size of the enemy force, and information was relayed from one village to another. If their situation was favorable, the men stayed and fought, sending women to the hills. If they were too weak in numbers, the men went to the hills too. Sometimes a village received a message from the city as to when the Kuomintang might arrive and how large the force was. If the peasants were strong enough, they ambushed it on the road before it could get near the village. If too weak, they always evacuated."[21]

While peasants actively protected their families and villages and the Communists who were hiding among them, the demoralized cadre tried to think of ways to "mobilize" the peasants. Before the Haifeng Communists could find value in the peasants' tenacious defense of their villages, they had to learn from the mistakes that had been made in May. Some began to see the potential for guerrilla warfare implicit in the peasants' spontaneous forms of collective action, struggle, and resistance: others derided these as manifestations of the dreaded "peasant localism." Both views, of course, were accurate.

In analyzing their strategy, Communist cadre concluded that they had failed to lead the peasants. In the choice of military tactics, for example, an alternative would have been the guerrilla action of "drawing the enemy in deep" in order to isolate and annihilate the invading army bit by bit. The major military mistake had been an "exclusive reliance on the Peasant Army" which consequently "demoralized" the masses. After the army fled, peasants complained that it was "as useless as a woman." The military debacle was but one symptom of the general failure of the Party to put forward slogans and programs to which peasants would respond. They realized that "our standpoint on the land problem was too confused. We did not lead the peasants in seizing the land." Other slogans such as creating a county People's Government, abolishing taxes, reducing rent, or eliminating rightists "simply did not concern the peasants." The result, of course, was that peasants "did not rise up or else decided to drop out." The general lesson, simple as it was, was difficult for a Leninist party to learn, and costly for peasants: "An uprising of the masses cannot be brought about at the drop of a command. Purely political slogans like 'Eliminate counterrevolutionaries' cannot arouse the masses. Only economic demands necessarily close to the masses can mobilize them for an uprising."[22]

The Rent Resistance Movement: Autumn 1927

Peasants made the demands themselves. With the return of landlords and the approach of the harvest, peasants raised the question of land and the issue of rent resistance. Communists and peasants did not completely agree. Some cadre felt that if under the prevailing conditions even a rent reduction could not be accomplished, to press for total rent resistance would surely invite a massacre. Outside help, they argued, was essential. Other cadre counseled that rent resistance was not necessary; an immediate uprising to take Haifeng city was. But having learned the lesson that "only economic demands necessarily close to the masses can mobilize them," the majority of cadre and peasants decided that rent resistance was the only possible path of action. Besides, the CCP Guangdong Regional Committee had finally allowed the Haifeng cadre to raise the slogan "Land to the Peasants."[23]

The immediate goal of the Communist campaign was to restore peasant faith in the Party by issuing demands that reflected peasant needs: rent resistance and "Land to the Peasants." In some places, peasants spontaneously enforced the rent resistance movement by dealing strictly with those who did not resolutely support it. In collective actions reminiscent of the 1880s, peasants attacked tax and rent collectors to frighten them from ever entering the villages, stole grain from lightly guarded stores, and destroyed grain in landlord fields. In those areas where enemy troop strength was too great, rent resistance took traditionally covert forms, while in other areas, it was an open and public act.[24]

The formation of a new Peasant Army also strengthened the rent resistance movement. Although the main force of the Peasant Army had fled Haifeng, remaining members soon began to train a new force. Throughout June and July, the forces of the new Peasant Army continued to multiply as the rent resistance struggle sharpened. In the area of the Meilong marketing system, the new Peasant Army frequently engaged and defeated enemy forces by using guerrilla tactics. One Guomindang source complained that the Communists did not make a good target, for when attacked, they dispersed, only to reassemble later. The struggle was particularly acute in the Meilong, Gongping, and Chishi marketing systems, around Xintian market in Lufeng, and extending west into Huiyang county. Although "enemy troops incessantly attacked the villages," the CP reported, "they could not completely subdue them. ... Everywhere, peasants harassed the rural militia and Peace Preservation Corps, who were prepared to flee."[25]

That the rent reduction movement and support for the Peasant Army should have centered around Meilong and Gongping is not surprising. These were areas of agricultural wealth where class distinctions between landlords and peasants were sharply drawn. To be sure, the agricultural lands around Meilong were more productive than those around Gongping; the former were level, sandy loam fields with access to irrigation, while the latter were somewhat more broken by hills with little or no irrigation. Furthermore, tensions between Lin landlords and their tenants in Meilong had a longer history than in Gongping. But Gongping had been in the thick of the sugar boom and bust, and it was near Gongping that the Haifeng landlord Zhu Mo in 1923 had tried to raise rents on peasants who tilled permanent tenure "manure investment" fields. Since 1922, peasants in these two areas, as well as those in the villages around Haifeng city, where tenancy also was high, had responded time and again to Peng Pai's message of "rent reduction" and "land to the tiller." For five years, two forms of social organization—the cult of Peng Pai and the peasant

242

unions—had guided peasants in collective action against land-lords. In the summer of 1927, the villages around Haifeng were quiet, but that can be attributed to the soldiers stationed nearby in the city. When the opportunity presented itself, peasants there too would rise up.

The Second Seizure of Power: September 1927

By late August, peasants and members of the peasant armies, very few armed with anything but spears, swords, and sharpened tools, had driven nearly all of the Peace Preservation Corps and rural militia from the countryside and into the market towns. As even a Guomindang supporter admitted, the peasant armies roamed freely throughout the countryside.[26] The defenders of order were holed up in the small towns, easy prey for these Armies. At night, peasants attacked an increasingly nervous and edgy militia. Soon, the siege paid off. On 7 September, the commander of one company in Gongping led his troops into the countryside; he was seeking the Peasant Army—not to engage in battle, but to switch sides. This was the break the Peasant Army needed. Lin Daowen, commander of the Peasant Army, accepted the surrender and held an impromptu celebration. During the festivities, Lin suggested that those assembled march on Yanqian village, some seven miles distant, where Dai Kexiong, the Peace Preservation Corps leader, lived. Such actions by then were not unusual, since the Peasant Army had been harassing landlords and their protectors for several months. What was unusual was that after completing their business at Yanqian, the band of peasants, now swelled by several hundred others, decided to march on Gongping, which they took easily. In the meantime, peasant forces elsewhere in Haifeng had been attacking other market towns. When news of what happened in Gongping spread, Peace Preservation Corps and rural militia retreated from the market towns of Meilong, Chishi, and Qinggang to Haifeng and Shanwei. On 11 September, the defenders of Shanwei hopped a boat for Xiamen.[27] That left only Haifeng city.

On 16 September, thousands of unarmed peasants repeatedly stormed the walls and gates of Haifeng city. When defending troops fled, peasants reoccupied the city. Although the CCP declared that a new government, a "Dictatorship of Workers and Peasants," had been formed, its only task in the little time left before Guomindang troops would return was to prepare for the retreat. Thus while the "Dictatorship of Workers and Peasants" made "despotic inroads" on the rights of private property, it did so with an eye toward evacuation. All the cloth of the Nanfeng Textile Mill was expropriated and transported to the countryside; all items of wealth were confiscated from pawn shops, while the pawned goods of peasants and poor people were returned; and the printing press of the *Lu-an Daily* was expropriated and moved to a remote village near the Haifeng-Lufeng-Zejin-Huiyang border region.[28]

The other task of the Provisional Revolutionary Government was to "eliminate counterrevolutionaries." A revolutionary court was established, "but because the masses were allowed to kill freely," according to one report, the cases heard by the court were few indeed. None of the documents indicate who was considered a "counterrevolutionary" or on what basis that judgement was made. The term probably referred primarily to the powerful landlord lineages, since it was claimed that some "counterrevolutionary villages were burned completely down."[29] Others, such as "local bullies, evil gentry, and lawless landlords," as the popular trilogy went, were probably also included. But since peasants were free to decide these matters themselves, it probably meant that old scores were being settled in which people besides landlords were killed.

Although peasants were willing to loot, burn, and some of them to kill, they were not willing to seize the land—at least not yet. It was not that CCP members and Peasant Army leaders such as Lin Daowen did not raise the slogan: "We were very resolute in wanting the immediate expropriation and redistribution of land, and constantly propagated those goals . . . to mobilize the peasants." Rather, through the years of struggle under the most adverse of circumstances, peasants had developed an acute sense of the real balance of power in the countryside. They simply did not act recklessly when the odds were against them. This, after all, was the primary rule of both daily peasant life as well as guerrilla warfare. Unlike conditions in 1926 when peasants demanded the land, it was obvious that friendly forces no longer controlled the state apparatus. Like the CCP itself, peasants knew that Guomindang troops would return soon to restore landlord rule. To most peasants, caution was the better part of valour. As some Lufeng peasants counseled the CCP after the September uprising, "Don't be too ferocious, since the Peasant Unions will soon be overthrown."[30]

And of course they were. When Guomindang troops under the command of Chen Xuexun began to march on Haifeng in mid-September, the Peasant Army and the CCP carried out its strategic retreat to the small village of Zhongdong in the mountainous border region north of Haifeng. To this "revolutionary base area" was moved the large amount of expropriated cotton cloth, ammunition, medical supplies, and the printing press. Here the revolutionary forces were to await the arrival of Ye Ting and He Long's army which, it was hoped, would spark a general uprising of peasants and workers not only in Haifeng, but throughout Guangdong, and then the rest of China.

Toward the Haifeng Soviet

Peasants and their leaders waited until late October. By that time a convergence of circumstances made another uprising possible; this time it would result in the establishment of China's first rural soviet.

In mid-October, fighting once again broke out between two generals contending for control of Guangdong province, Li Jishen and Zhang Fakui. Zhang had led his "Ironsides" army (composed of soldiers and officers from Guangdong) in the Northern Expedition, and then in July, seeing the alliance between the Left-Guomindang and the Communists crumble, marched back to Guangdong. Upon his return, Zhang proclaimed that he would "save Guangdong for the revolution" by ousting Li Jishen. But after some initial sparring, on 20 September Generals Li and Zhang came to a *modus vivendi* in which Zhang took Shantou and the surrounding area, while Li remained in control of the rest of Guangdong. The truce was to last only for a month, having been concluded in the first place only because of the threat posed to both by the southern march into Guangdong of the armies of the Communist commanders Ye Ting and He Long.[31]

Ye and He had seized Nanchang for a few days in the first of the CCP's abortive "Autumn Harvest Uprisings," and after being driven out by Zhang Fakui led their army south through Jiangsu and Jiangxi provinces toward Guangdong in the hope of rekindling the mass-based revolution. Accompanied by such Communist luminaries as Zhang Guotao, Tan Pingshan, Zhou Enlai, Zhu De, and Peng Pai, the Ye-He armies marched through the countryside hoping to attract peasants to their cause, but sending them in flight instead. After losing many troops to death and desertion, the army attacked Shantou, where they believed they could receive supplies from the Soviet Union. Defeated again by Zhang Fakui at Shantou, a thousand or so soldiers beat a hasty retreat to Haifeng. While Zhang Guotao, Zhou Enlai, Tan Pingshan, Peng Pai and other Communist leaders fled by small fishing boats to Hong Kong or Shanghai, the Communist commanders Ye Ting and He Long continued overland to Haifeng.[32]

The Haifeng Communists and peasants expected that Ye and He's ten-thousand-strong army would be marching victoriously through eastern Guangdong toward Haifeng. But when the few survivors arrived in the Haifeng base area on 19 October, a CCP member reported, "we knew they were a defeated army. But we never guessed they would never want to fight another battle. . . . They were too run-down. Their uniforms were in rags, and the majority did not have caps, rain hats, or straw sandals. It was rainy and cold, and the defeated troops were weary and undernourished. They were demoralized, countless numbers had fallen by the way . . ., and both officers and soldiers felt hopeless." But secure in the base area, the troops for the first time in months could rest and recuperate without fear of attack. The base area was in the Nanling marketing system, some twenty-five miles north of Haifeng city. Surrounded by mountains, Nanling was a natural fortress; the local inhabitants had long boasted that with "mountains high and emperor distant," it was an independent kingdom. Following the September uprising, its strategic importance was not lost on the CCP. Resting in the village of Zhongdong, the demoralized troops were entertained and visited by peasants who brought gifts of peanuts, turnips, pork, and rice. Rain hats and sandals were purchased, and peasant women made uniforms from the cloth expropriated from the Nanfeng Textile Mill.[33]

Although peasants in the immediately surrounding area knew that the Ye-He army was a defeated and demoralized one, peasants in areas of Haifeng farther away were not so well informed, and when they heard of the arrival of a "Communist army," they acted. In the Qinggang and Jiesheng marketing systems, it was reported that sometime around 25 October "over one hundred people were nabbed, and all clothing, artifacts, gold and silver were taken by peasants." Peasants weren't the only ones to draw the wrong conclusions about the arrival of a "Red Army." Panic was seizing the landlords, who began fleeing to Shanwei in order to board outward-bound steamers—or even small fishing boats. In the meantime, fighting resumed between Li Jishen and Zhang Fakui, and landlords knew they could not expect military protection from Li's lieutenants much longer.[34]

Landowners certainly preferred to remain in Haifeng at least another month or so. The harvest was just coming in, and for the first time in years they had a chance to collect rents: the fall of 1923 had seen the typhoon; in 1925 the Eastern Expeditions aided peasants in their rent resistance efforts; and by the fall of 1926 peasants had imposed rent reductions of 64 percent, while many others paid no rent at all. Perhaps fear of losing another year's rental income convinced many to remain in Haifeng just a little longer. The stakes were high, but so were the risks. Peasants too understood the risks. Within a few days the harvest would be in, but so would the rent collectors. And this time landlords would demand not simply this year's rent, but back rent as well. Peasants also realized that they would soon be freed from their otherwise daily tasks in the fields to fight for the fruits of their labor.[35]

Peasants knew that Peng Pai had returned, and was somewhere in Guangdong. Any doubts that they may have had about the wisdom of a third uprising vanished in his presence. As Peng the Bodhisattva, the Pusa, the Eternal One, he was an intangible force perhaps, but an important one nonetheless. According to one eyewitness, when Peng was absent from Haifeng during the White Terror, peasants who had fled their villages "looked down the hills and saw their homes burning. . . . [They] would lift their arms and cry out: 'When will Peng Pai come back to us? Everything will be all right again then.' "[36]

When informed of CP plans to seize the villages and towns, peasants responded. They needed no promises; the Communist party gave none. Both followed Peng Pai. On Saturday, 29 October, peasants throughout Haifeng gathered at dawn in their villages to converge on the market towns. As Dai Kexiong withdrew his few hundred Peace Preservation Corps troops to the safety of Haifeng city, peasants easily took most of their targets. The next day, Dai, his corps, and a company of Guomindang regulars fled to the coastal town of Jieshi in Lufeng. Haifeng was defenseless; peasants took it without encountering much resistance.[37]

Peasants did not take all of the rural market towns so easily, meeting heavy resistance at Meilong and Jiesheng. The Lin lineage of Meilong (the Guifeng landlords) were powerful and rich, holding the land of nearly all the neighboring villages. Even a report sympathetic to the Guomindang acknowledged that for good reason "the peasants especially hated the Lin lineage." Peasants were not merely Lin tenants; the Lin treated them as "tenant households," a throwback to Ming and Qing times when tenants had been considered servile. A young Lin tenant, Ye Zexin, had led the struggle against the Lin since 1923; presumably he led the attack. When the town fell, peasants rounded up thirty to forty Lin and had them shot.[38]

Unlike Meilong, Jiesheng was a walled market town and thus eminently more defensible. Mutual antagonism existed between the landowners of the town, who were predominantly merchants and members of the He lineage, and their tenants outside the walls. The defense inside the walls was coordinated by He Wuting, a 51-year-old Qing scholar, who marshalled all of the town's resources for the siege. Surrounded by peasants who deeply hated them, and without a means of escape, He Wuting and the townspeople engaged in a life-or-death struggle. For nearly three weeks, thousands of poorly armed peasants attempted to scale the walls, only to have the defenders pour burning oil on them. Only when peasants received aid from the Red Army did they take Jiesheng. Inflamed by thoughts of revenge, peasants burned Jiesheng, decapitated thirty-seven leaders, including He Wuting and Dai Kexiong, and reportedly took the heads to Haifeng in celebration.[39]

The New World

When peasants took Haifeng city on Tuesday, 1 November, their leaders established a Provisional Revolutionary Government (PRG) which cleared the way three weeks later for the formal proclamation of the Haifeng Soviet of Workers, Peasants, and Soldiers. The main task of the PRG, headed by a six-person steering committee, was to make preparations for the "land revolution" by preventing the collection of rents and debts. The PRG did not see as its goal confiscating or redistributing land, but only destroying landlord political power, as the Fundamental Law of the PRG promulgated on 6 November indicates:

1. All landlords who collect rent shall be executed.

2. Those who collaborate with landlords in illicit rent deals shall be executed.

3. All hidden land deeds shall be submitted to this government, or else the holders will be executed.

4. All debts are hereby abolished; those who collect debts from peasants shall be executed.

5. Underlings who collect rent for landlords shall be executed.

6. Those who conceal rental contracts shall be executed.

7. Those who have already collected rent from peasants must return it or be executed.[40]

The district and village peasant unions then prepared for elections to the Representative Assembly, scheduled to meet on 18–21 November. The unions estimated the population of each of Haifeng's nine districts and allocated representatives based on population. Delegates to the county assembly were then elected from each of the district representative assemblies. Workers were elected on the basis of the nature of their work and the number of people in that sector, while soldiers were elected directly from the army. Of the 311 representatives then elected, 60 percent were peasants, 30 percent workers, and 10 percent soldiers. One-quarter of all delegates were CP members.[41]

The four-day assembly was great theater, and Peng Pai was the main attraction. In addition to the 311 delegates, ten thousand peasants crowded into Haifeng for the opening day ceremonies. What they saw this first day was a dozen or so people on a podium, many or most of whom they did not know, singing the "Internationale," bowing three times to large pictures of the Westerners Marx and Lenin, and then giving way to Peng Pai. He held center stage for the rest of the day. The next morning, after a similar amount of ritual, Peng continued his talk, interrupting it long enough to announce a military victory at Jiesheng. On the next day, fifty thousand people gathered on a hill about three miles from Haifeng to celebrate the victory Peng Pai had told them about, and thirty "counterrevolutionaries" taken prisoner were publicly executed. And on the next and final day of the meeting, fifty thousand people jammed into Haifeng to hear Peng Pai discuss the "land revolution" and to hear the official proclamation of the "Haifeng Soviet" (Haifeng *su-wei-ai*). After this exhilarating experience, peasants returned to their villages to act on what they had heard Peng Pai say about "land revolution."[42]

Peng Pai was the one who held political power in Haifeng, and yet the formal organization of power was called a "soviet." The idea of establishing a soviet government, of course, had not originated with the peasants. After all, they had little idea what a *su-wei-ai*, the Chinese transliteration for "soviet," was. Peng Pai wasn't too sure about the idea either. As early as 1923, Peng had thought of calling the peasant unions "soviets," but had rejected the idea, realizing that peasants would have difficulty enough remembering the transliteration, let alone understanding what it meant.[43] But now, at Stalin's urging, the Central Committee of the CCP had agreed that it was time for soviets in China, and here in Haifeng the term was being used. An expected, but apparently not too widespread phenomenon, was some peasants' fetishistic understanding of the word *su-wei-ai*. Some thought that a "Mr. Suweiai" was arriving to deliver them from their sufferings, while others thought it meant "this is mine" (*zhe wei wo*), which indeed sounded somewhat similar.

Not only peasants, but also the Comintern and some members of the CCP, likewise attached a somewhat mystical quality to soviets. The issue of establishing soviets in China had arisen more out of the internal struggles in the Comintern between Stalin and Trotsky over the problem of what stage the Chinese revolution had entered than anything else. In the rarefied atmosphere of these Comintern China debates, the slogan of "soviets" had taken on a reified existence in which their Russian origin in spontaneous workers' actions and their future in the Soviet Union as powerless organs was replaced by an empty abstraction signifying solely the hope that the Chinese revolution had passed to the socialist stage. So with Stalin's call for soviets in late July, the Comintern decided that China had passed somewhat abruptly from the bourgeois-democratic "National Revolution" to the stage of proletarian-socialist revolution.[44]

The CCP center and Guangdong Regional Committee were not much help either in deciphering the historical content of soviets in China. Shortly after the 7 August emergency meeting deposing party chief Chen Duxiu, it was considered appropriate to propagate soviets, but not establish them. Soviets then were characterized as a "revolutionary form of political power, that is, a unique method of guaranteeing the growth and transformation of the democratic revolution of workers and peasants into the socialist revolution." By 30 September, after the establishment of these revolutionary organs had become Party policy, the CCP center clearly stated that soviets could be established only in large cities. But after the establishment of the PRG in Haifeng, the Party evidently decided at its mid-November Central Committee meeting in Hankou that a soviet government was now appropriate for rural Haifeng as well.[45]

Given the fact that in the Soviet Union the historical meaning of "soviet" had been lost, and that by the 1920s "party" had replaced "soviet" in ruling Russia, it should not be too surprising that there was a great deal of confusion in Haifeng over the difference between party and state organs. Although a thirteen-member executive committee comprising seven peasants, three workers, one soldier, and two intellectuals was elected to administer the soviet government, one report observed that "seemingly confused ideas prevailed among the comrades. The result was that the government could be distinguished only slightly from the East River Regional Committee of the Party. For example, in the Regional Committee, one comrade held the title of 'Finance Commissar,' a state post. Another held the post of 'War Commissar,' while the government had a 'Propaganda Department,' a Party function. Actually there was not much difference at all between the two organizations. Proclamations and decrees were occasionally signed by the Party and sometimes by the Soviet Government."[46]

It was not merely that the CP held power through the soviet, but that it held power outside of it. And even then the Party itself was not all that important; rather, one person was—Peng Pai. Peng never held an official post in the soviet government; he represented only the Central Committee of the Chinese Communist Party in Haifeng. His official post was head of the East River Committee of the CCP. Nonetheless, it was commonly believed that he was the chairman of the soviet.

Peng delivered all the major speeches at meetings of the soviet and presided over the soviet court, even though he was not a member. Despite the formal government structure, it was clear to at least one observer, the Korean Communist Kim San, that the real nature of political power in Haifeng rested on the cult of Peng Pai: "This Soviet government was actually a 'democratic dictatorship,' and Peng understood how to manage this form of government. He was a revolutionary dictator with plenary powers, but he derived these from the consent of the people. They followed his line by persuasion, not force. There was no party dictatorship, but one executive close to the people, who carried out their will; he led the people and they followed him."[47]

Political power in Haifeng had neither an elective nor a bureaucratic basis. Peng Pai held political power not by virtue of election to the soviet nor by virtue of his position in the Communist party bureaucracy—he held it by virtue. Political power was based on the cult of Peng Pai: the soviet and the Party received their powers from Peng Pai, not vice versa. Far from weakening since 1926, the cult of Peng Pai had become stronger. There was a difference between the real nature of political power and the power structure presumed to exist in Haifeng: one was created by the peasants, the other by their leaders. Clearly, there were two quite different interpretations of what was being created in Haifeng during the fall and winter of 1927.

Land Revolution

If the actual nature of political power was not commensurate with the formal democratic ideals of a soviet, neither was the economic and political program congruous with the historical task envisioned for a soviet—that of overseeing "the transformation of the democratic revolution of workers and peasants into the socialist revolution." The immediate task of the Haifeng Soviet, carying out the "land revolution," was not a socialist measure at all, but properly belonged to the period of the bourgeois-democratic revolution. But since the agent of that revolution, the Guomindang, had become a reactionary power protecting landlord interests, the party of the proletariat, the Chinese Communist Party, assumed that it had to carry out these tasks.

The CCP was not the only Communist party to have faced this seeming paradox: the Russian Bolsheviks had confronted a similar dilemma following the March Revolution when no other political party would take up the peasants' demand for land. As Rosa Luxemburg wrote of the Bolshevik land policy, "Surely the solution of the problem by the direct, immediate seizure and distribution of land by the peasants was the shortest, simplest, most clean-cut formula to achieve two diverse things: to break down large land ownership, and immediately to bind the peasants to the revolutionary government." But Luxemburg warned that the slogan "Go and take the land for yourselves" had "in general nothing at all in common with socialist economy." By confirming the landownership of small-holding peasants, she argued, the Bolshevik land policy created conditions for peasant opposition to the socialization of agriculture. Luxemburg insisted that a socialist transformation of agriculture had to include both the nationalization of large and middle-sized estates and the union of industry and agriculture.[48]

The Chinese Communist Party under the new leadership of Qu Qiubai had assumed that local uprisings, such as the one in Haifeng as well as those in the cities, would soon consolidate at least provincial-wide revolutionary bases. But CCP members did not recognize—at least, not openly—that the land revolution carried out under the slogan "Land to the Peasants" could become an obstacle to the ultimate socialist transformation of the economy. To be sure, the Communist party had had little experience with confiscating and distributing land, and even the limited experience it did have had been circumscribed by military considerations and limited to paper proclamations. Little was actually done. During the Land Committee meetings of the Left-Guomindang in Wuhan, it was generally thought that land could be easily expropriated, except for that belonging to army officers. Little concern was expressed for what socialist agriculture might look like. And even after the Nanchang Uprising when the Ye-He armies had decided to confiscate the land of landlords having over 200 mou, Guangdong peasants among the troops grumbled that that was as good as nothing. Although the limit was later lowered to 50 mou, the CCP subsequently felt that even this had been a mistake, since the peasants still did not flock to the support of the Ye-He army. The land policy of the CCP thus had been based almost exclusively on military expediency and attempts to attract peasant support, not on the promise of the socialist transformation of agriculture.[49]

When the Haifeng Representative Assembly met from 18 to 21 November, the primary problem discussed was the land revolution. A resolution on the confiscation and redistribution of land was submitted for the discussion and approval of the peasant-dominated assembly. The four major points of the resolution were

1. To burn all land deeds and rental contracts;

2. To destroy all field markers which hinder peasant work so that landlords will not know the location of their land;

3. To issue land-use certificates to peasants from the soviet government;

4. To redistribute the land.

Although peasants immediately accepted the provisions to burn all land deeds and rental contracts and to issue land-use certificates, they had many questions concerning points 2 and 4. Peasants asked how the field boundaries should be broken down, and when it should be done. Rather than attempt to set standardized regulations, the assembly agreed that each village soviet would decide which boundaries to destroy, but that it should be accomplished by mid-November on the lunar calendar.[50]

The problem of the means of land redistribution was much more complicated. The delegates discussed the issues of landless peasants and agricultural workers who did not rent any land, peasants who had a little surplus of land and either let it out or hired labor, fluctuations in family size, frequency of land redistribution (annually, biennually, or triennually), and the rate of taxation for public expenditures. Once again, the assembly decided that the village soviets should carry out the actual redistribution, but along guidelines proposed by Peng Pai and accepted by the assembly—according to the number of people in each family, according to the capacity for work of each member, depending on the family's nonagricultural sources of income, according to soil fertility—with periodic redistributions initiated by a majority vote of the village soviet. The assembly also decided to levy a 10 percent tax on the crop for soviet expenditures.[51]

Acting on these suggestions by Peng Pai, peasants carried out the "land revolution." The real power to make the crucial decisions of who got how much land, based on family size and land fertility, rested with the village peasant unions. How equitably these decisions were made depended in part on who controlled the villages unions. As William Hinton has shown in great detail for Long Bow village, inequitable distributions rendered land reform ineffective in satisfying peasant demands and keeping poor peasants and agricultural workers active in the revolution. When middle or rich peasants controlled the process, the revolutionary spirit of other peasants waned. Unfortunately, there is little information available to judge who controlled the village peasant unions in Haifeng, and that which is available is contradictory. One source claims that the village unions were composed mainly of tenant and poor peasants who pushed for the confiscation and redistribution of the land not only of landlords, but of freeholders as well, so that freeholders were allocated land on the same basis as everyone else.[52] Another source, however, claims that "agricultural and poor peasants had too little influence on the course of business of the unions." According to this account, "the distribution of land was carried out in different ways in various villages. Mostly, however, all village land was lumped together and then distributed to peasant families according to the number of able-bodied members. In villages where possible, land was apportioned for the care of the elderly and orphans."[53] Whoever controlled the process, by the end of January 1928, land redistribution in Haifeng was complete. Peasants tore up field markers and burned 471,088 land deeds and 58,027 rent books.[54]

Where land distribution had been completed, the institutions and world outlook peasants were creating hardly had a socialist aura. Peasants destroyed field boundaries and fences not merely to make later redistribution easier, but also to make it difficult for lords to reclaim their lands should they return. Peasants similarly hoped that the destruction of land deeds would make a return to old property relations impossible. Although the old land system was destroyed, making it at least possible for some to engage in cooperative or collective agriculture, only one village in northern Haifeng established a collective farm. In fact, rural Haifeng had come to resemble more a medieval European village, with its annual redivision of land, notions of equity, and absence of privately owned land, than a society in the process of socialist transformation. Rather than pointing to a future of large-scale, mechanized, and collective agriculture, the Representative Assembly resolution on the confiscation of land looked back to the nearly universal peasant longing for a world without lords. Echoing the old European peasant saying, "When Adam delved and Eve span, where then was the gentleman," the Haifeng resolution declared that "land is in the realm of nature. . . . How is it that some people can call themselves lords of the land?"[55]

The secular struggle over land was not the only manifestation of the rural revolution, for there was a strong religious undercurrent as well. Just prior to the November uprising, for example, Lin Daowen, a leader of the Peasant Army, saw a large group of peasants in a procession to a Buddhist temple, holding up a basket and burning incense. The pilgrims told Lin that they were going to ask the Bodhisattva to send troops to Haifeng to help them. While peasants destroyed Confucian temples and icons as well as the temples and gods of powerful landlord lineages, the centers of folk religion—Buddhist and Daoist temples—were not touched.[56]

The Representative Assembly which proclaimed the soviet also was laden with religious ritual and symbolism. When assembly meetings began, the representatives and spectators bowed three times to the flag of the Communist International and to the pictures of Marx and Lenin. And by sheer historical accident, the flags and banners that covered Haifeng were quite naturally revolutionary red, a color traditionally considered most auspicious. Accompanied by lion dances, singing, and ecstatic drum beating, peasants celebrated the assembly as if it were the New Year. As Peng Pai told the thousands in attendance: "In past New Years, our peasant brothers had no rice, no firewood, no honey, no pork. Without money, they sat on the street begging. . . . This great Representative Assembly . . . has now been called to carry out the land revolution. . . . This New Year is greater than all those in the past. From now on every day is New Year's Day!"[57] In a sense, then, the revolution changed even time itself.

Religious convictions also led to violence and a gruesome end for a colony of lepers. Two or three hundred lepers had gathered on the coast near the English Presbyterian Mission hospital in Shanwei, where some wealthy community members had built shelters and had given them wasteland to till. But the overwhelming majority of lepers depended on alms from merchants and rich families. Some also had collected rent for Christianized landlords, who probably thought they were showing charity by giving lepers work. Besides, peasants would not argue with a leper. When landlords and the wealthy fled Haifeng, no one remained to give them alms. So when they then began begging in the villages, peasants killed some lepers, evidently not out of the old fear of contracting leprosy, for to kill them required getting quite close, but rather out of the belief that lepers, both as lepers and representatives of Christians, were sources of pollution in their new world. When rumor got back to the colony that villagers planned to immolate them, the lepers committed mass suicide.[58]

The Haifeng Soviet

Revolutionary Justice

The Haifeng peasants' age-old dream of a world without lords was being fulfilled as they destroyed nearly every vestige of landlord property rights. And this included landlords themselves. Right after seizing power, the Provisional Revolutionary Government allowed peasants three days to settle accounts with lords, and many lords were executed. Following these more or less spontaneous executions, the soviet established a Revolutionary Court to hear evidence and pass judgement on those accused of being counterrevolutionaries. By the end of January, nearly two thousand landlords and other declared counterrevolutionaries had been executed. The number actually killed certainly exceeded this official total, as even the CCP admitted that "there were, of course, certain excesses and unnecessary atrocities committed by peasants in certain localities contrary to the policy and directives of the Party organizations."[59] But then it had been the peasants of Haifeng, not the Party, who had made the revolution. Table 5 reproduces a page from Haifeng's Newgate Calendar indicating that as late as February 1928, the executions continued.

Table 5: Executions in Haifeng's Third District, 15 February 1928

Name	Age	Sex	Address	Indictment
Lin Yasen	23	M	Guifeng	Murderer, rent collector
Lin Liangyu	53	M	Guifeng	Son member of counter-revolutionary group
Lin Yabo	20	M	Guifeng	Member of counter-revolutionary group
Lin Yayi	46	M	Guifeng	Gentry
Yang Yahua	19	M	Zunyi	Public Security Bureau
Yang Daxia	48	M	Zunyi	Warlock, rent collector
Yang Yabian	42	M	Zunyi	Prohibited son from joining youth corps
Zhong Mazhu	35	F	Jimucao	Murderess
Lin Mashui	28	M	Bucai	Paid rent
Lin Liangtian	58	M	Bucai	Too old to work

Source: Guomin geming jun di shiliu shi zhengzhi xunlian chu, *Hailufeng ping gong ji* (Suppressing Communists in Hailufeng) (Guangzhou, 1928), pp. 95–96.

259

The terror and executions raise the question asked of every revolution since the Jacobin Terror of the French Revolution about the cost and necessity of revolution. Although Barrington Moore, Jr., has raised the issue above the level of pure hysteria by pointing out the human costs to a society of going without revolution,[60] the problem is more complicated in the case of a revolution which ultimately fails, as did the Haifeng movement. And it is further complicated because in Haifeng, peasants not only executed a few thousand, but mutilated and tortured many more as well.

One way of looking at this violence is to place it in the context of collective action. Charles Tilly has argued that collective violence arises out of the same processes that produce collective *nonviolent* action.[61] We have often seen how peasant collective action began peacefully, only to become violent in the course of events. In all the forms of collective behavior that we have investigated here, a similar pattern can be observed: one group staked a claim to resources controlled by another group, whether it was Flag against Flag, lineage against lineage, peasant against state, or peasant against landlord. Food riots, for instance, began as peasants gathered to press their claims for assured local supplies of food at fair prices upon government officials and merchants. If violence occurred, it was because the state used force to disperse the gathering, or because the demands being raised were not met by the authorities. In other instances as well, collective action spilled over into collective violence only when the state or landlords reacted violently to claims made by peasants. In the Zhu Mo affair in 1923, six thousand peasants gathered peacefully in Haifeng city to demand the release of six of their members from jail. The magistrate did not use force to disperse the crowd, so no violence occurred on this occasion. Similar actions following the August 1923 typhoon, on the other hand, did result in violence. Peasants felt they had a right to rent reductions and refused to pay when a rent collector came to the village. The magistrate sent troops the next day, precipitating violence. When peasants then gathered peacefully to protest this violation of rights and to demonstrate their claims to a rent re-

duction, the magistrate waited until the next morning to un-
leash soldiers and militia on peasants and the peasant unions.
From 1925 to early 1927, when state power was in hands
sympathetic to peasants, there was much collective action, but
little violence. Peasants in "Little Moscow" held mass demonstrations, parades, and other expressions of solidarity or
claims of rights that did not result in violence.

It is clear that the state more often than not initiated violence by using force to disperse groups of peasants who had
gathered peacefully to claim a right. Violence occurred when
the state or landlords rejected those claims, choosing instead
to enforce their own claims. Violence, then, arose from the
interaction of groups with conflicting claims. Those resisting
more often than not were the state or landlords; those making
the claims were peasants. Furthermore, peasants saw their
claims not as new impositions, but as traditional rights that
had been respected in the past and should be respected in the
present.

Since 1926, peasants had been making claims for the land.
Peasants asked how it was that landlords, not they, had come
to own and control the land in the first place. In a Proudhonian
answer not far from the truth, peasants believed that landlords
had stolen the land from their ancestors. The landlord claims
to the land were no longer legitimate; their's were. When Peng
Pai then proclaimed during the establishment of the soviet that
"land belongs to the peasants," he merely articulated the peasants' wish to reclaim their birthright. The issue no longer was
how to share the produce of the land fairly, but who could
control the land itself.[62]

When the struggle reached this point, landlords had three
choices: to give up their claim to the land and receive a land
use certificate like everyone else; to flee; or to stay and resist
peasant claims. Only the last course of action resulted in violence. Perhaps those landlords who elected to stay in Haifeng
thought they could outlast the soviet.

Their chances were slim. Within Haifeng itself, all organized forms of opposition had been overcome by mid-November. The last outpost had been Jiesheng, and that fell just as

the soviet was being proclaimed. After that, all opposition was organized outside of Haifeng. To be overthrown, the soviet had to be invaded from outside. No attempts even were made until late January 1928.

Enemies of the Soviet

Ever since landlords fled Haifeng for the safety of Guangzhou, Shantou, Xiamen, or Hong Kong, they had issued plea after plea to General Li Jishen to topple the soviet and to suppress the "peasant bandits." But as long as Li had his hands tied with what he perceived to be the greater threat of the "Ironside Army" of General Zhang Fakui, he was unwilling to commit troops to Haifeng. His priorities were clear. That meant that any expeditionary force sent against Haifeng had to be organized by the exiled landlords themselves. The only attempt was launched in January by Zhong Xiunan. Sometime in December 1927, Zhong had arrived in Huangbu, a coastal market town west of Haifeng in Huiyang county. No doubt with funds collected from refugee landlords in Hong Kong, Zhong made plans with Cai Tenghui to invade Haifeng. Although Cai's base of operations was in Huiyang, he had been drawn into Haifeng earlier, in April 1927, when Liu Bingcui had been looking for armed forces capable of occupying Haifeng. Zhong Xiunan's visit provided another opportunity.

Striking quickly on 28 January, Cai's forces occupied Chishi, driving the three hundred or so defenders toward Meilong. Informed of Cai's advance, a thousand troops of Ye Yong's Red Army left Haifeng city for Meilong. On 29 January, the combined Communist forces headed west toward Chishi. In the meantime, Cai's expedition headed east toward Meilong, guided by a dozen or so members of the Meilong Lin lineage. The opposing armies met in a fierce two-hour battle on a plain west of Meilong. Cai was soundly defeated, and as he hastily retreated, peasants harrassed his troops from the hills.[63]

Zhong Xiunan observed later that he and Cai had met a solid wall of peasant resistance when they entered Haifeng. "Who would have known," he told the landlord refugees in Hong Kong, "that when we got into Haifeng, peasants everywhere would make it so hard on us." He told about freshly fortified villages, the hatred of peasants toward them, and how "when our army was in retreat, villagers on all sides attacked us."[64] In Haifeng, there were no Flags, lineages, or other social groups that would give landlords support. As even Zhong realized, Haifeng was cleanly divided along class lines.

The same was not true of Lufeng county, where opposition to the soviet was expressed earlier than in Haifeng. More than one observer had commented that Lufeng was generally more backward than Haifeng. Even one unsympathetic to the peasants remarked that "if Haifeng was a semi-feudal society, then Lufeng was a full-fledged feudal society."[65] Lufeng had never experienced the commercialization of agriculture and expansion of marketing systems that had so greatly altered rural class relations in Haifeng in the late nineteenth and early twentieth centuries. The reason is not hard to find. Lufeng simply was too far from the port of Shanwei for the commercializing influences emanating from there to have had much effect on the rural society and economy. Not surprisingly, in socioeconomic terms, Lufeng in 1927 looked much like Haifeng of 1877. Not only were lineage organizations powerful, but the Flag societies were still very active.

When Haifeng's Red Army marched into Lufeng just after the Haifeng Soviet had been established, it entered a world in which rural struggle was still primarily factional strife, not class warfare. According to one report, for example, "when the Red Army arrived flying red banners, the troops were greeted by landowners and peasants alike from Red Flag villages who thought they were allies in the struggle against the common enemy, the Black Flag villages."[66] Recognizing that the villagers had rallied to the right flag for the wrong reasons, Communists informed skeptical peasants of the goals of the land revolution. "This propaganda was not always so skillfully conducted," cadre reported, "and in some cases did not lead to the desired results."[67] One wonders if under these conditions any propaganda, skillful or otherwise, would have led to the "desired results."

The Haifeng Soviet

The police chief of Jiazi knew that traditional Red and Black Flag hostilities could be turned against the new "Red Flags," and spent most of December organizing a disparate group of these people into the anti-Communist "White Flags." Jiazi was a coastal fortress in easternmost Lufeng that had served since late Ming times for coastal defense. It was not an agricultural area, and most of the people were engaged in salt production, the salt trade, and various kinds of protection rackets. With profits from the salt business, local leaders had long been able to command the talents of the underworld, and they were able to do so again. In mid-December, more anti-Communist troops arrived in Jiazi, having been driven earlier from Jiesheng by Peng Pai and the Red Army. Their commander, Chen Zihe, was a leader of the ten-thousand-strong Chen lineage of Beihu, a large village complex some fifteen miles east of Lufeng city. All of the Chen belonged to the Black Flags, and Chen Zihe was willing to enlist their help in defeating the Communists. When Chen slipped back to his village to recruit fighters, he also contacted leaders of Red Flag villages, who by then knew that the Red Army was not really a Red Flag. They too agreed to fight the Communists. Returning to Jiazi, the Red Flags, Black Flags, and the criminal underworld trained together under the White Flag.[68]

On Monday, 8 January, the White Flag flew west out of Jiazi. Meeting little resistance as they marched through Nantang and Bomei markets, the White Flag troops surprised the defenders of Lufeng and took the city on Thursday. They held Lufeng for two days. Only when reinforcements arrived did the Fourth Red Army drive the White Flags back to their walled fortress, where they withstood all subsequent attempts to dislodge them. In the midst of the fighting, Chen Zihe and the White Flags received the assistance of the Long Hair Party, whose peasant members attacked the Red Army waving fans, burning incense, and doing their ritual dance.[69]

The situation was just as complex in northernmost Lufeng, where lineages reigned supreme and lineage conflict superseded all others.[70] Travel between northern Lufeng, which was separated from the coastal plains by low mountains, and the more densely populated south was confined to one or two trails. But in the mountainous north, neither lineages nor villages were small—they were just isolated. Indeed, it was here that populous and powerful lineages, ranging from a few thousand to several tens of thousands, lived almost exclusively in single-lineage villages. The Pengs, a large and socially differentiated lineage of perhaps thirty thousand people, controlled the market town of Hetian and inhabited nearly every village in the surrounding area. While most members tilled the land, the Peng also had long-established ties to officialdom: the first imperial degree was won in the sixteenth century, and members continued to hold degrees into the twentieth. The next strongest lineage, at least until the nineteenth century, was the Ye. The Ye also had degree-holding members, and in 1726 even produced a *jinshi* scholar. Following the Ye came the Zhuang, Luo, and Zhu, all lineages with about seven thousand members.

Thoughout most of the Qing period there had been a recognized pecking order among these lineages, with the Peng at the top and the rest following. But in the nineteenth century, the Zhuang of Shangsha, the northernmost market in Lufeng, challenged the existing order, and by the twentieth century began pressing the Peng for superiority, having already replaced the Ye as the second most powerful. In 1858, the Zhuang had compelled a tenant lineage of the Ye to pay rent to them instead of the Ye, and had successfully escaped prosecution, even though they did not have official connections. Throughout the rest of the century the Zhuang apparently continued their aggressive expansion, for by the 1920s they were reported in possession of Wuyundong, a village that had been a Peng village since the seventeenth century.

When peasant organizers began working the area in 1925, they had little success. Peasant loyalty remained with the lineage, and peasants still considered other lineages the enemy. The Zhuang and Luo lineages especially put up armed resistance to keep the union organizers out, and relented only when they encountered an armed force led by a Peng. Peng Pai, at the request of the activists, in late 1925 sent a contingent of the Peasant Self-Defense Army to aid the organizing drive. Leaders of the Peng lineage, pressed by the Zhuang for some time, saw an opportunity to reverse some of their losses, and when asked to join the Peasant Union, eagerly agreed. Lineage warfare then resumed at a renewed pitch. The Peng first raided Shangsha, kidnapped several Zhuang, and wrested their ancestral village of Wuyundong back from Zhuang hands. Next they turned their attention south to Jianmen, razing houses and temples of the Luo lineage, who had apparently allied with the Zhuang. Throughout 1927 and into the period of the soviet, the feud continued as each side sought retribution. Armed opposition in these northernmost valleys of Lufeng was not directed against the soviet *per se*: armed struggle just continued as before over issues and animosities centuries old. The only difference was that the Communists had made an alliance with the Peng lineage, which then was dubbed a revolutionary force. This was hardly the case. The Peng lineage remained an elite-directed social organization that continued to feud with other lineages. The only thing that distinguished the Peng is that it was a previously large and powerful lineage that was on the defensive. That it had the same surname as Peng Pai, and may even have been very distantly related to him, no doubt made it easier for them to cooperate with the Communists.

In Lufeng county during the 1920s, then, collective action was still patterned by the localistic concerns of marketing system–based social organizations of lineages and Flags. This factionalized environment was not very conducive to Communist organizing. Both Red and Black Flag organizations rebuffed the Communists, who were able to ally only with one declining lineage that conveniently shared Peng Pai's surname. The Flag and lineage organizations were woven into the socioeconomic fabric of Lufeng, and no amount of outside organization or agitation could break that pattern. Strands here and there might come loose, but the patterns of collective action and violence in Lufeng remained much the same as they had been for decades.

In Haifeng county, by contrast, these older patterns had passed from the scene. Changing socioeconomic patterns—a reformist-gentry landlord class divorced from the countryside, the sugar market crash, the destruction of traditional forms of tenure—had given rise to class, not factional, conflicts. In addition, by early 1928, Peng Pai and the peasant unions had provided peasants with five years of experience in acting together to pursue their interests. With Haifeng devoid of all factional conflict, but clearly divided along class lines, it is not surprising that landlords could find no cleavages to exploit in order to gain support. A wall of resistance had risen up when Zhong Xiunan and Cai Tenghui led a landlord army into Haifeng. No one supported them. The lesson that Zhong drew from his experience was that only a much larger force—maybe all of the rural militia from Huiyang county, or maybe a regular army—could subdue the Haifeng Soviet.

Internal Problems

After meeting the threat posed by the White Flags and turning back Zhong Xiunan's challenge, the Haifeng Soviet should have been in a strong position. The leadership was so confident of its strength that it was reported to have boasted: "We invite the enemy to come down here!"[71] As if to tempt them, Peng Pai led an army east into Puning and Huilai counties at the beginning of February 1928 to extend the base of Soviet power. The decision to defend Haifeng against all outside threats, however, had been made only in early January. Earlier, such resolve and confidence was not apparent. As a fiasco known as the "December 28 Incident" clearly demonstrates, the Communist leadership more than a month after the soviet was formed had been prepared to evacuate to the hills at the first sign of enemy troops.

On the morning of 28 December 1927 Peng Pai received a telegram from Zheng Zhiyun, who was in Lufeng at the Peng lineage stronghold of Hetian, warning of the approach of six hundred enemy troops. Peng called an emergency meeting of the East River Special Committee of the CCP and decided to evacuate. That afternoon, members of the East River Committee and "other organs" left for a safe place in the mountains. Soon it was learned that it was a false alarm, and Peng and the others returned on December 30. The bad omens had only begun. During a New Year's Day meeting to celebrate a "Red New Year" and to explain that the retreat really had been an attempt to "deceive the enemy," the red flag of the peasant union suddenly fell down. Startled, the crowd rushed from the square, trampling several women and children in the crush.[72]

Communist party members feared that peasants' reaction to the falling flag showed that their faith in the Communist leadership had been shaken. They were at least partially right. In Haifeng, there actually were two Communist party organizations: the County Committee, headed by Chen Shunyi, and the East River Committee, headed by Peng Pai. The East River Committee had its headquarters in the Longshan Temple near Peng's house. This was where the original peasant union had its headquarters, which, it will be recalled, had been raided and shut down in 1923 by Wang Zuoxin. The East River Committee had few members, but they were all familiar names long associated with Peng and Haifeng. The County Committee, by contrast, had its headquarters in town, was led by a native of Zhejiang province, had other members who were outsiders as well, and was more interested in organizing workers than peasants. It was the County Committee, not Peng Pai and the East River Committee, that was most disturbed by the December 28 Incident and what it believed to be the consequences.

In order to remedy the harm it thought had been done to Communist leadership of the masses, the County Committee called a plenary session for 22–23 January. The County Committee no doubt also wanted to gain some control over the Communist party membership, which had exploded from 700 in April 1927 to 11,500 by January 1928. Most of these new members were peasants, whom Chen Shunyi and his more orthodox County Committee looked upon rather suspiciously in any case. The plenary session, Chen thought, would be a good opportunity to instill some discipline into this rather unorthodox Communist party. At first glance, the plenary session appeared to be an exemplar of Communist organizational skill. The membership was divided into groups of 50, each of which was to elect a representative, for a total of 230 delegates to the session. The delegates were to be given reports on the December 28 Incident, the leadership would offer self-criticism, and then the delegates would offer their criticism. This would draw the members into the decision-making process and make them feel even more a part of the organization. Filled with revolutionary vigor, the delegates then would return to their villages, unity would be strengthened, and Communist leadership of the masses would be reaffirmed.[73] Communist leadership of the masses is always supposed to go that way. But things didn't turn out quite as planned. Peasants it seems, just didn't seem to know that they were supposed to be "astonished" by Communist organizational skills.

The election of delegates proceeded without problem, and the sessions opened as scheduled with reports by representatives of the East River Committee (Peng Pai), the County Committee (Chen Shunyi), and the Guangdong Provincial Committee. Presumably these reports contained some self-criticism. Some delegates then offered criticisms, such as "the East River Committee failed to pay attention to intelligence work," "the East River Committee was afraid," or "the County Committee failed in leadership." According to the County Committee, at this point things were going pretty much as planned, and "the revolutionary spirit was especially high." But when the East River Committee and Peng Pai came in for criticism, probably from members of the County Committee, Peng Pai shot back counterarguments in a most unexpected manner. Thereafter, no one except a few intellectuals was willing to offer any more criticism of Peng.

This was particularly galling to Chen Shunyi and the County Committee. The County Committee later complained bitterly to their higher-ups about Peng Pai and the peasant makeup of the Communist party in Haifeng. They charged that some delegates had been Party members for as little as twenty days before the plenary session, some slept through meetings, others left without telling anyone, and many simply didn't pay attention. But worst of all, peasants simply refused to criticize Peng Pai. The County Committee attributed this to the delegates' "feudal ideas" and irrational but "complete faith in Peng Pai." Furthermore, peasants were downright "hostile to the County Committee."[74]

If the worker-oriented County Committee had little support among peasants, Peng Pai emerged from "December 28 Incident" and the 22–23 January meetings with his reputation intact. Not only that, peasants shifted all the blame for the "December 28 Incident," the falling flag, and anything else that could go wrong, to the County Committee. It was a convenient separation. Peasants could attribute every success and everything good to Peng Pai, and every failure or problem to Chen Shunyi and the County Committee. Peasants still believed in Peng Pai, and the cult of Peng Pai remained strong. Indeed, it is doubtful that anything could have shaken peasant faith in Peng Pai or undermined the cult. Even after the soviet was crushed and Zhong Xiunan's armies were sweeping through the countryside, peasants still called him "Peng Pusa, the one who saves the poor from suffering and hardship."[75]

By the end of January, Haifeng seemed secure. Land had been distributed, attempts to overthrow the soviet repulsed, and Peng Pai's standing among peasants was untarnished. But under the surface, economic problems cropped up. The soviet, by its very existence, had severed Haifeng's economy not only from the rest of Guangdong, but even from neighboring counties as well. This caused severe strains. For well over a century, and perhaps longer, Haifeng had been integrated into a broader economic network. Agricultural and forest products had been exported up the coast to the Chaozhou-Shantou region, and down the coast to Hong Kong and Guangzhou. In return, all sorts of commodities were imported, including daily necessities and raw materials for the various industries in Haifeng and Shanwei. In addition, Haifeng was part of the capitalist world economy, as Peng Pai reminded his audience in November when the soviet had proclaimed: "Take a look at your clothes, everyone, and see how much comes from England. How much stuff in your pockets comes from England?"[76] The point was simple: Haifeng's economy could not exist in isolation from the rest of the world.

During the first month or so of the soviet, economic conditions seemed good. The harvest was just in, the peasants didn't have to pay rent. Believing that they would have large surpluses and sufficient cash reserves, peasants had gone on a spending spree. But from then on, trade gradually ground to a halt as local stocks of goods were depleted. Besides problems encountered in the fish and salt trade, supplies of manufactured goods and raw materials used in Haifeng's industries dried up, as trade with Hong Kong became more difficult. In January, the soviet tried to resolve the economic problems caused by shortages. Running a weekly voyage to Hong Kong, the soviet organized the direct purchase of manufactured goods and some foodstuffs from Hong Kong.[77]

This trade was not sufficient to stimulate the economy and generate the revenues necessary to run the government and pay the soldiers. Besides, the soviet needed a source of "foreign exchange" even to begin trading in Hong Kong for daily necessities and ammunition. But the greatest need for revenue was to get agricultural production going again. Replacing the thousand or so draft animals and repairing the irrigation works and roads, not to mention rebuilding the destroyed buildings and granaries, would require huge amounts of money. Estimates after the suppression of the soviet indicated that 750,000 yuan was needed for the job (one buffalo alone cost about 60 yuan).[78] The soviet was hardly able to raise that kind of capital from its own meager resources.

The soviet government initially had at its disposal a considerable amount of funds that had come from the confiscation of the goods and specie of the wealthy. But by early 1928, the soviet faced problems affecting both government revenues and the economic life of the populace. Although the government knew that its monthly expenses amounted to about 19,000 yuan, it had not felt the need to establish an accounting system. In January, its leaders suddenly discovered that they had an income of only 7,300 yuan.[79]

In the face of these mounting problems, the workaday world reasserted itself, cooling the chiliastic expectations that had fueled the revolution. With the inexorable turn of the annual agricultural cycle, peasants' thoughts turned to the spring planting. The fields had to be plowed and harrowed, manure collected and spread, shoots prepared and transplanted, and tools repaired and tested. In Haifeng, where field markers and irrigation works had been destroyed, peasants demanded order in property and water rights. And in Lufeng, peasants resisted land redistribution because, they complained, it interfered with spring planting.[80] Where was the new world? Where was the perpetual New Year?

These questions might have caused peasants to doubt that Peng Pai could lead them out of their hardship and suffering. He had promised them a new world with electricity and running water for their homes, tractors for their farms, schools for their children, and museums for their cultural development. He had even shown them the way to get there—seize and divide the land, drive away landlords, and burn rental books and deeds. These things they had done. But by February, things seemed to be getting worse, not better. Why didn't Peng Pai do something? He couldn't; he wasn't in Haifeng.

One week after the 22–23 January plenary session, Peng Pai led troops of the Fourth Red Army east into Huilai and Puning counties. The peasants of Puning had long held Peng Pai in high esteem, having called him the "Eternal One" (*wan-sui*) in 1926 when he helped them deal with the Fang lineage landlords. He could expect support in this area, and he got it. In the middle of February, the Puning Soviet was formed. A few days later, the Red Army attacked and captured the market town of Kuitan in Huilai county, a stronghold of Long Hair Party support.

Peng Pai would remain in Huilai and Puning counties until May 1928 before trying to return to Haifeng. But by then the Haifeng Soviet would be crushed, and his attempt to seize Haifeng would be thwarted by the occupying Guomindang troops. In the critical month of February, then, when serious economic problems cropped up, and when later in the month

GMD troops attacked in large numbers, Peng Pai was not in Haifeng. From the perspective of peasants, how could he have had anything to do with these things? Wouldn't things have been all right if Peng had remained in Haifeng? Peasants had good reason to think that others were responsible for their problems. On 10 February, shortly after Peng Pai left Haifeng, it was announced that the Haifeng Soviet had been reorganized into the Haifeng Soviet People's Government. The stated reason for the change was that a new stage in the revolution had been reached—the stage of socialist reconstruction—and that new governmental institutions were needed to oversee this new stage. Actually, this "reorganization" had all the earmarks of a power seizure, or maybe even a coup, by Chen Shunyi and the County Committee. According to documents issued by the new Soviet People's Government, Chen Shunyi and twenty-four others had been elected at a "Second Representative Assembly." Perhaps—but it certainly had been kept a secret. Compared to the first one, which had 311 delegates and 50,000 observers to proclaim the soviet, the second one was very quiet indeed. No record of its deliberations exists, no mention of delegate selection is made in any documents, and no mass meetings were held in conjunction with it. The only record is the one issued after the fact. In addition, only three members of the original Soviet Executive Committee of thirteen reappeared as members of the second one.[81]

The leaders of the new soviet considered themselves representatives of workers, not of peasants. Chen Shunyi was a labor movement organizer to begin with and, as was clear in the 22–23 January plenary session, held peasants in contempt. Chen and others felt that the first soviet leadership, concerned mainly with peasants and the "land revolution," had ignored workers and their problems. According to one document written in May 1928, after the November seizure of power workers faced serious problems that the soviet did not address. When owners of the textile mills fled, the plants shut down. Artisans who depended on the business of the wealthy likewise lost employment because of the flight or execution of their patrons.

And for all workers, raw materials that had been imported from Hong Kong or elsewhere were no longer available. In short, workers were unemployed, and the leaders of the first soviet government, in Chen's view, had not done anything about it.[82]

Unemployment was not the only problem facing the second soviet leadership. The financial footing of the government was shaky, larger economic problems were looming, and the military had to be enlarged. To deal with these problems, the new soviet government created several bureaus, such as the Economic, Construction, Military Affairs, Commerce, and Communication bureaus.[83] No doubt this reorganization also was designed to correct the earlier confusion between state and party organizations.

To stimulate the economy and to finance the state and military, Chen and the new soviet leaders issued their own money. On 20 February, just nine days before Guomindang troops descended on Haifeng, the soviet announced that the "Labor Bank" was open for business. Since the bank had not had time to print its own money, it issued chits that had been used by the Nanfeng Textile Mill. The soviet leaders hoped to obtain hard cash for the paper money in order to buy supplies outside of Haifeng, especially ammunition. These chits were declared legal tender, and anyone refusing to honor them was to be considered a counterrevolutionary and shot. Despite the threat of executions, the chits were not accepted, and this effort collapsed. The soviet leaders then confiscated stocks of salt and other goods to barter directly for the increasingly crucial ammunition.[84]

By this time, reports that GMD troops were poised to descend on Haifeng had been confirmed. To bolster its defenses, the soviet needed more recruits for the army. In order to gain volunteers, the soviet set aside a week for "comforting and supporting the Red Army." In several mass meetings, it was pointed out that the army had fought side-by-side with peasants and that although ever-victorious, it had lost many men. But the plea for volunteers fell on deaf ears. Therefore, on 20 February, the new soviet leaders issued a general conscription order, inducting one-tenth of all males between the ages of eighteen and thirty into the army. But this was not all; the recruits also had to be revolutionary. After the new soviet leaders had been installed, there were reports of soldiers executed for being "insufficiently revolutionary." And on 19 February, the soviet acknowledged that fifty-seven soldiers had deserted.[85]

Of all the dictates coming down from the new soviet leaders, the conscription order was the most onerous to peasants. Spring planting was just beginning, and here was a demand that most productive members of the family be snatched from the fields for military duty. To be sure, the conscription order also included provisions to support peasant families with labor power, loans, free schooling, tax exemptions, and parent funeral expenses. But the burden on peasant families was great, and the quota of 3,500 was not met.[86] One can only wonder whether an appeal direct from Peng Pai would have had greater response.

But Peng was not in Haifeng, and there is more than a hint of desperation in the actions of the new soviet leaders. They tried to lead, but nobody followed. To be sure, the economic and financial problems they faced were formidable. In addition, enemy troops had begun to probe Haifeng's defenses, and on 20 February, four enemy gunboats began patrolling the waters off Haifeng. But the administrative fiats issued to deal with these problems had not been obeyed, so the soviet leaders resorted to terror to force compliance. What this reveals, of course, is that peasants did not follow the orders of the new soviet leaders—and maybe nobody at all did. This is not surprising, since political power in Haifeng never had been based on the control of organizations, mass or otherwise. The form of political power was not the soviet or the Communist party; it was the cult of Peng Pai.

Defeat

The end of the Haifeng Soviet came swiftly. By 26 February, enemy troops had surrounded Haifeng. It was only a question of time before they attacked. The differences between Generals

Li Jishen and Zhang Fakui had been patched up, so all of Guangdong, in the words of a member of the East River Committee, "was under the unified control of reactionary power." Skirmishes with landing parties from the gunboats already had been reported around Shanwei, and soviet leaders knew the commanders and troop strengths of the opposing armies. The defenders thought they had as much as a month's time before the attack began in earnest. There was, they hoped, just enough time to plan for the resistance.

When the invasion began, according to these plans, the Red Army and soviet leaders would melt back into the countryside. In the meantime, a resistance network would be created, starting at the level of the village and working up to the district. The plan was to have an armed and organized populace confronting the occupying forces. When GMD forces attacked, they would be allowed to take the cities, but the countryside would remain in Red Army hands. Villagers would wait for tactical advantages to surround and wipe out enemy units. At the same time, according to the plan, propaganda would be aimed at the enemy soldiers to demoralize them, and any landlords who returned would be captured or killed. Similar tactics had worked after the second seizure of Haifeng city, and soviet leaders were hopeful that they would work again.[87]

They were overly optimistic. In the first place, Li Jishen and Zhang Fakui had stopped fighting, freeing army regulars to be used against Haifeng. Second, Peng Pai had left Haifeng with a detachment of the Red Army, which meant the absence not only of a trained military force but of the peasants' leader as well. And third, Chen Shunyi and the new soviet leaders had squandered whatever support peasants once may have given them. Given all these factors, the deck this time was stacked in the enemy's favor. And to make matters worse, GMD troops attacked sooner than anyone had anticipated, and much sooner than the plan for resistance could be implemented.

On 28 February, just two days after the East River Committee had described the precarious situation to the Provincial Committee and had outlined the resistance plans, GMD troops attacked. Advancing from Jieyang county to the east, two divisions of enemy troops easily took Lufeng city and advanced on to Gongping. Taking that city the next day, the enemy troops pushed immediately to Haifeng city. Preparations for an orderly retreat were rendered useless, and after a disorganized and futile attempt to stop the GMD troops between Gongping and Haifeng, Haifeng fell. Meanwhile, two more GMD divisions attacked from the west and the north. Skirmishes continued for the next few days, and on 6 March, the Red Army launched a counterattack to retake Haifeng. The attempt failed, and hopes for a quick return to power faded. Guomindang forces then went about strengthening their grip first on the towns, and then on the countryside. Communist forces were totally disorganized, dispersing into any village, gully, or hilltop that provided shelter. Some hid out as long as possible; others escaped by land or by sea to Hong Kong or Shanghai.[88]

As GMD military forces widened their scope of attacks in the countryside, landlord forces returned to reestablish their rule. Under the stewardship of Zhong Xiunan, the "Haifeng Reconstruction Committee" submitted plans to Li Jishen's provincial government for rebuilding roads, establishing a bank, and requesting tax remissions and food relief. The major task, however, was the reconstruction of the landlords' economic and political power. With land deeds and field markers destroyed, landlords returning from Hong Kong, Guangzhou, and Shantou had only to pay a five-cent fee to have new deeds issued, after having three neighbors vouch for their ownership. With rights to the land officially secured, landlords had only to collect the produce of the land. As the autumn harvest approached, rent collectors and smaller landlords who ventured into the countryside were ambushed and killed by remaining guerrilla bands. "After this," according to a Guomindang report, "landlords from the towns wanting to collect rent in the villages exercised great care. The county Public Security Bureau, responding to the needs of the citizens, sent ten soldiers with each [rent-collecting landlord]."[89]

Although uncoordinated resistance in the countryside continued throughout the summer and fall of 1928, Zhong Xiunan's strategy of "surrounding the villages and sweeping the hills" began to pay off. Week by week, month by month, military order was clamped on Haifeng. By laying ambushes, using bribery, and holding military supremacy, Guomindang troops and agents soon either killed or arrested and executed most of the leaders of the Haifeng peasants: on 6 July, Lin Tieshi, Peasant Union activist and Peasant Army leader, was captured in battle and executed; on 18 July, Zhang Wei, peasant organizer in Lufeng and chairman of the Lufeng Soviet, was captured and executed; in mid-August, Yang Wang, Peasant Union leader, and Peng Pai's closest aide, was killed in battle; and throughout this period, thousands of nameless peasants were killed defending their homes and families.[90]

Peng Pai had left Haifeng in early February, it will be recalled, leading a detachment of the Red Army east into Puning and Huilai counties. When Guomindang troops attacked Haifeng, Peng was somewhere in Huilai. On 12 March and again on 22 March, his forces attacked and captured Huilai, the second time holding on until 5 April, hoping to draw GMD troops from Haifeng. This stratagem failed, and GMD forces recaptured Huilai as well, driving Peng Pai and his small army into the surrounding mountains. In desperate need of food, ammunition, and money, they made plans to attack Haifeng. Peng remained in the mountain hideout while six hundred soldiers slipped back into Haifeng, mobilizing another two thousand peasants along the way. In the early morning hours of 3 May, they attacked Haifeng. According to Kim San, a Korean Communist with the troops, the goal was not to retake the city, but to sieze the 400,000 yuan that GMD forces reportedly had brought with them, and then to retreat. This failed miserably, and the surviving four hundred soldiers split into smaller groups for the retreat into the mountains.[91]

It took weeks before these groups could pick their way through the mountains to find where Peng Pai and the others had now hid. Along the way, according to Kim San, the bands had adopted a Robin Hood–like existence: "During the daytime we ate in the villages, and hid in the mountains at night. . . . We began partisan warfare against landlords to get food, as the poor people could not support us. We took from the land-lords and distributed to the villagers, so the poor people came to love us very much."[92] Toward the end of May, they found Peng and their other comrades hiding in a cave whose entrance was hidden by a big waterfall. As spring turned into summer, plans were made and remade for various kinds of "uprisings," but nothing much came of them. Peng Pai recuperated from a serious illness and began going into villages at night to do some organizing work. On 29 September 1928, while he and Zheng Zhiyun were in a village, it was surrounded by GMD troops. Zheng was killed, but Peng managed to escape.[93]

Peng had been elected *in absentia* to the Central Committee of the CCP at its Sixth Congress (meeting in the safety of Moscow), and when he was ordered to leave the mountains for clandestine work in Shanghai, he did so. He would not return to Haifeng. After almost a year of work in the Shanghai underground, he was betrayed by a fellow Party member and arrested on 26 August 1929. After positive identification was made, on 30 August Peng Pai was tortured to death in a Shang-hai police station.[94]

The chances of the Haifeng Soviet lasting much longer than it did never were very good from the start. It existed just as long as squabbles between Generals Li Jishen and Zhang Fakui created an opening for peasants and their Communist leaders to take power from weaker local military forces. But as soon as the generals' differences were patched up, the military force thrown against Haifeng crushed the soviet quickly and easily. Clearly, overwhelming military might was the immediate cause of the destruction of the Haifeng Soviet.

But that only begs the question. Why were peasant forces so much weaker than those of their landlord opponents? From a long-term historical perspective, the establishment and defeat of the Haifeng Soviet was the climax of a conflict between classes whose historical development from early Qing times conditioned their twentieth-century struggle. The defeat of the soviet, then, is a question of the relative class strengths of landlords and peasants. As Robert Brenner has argued, the outcomes of rural class conflicts are dependent upon *"historically specific* patterns of development of the contending classes and their relative strength . . . : their relative levels of internal solidarity, their self-consciousness and organization, and their general political resources—especially their relationships to the non-agricultural classes (in particular, potential urban class allies) and to the state . . . ."[95]

On all of these counts, the peasants of Haifeng were weak. To be sure, the moral economy of the Haifeng peasants and their experiences with various forms of collective action provided them with an impressive solidarity when landlords or others transgressed what were considered to be fair and just practices, but these were defensively oriented and designed to maintain the status quo, not change it. The peasants' tenacious defense of the social and economic rights they had won in the early Qing explains the persistence of the smallholding economy for nearly three centuries in the face of tremendous demographic and commercial forces, as well as the source of peasant anger against landlords in the 1920s, but peasant collective action directed toward overthrowing landlordism had to be organized in a form that could overcome the remaining geographic isolation and petty differences that divided peasants: the cult of Peng Pai.

The cult had become the primary form of peasant collective action in Haifeng. Even though Peng Pai himself had recognized that peasant dependence on an outside leader weakened their ability to act for themselves, he had acquiesced in the use of the cult in late 1926 when he came to believe that not to do so would have resulted in the suppression of the revolutionary movement in the countryside. The result was a peasantry that acted not for itself but in the name of Peng Pai. Thus when Peng was not in Haifeng, the Communist party had little success in mobilizing peasant support.

Given the later Communist victory in 1949 and the subsequent celebration of the "Great Revolution of 1925–27," there is a tendency to consider the advances peasants made during those years as a victory. But let there be no mistake: in the class conflicts in Haifeng, it was landlords who won. To be sure, from 1925 to early 1928, the peasants of Haifeng had been on the offensive, having found new urban allies in the working class of Guangzhou and among the young inteligentsia. But with the collapse of the Hong Kong–Guangzhou Strike and Boycott in late 1926 and Jiang Jieshi's coup in April 1927, the peasants of Haifeng became isolated from their urban allies. Haifeng landlords, on the other hand, had developed strong ties to the urban reformist elite of Guangzhou and their counterparts in Haifeng. Indeed, in Haifeng the landlord class shaded imperceptibly into the reformist elite that had emerged around the time of the 1911 Revolution. Thus to overthrow the Haifeng Soviet, Zhong Xiunan traveled back and forth between Hong Kong and Guangzhou using those ties first to raise a small army for an abortive invasion and then to use Li Jishen's Guomindang armies to return Haifeng to landlord rule.

CONCLUSION

PENG PAI and the Haifeng Soviet, from one historical perspective, are the stuff out of which history is made and about which history is written. The documents that chronicle the lives of Peng Pai and his contemporaries, and the events of the memorable 1920s, are filled with the passions, desires, and political intrigues of the moment, and as such are fascinating to read. Histories based on these sources likewise are interesting for what they tell us about a few individuals and their passions, desires, and politics. Whether they tell us anything about rural revolution is questionable. As Theda Skocpol has argued, "It simply will not do . . . to try to decipher the logic of the processes or outcomes of a social revolution by adopting the perspective or following the actions of any one class or elite or organization—no matter how important its participatory role."[1] From this perspective, these documents, lives, and events are like "frail barks," in the words of Fernand Braudel, "tossed like cockleshells" on deeper currents of history "whose direction can only be discerned by watching them over long periods of time. Resounding events are often only momentary outbursts, surface manifestations of these larger movements and explicable only in terms of them."[2] If this study has leaned in any direction, it has been toward a structuralist approach akin to that of Skocpol, strongly tempered by E.P. Thompson's concern for viewing history as "process with people."

The central conclusion that emerges from this approach is that the peasants of Haifeng made their own history: they were not the passive objects of someone else's history. Peasants made the more visible history chronicled in the documentary record—the riots, uprisings, or other types of collective action evident in the 1920s; moreover, through these actions, peasants had a hand in making the very structures that patterned subsequent action as well.

Conclusion

Consider the rural class structure itself. The smallholding characteristic of rural China was not a part of the natural environment. It was made by people. That form was not predetermined, for in the Ming another kind of social order—one dominated by large estates—could have dominated rural China. By fighting for and protecting rights to till the land, peasants laid the foundation for a different order. Holding economic decision-making firmly in their own hands and on their own farms, peasants in the seventeenth and eighteenth centuries settled the question of who would manage the rural economy. From then on, even outright ownership of the land did not confer on landowners the right to remove peasants from the land. It conferred only the right to a certain portion of the produce of the land as rent. And it was this issue—the amount of rent and the terms of tenancy—and not such issues as agricultural labor and wages that was to become the crucial question in Haifeng in the 1920s. It was a legacy of landholding patterns that had emerged in the early Qing.

If the nature of the modern conflict was determined by the seventeenth-century settlement between lords and peasants, the outcome of the conflict itself was not. For the seventeenth-century uprisings created conditions initially favorable not for class conflict but for other forms of rural conflict. The rural marketing systems reinforced factional conflict between lineages, and between Red and Black Flags, by providing a base rooted in the socioeconomic structure, while food riots reflected the endemic conflict between state and society. In both cases, conflict cut across class lines, accentuating other divisions in the countryside. What is interesting and historically significant is that these forms of social conflict began to give way in the second half of the nineteenth century to class conflict as a result of China's integration into the capitalist world market.

The evidence presented here supports the view that the irruption of the capitalist world market into China created socioeconomic conditions favorable for rural revolution. The reason was not, as is sometimes argued, that imperialism caused the peasants' standard of living to fall, creating the rural impoverishment and misery that fueled revolutionary movements. Rather, it was because imperialism changed the rural social structure in certain ways. Just as the fact of a bad harvest only made its impact felt through existing social relations, so too was the impact of imperialism mediated through class structure. To the peasants in Haifeng, the integration of China into the capitalist world market may have seemed a fortuitous event, but the way it worked its consequences out in Haifeng was not. That was determined by the class structure. What it meant initially was that factional conflict between lineages and Flags escalated because of the expansion of marketing systems. Only after the crash of the sugar market, when landlords began to alter the terms of tenancy more to their advantage, and the destruction of handicraft spinning and weaving cut off peasants' sideline income, were the conditions for the emergence of class conflict created. The outcome of that struggle, moreover, was determined, not by imperialism, but by factors which affected the strengths and weaknesses of the contending classes. The ways things worked out, it was landlords who emerged stronger. But as the experience of peasants in the 1911 Revolution demonstrates, they had acquired a certain rough sense of class in the process.

Peasant collective action in all of its forms was embedded in the structure of society. As the rural social structure changed, so too did the forms of collective action. What was significant about rural social conflict in the 1920s was that the combatants were social classes: landlords and peasants. This does not mean that peasant collective action along class rather than factional lines had been the immediate result of changes in rural social structure occasioned by imperialism and the 1911 Revolution. The evidence does not support a determinist explanation of peasant collective action. Mediating structural change and forms of collective action was peasant experience. E. P. Thompson defines human experience "as persons experiencing their determinate productive situations and relationships, as needs and interests and as antagonisms, . . . 'handling' this experience within their *consciousness* and their *culture* in the most complex . . . ways, and then (often but not always through the ensuing structures of class) acting upon their determinate situation in turn."[3]

The way the peasants of Haifeng "handled" their experiences in the first two decades of the twentieth century was in terms of their moral economy. The moral economy of the peasants of Haifeng, it must be emphasized, was a historical phenomenon that had come into being along with the freeholding peasantry. It was a class-based system of values by which peasants judged the actions of others. As James C. Scott has argued, "A study of the moral economy of peasants can tell us what makes them angry and what is likely, other things being equal, to generate an explosive situation."[4] This of course is only part of the story: class structure and the forms of peasant organization also must be considered to explain particular forms of collective action.

Seen from this perspective, the Haifeng peasant movement of the 1920s was a form of peasant collective action that had its roots in the rural class structure and the historical experiences of peasants: it was not the creation *ex nihilo* of a revolutionary elite. Explanations of revolutionary movements in terms of elite politics ignore the underlying historical currents—how particular class structures give rise to social classes and groups and how those groups articulate their interests and act in pursuit of them—which carry those movements along and in the final analysis account for their direction and fate.

What was the historical role of an outsider like Peng Pai? It should be noted first that Peng was not that much of an outsider. To be sure, he spoke differently and had a different culture from the peasants of Haifeng, but he was as much a product of the rural class structure as they were. His family lived in Haifeng city because peasants had wrested control of agricultural production from landlords, among them, Peng's ancestors, a century before. His family then was caught up in the processes that made landlords into urban rentiers, providing the raw material for Haifeng's reformist gentry class. As a result of his contact with these reformers, Peng Pai went abroad to study, returning from Japan with socialist ideas and some thoughts about the role of peasants in China's revolution.

Conclusion

Peng Pai did not manufacture a "peasant movement" out of thin air, as he is sometimes supposed to have done. From the perspective of peasant collective action, what he did was to articulate peasant interests in ways that resounded with the values and experiences as expressed in their moral economy, defining goals toward which collective action could be directed. The form that the collective action of peasants then took was a charismatic cult. There were several reasons for this. The changes in land tenure relations were relatively recent, and peasants had little experience under the new conditions. Besides, factional conflict still echoed peasant distrust of their neighbors. Finally, folk beliefs provided peasants with categories to explain why someone as different from them as Peng Pai would want to help them.

Peng Pai was not the only Chinese Communist peasant leader to have had a cult following. The other of course was Mao Zedong. As early as 1937, Edgar Snow commented on the "charmed life" that Mao seemed to lead,[5] and stories about the fabled "Chu Mao" who could appear in two places at once had circulated among peasants near Jinggangshan. The cult of Mao was consciously fostered during the Rectification Campaign of 1942 with the study of the thoughts of Mao,[6] and reached what Snow termed "immoderate" proportions on the eve of the Cultural Revolution.[7] When Snow interviewed Mao in 1937 before hardly anyone else in the world knew who Mao was, he captured a sense of what would contribute to the Mao cult—and to Mao's greatness:

> You feel that whatever there is extraordinary in this man
> grows out of the uncanny degree to which he synthesizes
> and expresses the urgent demands of millions of Chinese,
> and especially the peasantry—those impoverished,
> underfed, exploited, illiterate, but kind, generous,
> courageous and just now rather rebellious human beings
> who are the vast majority of the Chinese people. If these
> demands and the movement which is pressing them
> forward are the dynamic which can regenerate China,
> then in this deeply historical sense Mao Tse-tung may
> possibly become a very great man.[8]

286

Conclusion

Kim San, a man as perceptive as Snow, knew both Peng Pai and Mao, and characterized Peng very similarly to the way Snow had described Mao:

P'eng P'ai would surely have become one of the greatest mass leaders China has ever known, had he not met an untimely death. Nobody I have met in China except Mao Tse-tung shares equally with him that rare quality of inborn leadership. He created the Hailufeng peasant movement, and his influence spread all through the province, including Canton city. He was the first organizer of the new agrarian revolution and had led the peasant movement for ten years.[9]

Edgar Snow and Kim San saw something special about Mao and Peng. But why did peasants in addition attribute such extraordinary powers to them? Was there something about Chinese peasant mentality that created cults around peasant leaders? Chinese historians in the early 1960s debated the issue of peasant "monarchism," or the tendency of peasants in China toward emperor worship,[10] and a vice-minister of foreign affairs commented on what happened when Mao took the rostrum on the Gate of Heavenly Peace: "When the peasants came to the October anniversary and went past the reviewing stand, many did the k'ou-t'ou before Chairman Mao. We had to keep guards posted there to prevent them from prostrating themselves. It takes time to make people understand that Chairman Mao is not an emperor or a god but a man who wants the peasants to stand up like men."[11] Indeed it does.

Karl Marx paid attention to this problem in his analysis of the political power of Louis Bonaparte (Napoleon III). The freeholding peasants of France, Marx observed, were incapable of taking political action to defend their interests, requiring instead a representative who "must at the same time appear as their master, as an authority over them, as an unlimited governmental power that protects them against the other classes and sends them the rain and sunshine from above." French peasants had come to believe "in a miracle that a man named Napoleon would bring all the glory [of the first Napoleon] back to them." "Bonapartism," it is tempting to conclude, is the characteristic form of political expression of the peasantry. But Marx was talking about the smallholders of France, who formed a class only inasmuch as "potatoes in a sack form a sack of potatoes." The French peasants were so isolated from each other, and so economically self-sufficient, that regardless of their similar conditions of life, "the identity of their interests begets no community, no national bond, and political organization among them, [and hence] they do not form a class."[12] Marx's analysis suggests that the less peasants are able to engage in collective action, the greater the likelihood that their political expression will take the form of Bonapartism or some other form of cult.

Comparatively, the peasants of Haifeng were not nearly as isolated nor as incapable of collective action as were the French peasants, and yet they too attributed rather extraordinary powers to Peng Pai. They interpreted Peng's action in terms of familiar categories, handed down by a folk tradition with strong millenarian strains, as that of a Bodhisattva or an "Eternal One." Still, there was an important difference between Bonapartism and the cult of Peng Pai (I am not so sure about the cult of Mao, especially during the Cultural Revolution): the cult was a form of social organization that organized collective action along class lines. And in the process of taking action and working through other organizations, the cult had the distinct historical possibility of being transcended, or replaced, by other forms of social organization, such as the peasant unions.

That the cult of Peng Pai should have flourished was not inevitable but is attributable to the specific historical situation in 1926–27, when both of China's modern political parties, the Guomindang and the Communist party, refused to give programmatic form to peasant demands. The political power then created by peasants found its expression as a charismatic cult, and that is the form it retained in the Haifeng Soviet. It was ironic but understandable that a "soviet"—what Communists considered the most advanced political formation—was based in Haifeng on a most archaic social formation.

Conclusion

Peasant participation in modern revolution has come about in different ways in various parts of China. In Haifeng, it was contingent upon changes in social structure and class relations that occurred in the context of an expansive world capitalism. That this was not the only route, at least in China, seems clear enough when Haifeng is compared to North China. In Huaibei, Elizabeth Perry has shown, a more or less unchanging natural and social environment produced forms of peasant collective action which issued over into rebellion under certain conditions, but did not lead to peasant participation in the modern revolution led by the Chinese Communist Party. Only when new Communist party policies in the mid-1940s "pointed the way to a more efficient method of group survival," Perry observes, "was [it] possible to transform peasant behavior" and "to alter the structure of collective action."[13] What the action of the Communist party demonstrates, Perry concludes, is that "group action to overcome—rather than reflect—prior conditions was also within the range of human possibility."[14]

The results of this study of Haifeng point to different—structural rather than voluntarist—explanations for changes in the forms of peasant collective action and for peasant participation in modern revolution. Much of what the Communist party apparently had to do in Huaibei "to transform peasant behavior," in Haifeng had been accomplished by changes in rural social relations occasioned by contact with the capitalist world market. The routes in Huaibei and Haifeng were different, but through both, peasants did come to participate in modern revolution.

289

Notes and Index

NOTES

Introduction

1 This should not be mistaken for structural*ism* or structural *determinism*. See the argument that follows. For a full discussion of the relationship between social structure, historical process, and human experience, see E. P. Thompson, *The Poverty of Theory* (New York: Monthly Review Press, 1978); for a discussion of the relationship between narrative history and social history that touches on similar issues, see E. J. Hobsbawm, "The Revival of Narrative: Some Comments," *Past and Present* 86 (1980): 3–8.

2 For the former, I am thinking especially of Roy Hofheinz, Jr., *The Broken Wave: The Chinese Communist Peasant Movement, 1922–1928* (Cambridge: Harvard University Press, 1977); and for the latter, Mark Selden, *The Yenan Way in Revolutionary China* (Cambridge: Harvard University Press, 1971). More will be said about Hofheinz's approach below.

3 See Charles Tilly, *From Mobilization to Revolution* (Reading, Mass.: Addison-Wesley, 1978); Charles, Louise, and Richard Tilly, *The Rebellious Century, 1830–1930* (Cambridge: Harvard University Press, 1975); and Elizabeth Perry, *Rebels and Revolutionaries in North China, 1845–1945* (Stanford: Stanford University Press, 1980).

4 Theda Skocpol, *States and Social Revolutions* (New York: Cambridge University Press, 1978), esp. chap. 1.

5 New source material uncovered by Chinese historians has been just published as *Peng Pai yanjiu shiliao* (Historical materials for the study of Peng Pai) (Guangzhou: Renmin chuban she, 1981). The organizing principle for the selection of material is Peng Pai, not peasant collective action or the rural socioeconomic system. What conclusions Chinese historians will reach on the basis of these materials remains to be seen, but the precedent of focusing exclusively on Peng Pai has been set. An exception is Guo Chengxiang, "Haifeng tudi wenti chutan" (A preliminary investigation of the land problem in Haifeng), in *Canjia jinian Peng Pai xueshu taolunhui lunwen* (Guangzhou: Guangzhou waiguoyu xueyuan, 1981).

293

6 Hofheinz, *The Broken Wave*. This criticism also applies to one of the two recent doctoral dissertations on Peng Pai. Yong-pil Pang, in "Peng Pai and the Origins of Rural Revolution under Warlordism in the 1920s: Haifeng County, Guangdong Province" (Ph.D. diss., University of California—Los Angeles, 1981), argues that in the 1920s Haifeng "was objectively ripe for a revolution. Only leadership was lacking." The other dissertation, F. Galbiati, "P'eng P'ai, the Leader of the First Soviet: Hai-lu-feng, 1898–1930" (D. Phil., Oxford University, 1982), is not available as of this writing.

7 On the availability of Chinese archival sources, see Philip C. C. Huang, "County Archives and the Study of Local Social History," *Modern China* 1 (January 1982): 133–43.

8 E. P. Thompson discusses the difficulties of interrogating discrete facts for structure-yielding evidence in *The Poverty of Theory*, pp. 29–30.

9 Evelyn Rawski, *Agricultural Change and the Peasant Economy of South China* (Cambridge: Harvard University Press, 1972), p. 4.

10 Fu-mei Chang Chen and Ramon H. Myers, "Customary Law and the Economic Growth of China during the Ch'ing Period," *Ch'ing-shih wen-t'i* 5 (November 1976): 1–32.

11 See Hofheinz, *The Broken Wave*, chap. 6.

12 See Perry, *Rebels and Revolutionaries*, chap. 1.

13 E. P. Thompson sees the problem in terms of structure and process, and discusses the difficulties of Marxist political economy and historical materialism in finding "a common junction and a theoretical vocabulary capable of encompassing both process and structure." See *The Poverty of Theory*, pp. 68, 84, 86. No claim is made here to having found that vocabulary.

14 Braudel asks: "Is it possible somehow to convey simultaneously both that conspicuous history which holds our interest by its continual and dramatic changes—and that other, submerged history, almost silent and always discreet, virtually unsuspected either by its observers or its participants which is little touched by the erosion of time? This fundamental contradiction, which must always lie at the centre of our thought, can be a vital tool of knowledge and research." *The Mediterranean and the Mediterranean World in the Age of Philip H* (New York: Harper and Row, 1972), p. 16.

15 Ibid., pp. 20–21. See also his essay "Time, History, and the Social Sciences," in Fritz Stern, ed., *The Varieties of History* (New York: Vintage Books, 1973).

16 See Tilly, *From Mobilization to Revolution*, chap. 2.

17 Tilly lists a number of examples in other areas. From the China field might be added Edward J. M. Rhoads, *China's Republican Revolution: The Case of Kwangtung, 1895–1913* (Cambridge: Harvard University Press, 1975), in the Durkheimian tradition; and in the Marxian tradition a number of comparative studies: Barrington Moore, Jr., *The Social Origins of Dictatorship and Democracy* (Boston: Beacon Press, 1966); Eric Wolf, *Peasant Wars of the Twentieth Century* (New York: Harper Torchbooks, 1969); and Theda Skocpol, *States and Social Revolutions.* Hofheinz's *The Broken Wave* draws on Millian perspectives and what Tilly calls pseudo-Mill, the "eclectic effort to assemble individually plausible variables into equations which state their joint effects and interrelations." See Tilly, *From Mobilization to Revolution,* chap. 2.

18 See esp. Jeffrey Paige, *Agrarian Revolution* (New York: Free Press, 1975).

19 This is the main criticism that can be made of Theda Skocpol, *States and Social Revolutions.* See Peter Manicas' review of Skocpol in *History and Theory* 2 (1981): 204–18.

20 The phrase is from Thompson, *The Poverty of Theory,* p. 99.

21 Robert Brenner, "Agrarian Class Structure and Economic Development in Pre-Industrial Europe," *Past and Present* 60 (February 1976): 30–75. Brenner's understanding of determinism is very close to that given by Thompson in *The Poverty of Theory,* p. 110.

22 E. P. Thompson, *The Making of the English Working Class,* 2nd rev. ed. (Middlesex, England: Penguin Books, 1968), p. 9.

23 E. P. Thompson, "The Moral Economy of the English Crowd in the Eighteenth Century," *Past and Present* 50 (1971): 71–136; James C. Scott, *The Moral Economy of the Peasant: Rebellion and Revolution in Southeast Asia* (New Haven: Yale University Press, 1976).

24 Charles, Louise, and Richard Tilly, *The Rebellious Century,* p. 290.

25 For succinct summaries of the opposing views see Joseph Esherick, "Harvard on China: The Apologetics of Imperialism," and Andrew Nathan, "Imperialism's Effects on China," both in *Bulletin of Concerned Asian Scholars* 4 (December 1972); for a critique of this debate, see Elizabeth Lasek, "Imperialism in China: A Methodological Critique," *Bulletin of Concerned Asian Scholars* 15:1 (January 1983). For a general approach to understanding the relationship between imperialism and social revolution, see James Petras, *Critical Perspectives on Imperialism and Social Class in the Third World* (New York: Monthly Review Press, 1978), esp. chap. 1, "Liberal, Structural, and Radical Approaches to Political Economy: An Assessment and an Alternative" (with Kent Trachte).

26 See esp. Rhoads, *China's Republican Revolution,* and Joseph Esherick, *Reform and Revolution in China: The 1911 Revolution in Hubei and Hunan* (Berkeley and Los Angeles: University of California Press, 1976). A notable exception is Edward Friedman, *Backward Toward Revolution* (Berkeley and Los Angeles: University of California Press, 1974), which deals with rural social movements *after* 1911.

27 Peter Worsley, *The Trumpet Shall Sound: A Study of "Cargo" Cults in Melanesia* (New York: Schocken Books, 1968); George Rudé, *Ideology and Popular Protest* (New York: Pantheon Books, 1980); and Carlo Ginzburg, *The Cheese and the Worms: The Cosmos of a Sixteenth-Century Miller* (New York: Penguin Books, 1980).

Chapter 1: Late Ming Land Tenure Relations

1 Estates worked by slave, serf, and hired labor were not a creation of Ming times, having existed for centuries and becoming a common feature of the rural order by late Tang or early Song times. See for instance Yang Guoyi, "Nan Song da dizhu tudi suoyouzhi de fazhan" (The development of large landlord landownership in the southern Song), in *Zhongguo fengjian shehui tudi suoyouzhi xingshi wenti taolun ji* (Beijing: Sanlian shudian, 1962), pp. 687–703.

2 Gu Yanwu, *Ri zhi lu* (Record of daily knowledge) (Taibei: Minglun chuban she, 1970), pp. 401–2; Mark Elvin, *The Pattern of the Chinese Past* (Stanford: Stanford University Press, 1973), p. 235; Huang Peijin, "Guanyu Ming dai guonei shichang wenti de kaoji" (Inquiry into the problem of the domestic market during Ming times), in *Ming Qing shehui jingji xingtai de yanjiu* (Shanghai: Renmin chuban she, 1957), p. 231.

3 Hu Pu-an, *Zhongguo quan guo fengsu zhi* (Compendium of customs in China) (Shanghai: Dada tushu gongying she, 1935), vol. 2, ch. 8:7. See also Li Diaoyuan, *Yuedong biji* (Guangdong sketches) (Shanghai: Huiwentang, 1915), ch. 2:7b.

4 As Marc Bloch observed of medieval France: "Where studies concerning medieval studies are concerned, it is a good general rule never to linger over particular terms, since they vary enormously. . . . If instead we concentrate on fundamental principles, it is obvious that the basic ideas . . . are at once very simple and almost everywhere identical." See his *French Rural Society,* trans. Janet Sondheim (London: Routledge and Kegan Paul, 1966), p. 89. On

Russia, see Jerome Blum, *Lord and Peasant in Russia from the Ninth to the Nineteenth Century* (New York: Atheneum, 1969), pp. 601 ff.

5 Quoted in Elvin, *Pattern of the Chinese Past*, p. 239.

6 Wei Jinyu, "Ming Qing shidai diannong de nongnu diwei" (The serflike status of tenants in the Ming and Qing times), in *Zhongguo jin sanbai nian shehui jingji taolun ji* (Hong Kong: Cuncui xueshe, 1972), 1:156–57.

7 Li Wenzhi, "Lun Qing dai qianqi de tudi zhanyou guanxi" (On land tenure relations in early Qing times), in *Zhongguo jin sanbai nian shehui jingji taolun ji*, 1:42.

8 Quoted in Charles R. Boxer, ed., *South China in the Sixteenth Century* (London: Hakluyt Society, 1953), p. 274.

9 Xie Guozhen, *Ming Qing zhi ji dang she yundong kao* (Inquiry into factionalism in the Ming-Qing interregnum) (Taibei: Shangwu yinshu guan, 1967), p. 263.

10 Peter Mundy, *The Travels of Peter Mundy in Europe and Asia, 1608–1667*, ed. Richard C. Temple (London: Hakluyt Society, 1919), 3:263. See also Wei Jinyu, "Ming Qing shidai diannong," pp. 138 ff.

11 Fu Yiling, *Ming Qing nongcun shehui jingji* (Rural society and economy during Ming and Qing times) (Beijing: Sanlian shudian, 1961), pp. 5–6. The serf population of Europe had expanded by the practice of commendation, and for many of the same reasons as in China. See Marc Bloch, *Feudal Society*, trans. L. A. Manyon (Chicago: University of Chicago Press, 1961), 1:183.

12 Wei Jinyu, "Ming Qing shidai diannong," p. 141.

13 Ibid.

14 Elvin, *Pattern of the Chinese Past*, p. 244. See also Wei Jinyu, "Ming Qing shidai diannong," p. 142.

15 Huang Peijin, "Guanyu Ming dai guonei shichang," pp. 231–33; Peng Xinwei, *Zhongguo huobi shi* (A history of money in China) (Shanghai: Renmin chuban she, 1965), p. 705; Fu Yiling, *Ming Qing nongcun shehui jingji*, p. 1.

16 Elvin, *Pattern of the Chinese Past*, pp. 236–43.

17 Wang Zhen, *Nong shu* (Treatise on agriculture), ch. 19:3a–12b, and ch. 20; Pang Shangpeng, *Pang shi jia xun* (Pang family instructions) (1572 text, reprinted in *Baibu congshu jicheng* 93, *Lingnan guishu*, vol. 39), p. 2a.

18 Wang Zhen, *Nong shu*, ch. 11:9b–10a; ch. 12:4a–b; ch. 13:15a.

19 Pang Shangpeng, *Pang shi jia xun*, p. 10a.

20 Ibid., pp. 2a, 3a, 10a–b.

21 Ibid., pp. 3b, 2a.

22 Ibid., pp. 2a, 10b.
23 Cited in Niida Noboru, *Chugoku heseishi kenkyu* (Historical studies of China's legal system) (Tokyo: Tokyo University Press, 1962), 3:223. Emphasis added.
24 Ibid., pp. 267–68.
25 Wei Jinyu, "Ming Qing shidai diannong," pp. 142–43.
26 Xie Guozhen, *Ming Qing zhi ji dang she yundong,* p. 260. On what the Chinese state considered to constitute customary servitude, see Bao Shuyun, comp. *Xing an hui lan* (Compendium of legal cases) (Shanghai, 1887), ch. 39:4a–6b.
27 Evelyn Rawski, *Agricultural Change and the Peasant Economy of South China* (Cambridge: Harvard University Press, 1972), chap. 2.
28 Pang Shangpeng, *Pang shi jia xun,* pp. 8a–b.
29 Fu Yiling, *Ming Qing nongcun shehui jingji,* pp. 82 ff.; Peng Shangpeng, *Pang shi jia xun,* p. 8a.
30 Li Wenzhi, "Lun Qing dai qianqi de tudi," p. 44.
31 Xie Guozhen, *Ming Qing zhi ji dang she yundong,* pp. 277–81.
32 Xie Guozhen, *Qing chu nongmin qiyi ziliao jilu* (Collected source materials on peasant uprisings in the early Qing) (Shanghai: Xin zhishi chuban she, 1956), pp. 310, 323.
33 For a political history of the revolts in the north, see James B. Parsons, *The Peasant Rebellions of the Late Ming Dynasty* (Tucson: University of Arizona Press, 1970).
34 Elvin, *Pattern of the Chinese Past,* chap. 15.

Chapter 2: Peasants, Lords, and the State

1 *Huizhou fuzhi* (1888), ch. 14:24a.
2 Ibid., ch. 14:12a–25b. For a discussion of the Ming tax system, see Ray Huang, *Taxation in Sixteenth-Century Ming China* (London: Cambridge University Press, 1974).
3 *Lufeng xianzhi* (1747), ch. 12:1a–3b.
4 The single-whip method of taxation arose in several different areas during the sixteenth century as a means by which various kinds of taxes on land and persons were merged and/or converted into payment in silver. See Liang Fang-chung, *The Single-Whip Method of Taxation in China* (Cambridge: Harvard University Press,1956); Wang Fangzhong, "Ming dai yitiaobian fa de shengchan ji qi zuoyong" (The development and use of the single-whip method of taxation), in *Ming Qing shehui jingji xingtai de yanjiu* (Beijing:

Renmin daxue, 1957); and Huang, *Taxation in Sixteenth-Century Ming China*.

5 Peng Xinwei, *Zhongguo huobi shi* (Shanghai: Renmin chuban she, 1965), p. 705.

6 We know of people from Haifeng trading in Japan from a rescript written by Hideoshi in 1590. See Charles R. Boxer, ed. and trans., *The Great Ship from Amacon: Annals of Macao and the Old Japan Trade, 1555–1640* (Lisbon: Centro de Estudos Historicus Ultramarinos, 1959), pp. 321–22.

7 *Huizhou fuzhi* (1888), ch. 17:38b.

8 *Haifeng xianzhi* (1750), ch. 2:37a; *Huizhou fuzhi* (1888), ch. 17:36b–37a, 38b.

9 Xie Guozhen, *Qing chu nongmin qiyi ziliao* (Shanghai: Xin zhishi chuban she, 1956), p. 310; *Lufeng xianzhi*, ch. 12.

10 *Haifeng xianzhi* (1750), ch. 2:37a–38a.

11 Xie Guozhen, *Qing chu nongmin qiyi ziliao*, p. 310.

12 *Haifeng xianzhi* (1750), ch. 2:37a–39b.

13 Xie Guozhen, *Qing chu nongmin qiyi ziliao*, p. 319.

14 Ibid., p. 323; *Haifeng xianzhi* (1750), 2:40a.

15 Xie Guozhen, *Qing chu nongmin qiyi ziliao*, p. 321.

16 *Haifeng xianzhi* (1750), ch. 2:40b–41a; Li Diaoyuan, *Yuedong biji* (Shanghai: Huiwentang, 1915), ch. 5:2a–b.

17 Xie Guozhen, *Ming Qing zhi ji dang she yundong* (Taibei: Shangwu yinshu guan, 1967), p. 277.

18 Ibid., p. 280; Zhang Weihua, *Ming dai haiwai maoyi jian lun* (A short discourse on overseas trade in Ming times) (Shanghai: Renmin chuban she, 1956), pp. 96–97; Kwan-wai So, *Japanese Piracy in Ming China during the Sixteenth Century* (East Lansing?: Michigan State University, 1975), pp. 15–40.

19 Li Wenzhi, "Lun Qing dai qianqi de tudi zhanyou quanxi," in *Zhongguo jin sanbai nian shehui jingji taolun ji* (Hong Kong: Cuncui xueshe, 1972), 1:44; Wei Jinyu, "Ming Qing shidai diannong de nongnu diwei," ibid., p. 156; Mark Elvin, *The Pattern of the Chinese Past* (Stanford: Stanford University Press, 1973), p. 248.

20 *Qing shilu jingji ziliao jiyao* (A compilation of economic source material from the Veritable Records of the Qing Dynasty) (Shanghai: Zhonghua shuju, 1959), pp. 287–88.

21 Li Wenzhi, "Lun Qing dai qianqi de tudi," pp. 46–47.

22 Ibid., pp. 48–49.

23 Ibid.

24 Wei Jinyu, "Ming Qing shidai diannong," p. 144.

25 Ibid., p. 149; Rong Sheng, "Taolun Ming Qing jian nongmin jieji douzheng de mouxie tedian" (A discussion of a few special points about peasant class struggles in the Ming-Qing transition), in Shi Zhaobin, ed., *Zhongguo fengjian shehui nongmin zhanzheng wenti taolun ji* (Beijing: Sanlian shudian, 1962), p. 25.

26 *Haifeng xianzhi* (1750), ch. 1:49a; ch. 2:30b–31a.

27 Ibid., ch. 2:41a–b.

28 Wei Jinyu, "Ming Qing shidai diannong," p. 156; *Haifeng xianzhi* (1750), ch. 2:47b–55b. Land reclamation continued into the eighteenth century, albeit at a slower pace. In 1745, for instance, the Qianlong emperor approved a memorial from the governor of Guangdong province requesting that one-hundred-mou tracts of hilly land be given tax free for ten years to "landless, poor peasants." See *Qing shilu jingji ziliao jiyao*, pp. 68–95, 141.

29 *Qing shilu jingji ziliao jiyao*, p. 81.

30 Chen Han-seng, *Agrarian Problems in Southernmost China* (Shanghai: Kelly and Walsh, 1936), pp. 59–60; see also *Qing shilu jingji ziliao jiyao*, p. 288.

31 Tieren (pseud.), "Min'guo shiliu nian Hailufeng chihuo zhi huiyi" (Memoir of the 1927 Red holocaust in Hailufeng) (manuscript in the author's possession). The details of this system are drawn from Zhang Youyi, "Taiping tianguo geming qianqi Huizhou dichu tudi guanxi de yige shilu: Yi xian dizhu 'Jiang Zong Yi Tang Zhichan Bu' pou xi" (A record of land tenure relations in the Huizhou region on the eve of the Taiping revolution: Disclosures from the 'Property Registers of the Jiang Zong Yi Family Hall' landlords of Yi county), *Wenwu* 6 (1975): 34–46.

32 The notion of dual rights to the land was not unique to China. In many parts of Europe the feudal principle of *nulle terre sans seigneur* continued to exist in the late eighteenth century. As Jerome Blum described the institution: "That meant that the seignor had the legal ownership—or the *dominum directum*, as the lawyers called it—of the land within the fief or seignory. Those peasants who held land in the seigniory by hereditary tenure had most of the rights of ownership. In popular speech, in government reports, and even in legal texts they were called proprietors. Actually they owned only the right to the use of the land, the *dominum utile*. In recognition of the superior ownership of the seignor, the occupant of the land owed certain obligations to the lord and stood in servile relationship to him." As in China, the lord could own outright both types of rights to the land. Land held this way in

France was called the lord's *domaine* or *reservé*. But in China, unlike France, peasants too could own both rights to the land, conferring absolute ownership, and likewise could sell one or both rights. See Jerome Blum, *The End of the Old Order in Rural Europe* (Princeton: Princeton University Press, 1978), pp. 20, 60, 99.
33 See my Ph.D. dissertation, "Peasants and Peasant Society in South China: Social Change in Haifeng County, 1630–1930" (University of Wisconsin—Madison, 1978), pp. 166 ff. for a fuller discussion.
34 Li Wenzhi, "Lun Qing dai qianqi de tudi," pp. 67, 70.
35 Wei Jinyu, "Ming Qing shidai diannong," pp. 145, 147–48.
36 Ibid., p. 157.
37 Bao Shuyun, comp., *Xing an hui lan* (Shanghai, 1887), ch. 39:4a–6b.
38 Wei Jinyu, "Ming Qing shidai diannong," p. 149.
39 Ibid., p. 158.
40 Li Wenzhi, "Lun Qing dai qianqi de tudi," pp. 45, 49, 53, 62–64.
41 Wei Jinyu, "Ming Qing shidai diannong," p. 150; Fu Yiling, *Ming Qing nongcun shehui jingji* (Beijing: Sanlian shudian, 1961), pp. 54–57.

Chapter 3: A New Pattern to Rural Life

1 Li Wenzhi, "Lun qing dai qianqi de tudi zhanyou guanxi," in *Zhongguo jin sanbai nian shehui jingji taolun ji* (Hong Kong: Cuncui xueshe, 1972), p. 152.
2 *Haifeng xianzhi* (1750), ch. 1:38a.
3 Huang Beijin, "Guanyu Ming dai quonei shichang wenti de kaoji," in *Ming Qing shehui jingji xingtai de yanjiu* (Shanghai: Renmin chuban she, 1957), p. 231; Li Wenzhi et al., comps., *Zhongguo jindai nongye shi ziliao* (Source materials on the study of agriculture in modern China) (Beijing: Sanlian shudian, 1957), 1:472.
4 Ping-ti Ho, *Studies on the Population of China* (Cambridge: Harvard University Press, 1959), p. 203; Li Wenzhi et al., *Zhongguo jindai nongye shi ziliao*, 1:472.
5 Dwight H. Perkins, *Agricultural Development in China, 1368–1968* (Edinburgh: Edinburgh University Press, 1969), p. 136; Li Zhiqin, "Lun yapian zhanzheng yiqian Qing dai shangyexing nongye de fazhan" (On the development of commercialized agriculture before the Opium War), in *Ming Qing shehui jingji xingtai de yanjiu* (Shanghai: Renmin chuban she, 1957), pp. 281–303.
6 *Haifeng xianzhi* (1750), ch. 1:6a–b.

7 *Haifeng xianzhi* (1874), p. 7a. See also Ping-ti Ho, "Early-ripening Rice in Chinese History," *Economic History Review*, 2nd ser., 2 (1956); and C. K. Yang, *Chinese Communist Society: The Family and the Village* (Cambridge: MIT Press, 1965), p. 37.

8 Li Diaoyuan, *Yuedong biji* (Shanghai: Huiwentang, 1915), ch. 1:3a–b. The other major handicraft industries were textile spinning, weaving, and dyeing. Because of the importance of these handicraft industries and their relationship to the world market, they will be treated in more detail in Chapter 5.

9 "Haifeng tianzhujiao qishiwunian da shi ji" (Seventy-five-year chronology of Catholicism in Haifeng) (Handwritten manuscript at P.I.M.E. Fathers Mission, Hong Kong), 1892, 1893.

10 Liang Tingnan, comp., *Yue hai guan zhi* (Guangdong maritime customs records), reprinted in *Jindai zhongguo shiliao congkan xunbian* (Taibei: Wenhai chuban she, n.d.), vols. 181–84, pp. 621–28.

11 Ibid., pp. 735–37, 703, 734.

12 *The Story of Swabue* (London: F. E. Philip and Sons, 1911), pp. 9–10.

13 Li Diaoyuan, *Yuedong biji*, ch. 1:4a; G. William Skinner, "Marketing and Social Structure in China, Part 1," *Journal of Asian Studies* 1 (1964): 34; Daniel Harrison Kulp, *Country Life in South China* (New York: Columbia University Press, 1925), p. 93; "Haifeng tianzhujiao", 1889.

14 *Story of Swabue*, p. 10.

15 Qiu Guochen, *Fengdi yusheng lu* (A record of surviving) (Hong Kong: Tianfeng yinshu chang, 1972), pp. 347–48; Skinner, "Marketing, Part 1," p. 21.

16 Qiu Guochen, *Fengdi*, pp. 347–48. On the role of the teahouse in rural China, see Jiao Jiming, *Jiangning xian xunhua zhen xiangcun shehui zhi yanjiu* (A study of Shunhuachen rural community interests), University of Nanjing College of Agriculture and Forestry, Bulletin no. 23, new series (Nanjing, 1934), p. 13.

17 Skinner, "Marketing, Part 1," pp. 3, 6, 18, 33, 35–37.

18 The discussion of Xunhua is based on Jiao Jiming, *Jiangning xunhua zhen*.

19 Ibid., p. 21.

20 Philip A. Kuhn, *Rebellion and Its Enemies in Late Imperial China: Militarization and Social Structure, 1796–1864* (Cambridge: Harvard University Press, 1970), p. 83.

21 Qiu Guochen, *Fengdi*, p. 7.

22 Adele Fielde, *A Corner of Cathay* (New York: Macmillan, 1894), pp. 128–31. For further analysis, see Maurice Freedman, *Lineage*

Organization in Southeast China (New York: Humanities Press, 1965), pp. 107 ff.

23 Xu Gengbi, *Buziqie zhai man cun* (Random papers from the studio of discontent) (Taibei: Wenhai chuban she, n.d.), pp. 455–57; Hsien-chin Hu, *The Common Descent Group in China and Its Functions* (New York: The Viking Fund, 1948), p. 91.

24 George Jamieson, *Chinese Family and Commercial Law* (Shanghai: Kelly and Walsh, 1921), pp. 103–4; Bao Shuyun, comp., *Xing an hui lan* (Shanghai, 1887), ch. 29:15a.

25 *Huazi ribao*, 22 January 1926. As late as 1950, some lineages in Haifeng were reported to be fighting over water rights. See *Nanfang ribao*, 13 August 1950, p. 2.

26 William Ashmore, "A Clan Feud near Swatow," *The Chinese Recorder* 5 (1897): 214.

27 Ibid., p. 215. See also *South China Morning Post*, 30 May 1912. The Fang lineage was the wealthiest in Puning county, owning shops in the city and land in the countryside. Struggles with the Fang continued for several decades, reaching a new height in the 1920s. For a discussion of the Puning struggles, see my article, "The World Can Change! Guangdong Peasants in Revolution," *Modern China* 1 (1977):89–96.

28 Kulp, *Country Life in South China*, p. 13; *Hong Kong Telegraph*, 14 January 1911.

29 Information on the Lin lineage came from Chen Xiaobai, *Hailufeng chihuo ji* (The Red holocaust in Hailufeng) (Guangzhou: Peiyang yinwu ju, 1932), pp. 29–31; on the He, from the same source, pp. 31–33. For more on these lineages, see Chapters 7–9.

30 Zhong Yimou, *Hailufeng nongmin yundong* (Guangzhou: Renmin chuban she, 1957), p. 100.

31 Qiu Guochen, *Fengdi*, pp. 26–27; Hsien-chin Hu, *Common Descent Group*, p. 94.

32 Xu Gengbi, *Buziqie zhai man cun*, pp. 440–41.

33 Ibid., pp. 519–21.

34 This information was supplied by an informant in Hong Kong.

35 Xu Gengbi, *Buziqie zhai man cun*, p. 561.

36 Ibid., p. 446.

37 Ibid., pp. 470, 489, 491–92.

38 Harry Lamley, "Hsieh-tou: The Pathology of Violence in Southeastern China," *Ch'ing-shih wen-t'i* 7 (1977): 29.

39 Elizabeth Perry, *Rebels and Revolutionaries in North China, 1845–1945* (Stanford: Stanford University Press, 1980).

40 Ibid., p. 250.

41 Ibid., p. 33.

Chapter 4: Markets and Morals

1 *Haifeng xianzhi* (1750), ch. 2:44b.

2 The literature showing the "riot" as a rational act, rather than as "mob" action, is extensive. See George Rudé, *The Crowd in the French Revolution* (New York: Oxford University Press, 1967); E. P. Thompson, "The Moral Economy of the English Crowd in the Eighteenth Century," *Past and Present* 50 (1971); Richard Cobb, *The Police and the People: French Popular Protest, 1789–1829* (New York: Oxford University Press, 1972); and Dirk Hoerder, *Crowd Action in Revolutionary Massachusetts, 1765–1780* (New York: Academic Press, 1977).

3 *Haifeng xianzhi* (1750), ch. 2:45a–46b.

4 Ibid., p. 45a.

5 *Haifeng xianzhi* (1874), p. 33a. See also Lao Dong, *Jiu huang bei lan* (Guide to famine preparedness), in *Baibu congshu jicheng* 93, *Lingnan guishu*, vol. 39.

6 *Gugong wenxian* (Documents from the palace museum archives) (Taibei), 1, no. 2:78–108. For other reports of rice prices, see ibid., 2, no. 4:101, 147–48; 3, no. 1:89, 112, 118, 120.

7 Lao Dong, *Jiu huang bei lan*, p. 13a.

8 Ibid., pp. 1b–2a; *Haifeng xianzhi* (1750), ch. 2:46a; *Haifeng xianzhi* (1874), p. 33a.

9 Lao Dong, *Jiu huang bei lan*, p. 9a. One strongly suspects that Chinese peasants and eighteenth-century British poor would have understood each other quite well. Food rioters in England took actions similar to those of Chinese peasants, preventing exports, setting prices, and forcing the wealthy to sell grain at popularly determined prices. According to an eighteenth-century English sheriff, food rioters "visited Farmers, Millers, Bakers, and Hucksters shops, selling corn, flower, bread, cheese, butter, and bacon at their own prices. They returned in general the produce [i.e. money] to the proprietors or in their absence left the money for them; and behaved with great regularity and decency where they were not opposed, with outrage and violence where they was: but pilferd very little." Quoted in Thompson, "The Moral Economy of the English Crowd," p. 111.

10 Bao Shuyun, comp., *Xing an hui lan* (Shanghai, 1887), ch. 16:9a.

11 Lao Dong, *Jiu huang bei lan*, p. 8b.
12 *Haifeng xianzhi* (1750), ch. 1:6b.
13 Xu Gengbi, *Buziqie zhai man cun* (Taibei: Wenhai chuban she, n.d.), pp. 395–97.
14 *Zhongguo lidai shihuo zhi sanbian* (Economic annals from China's dynastic histories) (Taibei: Xuehai chuban she, 1972), p. 1281. See also Feng Liutang, *Zhongguo lidai minshi zhengce shi* (History of China's food policies) (Shanghai: Shangwu yinshu guan, 1937), p. 232.
15 For a discussion of the concept of moral economy, see Thompson, "The Moral Economy of the English Crowd," and James C. Scott, *The Moral Economy of the Peasant: Rebellion and Subsistence in Southeast Asia* (New Haven: Yale University Press, 1976).
16 *Zhongguo lidai shihuo zhi sanbian*, p. 1313; Feng Liutang, *Zhongguo lidai minshi zhengce*, pp. 233–34.
17 *Zhongguo lidai shihuo zhi sanbian*, p. 2094; *Haifeng xianzhi* (1874), p. 33a.
18 *Zhongguo lidai shihuo zhi sanbian*, pp. 2096–97.
19 *Hong Kong Telegraph*, 14 September 1907. For other examples, see *Haifeng xianzhi* (1874), pp. 38a–39a, and Li Wenzhi et al., comps., *Zhongguo jindai nongye shi ziliao* (Beijing: Sanlian shudian, 1957), 1:982.
20 Quoted in Kung-chuan Hsiao, *Rural China* (Seattle: University of Washington Press, 1960), p. 189. For Haifeng, see *Haifeng xianzhi* (1874), p. 42b.
21 Ping-ti Ho, *Studies on the Population of China* (Cambridge: Harvard University Press, 1959), pp. 13–14; Xu Gengbi, *Buziqie zhai man cun*, pp. 451–54.
22 Han-seng Chen, *Agrarian Problems in Southernmost China* (Shanghai: Kelly and Walsh, 1937), pp. 59–60. This was the origin of the type of permanent tenure in Haifeng known as the *zuoge* system.
23 L. Mad'iar, *Zhongguo nongcun jingji yanjiu* (Studies in China's rural economy), trans. Chen Daiqing and Peng Guiqiu (Shanghai: Shenzhou guoguang she, 1930), pp. 226–27. This example was not taken from Haifeng, but conversations with Haifeng natives indicate that it was typical.
24 Liu Wanzhang, "Haifeng qingming" (The Qingming festival in Haifeng), in *Guangdong fengsu juilu* (Hong Kong, 1972), pp. 417–18. See also Hsien-chin Hu, *The Common Descent Group in China and Its Functions* (New York: The Viking Fund, 1948), pp. 88–89; and Mad'iar, *Zhongguo nongcun jingji*, p. 227.

25 On rice prices, see Peng Xinwei, *Zhongguo huobi shi* (Shanghai: Renmin chuban she, 1965), p. 850. For merchant purchases of land, see Li Wenzhi, "Lun Qing dai qianqi de tudi zhanyou guanxi," in *Zhongguo jin sanbai nian shehui jingji taolun ji* (Hong Kong: Cuncui xueshe, 1972), pp. 60–62, 53. On merchants renting land to grow market crops, see Li Min, "Qianlong xingke tiben zhong youguan nongye zibenzhuyi mengya de cailiao" (Materials concerning the sprouts of capitalism found in the archives of the Board of Punishments for the Qianlong period), *Wenwu* 9 (1975).

26 Ma-lie zhuyi jiaoyanwo zhonggong dang shi jiaoyanzu, *Peng Pai zhuan lue* (Biography of Peng Pai) (Guangzhou: Guangzhou waiguo yu xueyuan, 1980), p. 2.

27 Tieren (pseud.), "Min'guo shiliu nian hailufeng chihuo zhi huiyi" (MS in author's possession), ch. 1:11b–12a.

28 *Guangdong nongmin yundong baogao* (Report on the Guangdong peasant movement) (Guangzhou: n.p., 1926), pp. 25–27; Mad'iar, *Zhongguo nongcun jingji*, p. 314.

29 Feng Hefa, *Zhongguo nongcun jingji ziliao* (Source materials on China's rural economy) (Shanghai: Liming shuju, 1933), p. 914.

30 Tieren, "Hailufeng chihuo zhi huiyi," ch. 1:7b.

31 Feng Hefa, *Zhongguo nongcun jingji ziliao*, pp. 915–16.

32 This discussion of paternalism is based on the analysis put forward by Eugene D. Genovese, *Roll, Jordan, Roll: The World the Slaves Made* (New York: Pantheon Press, 1974); see Genovese's index for his numerous discussions of paternalism.

Chapter 5: New Forces and Old Enemies

1 The information on Cai Shunling is drawn from "Haifeng tian-zhujiao qishiwunian da shi ji" (MS at P.I.M.E. Fathers Mission Hong Kong), 1871–85.

2 Xu Gengbi, *Buziqie zhai man cun* (Taibei: Wenhai chuban she, n.d.), pp. 460, 475, 482, 491, 610, 612.

3 *The Story of Swabue* (London: F. E. Philips and Sons, 1911).

4 Kwang-ching Liu, *Anglo-American Steamship Rivalry in China* (Cambridge: Harvard University Press, 1962), pp. 60–61.

5 Wang Jingyu, "Shijiu shiji waiguo chin hua qiye zhong de hua hang fugu huodong" (The role of Chinese management–foreign ownership enterprises in foreign aggression against Chinese enterprises in the nineteenth century), *Lishi yanjiu* 4 (1965):60; Yan Zhongping et al., comps., *Zhongguo jindai jingji shi zongji ziliao*

xuanji (Selected statistical source materials on modern Chinese economic history) (Beijing: Kexue chuban she, 1955), pp. 120, 258; "A Study of the Sugar Industry in China," *Chinese Economic Journal* 10 (October 1927): 868.

6 Peng Zeyi et al., comps., *Zhongguo jindai shougongye ziliao* (Source materials on the history of modern Chinese handicrafts) (Beijing: Sanlian shudian, 1957), 2:324, 54; Sun Ching-chih, *Economic Geography of South China*, trans. Joint Publications Research Service no. 14,954 (Washington, D.C., 1957), pp. 42–43; H.C.P. Geerligs, "The World's Cane Sugar Industry" (Manchester: Norman Rodger, 1912), p. 75.

7 Yan Zhongping et al., *Zhongguo jingji ziliao*, pp. 223–24; "Haifeng tianzhujiao qishiwunian da shi ji," 1893.

8 "A Study of the Cane Sugar Industry in China," *Chinese Economic Journal* 11 (November 1927): 968; Governor Zhang Zhidong, cited in Peng Zeyi et al., *Zhongguo jindai shougongye ziliao*, 2:167.

9 "Sugar Trade in Shanghai," *Chinese Economic Journal* 6 (December 1928) 1072; Li Zhiqin, "Lun yapian zhanzheng yiqian Qing dai shangyexing nongye de fazhan," in *Ming Qing shehui jingji xingtai de yanjiu* (Shanghai: Renmin chuban she, 1957), p. 295; Daniel Harrison Kulp, *Country Life in South China* (New York: Columbia University Press, 1925), pp. 88–89.

10 Li Min, "Qianlong xingke tiben zhong youguan nongye zibenzhuyi mengya de cailiao," *Wenwu* 9 (1975):72.

11 Liu, *Steamship Rivalry*, pp. 63–64, 131; Sha Weizhai, *Zhongguo maiban zhi* (The Chinese compradore system) (Shanghai: Shangwu yinshu guan, 1927).

12 "Sugar Trade," p. 1074–75; Zhang Youyi et al., comps., *Zhongguo jindai nongye shi ziliao* (Beijing: Sanlian shudian, 1957), 2:529; China, Imperial Maritime Customs, *Decennial Reports, 1892–1901*, 2:155.

13 Liu, *Steamship Rivalry*, p. 66.

14 *Haifeng xianzhi* (1874), p. 14b; *Guangdong yu ditu shuo* (Explanation of the Guangdong atlas) (Guangzhou, 1908), p. 175. See also Chapter 3, above.

15 *Hong Kong Telegraph*, 30 March 1907, 4 June 1910.

16 Peng Zeyi et al., *Zhongguo jindai shougongye ziliao*, 2:287, 165–66; China, Imperial Maritime Customs, *Decennial Reports, 1912–1921*, 2:154.

17 Peng Pai, "Haifeng nongmin yundong," in *Diyici guonei geming zhanzheng shiqi de nongmin yundong* (The peasant movement dur-

ing the period of the first revolutionary civil war) (Beijing: Renmin chuban she, 1953), p. 45.

18 Tieren (pseud.), "Min'guo shiliu nian hailufeng chihuo zhi huiyi" (MS in author's possession), ch. 1:11b.

19 Adele Fielde, as quoted in George Jamieson et al., "Tenure of Land in China and the Condition of the Rural Population," *Journal of the China Branch of the Royal Asiatic Society* 23 (1889):113.

20 Direct evidence for the transformation of permanent tenure into oral leases in Haifeng is lacking, but is known to have occurred elsewhere. See Zhang Youyi,"Taiping tianguo geming qianqi weizhou diqu tudi quanxi de yige shilu" (A record of land tenure relations from the area of Weizhou on the eve of the Taiping revolution), *Wenwu* 6 (1975).

21 *Guangdong nongmin yundong baogao* (Guangzhou, 1926), pp. 25 ff; *Zhongguo jingji nianyan* (Chinese economic yearbook) (Shanghai?, 1933), pt. 1, sec. G, pp. 236–37.

22 Tieren, "Hailufeng chihuo zhi huiyi," ch. 1:11b.

23 *Guangdong nongmin yundaong baogao*, p. 37; *Zhongguo jingji nianyan*, pt. 1, sec. G, p. 236.

24 Peng Xinwei, *Zhongguo huobi shi* (Shanghai: Renmin chuban she, 1965), pp. 843–44, 850.

25 Ibid., pp. 844–46.

26 Qiu Guochen, *Fengdi yusheng lu* (Hong Kong: Tianfeng yinshua chang, 1972), p. 377.

27 Kulp, *Country Life in South China*, p. 88.

28 Li Diaoyuan, *Yuedong biji* (Shanghai: Huiwentang, 1915), ch. 5:6a.

29 *Haifeng xianzhi* (1874), p. 9a; Kulp, *Country Life in South China*, p. 88.

30 Edward LeFevour, *Western Enterprise in Late Ch'ing China: A Selective Survey of Jardine, Matheson & Company's Operations, 1842–1895* (Cambridge: Harvard East Asian Monographs, 1970), p. 76.

31 Jamieson et al., "Tenure of Land," p. 114.

32 Charles F. Remer, *The Foreign Trade of China* (Shanghai: The Commercial Press, 1926), pp. 86–87; Peng Zeyi et al., *Zhongguo jindai shougongye ziliao*, 2:298–99.

33 Li Wenzhi et al., *Zhongguo jindai nongye*, 1:502; Kang Chao, "The Growth of a Modern Cotton Textile Industry and the Competition with Handicrafts," in Dwight H. Perkins, ed., *China's Modern Economy in Historical Perspective* (Stanford: Stanford University Press, 1975), p. 181; Peng Zeyi et al., *Zhongguo jindai shougongye ziliao*, 2:489.

34 Chao, "Modern Cotton Textile Industry," pp. 190–91.

35 Guomin geming jun di shiliu shi zhengzhi xunlian chu, *Hailufeng ping gong ji* (Suppressing Communists in Hailufeng) (Guangzhou, 1928), p. 117.

36 Ibid.

37 Ibid. Information on the ownership of the mills was provided by Peng Hengli (Bro. Henry Pang) in private correspondence with the author.

38 *Hailufeng ping gong ji*, p. 117; *Chen Jingcun xiansheng nianpu* (A biography of Chen Jiongming) (n.p., n.d.), p. 28.

39 Albert Feuerwerker, *The Chinese Economy, ca. 1870–1911*, Michigan Papers in Chinese Studies, no. 5 (Ann Arbor: University of Michigan Center for Chinese Studies, 1969), p. 27.

40 Roy Hofheinz, Jr., *The Broken Wave: The Chinese Communist Peasant Movement, 1922–1928* (Cambridge: Harvard University Press, 1977), p. 139.

Chapter 6: "A Matter for the Police and the Courts"

1 Chai Degeng et al., eds., *Xinhai geming* (The 1911 Revolution) (Shanghai: Renmin chuban she, various dates), 7:258.

2 For Censor Wan's proposal, see Chai Degeng et al., *Xinhai geming*, 7:259–61.

3 Chai Degeng et al., *Xinhai geming*, 7:256–58.

4 Qiu Guochen, *Fengdi yusheng lu* (Hong Kong: Tianfeng yinshua chang, 1972), pp. 31–33.

5 *Chen Jingcun xiansheng nianpu* (n.p., n.d.), pp. 11–12.

6 See Winston Hsieh, "Ch'en Chiung-ming: The Ideas and Ideals of a Warlord (1878–1933)," *Papers on China* 16 (1962).

7 *Chen Jingcun xiansheng shilue* (A biography of Chen Jiongming) (n.p., n.d.), p. 1; *Chen Jingcun nianpu*, p. 7.

8 Qiu Guochen, *Fengdi*, p. 30; *Haifeng xianzhi* (1970), p. 17.

9 See Joseph Esherick, *Reform and Revolution in China: The 1911 Revolution in Hunan and Hubei* (Berkeley and Los Angeles: University of California Press, 1966), pp. 66 ff.

10 Edward J. M. Rhoads, *China's Republican Revolution: The Case of Kwangtung, 1895–1913* (Cambridge: Harvard University Press, 1975), pp. 55, 75, 103, 107, 160, 247.

11 *Chen Jingcun nianpu*, pp. 11–13.

12 *Chen Jingcun shilue*, pp. 2–3; *Chen Jingcun nianpu*, pp. 13–14.

13 John Lust, "Secret Societies, Popular Movements, and the 1911 Revolution," in Jean Chesneaux, ed., *Popular Movements and Secret Societies in China, 1840–1950* (Stanford: Stanford University Press, 1972); Mary Backus Rankin, "The Revolutionary Movement in Chekiang: A Study in the Tenacity of Tradition," in Mary C. Wright, ed., *China in Revolution: The First Phase, 1900–1913* (New Haven: Yale University Press, 1968), pp. 321 ff.

14 Jean Chesneaux, "Secret Societies in China's Historical Evolution," in Chesnaux, *Popular Movements*, p. 3.

15 Frederick Wakeman, Jr., *Strangers at the Gate: Social Disorder in South China, 1839–1861* (Berkeley and Los Angeles: University of California Press, 1966), p. 118. See also his essay "The Secret Societies of Kwangtung, 1800–1856," in Chesneaux, *Popular Movements*.

16 See the reference in Chesneaux, "Secret Societies in China's Historical Evolution," in Chesneaux, *Popular Movements*, p. 17.

17 *Haifeng xianzhi* (1874), p. 33b.

18 Wakeman, "The Secret Societies of Kwangtung."

19 *Haifeng xianzhi* (1874), pp. 34b–37b. The gentry-led militia in Haifeng closely resembled those in other parts of Guangdong, although they apparently were not called *tuan* or *tuan-lian*, which implied official status. See Philip Kuhn, *Rebellion and Its Enemies in Late Imperial China: Militarization and Social Structure, 1796–1864* (Cambridge: Harvard University Press, 1970), esp. chap. 3.

20 Lust, "Secret Societies," p. 165.

21 See Winston Hsieh, "Triads, Salt Smugglers, and Local Uprisings: Some Observations on the Social and Economic Background of the Waichow Revolution of 1911," in Chesneaux, *Popular Movements*, pp. 145–64.

22 Qui Guochen, *Fengdi*, pp. 31–33; Li Langru and Lu Man, "Xinhai geming shiqi Guangdong minjun gaikuang" (The Guangdong People's Army at the time of the 1911 Revolution), in *Xinhai geming huiyilu* (Beijing: Zhonghua shuju, 1962), 2:410–12; *Haifeng xianzhi* (1970), pp. 14–15.

23 Chen Jinglü, "Huizhou guangfu ji" (Memoir of the 1911 Revolution in Huizhou), *Jindai shi ziliao* 2 (1958): 51–61.

24 Chai Degeng et al., *Xinhai geming*, 7:227–35. See also Rhoads, *China's Republican Revolution*, pp. 204 ff.

25 Chai Degeng et al., *Xinhai geming*, 7:232. See also *Hong Kong Telegraph*, 23 December 1911.

26 *Zhonghua min'guo wushi nian wenxian* (Documents celebrating the fiftieth anniversary of the Republic of China) (Taibei), 2, no. 4:419, 463–64.

27 Chai Degeng et al., *Xinhai geming*, 7:240–44. See also *South China Morning Post*, 4 January 1912.

28 Qiu Guochen, *Fengdi*, p. 34. See also *South China Morning Post*, 12 March, 9 July, and 16 August 1912.

29 Peng Pai, "Haifeng nongmin yundong," in *Diyici guonei geming zhanzheng shiqi de nongmin yundong* (Beijing: Renmin chuban she, 1953), p. 41; Hsieh, "Ch'en Chiung-ming," p. 204.

30 *South China Morning Post*, 14 February 1912. Similar interpretations of political events can be found among some early-nineteenth-century British workers. A "provisional government" was taken by some to mean one which would ensure a more plentiful supply of "provisions," while "universal suffrage" was taken by some to mean that "if one must suffer, all must suffer." See E. P. Thompson, *The Making of the English Working Class* (Harmondsworth: Penquin Books, 1968), p. 763.

31 Edward Band, *Working His Purpose Out: The History of the English Presbyterian Mission, 1847–1947* (London, 1948), p. 285.

32 As Peter Worsley has warned, we should not project a "spurious unity" onto other people's beliefs. See *The Trumpet Shall Sound: A Study of "Cargo" Cults in Melanesia* (New York: Schocken Books, 1968), pp. xvii–xxv, for a discussion of belief systems of the inarticulate.

33 Henry Doré, *Researches into Chinese Superstitions*, trans. D. J. Finn (Taibei: Ch'eng-wen Publishing Co., 1966–67), 10:3 ff.; William Soothill and Louis Hodous, *A Dictionary of Chinese Buddhist Terms* (Taibei: Ch'eng-wen Publishing Co., 1960), pp. 148–49.

34 Fr. Gerado Brambilla, *Il Pontificio Instituto Della Mission Estere e le Sue Missioni* (Milan, 1943), 5:302; Band, *Working His Purpose Out*, pp. 265–66; Xu Gengbi, *Buziqie zhai man cun* (Taibei: Wenhai chuban she, n.d.), pp. 461–62, 477.

35 "Haifeng tianzhujiao wushiqi nian dashiji" (MS at P.I.M.E. Fathers Mission, Hong Kong), 1900; Xu Gengbi, *Buziqie zhai man cun*, pp. 477–79.

36 "Haifeng tianzhujiao", 1906, 1907.

37 Ibid., 1911. Guo was not the only person executed in Haifeng. According to Qiu Guochen, *Fengdi*, p. 34, the execution ground was littered with people's heads.

38 This phrase is taken from Antonio Gramsci, *Selections from the Prison Notebooks* (New York: International Publishers, 1971), pp. 90 ff.

39 Hou Feng, *Peng Pai lieshi zhuanlue* (The biography of Peng Pai, revolutionary martyr) (Guangzhou: Renmin chuban she, 1959), p. 7; Zhong Yimou, *Hailufeng nongmin yundong* (The Hailufeng peasant movement) (Guangzhou: Renmin chuban she, 1957), pp. 10, 27; *The Story of Swabue* (London: F. E. Philips and Sons, 1911), p. 9.

40 *South China Morning Post*, 28 February 1913. See also Rhoads, *China's Republican Revolution*, p. 257.

41 Peng Pai, "Haifeng nongmin yundong," p. 42.

42 *Guangdong nongmin yundong baogao* (Guangzhou, 1926), p. 34; *Zhongguo jingji nianyan* (Shanghai?, 1933), pt. 1, sec. G, p. 237.

43 Peng Pai, "Haifeng nongmin yundong," p. 136; Feng Hefa, *Zhongguo nongcun jingji ziliao* (Shanghai: Liming shuju, 1933), pp. 913–14.

44 Guo Chengxiang, "Haifeng tudi wenti chutan," in *Canjia jinian Peng Pai xueshu taolunhui lunwen* (Guangzhou: Guangzhou waiguo yu xueyuan, 1981).

45 Tieren (pseud.), "Min'guo shiliu nian hailufeng chihuo zhi huiyi" (manuscript in author's possession), ch. 1:11b; Peng Pai, "Haifeng nongmin yundong," p. 70; *Guangdong nongmin yundong baogao*, p. 25; *Zhongguo jingji nianyan*, pt. 1, sec. G, p. 236.

46 Guo Chengxiang, "Haifeng tudi wenti," pp. 1–2.

47 Feng Hefa, *Zhongguo nongcun*, p. 914.

48 Daniel Harrison Kulp, *Country Life in South China* (New York: Columbia University Press, 1925), pp. 214, 109.

49 *Gongren ribao*, 7 July 1962, p. 4. Information on the Flags was supplied by an informant in a 1975 interview in Hong Kong.

50 See Chapter 9 for a fuller discussion of these north Lufeng lineages.

Chapter 7: The Politics of Backwardness

1 Peng Pai, "Haifeng nongmin yundong," in *Diyici guonei geming zhanzheng shiqi de nongmin yundong* (Beijing: Renmin chuban she, 1953), pp. 51–53. For a more accessible version, see *Peng Pai wenji* (The Collected Works of Peng Pai) (Beijing: Renmin chuban she, 1981), pp. 3–7. Many of the quotations from this source are based on translations first made by Donald Holoch in *Seeds of Peasant Revolution* (Cornell University East Asia Paper) (Cornell: Cornell University Press, 1973).

2 Ibid., p. 54.

3 Ibid., p. 55.

4 Ibid., pp. 56–58.

5 Information on the Peng family, unless otherwise noted, was kindly supplied to me by Bro. Henry Pang (Peng Hengli).

6 Peng Pai, "Haifeng nongmin yundong," p. 52.

7 Ma-lie zhuyi jiaoyan wo zhonggong shi jiaoyan zu, *Peng Pai zhuanlue* (Guangzhou: Guangzhou waiguo yu xueyuan, 1980), pp. 1–5.

8 Yuan Ying, "Auntie Peng," in *Chinese Women in the Great Leap Forward* (Beijing: Foreign Languages Press, 1960), p. 91; Hou Feng, *Peng Pai lieshi zhuanlue* (Guangzhou: Renmin chuban she, 1959), p. 3.

9 Qiu Guochen, *Fengdi yusheng lu* (Hong Kong: Tianfeng yinshua chang, 1972), pp. 35–36; *Haifeng xianzhi* (1970), 4:9.

10 *Peng Pai zhuanlue*, pp. 4–5.

11 *Chen Jingcun xiansheng nianpu* (n.p., n.d.), p. 24.

12 See Tse-tung Chow, *The May Fourth Movement* (Stanford: Stanford University Press, 1967), pp. 84–115.

13 Wang Gongbi, "Dong you hui han lu" (Memoir in sweat of study in Japan), *Jindai shi ziliao* 2 (1955): 110–23.

14 *Peng Pai yanjiu shiliao* (Historical source materials for the study of Peng Pai) (Guangzhou: Renmin chuban she, 1981), pp. 368–69.

15 Li Zhendao, "Haifeng nongmin yundong ji qi lingdaozhe Peng Pai" (The Haifeng peasant movement and its leader Peng Pai), originally published in *Chenguang* 1 (30 January 1924), reprinted in *Peng Pai yanjiu shiliao*, pp. 282–83. Li's article is a major source for the early period of Peng's activities, paralleling and confirming much of what Peng wrote in "Haifeng nongmin yundong."

16 Henry D. Smith, *Japan's First Student Radicals* (Cambridge: Harvard University Press, 1972), pp. 50–56. See also Yong-pil Pang, "Peng Pai from Landlord to Revolutionary," *Modern China* 3 (July 1975): 314; and Rong Souying (?), "Peng Pai he jianshezhe tongmeng," in *Canjia jinian Peng Pai xueshu taolunhui lunwen* (Guangzhou: Guangzhou waiguo yu xueyuan, 1981).

17 Quoted in Chow, *May Fourth Movement*, pp. 45–46.

18 Smith, *Japan's Student Radicals*, p. 54.

19 Ibid., pp. 56–57.

20 Ibid., p. 55.

21 Inoue Kiyoshi, *Riben nongmin yundong shi* (History of the Japanese peasant movement), trans. Fukatani Takeseki (Beijing: Sanlian shudian, 1957), pp. 75–85.

22 Bai Shi, "Peng Pai zaoqi geming sixiang chutan" (A preliminary investigation into Peng Pai's early revolutionary ideas), *Xueshu* 3 (1980), p. 81, n. 13.
23 Li Zhendao, "Haifeng nongmin yundong," pp. 282–83. See also Bai Shi, "Peng Pai zaoqi," p. 77.
24 *South China Morning Post*, 23 February 1921.
25 Guangdong zizhi hui, ed., *Guangdong difang zizhi* (Guangdong local self-government) (Shanghai, 1922).
26 *Peng Pai yanjiu shiliao*, pp. 102–9.
27 Li Zhendao, "Haifeng nongmin yundong," p. 285.
28 *Peng Pai yanjiu shiliao*, pp. 102–3.
29 Zhonggong zhongyang makesi engesi liening sidalin zhuzuo bianyi ju yanjiu wo, ed., *Wusi shiqi qikan jieshao* (Introduction to the periodicals of the May Fourth period) (Beijing: Renmin chuban she, 1959), 3:443.
30 Ibid., p. 444.
31 Bai Shi, "Peng Pai zaoqi," pp. 77–79.
32 All quotations from "Gao tongbao" are from the version printed in Zhong Yimou, *Hailufeng nongmin yundong* (Guangzhou: Renmin chuban she, 1957), pp. 15–20.
33 Ibid., p. 20.
34 Ibid., pp. 17–18.
35 *Peng Pai zhuanlue*, pp. 14–15.
36 *Wusi shiqi qikan jieshao*, 3:539.
37 *Peng Pai yanjiu shiliao*, pp. 102–8.
38 Ibid., pp. 107–13.
39 Peng Pai, "Haifeng nongmin yundong," p. 51; Zhong Yimou, *Hailufeng nongmin yundong*, p. 10.
40 *Peng Pai yanjiu shiliao*, p. 109.
41 See, for example, Edward Friedman, *Backward toward Revolution* (Berkeley and Los Angeles: University of California Press, 1974), pp. 15, 17, 19.
42 Peng Pai, "Shei yingdang chulai tichang shehuizhuyi" (Who Should Advocate Socialism?), in *Peng Pai wen ji*, pp. 8–9. See also Li Zhendao, "Haifeng nongmin yundong," pp. 287–88.
43 Ibid., p. 288.
44 Peng Pai, "Haifeng nongmin yundong," pp. 51–52.
45 Ibid., p. 52.
46 Li Zhendao, "Haifeng nongmin yundong," p. 290.
47 *Peng Pai zhuanlue*, p. 20.
48 Li Zhendao, "Haifeng nongmin yundong," pp. 289–90.

49 Peng Pai, "Haifeng nongmin yundong," p. 59.
50 Ibid., pp. 60–61.
51 Chen Xiaobai, *Hailufeng chihuo ji* (Guangzhou: Peiying yinwu ju, 1932), p. 29.
52 Li Zhendao, "Haifeng nongmin yundong,'', p. 290.
53 Zhong Yimou, *Hailufeng nongmin yundong*, pp. 9, 20–21; Peng Pai, "Haifeng nongmin yundong," p. 63.
54 Peng Pai, "Haifeng nongmin yundong," pp. 49–50.
55 Ibid., p. 49. See also *Gongren ribao*, 7 July 1962, p. 4.
56 Li Zhendao, "Haifeng nongmin yundong," p. 289.
57 Shu Huai, "Wo ye tantan jiuli xin nian—Haifeng de" (I will also talk about the old lunar New Year—Haifeng's), in *Guangdong fengsu juilu* (Hong Kong, 1972), pp. 402–4.
58 Cited in *Zhongguo qingnian* 13 (5 January 1924): 5. The source of this story probably was Peng Pai's report, "The Organization of the Guangdong Peasant Union and Its Experiences," written to the central committee of the Socialist Youth Corps in September 1923. See Peng Pai, "Guangdong nonghui zhi zuzhi ji jingguo," in *Peng Pai wen ji*, pp. 46–49.
59 Zhong Yimou, *Hailufeng nongmin yundong*, p. 31, n. 1.
60 Li Zhendao, "Haifeng nongmin yundong," p. 289.
61 Peng Pai, "Haifeng nongmin yundong," pp. 73–74.
62 Ibid., pp. 70–71.
63 Chen Xiaobai, *Hailufeng chihuo ji*, p. 30.
64 Peng Pai, "Haifeng nongmin yundong," pp. 71–73.
65 Ibid., pp. 73–74.
66 Ibid., p. 75.
67 Ibid., pp. 75–76; Xu Xiangqian, "Ben xiang Hailufeng" (Fleeing to Hailufeng), in *Xing huo liao yuan* (Beijing: Renmin chuban she, 1958), p. 215; Vera Vladimira Vishnyakova-Akimova, *Two Years in Revolutionary China, 1925–27*, trans. Steven I. Levine, Harvard East Asian Monographs (Cambridge: Harvard University East Asian Research Center, 1971), p. 163.
68 Peter Worsley, *The Trumpet Shall Sound: A Study of "Cargo" Cults in Melanesia"* (New York: Schocken Books, 1968), pp. xiii–xiv.
69 Li Zhendao, "Haifeng nongmin yundong," pp. 301–8.
70 Peng Pai, "Haifeng nongmin yundong," p. 86.
71 Ibid., pp. 88–89.
72 Li Zhendao, "Haifeng nongmin yundong," p. 308.
73 Ibid., p. 310. There is a possibility that this report was not written by Peng Pai. See *Peng Pai wen ji*, p. 41 note 2.

315

74 Peng Pai, "Haifeng nongmin yundong," pp. 97–99, 113. By January 1924, 25 of those arrested had been released. See *Peng Pai wen ji*, p. 54. The Haifeng peasant union was reestablished briefly in February 1924 after Peng Pai had obtained the approval of Chen Jiongming. After a few days, the magistrate Wang Zuoxin again disbanded it. Peng Pai was in Guangzhou at the time, but his brother and others who were active in the union managed to escape to Guangzhou via Shantou and Hong Kong. See *Peng Pai wen ji*, p. 56, and Zhong Yimou, *Hailufeng nongmin yundong*, p. 29.

75 Ibid., pp. 99, 113.

76 Roy Hofheinz, Jr., *The Broken Wave: The Chinese Communist Peasant Movement, 1922–1928* (Cambridge: Harvard University Press, 1977), p. 67.

77 Ibid., p. 162.

Chapter 8: The Cult of Peng Pai

1 *Huazi ribao*, 17 July 1923.

2 Liao Zhongkai, *Liao Zhongkai ji* (The collected works of Liao Zhongkai) (Beijing: Zhonghua shuju, 1963), p. 188.

3 Luo Qiyuan, "Ben bu yinian lai jingguo baogao gaiyao: nongmin bu zhi zuzhi" (General report on the work of this department in the past year: The organization of the peasant department), *Zhongguo nongmin* 2 (February 1926): 4–5; *Guomindang zhoukan*, 3 July 1924, p. 4.

4 *Liao Zhongkai ji*, pp. 169–74.

5 Gan Naiguang, "Shei shi guomin geming de li jun?" (Who is the main force of the National Revolution?), *Zhongguo nongmin* 8 (October 1926): 1–11.

6 Zou Lu, *Huigulu* (My memoirs) (Guangzhou: Jindai zhongguo shiliao congkan, 1938), p. 161.

7 *Peng Pai yanjiu shiliao*, (Guangzhou: Renmin chuban she, 1981), pp. 4–7.

8 *Guomindang zhoukan*, 3 July 1924, p. 4; *Nonggong xunkan*, 1 September 1924, pp. 9–10; Luo Qiyuan, "Ben bu yinian lai," p. 5; *Peng Pai yanjiu shiliao*, pp. 12–13. See also Gerald W. Berkley, "The Canton Peasant Movement Training Institute," *Modern China* 1, no. 2 (April 1975).

9 Figures do not exist for all sessions, but percentages from the second and third sessions break down as follows: of 225 students

in the second class, 30% were peasants, 30% students, 22% workers, and the rest "others"; of the 138 students in the third session, 72% were peasants. *Zhongguo nongmin* 2 (February 1926): 1–44; Luo Qiyuan, "Ben bu yinian lai," pp. 8–18.

10 *Nonggong xunkan*, 1 August 1924, pp. 15–16.

11 *South China Morning Post*, 17 July 1923, 3 July 1922, 20 July 1923, 24 July 1919, 29 May 1924.

12 *Geming wenxian* (Taibei, various dates), p. 1766. Eighty-five rifles were given to the Peasant Army, and 220 rifles to the Worker's Army. For various accounts, see Luo Qiyuan, "Ben bu yinian lai," pp. 18–19; *Nonggong xunkan*, 11 September 1924, p. 23; and *China Illustrated Review*, 20 September 1924.

13 For an account sympathetic to the Merchant Volunteer Corps, see *Guangdong kouxie chao* (English title: *The Canton Volunteer Arms Case*) (Hong Kong: Huazi ribao, 1924). For a brief account in English, see Jean Chesneaux, *The Chinese Labor Movement, 1919–1927*, trans. Arthur F. Wright (Stanford: Stanford University Press, 1968), pp. 248–49.

14 *China Illustrated Review*, 6 December 1924; *South China Morning Post*, 3 September 1924.

15 Liu Bingcui, *Geming jun diyici dongzheng shi zhan ji* (A factual record of the First Eastern Expedition) (Guangzhou?: Zhonghua shuju, 1928), pp. 192, 196–97, 203. See also *Geming wenxian*, p. 1611.

16 *Guangdong nongmin yundong baogao* (Guangzhou, 1926), pp. 125–26; Ruan Xiaoxian, "Huiyang nongmin xiehui chengli zhi jingguo" (Experiences in establishing the Huiyang peasant union), *Zhongguo nongmin* 3 (March 1926): 20.

17 Zhong Yimou, "Hailufeng nongmin de ba nian douzheng" (The eight-year struggle of the Hailufeng peasants), *Jindai shi ziliao* 4 (1955): 189; *Huazi ribao*, 4 March 1925; *South China Morning Post*, 9 March 1925.

18 Quoted in Cai Hesen, "Jin nian wuyi zhi Guangdong nongmin yundong" (The Guangdong peasant movement as of this year's May Day), *Xiangdao zhoubao* 151 (28 April 1925): 1031.

19 *Peng Pai yanjiu shiliao*, pp. 120–26.

20 *South China Morning Post*, 29 August 1925. See also ibid., 1 October 1925; *China Illustrated Review*, 4 December 1925.

21 Zhong Yimou, "Hailufeng nongmin de ba nian douzheng," p. 191; *Hailufeng suweiai* (The Hailufeng soviet) (Shanghai?, 1928), p. 6.

22 See Zhou Enlai's speech upon taking Shantou in *China Illustrated Review*, 4 December 1925.

23 *Geming wenxian*, p. 1671; Fr. Gerado Brambilla, *Il Pontificio Instituto Della Mission Estere e le sue Missioni* (Milan, 1943), 5: 291–92; *South China Morning Post*, 28 October 1925.

24 *Huazi ribao*, 4 March 1925; Tieren (pseud.), "Min'guo shiliu nian Hailufeng chihuo zhi huiyi" (MS in author's possession), ch. 1:19a; Zhong Yimou, "Hailufeng nongmin de ba nian douzheng," p. 190.

25 *Huazi ribao*, 4 March 1925.

26 Zhong Yimou, *Hailufeng nongmin yundong* (Guangzhou: Renmin chuban she, 1957), p. 40; *Guangzhou minguo ribao*, 10 August 1926; *Hailufeng suweiai*, pp. 6–8. Peng Pai's older brother, Hanyuan, was Haifeng magistrate, while the Lufeng post was held by Zhang Wei. Both were replaced shortly after Jiang Jieshi's 20 March 1926 coup.

27 *Guangzhou minguo ribao*, 8 July 1926.

28 Tieren, "Hailufeng chihuo zhi huiyi," ch. 1:5b, 23b–24a.

29 Zhong Yimou, *Hailufeng nongmin yundong*, p. 36; *Hailufeng suweiai*, p. 8; L. Mad'iar, *Zhongguo nongcun jingji yanjiu* (Shanghai: Shenzhou guoguang she, 1930), p. 337; Zhong Yimou, "Hailufeng nongmin de ba nian douzheng," p. 195.

30 Zhong Yimou, *Hailufeng nongmin yundong*, pp. 40–49.

31 *Hailufeng suweiai*, p. 8; Zhong Yimou, *Hailufeng nongmin yundong*, p. 36. In a speech on 25 October 1925 reinstating the Peasant Union, Peng Pai had licensed the revenge: "We must resolutely and pitilessly eliminate the enemy. We must seek an eye for an eye, a tooth for a tooth. . . . We cannot show compassion. . . . To be compassionate only hurts the revolution." Zhong Yimou, *Hailufeng nongmin yundong*, p. 40.

32 *Hailufeng suweiai*, p. 9.

33 Ibid.

34 Ibid. See also James P. Harrison, *The Long March to Power: A History of the Chinese Communist Party, 1922–1972* (New York: Praeger, 1972), p. 99.

35 *Peng Pai yanjiu shiliao*, pp. 205–6.

36 *Guangzhou minguo ribao*, 20 August 1926.

37 Zhong Yimou, "Hailufeng nongmin de ba nian douzheng," p. 195.

38 See Conrad Brandt, *Stalin's Failure in China* (New York: W. W. Norton, 1966), pp. 57–58, for a discussion of Dai's views.

39 *Guomindang zhoubao*, 10 October 1926, pp. 22–23.

40 *Guangdong nongmin yundong baogao*, pp. 113–14.

41 Zou Lu, *Huigulu*, pp. 165–66.

42 He Yangling, *Nongmin yundong* (The peasant movement) (Nanjing, 1928), bk. 8, p. 14. Biographies of the assassinated special

deputies can be found on the unpaginated endplates of *Zhongguo nongmin* 10 (December 1926).

43 "Zenyang jiejue nongjun yu mintuan jiufen" (How to resolve the conflict between the peasant army and the rural militia), *Litou zhoubao* 14 (15 September 1926): 1. Neither the function nor membership of the Rear Area Working Committee is known.

44 *Guangdong nongmin yundong baogao,* pp. 63, 160.

45 *Litou zhoubao* 15 (23 September 1926): 34; *Guangdong nongmin yundong baogao,* pp. 160–64. The Guangdong CCP Regional Committee proposed that at least two investigators be sent to survey conditions in each of eleven counties: Haifeng, Puning, Jieyang, Shunde, Zhongshan, Nanhai, Dongguan, Houshan, Guangning, Qingyuan, and Xinyi. The criteria for selecting the investigators—most of whom, it was assumed, would be special deputies—included familiarity with local conditions, fluency in the local dialect, and experience in the peasant movement. The investigators were to receive training in Guangzhou during late August. Five classes for a total of 84 hours of instruction were planned, with classes taught by Soviet advisors and Mao Zedong, among others. Based on these investigations, the committee hoped to "make new policies for the peasant movement." For a discussion of how the "rural investigation plan" was subsequently implemented through the Guangdong Provincial Peasant Union, see "Guangdong sheng nongmin xiehui ba nian lai de zhongyao gongzuo," *Zhongguo nongmin* 10 (December 1926): 64–74, and *Guangzhou minguo ribao,* 9 October 1926, p. 11. It is my guess that these investigations were the basis of a massive report in English by the Soviet advisors M. Volin and E. Yolk, *The Kwangtung Peasant Movement.* This study was mimeographed just before Jiang Jieshi's 12 April 1927 coup, and reportedly most copies were destroyed at the printer's. At least two copies are known to exist: one at the Academy of Sciences in Moscow, and one either in Beijing or Guangzhou. I have been unable to obtain a copy from either place.

46 Luo Qiyuan, "Ben bu yinian lai,", pp. 2–4.

47 *Guangdong nongmin yundong baogao,* pp. 51–52, 82.

48 Ibid., p. 63.

49 Chang Kuo-t'ao, *The Rise of the Chinese Communist Party, 1921–1927* (Lawrence: University of Kansas Press, 1971), 1:600.

50 Ibid., pp. 599–600. See also *Guangdong nongmin yundong baogao,* pp. 156–57.

51 *Litou zhoubao* 12 (4 August 1926): 12–16, 16–19.

52 *Litou zhoubao* 15 (23 September 1926): 22–23.
53 He Yangling, *Nongmin yundong*, bk. 8, pp. 15–16.
54 See *Guangzhou minguo ribao*, 8 October 1926, p. 11; 23 October 1926, p. 11; 30 October 1926, p. 7; 27 November 1926, p. 11.
55 *Litou zhoubao* 17–18 (October 1926): 45.
56 Ibid., pp. 44–45.
57 For a discussion of how varying relations between town and countryside affect the outcome of revolutionary movements, see my "Peasant Society and Peasant Uprisings in South China: Social Change in Haifeng County, 1630–1930" (Ph.D. diss., University of Wisconsin—Madison, 1978), pp. 247 ff.; Antonio Gramsci, *Selections from the Prison Notebooks*, ed. and trans. Quintin Hoare and Geoffrey Nowell Smith (New York: International Publishers, 1971), pp. 1–15, 90–94; Charles Tilly, "Town and County in Revolution," in John W. Lewis, ed., *Peasant Rebellion and Communist Revolution in Asia* (Stanford: Stanford University Press, 1971).
58 *Litou zhoubao* 21 (3 December 1926): 13.
59 *Guangdong nongmin yundong baogao*, p. 110. *Wansui* had been used as an adjectival honorific for emperors, but I have chosen to translate it here as "Eternal One" because peasants clearly used it as a noun.
60 *Litou zhoubao* 16 (1 October 1926): 25.
61 *Guangdong nongmin yundong baogao*, pp. 121–22.
62 *Hailufeng suweiai*, p. 9.

Chapter 9: The Haifeng Soviet

1 Antonio Gramsci, *Selections from the Prison Notebooks*, ed. and trans. Quintin Hoare and Geoffrey Nowell Smith (New York: International Publishers, 1971), p. 210. For an analysis of Jiang Jieshi's 12 April 1927 coup in terms of a "crisis of authority" and a comparison with Harold Isaacs' Bonapartist analysis (in *The Tragedy of the Chinese Revolution*, 2nd rev. ed. [New York: Antheneum, 1968], pp. 180–82), see Robert B. Marks, "Peasant Society and Peasant Uprisings in South China: Social Change in Haifeng County, 1630–1930" (Ph.D. diss., University of Wisconsin—Madison, 1978), pp. 453–64.
2 Quoted in Stuart R. Schram, *The Political Thought of Mao Tse-tung*, rev. and enl. ed. (New York: Praeger, 1969), pp. 250–51.
3 Ibid., p. 250.
4 *South China Morning Post*, 11 January 1927.

5 See Jean Chesneaux, *The Chinese Labor Movement, 1919–1927*, trans. Arthur F. Wright (Stanford: Stanford University Press, 1968), pp. 345–71; and Isaacs, *Tragedy of the Chinese Revolution*, chaps. 8–11.

6 Angus McDonald, *The Urban Origins of Rural Revolution* (Berkeley and Los Angeles: University of California Press, 1978), p. 315.

7 Ibid., p. 309.

8 Isaacs, *Tragedy of the Chinese Revolution*, p. 182.

9 Edward Band, *Working His Purpose Out: The History of English Presbyterian Mission, 1847–1947* (London, 1948), p. 373.

10 *Zhongyang zhengzhi huiyi Guangzhou fenhui shiliu nian fen yuekan* (1927 monthly calendar for the Guangzhou branch of the central political assembly), (Guangzhou, 1928), 1:165; Zhong Yimou, *Hailufeng nongmin yundong*, (Guangzhou: Renmin chuban she, 1957), pp. 53–54.

11 While in Wuhan, Peng attended the Guomindang Land Committee deliberations in March and April 1927. He also held the post of head of the Peasant and Worker Bureau of the Hubei provincial government. See *Peng Pai zhuanlue* (Guangzhou: Guangzhou waiguo yu xueyuan, 1980), pp. 54–55; *Hailufeng suweiai* (Shanghai?, 1928), p. 14; and Chen Xiaobai, *Hailufeng chihuo ji* (Guangzhou: Peiying yinwu ju, 1932), p. 8.

12 *Hailufeng suweiai*, p. 14.

13 Ibid.

14 Zhong Yimou, *Hailufeng nongmin yundong*, pp. 54–55; *Hailufeng suweiai*, pp. 15–16.

15 *Hailufeng suweiai*, p. 18.

16 Pages of Lin's diary were later printed by the Guomindang army after the diary was captured in a raid into the villages. See Guomin geming jun di shiliu shi zhengzhi xunlian chu, *Hailufeng ping gong ji* (Suppressing Communists in Hailufeng) (Guangzhou, 1928), pp. 92–93.

17 Zhong Yimou, *Hailufeng nongmin yundong*, p. 57; *Hailufeng suweiai*, p. 23.

18 Zhong Yimou, *Hailufeng nongmin yundong*, p. 58; Chen Xiaobai, *Hailufeng chihuo ji*, pp. 9, 12–13.

19 Chen Xiaobai, *Hailufeng chihuo ji*, p. 11; Zhong Yimou, *Hailufeng nongmin yundong*, pp. 59–60; *Nanfang ribao*, 24 August 1952; Liu Youliang, 1975 interview with the author.

20 *Hailufeng suweiai*, pp. 21–22, 25, 28; Zhong Yimou, *Hailufeng nongmin yundong*, p. 60.

21 Helen Snow, *The Chinese Communists: Sketches and Autobiographies of the Old Guard* (Westport, Conn.: Greenwood, 1972), p. 208.

22 *Hailufeng suweiai*, pp. 19–21, 31.

23 Ibid., p. 29.

24 Ibid., pp. 29–30.

25 Ibid., pp. 30–33; Zhong Yimou, *Hailufeng nongmin yundong*, pp. 60–61, 67–68.

26 Chen Xiaobai, *Hailufeng chihuo ji*, pp. 10–13.

27 Zhong Yimou, *Hailufeng nongmin yundong*, pp. 60–61, 62, 63, 66–68; Chen Xiaobai, *Hailufeng chihuo ji*, p. 10; *Hailufeng suweiai*, pp. 32–33.

28 *Hailufeng suweiai*, p. 36.

29 Ibid.

30 Ibid., pp. 35–37.

31 *Guangzhou shibian yu Shanghai huiyi* (The Guangzhou incident and the Shanghai conference) (Guangzhou?: Guangzhou pingshe, 1928), pp. 16–19; *South China Morning Post*, 9 June, 31 August, 12 September, and 20 September 1927. Peng Pai clearly understood that the fighting between Zhang Fakui and Li Jishen had provided the opportunity to seize power once again. When the Haifeng Soviet was proclaimed, he pointedly reminded the people of Haifeng of that fact in order to strengthen their resolve to carry out the land revolution and prevent the return of the Guomindang armies. See *Peng Pai wen ji* (Beijing: Renmin chuban she, 1981), pp. 292–93.

32 Chang Kuo-t'ao, *The Rise of the Chinese Communist Party, 1928–1938* (Lawrence: University of Kansas Press, 1972), 2:28, 35. For the CCP analysis of the Nanchang Uprising, the southern march, and the subsequent debacle, see Hyobom Pak, ed. and trans., *Documents of the Chinese Communist Party, 1927–1930* (Hong Kong: Union Research Institute, 1971), pp. 147–58; the documents translated by C. Martin Wilbur in "The Ashes of Defeat," *China Quarterly* 18 (April–June 1964): 3–54; L. P. Deliusin, "From the August Conference to the Guangzhou Uprising (August–December 1927)," *Chinese Studies in History* 4 (Summer 1974): 36–91; and *Peng Pai zhuanlue*, pp. 55–58.

33 *Hailufeng suweiai*, pp. 42–44.

34 *Hailufeng suweiai*, pp. 41, 40, 39, 45; Zhong Yimou, *Hailufeng nongmin yundong*, p. 76; *Buersaiweike* (*Bolshevik*) 5 (21 November 1927): 121–22. See also *South China Morning Post*, 12 October 1927.

35 *Hailufeng suweiai*, p. 45.

36 Snow, *Chinese Communists*, p. 209.

37 *Hailufeng suweiai*, pp. 45–47; "Vier Monate Rätemacht in Hailu-föng: Ein Brief aus Kwangtung," in *Räte-China: Dokumente der chinesischen Revolution (1927–1931)* (Frankfurt: Verlag Ullstein, 1973), p. 31.

38 *Hailufeng suweiai*, p. 47. Chen Xiaobai, *Hailufeng chihuo ji*, p. 30, implies that hundreds were killed.

39 Chen Xiaobai, *Hailufeng chihuo ji*, pp. 31–33; *Hailufeng suweiai*, pp. 47, 62; Zhong Yimou, *Hailufeng nongmin yundong*, pp. 101–2.

40 Zhong Yimou, "Hailufeng nongmin de ba nian douzheng," *Jindai shi ziliao* 4 (1955): 208.

41 *Peng Pai yanjiu shiliao* (Guangzhou: Renmin chuban she, 1981), pp. 22–23; *Hailufeng suweiai*, pp. 57, 63. The distribution of the representatives had been set by the CCP Guangdong Regional Committee on September 30 in its "Outline of Post-Uprising Work in the Counties and Municipalities." See Pak, *Documents*, pp. 117–22.

42 Presumably the substance of what Peng said about the "land revolution" is contained in an article of the same title published about the same time in the CCP journal *Red Flag*. See Peng Pai, "Tudi geming," in *Peng Pai wen ji*, pp. 277–79. The text of Peng's speeches at the Assembly are in *Peng Pai wen ji*, pp. 280–93, while a description of the Assembly is in *Peng Pai yanjiu shiliao*, pp. 22–23.

43 Li Zhendao, "Haifeng nongmin yundong ji qi lingdaozhe Peng Pai," in *Peng Pai yanjiu shiliao*, p. 293.

44 The discussion of the fate of soviets in Russia is based on Edward H. Carr, *The Bolshevik Revolution, 1917–1923* (Middlesex, England: Penguin Books, 1973), 1: 224 ff., 249–50.

45 Pak, *Documents*, pp. 24, 131.

46 "Vier Monate," p. 43. See also *Hailufeng suweiai*, pp. 68–69.

47 Nym Wales (Helen Snow) and Kim San, *Song of Ariran: A Korean Communist in the Chinese Revolution* (San Francisco: Ramparts Press, 1972 renewal of 1941 copyright), p. 207.

48 Rosa Luxemburg, *The Russian Revolution and Leninism or Marxism* (Ann Arbor: University of Michigan Press, 1967), pp. 41–46.

49 Wilbur, "Ashes of Defeat," pp. 16, 41. Even after the CCP had gained some practical experience with the "land problem" through the Haifeng Soviet, it was still grappling with it in 1928 in an abstract and pedantic manner in the pages of its journal, the *Bol-*

shevik. See esp. *Buersaiweike* 6 (28 November 1927): 154–65; 15 (30 January 1928): 492–98; and 19 (27 February 1928): 646–51.

50 *Hailufeng suweiai*, pp. 81–82. Peng Pai also saw a strategic value to carrying out the land revolution as rapidly as possible: he hoped that by killing or driving away landlords, an attack on Haifeng by Guomindang troops would be forestalled if not prevented. See *Peng Pai wen ji*, p. 293.

51 *Hailufeng suweiai*, p. 81. See also Deliusin, "From the August Conference," p. 70.

52 *Hailufeng suweiai*, pp. 49–50.

53 "Vier Monate," pp. 36, 38.

54 Deliusin, "From the August Conference," p. 71.

55 *Hailufeng suweiai*, p. 80; Deliusin, "From the August Conference," p. 71; Zhong Yimou, *Hailufeng nongmin yundong*, p. 86. The most recent biography of Peng Pai likewise comments that the land revolution reflected the "thousand-year-old peasant ideal of 'land equalization' and 'equality between poor and rich.' " See *Peng Pai zhuanlue*, p. 61.

56 "Hailufeng de hong qi" (The red flag of Hailufeng), in *Xing huo liao yuan* (Beijing: Renmin chuban she, 1958), pp. 238–39. Their prayers, of course, were soon answered.

57 *Hailufeng suweiai*, pp. 57–59.

58 Tieren (pseud.), "Min'guo shiliu nian Hailufeng chihuo zhi huiyi" (MS in author's possession), ch. 1:41a–42b; Fr. Gerado Brambilla, *Il Pontificio Instituto Della Mission Estere e le sue Missioni* (Milan, 1943), 5:307.

59 "Vier Monate," pp. 36–37. See also Deliusin, "From the August Conference," p. 71; *Hailufeng suweiai*, pp. 88–95; Tieren, "Hailufeng chihuo zhi huiyi," ch. 1:36b–37a.

60 Barrington Moore, Jr., *The Social Origins of Dictatorship and Democracy: Lord and Peasant in the Making of the Modern World* (Boston: Beacon Press, 1966).

61 Charles Tilly, *From Mobilization to Revolution* (Reading, Mass.: Addison-Wesley, 1978), chap. 6.

62 See Jeffrey Paige, *Agrarian Revolution* (New York: Free Press, 1975), pp. 24 ff., for a discussion of a "zero-sum" conflict.

63 Chen Xiaobai, *Hailufeng chihuo ji*, pp. 49–51.

64 Ibid., p. 51.

65 Tieren, "Hailufeng chihuo zhi huiyi," ch. 1:22b.

66 "Vier Monate," p. 45. See also Zhong Yimou, *Hailufeng nongmin yundong*, pp. 109–11; Chen Xiaobai, *Hailufeng chihuo ji*, pp. 49–54.

67 Ibid.
68 Chen Xiaobai, *Hailufeng chihuo ji*, pp. 32–39, 46–47; Zhong Yimou, *Hailufeng nongmin yundong*, pp. 107–8.
69 Zhong Yimou, *Hailufeng nongmin yundong*, pp. 108–09; Chen Xiaobai, *Hailufeng chihuo ji*, pp. 46, 48.
70 The information on northern Lufeng was pieced together from Xu Gengbi, *Buziqie zhai man cun* (Taibei: Wenhai chuban she), pp. 614–17, 753; *Lufeng xianzhi* (1747), ch. 2:15a–16b, ch. 7:3b–14a; *Huizhou fuzhi* (1688), ch. 4; Chen Xiaobai, *Hailufeng chihuo ji*, pp. 39–41; Tieren, "Hailufeng chihuo zhi huiyi," ch. 1:31b; Zhong Yimou, *Hailufeng nongmin yundong*, pp. 35, 107–9; *Nanfang ribao*, 11 April 1950; "Vier Monate," pp. 45–46.
71 Chen Xiaobai, *Hailufeng chihuo ji*, p. 50.
72 *Peng Pai yanjiu shiliao*, p. 34.
73 Ibid., pp. 32–33.
74 Ibid., pp. 33–34.
75 *Peng Pai zhuanlue*, p. 68.
76 *Hailufeng suweiai*, pp. 71–72.
77 Ibid., p. 53. See also "Vier Monate," pp. 48–50.
78 Chen Xiaobai, *Hailufeng chihuo ji*, pp. 129–33.
79 "Vier Monate," p. 49.
80 Ibid., pp. 51, 38.
81 Zhong Yimou, *Hailufeng nongmin yundong*, pp. 111–13; Chen Xiaobai, *Hailufeng chihuo ji*, pp. 63–66.
82 "Vier Monate," pp. 48–49.
83 Chen Xiaobai, *Hailufeng chihuo ji*, p. 65.
84 Zhong Yimou, *Hailufeng nongmin yundong*, pp. 113–16; Chen Xiaobai, *Hailufeng chihuo ji*, pp. 65–67.
85 Chen Xiaobai, *Hailufeng chihuo ji*, pp. 69, 72–73.
86 Zhong Yimou, *Hailufeng nongmin yundong*, pp. 113–16; "Vier Monate," p. 39.
87 *Peng Pai yanjiu shiliao*, pp. 37–42.
88 Zhong Yimou, *Hailufeng nongmin yundong*, pp. 116–18; *Hailufeng ping gong ji*, pp. 46–49; Nym Wales and Kim San, *Song of Ariran*, pp. 192–97.
89 Chen Xiaobai, *Hailufeng chihuo ji*, pp. 135–37, 151–52.
90 The losses in the "White Terror" of 1928 reportedly amounted to 5,932 people killed, 7,246 houses razed, and 2,994 oxen killed. See *Peng Pai zhuanlue*, p. 66.
91 Nym Wales and Kim San, *Song of Ariran*, pp. 197–201; *Peng Pai yanjiu shiliao*, pp. 385–86.

92 Nym Wales and Kim San, *Song of Ariran*, p. 202.
93 *Peng Pai zhuanlue*, p. 68. On the East River Committee uprising plans and the response by the Guangdong Regional Committee, see *Peng Pai yanjiu shiliao*, pp. 51–81.
94 *Peng Pai zhuanlue*, pp. 69–72.
95 Robert Brenner, "Agrarian Class Structure and Economic Development in Pre-Industrial Europe," *Past and Present* 60 (February 1976): 52.

Conclusion

1 Theda Skocpol, *States and Social Revolutions* (New York: Cambridge University Press, 1978), p. 18.
2 Fernand Braudel, *The Mediterranean and the Mediterranean World in the Age of Philip II* (New York: Harper and Row, 1972), p. 21.
3 E. P. Thompson, *The Poverty of Theory* (New York: Monthly Review Press, 1978), p. 164.
4 James C. Scott, *The Moral Economy of the Peasant* (New Haven: Yale University Press, 1976), p. 4.
5 Edgar Snow, *Red Star Over China* (New York: Grove Press, 1961), p. 72.
6 Mark Selden, *The Yenan Way in Revolutionary China* (Cambridge: Harvard University Press, 1971), p. 199.
7 Edgar Snow, *The Long Revolution* (New York: Vintage Books, 1973), p. 68.
8 Snow, *Red Star Over China*, p. 71.
9 Nym Wales and Kim San, *The Song of Ariran: A Korean Communist in the Chinese Revolution* (San Francisco: Ramparts Press, 1972 renewal of 1941 copyright), p. 206.
10 See the essays by Bai Shouyi, "Zhongguo lishi shang nongmin zhanzheng de tedian," Ning Ke, "Zhongguo nongmin zhanzheng shi shang de huangchuanzhuyi," and Dong Jiazun, "Tan tan 'huangchuanzhuyi' wenti," in Shi Zhaobin, ed., *Zhongguo fengjian shehui nongmin zhanzheng wenti taolun ji* (Beijing: Sanlian shudian, 1962).
11 Snow, *The Long Revolution*, p. 69.
12 Karl Marx, "The Eighteenth Brumaire of Louis Bonaparte," in *Selected Works in One Volume* (New York: International Publishers, 1970), p. 172.
13 Elizabeth Perry, *Rebels and Revolutionaries in North China, 1845–1945* (Stanford: Stanford University Press, 1980), pp. 246–47.
14 Ibid., p. 239.

INDEX

Agrarian economy: conceptions of, xvii; specialization of, 47–48; affected by Ming-Qing troubles, 48–49; place of rice in, 49; and exports, 53; sugar cane in, 101–4. *See also* Guangdong province; Handicraft industries; Land tenure relations; Marketing systems; Markets; Peanuts; Rice; Sugar cane

Agriculture. *See* Agrarian economy

April 12 Coup, 232. *See also* Jiang Jieshi

Arrow War of 1856, 96

August 5 Movement, 188–90; commemorated, 212; as collective violence, 260–61

Autumn Harvest Uprising, 246

Baling Hui. *See* Baling sect

Baling sect, 140–43. *See also* Buddhism; Lin lineage of Meilong; Meilong; Religion

Bandits: and disintegration of estates, 15; peasants defined by state as, 23–24, 26; and 1911 Revolution, 121–22, 123; government suppression plans of, 122–23, 132; and crop-watching societies, 123; presence in Guangdong province of, 123; in Haifeng, 123–24. *See also* Peasants; Peasant uprisings; People's Armies; Pirates; Popular societies; Triad society

Baojia registers, 37

Black Flags. *See* Red and Black Flags

Bonapartism, 287–88. *See also* Cults; Peng Pai, cult of

Braudel, Fernand, xii, xviii, 282, 294n14

Brenner, Robert, xx, 279–80

Bubonic plague, 122, 139

Buddhism, 140–43; and the cult of Peng Pai, 186, 225–26; and the Haifeng Soviet, 257–58. *See also* Religion

Butterfield Swire and Company, 99–107 *passim*

Cai Suping, 155, 177

Cai Tenghui, 239, 262

Canton. *See* Guangzhou

Capitalism, 94–95

Chang fa dang. *See* Long Hair Party

Chan Lim-pak, 201

Charismatic cults. *See* Cults

Chen Duxiu: and May Fourth Movement, 156–57; Peng Pai and, 157, 165–66; ideas of compared with Japanese radicals, 159–60; organizes Socialist Youth Corps, 165–66; deposed as leader of Chinese Communist Party, 251. *See also* Chinese Communist Party

Chen Jiongming: and industrialization in Haifeng, 116, 126; political views of, 124, 125, 127–28, 163–64, 169; leader of reform in Haifeng, 124–27; family background of, 125; and urban reformist elite, 126; in the 1911 Revolution, 134, 136, 137, 138–39; family of benefits from 1911 Revolution, 146; and Peng Pai, 157, 195; and Sun Yat-sen, 162; and Merchant Volunteer Corps, 201;

Index

Cults: Peter Worsley on, 186–87; Karl Marx on, 287–88. *See also* Peng Pai, cult of

Dai Jitao, 213
Dai Kexiong, 238, 243, 248, 249
Daoism, 258. *See also* Baling sect; Religion
Dearth: and food riots, 76–86 *passim*
December 28 Incident, 267–68
Demesne, 10–12. *See also* Pang Shangpeng; Serfdom; Serfs
Deng Zhongxia, 219
Dianpu. *See* Serfs
"Dictatorship of Workers and Peasants," 243–45

Eastern Expeditions, 200–207
East River Committee. *See* Chinese Communist Party
East River region: described, 123
Education, 163–64. *See also* Students
Elite, urban reformist. *See* Urban reformist elite
Emperors. *See* Qing dynasty
Estates, 4–5, 9–15 *passim*. *See also* Land tenure relations; Serfdom; Serfs; Servility; Tenants

Famine, 27, 81–82, 190; relief, 78–86, 204–5. *See also* Dearth; Food riots; Haifeng county
Feuds: lineages and, 42–43, 61–62, 62–63, 65, 66, 68, 176, 303n25, 303n27; prevalence of, 72; analyzed, 72–75, 260; lineage use of Christianity in, 98–99; in Lufeng county, 264–66. *See also* Class conflict; Red and Black Flags
Fixed rents, 91–92. *See also* Land tenure relations; Tenancy
Folk religion. *See* Baling sect; Buddhism; Daoism; Religion
Food riots, 76–86 *passim*, 260, 304n9. *See also* Class conflict; Famine, relief; Moral economy of the peasant

Gan Naiguang, 197, 220
Ganqing, 93
Genovese, Eugene: on paternalism, 93
Gentry: killed by peasant rebels, 28; punishment of tenants by, 42; and local festivals, 57–59; and bandit suppression, 122–23; and local defense, 131; in 1911 Revolution, 136. *See also* Landlords
Gongping, 28, 101, 106, 242, 243, 277
Gramsci, Antonio, 230
Granaries, 78–79, 84–85
Guangdong province: serfdom in, 5; peasant uprisings in, 17; economy of, 47–48, 107–8; feuds in, 72; lineage land in, 87; bandits in, 121–24; politics in, 124–25; 1911 Revolution in, 133–39 *passim*; peasant unions in, 187, 196, 199–200, 208, 214, 221, 222, 224–25; possibility for rural revolution in, 223; White Terror in, 234; inter-militarist battles in, 245
Guangdong Provincial Peasant Union, 187, 220
Guangdong Regional Committee. *See* Chinese Communist Party
Guangzhou: peasant uprisings around, 17; imports of rice into, 47–48; 1911 Revolution in, 128, 133–39 *passim*; politics in, 195–201; and peasant unions, 196; Guomindang in, 196–202 *passim*; workers' movement in, 231–32
Guerrilla warfare, 240, 242
Guomindang: alliance with Chinese Communist Party of, 194; peasant movement of, 195–96, 196–97, 212–13, 214, 215, 220–21; army of, 196, 201–2, 237–38, 276–78; Peasant Department of, 197–98, 202; Peng Pai and, 198; and conflict with the Merchant Volunteer Corps, 200–202;

Index

Guomindang *(continued)*: mounts
Eastern Expeditions, 200–206 *passim*; receives assistance from peasants in Eastern Expeditions, 203,
207; peasant perceptions of, 211;
split between Left and Right in 212,
232; Left-wing of, 214, 232–33;
Right-wing of, 214, 231–32; alliance with Chinese Communist
Party threatened, 220
Guomindang Weekly, 213

Haifeng county: political affairs in,
124–25, 127, 133, 143, 145, 162–73
passim, 170–71; urban reformist elite
in, 126; Triad society in, 130–31;
1911 Revolution in, 133, 140–43;
May Fourth Movement in, 158–59;
student politics in, 162–74 *passim*;
excluded from plans to organize
peasant unions in, 200; in the Eastern Expeditions, 203–7; controlled
by peasant unions in 1926, 207–12;
as "Little Moscow," 212; as model
for the revolution, 212, 230; es-
capes White Terror, 234–35; first
uprising in, 234–37; occupied by
Guomindang troops, 237–38; second uprising in, 243–44; Communist armies retreat to, 246; establishment of soviet, 249; falls to
Guomindang army, 277. *See also*
Chen Jiongming; Haifeng Peasant
Union; Haifeng Soviet; 1911 Revolution; Peng Pai; Urban reformist
elite
—socioeconomic conditions in, 112–
13, 116–17, 270–72; land tenure relations, 5, 23, 109, 88–94 *passim*,
144–49 *passim*; physical environment, 19–22, 27, 47, 124; the Ming-
Qing transition and, 19–31; taxation, 22; population, 22–23, 25, 60;
famine and famine relief, 27, 76–
78, 79, 84, 85, 86; agriculture, 49–
53, 101–2, 106, 107–8, 271–72;

handicrafts, 52, 113–18; marketing
systems, 52–55 *passim*; exports, 53,
90; lineages, 61–66, 88, 149, 176;
Red and Black Flag conflict, 66–72;
compared with Huaibei, 73–75, 289;
food riots, 76–77; rural class conflict and, 96; Christianity, 97–99,
142–43; steamship service established, 101; inflation, 111–13; textile industry, 113–18; effect of imperialism on, 118–20; and banditry,
121–24; and urban reformist elite,
126; and Triad society, 130–31; education, 155–57. *See also* Agrarian
economy; Feuds; Gongping; Imperialism; Land tenure relations;
Lineages; Lin lineage of Meilong;
Meilong; Red and Black Flags; Sugar
cane
Haifeng Middle School, 155, 156
Haifeng "peasant movement"; interpretations of, xv–xvi, 191–93
Haifeng Peasant Union: early activities of, 175–77, 182, 184, 189;
membership and growth of, 175–
77, 179–80, 182, 187–88, 208; established, 179; goals of, 182; structure of, 182; reorganized into
Guangdong Provincial Peasant
Union, 187; suppression of, 190,
195, 206, 316n74; Chen Jiongming
supports reestablishment of, 195;
control of county government by,
210; suppression of, compared with
12 April coup, 233–34. *See also* Peng
Pai
Haifeng Reconstruction Committee,
239, 277–78
Haifeng Representative Assembly,
250, 255–58 *passim*; second, 273
Haifeng Soviet: origins of, xvi; interpretations of, xxv; establishment of,
249–50; land revolution in, 249–50,
253–58; revolution and, 256, 271;
executions in, 259–60; enemies of,
262–68 *passim*, 275–78; political

330

Index

problems in, 268–70, 274–75; economic problems of, 270–72, 273–74; possible coup in, 273; reorganization of, 273–75; suppression of, 275–78. *See also* Land revolution; Peng Pai

Haifeng Student Association, 164

Handicraft industries, 302*n8*; types of in Haifeng, 52; sugar cane refining, 102–4; textiles, 113–16

He lineage of Jiesheng, 64

He Long, 246

Hofheinz, Roy Jr., xvi, 119, 192

Hong Kong-Guangzhou Strike and Boycott, 231

Huaibei: Haifeng compared to, 73–75, 289

Huangbu Military Academy, 199, 202

Hu Hanmin, 136, 138, 145

Huizhou prefecture, 123, 134

Imperialism: and revolution, xxi; and rural class relations, xxii, 105–11; 119–20, 283–84; and the moral economy of the peasant, 95; Arrow War, 96; Opium War, 96; missionaries and, 96–99; impact on Haifeng county of, 119; Liao Zhongkai on, 197; Dai Jitao on, 213

Inflation, 111–13

Jardine, Matheson and Company, 105, 114; and opium, 99; and steamship transportation, 99–100; role in the sugar market of, 100–107

Jiang Jieshi, 230; in Eastern Expeditions, 203; and 20 March 1926 coup, 210; Peng Pai on, 222; and 12 April 1927 coup, 232

Jiesheng, 248–49

Kensetsusha Domei (Builders' League), 159–62

Kim San, 253

Kwangtung. *See* Guangdong province

Land deeds: burned by peasants, 257

Landlordism: development during Qing dynasty of, 40, 43, 88–89, 90–91; peasant economy and, 41; and corporal punishment of tenants, 42; in Ming and Qing dynasties, compared, 88–89; changes after 1911 Revolution in, 144–51; urban reformist elite and, 145; reestablished after Haifeng Soviet, 277. *See also* Landlords; Land tenure relations; Tenancy; Tenants

Landlords: and Ming estates, 6–10 *passim*; punishment of tenants by, 8, 43, 147; urbanization of, 17; tenant conflict with, 23–26, 92–94, 150–51, 176–77, 188, 209–10, 224–25, 237, 239–40, 241–42, 244, 247–48, 260, 261, 262–63; power of attacked by Qing state, 33–34, 36–37; sharecropping disliked by, 111; "newly arisen," 144–47; benefit from 1911 Revolution, 147; rent collection methods of, 147–48, 153; organize "Society for Maintaining Grain Production," 184; flee Haifeng, 209, 243, 247; return to Haifeng, 238, 239; killed by peasants, 244, 259, 261–62; and overthrow of Haifeng Soviet, 262–63. *See also* Class conflict; Estates, Gentry; Landlordism; Land tenure relations; Serfs; Tenancy; Tenants; Zhu Mo Affair

Land reclamation, 25, 32, 33, 35, 37, 300*n28*

Land revolution: and peasants, 211, 236, 261; Chinese Communist Party on, 218 235–36, 241; preparations in soviet for, 249–50, 255–56; Peng Pai on, 250, 323*n42*, 324*n50*; and socialist revolution, 253–54; carried out, 253–58; Chinese Communist Party experience with, 254–55, 323*n49*; resistance in Lufeng county to, 272

Index

Land tenure relations: during Ming dynasty, 4–15, 25–26; rent resistance and, 26, 92–94, 150–51, 176–77, 188; during early Qing, 32–40; peasant security in, 33–43 *passim*, 88, 90, 92–93, 109–11, 147, 148, 188; smallholding becomes norm of, 33–43 *passim*; and land reclamation, 37; permanent tenure, 37–38, 39, 40, 44, 88–89, 90, 91, 109–10, 147–48, 183–84, 300n32; peasant rights and, 88, 90, 92–93, 188; sharecropping and, 91–92, 111; contractual leases, 109–10 147–48; affected by imperialism, 109–11; during late Qing dynasty, 109–11; oral (*koutou*) leases, 110, 148; during the Republic, 144–51, 188–89, 209–10; altered by landlords, 147; during the Haifeng Soviet, 253–58. *See also* Class conflict; Haifeng county; Landlordism; Landlords; Tenancy; Tenants; Serfdom
Lepers, 257
Liao Zhongkai, 197, 200
Li Dazhao, 157
Li Guochen, 157
Li Jiming, 212
Li Jishen, 234, 245, 247, 262, 276–77
Li Laogong, 179, 209
Lin Daowen, 177, 235, 237, 243, 244, 257
Lineages: feuds between, 42–43, 61–62, 62–63, 65, 66, 68, 72–75, 98–99, 176, 260, 264–66, 303n25, 303n27; and rural social conflict, 61–66, 68, 283; and marketing systems, 64, compared with Red and Black Flags, 71; social composition of, 72; and land tenure relations, 87–88, 149; and the 1911 Revolution, 121; disintegration of, 149–50; and Haifeng Soviet, 244, 263. *See also* Lin lineage of Meilong
Lin lineage of Meilong: controls Meilong, 64; origins of, 64, 90; member

of opens textile mill, 117; and 1911 Revolution, 125–26, 141–43; and the urban reformist elite, 125–26, 144; and local self-defense, 131; as landlords, 141, 177, 248; and the Baling sect, 141–42; members of convert to Catholicism, 142; suppresses Baling sect, 143; triples rental income, 148; and Haifeng Soviet, 259, 262. *See also* Lineages; Meilong
Lin Tieshi, 157, 278
"Little Moscow": Haifeng county as, 212
Liu Gancai, 156
Li Zhendao, 157, 172, 313n15
Li Zicheng, 17
Long Hair Party, 238, 263
Lu-an Daily News: established, 163; Peng Pai attacked by, 172–73; press expropriated from, 244
Lu-an Normal School, 156, 158–59
Lu Chuyong, 177, 190
Lufeng county: created, 22; population of, 60; lineage feuds in, 62, 66, 98–99, 150, 264–66; Red and Black Flag conflict in, 66–72; famine relief in, 82–83; tax resistance in, 86–87; missionaries in, 98–99; schools in, 156; peasant unions in, 263; compared with Haifeng county, 263, 266–67; and Haifeng Soviet, 263–66; land revolution resisted in, 272
Luo Qiyuan, 216, 219, 220
Luxemburg, Rosa, 254

Manchus, 31–32. *See also* Qing dynasty
Manorial estates. *See* Estates
Manure investment system. *See* Land tenure relations, permanent tenure
Mao Zedong: leads Peasant Movement Training Institute students to Haifeng, 211–12; selected to head Chinese Communist Party Peasant Department, 218; "Report on the

Index

Peng Hanyuan: writes for *New Haifeng*, 169; elected to county assembly, 170; helps Peng Pai, 177; leads Haifeng underground, 203; replaced as county magistrate, 210; leads uprising in Haifeng, 235

Peng Pai: and explanations of Haifeng peasant movement, xvi; as owner of textile mill, 117; teaches in Peasant Movement Training Institute, 198–99; and Eastern Expeditions, 202–4; oratory powers of, 208; executed, 279; interpretations of, 282, 285–89, 324*n*55; compared with Mao Zedong, 287

—and peasant organizing: first meets peasants, 152–54; learns from peasants, 154; family opposition to, 154, 173–74, 175; introduced to peasant organizing, 161; decides to organize peasants, 173; goes into villages, 175; returns land to peasants, 175; writes folk songs, 181, 212; and the Zhu Mo Affair, 184–85; view of peasants and, 184–85; seeks support from Guomindang, 195; becomes secretary of Guomindang Peasant Department, 197–98; and Peasant Movement Training Institute, 198–99; around Guangzhou, 200; in Haifeng 207–8; in Hua county, 221–22; in Puning county, 225. *See also* Haifeng Peasant Union; Peasant unions

—and the Chinese Communist Party: joins Socialist Youth Corps, 165, 170, 171; elected to Guangdong Regional Committee executive committee; 198; joins the party, 198; advocates party leadership of peasants, 215; opposes party policy, 217, 221; debates Luo Qiyuan on party peasant policy, 219; opposes party policy on the Northern Expedition, 219; in Wuhan, 227; 321*n*11; in the Autumn Harvest Uprising, 246;

elected to Central Committee, 279. *See also* Chinese Communist Party

—and the Haifeng Soviet; establishment of, 250; discusses land revolution, 250, 324*n*50; as leader of, 252–53; and lineage feuds, 265–66; leads soviet forces to Puning, 267, 272, criticized during, 269; defeat of, 278

—cult of, 193, 248; interpretation of, xxiv, 228–29, 286–89; and peasant grievances, 184–85, 187, 224, 227–28, 261; and peasant perceptions of Peng Pai, 185–86, 224–25; charisma and, 186; and peasant collective action, 186–87, 226–27, 228, 280; and class conflict, 187; and Peasant unions, 207–8; and the Chinese Communist Party, 224; flourishes, 226; and political legitimacy, 253. *See also* Collective action; Haifeng Peasant Union; Moral economy of the peasant; Peasants; Peasant unions; Religion

—in Haifeng county politics: writes for *New Haifeng*, 160; enters county politics, 162, 170; and Haifeng's urban reformist elite, 163–64, 169–70; as education commissioner, 164, 169; and views of society, 164–70; leads May Day parade, 171; resigns as education commissioner, 171–72; publishes *Chixin Weekly*, 172; splits with urban reformist elite, 172; responds to Zhu Mo Affair, 184–85; leads peasant demonstration, 188; nearly arrested, 190; seeks aid from Chen Jiongming, 194–95; reorganizes Haifeng Peasant Union

—views of: on Chen Jiongming, 139; on rent reduction, 153–54, 183; influenced by nationalism, 159; influenced in Japan, 159; influenced by Russian Populism, 160–61; influenced by socialist ideas, 161, 162, 165–68; on society, 164–70 *passim;*

Index

257–58. *See also* Baling sect; Buddhism; Peng Pai, cult of

Rent books, 257

Rent reduction: claimed as peasant right, 148; Peng Pai on, 153–54, 182; Chen Jiongming supports idea of, 195; pushed by peasants, 209; supported by Chinese Communist Party, 218; Guomindang policy toward, 239; demanded by peasants, 241–42. *See also* Landlords; Land tenure relations; Moral economy of the peasant; Rent resistance; Tenants

Rent resistance, 26, 92–94, 150–51, 176–77, 188. *See also* Landlords; Land tenure relations; Moral economy of the peasant; Tenants

Revolution: theories of, xi, xv, xix, xxii; Peng Pai on, 166–68, 172, 221, 222–23, 226; division between town and countryside and, 223; costs of, 260; in Haifeng and Huaibei compared, 289

Rice: price of, 9, 12, 24, 77, 79, 81–82, 89, 112; demand for, 48, 81–82; exports of prohibited, 48, 79, 82, 83, 204; double-cropping of, 49–50; planting techniques of, 50; varieties in Haifeng of, 50; and food riots, 79; stealing of, 80; price of set by crowds, 80–81, 137; market for regulated, 82, 83, 84. *See also* Agrarian economy; Haifeng county, socioeconomic conditions in

Rice riots. *See* Food riots

Ruan Shipeng, 37–38

Ruan Xiaoxian, 202, 219, 220

Rural militia: and bandits, 122–23, 310n19; Zou Lu on, 214; attacks on peasant unions of, 214, 221; problem of, 215, 220–21; Chinese Communist Party on, 220; and the Chinese Communist Party, 238; driven from countryside, 243

Salt smuggling, 28–29, 31, 98, 129

Schools: after the 1911 Revolution, 155–62 *passim*, 163–64. *See also* Students

Self-government, 162–63, 169–70, 205

Serfdom: development in Ming dynasty of, 4; and estates, 4–5; tenants and, 13, 14–15; destruction of, 15–16, 17–18, 32–33; and the Qing state, 41–45 *passim*. *See also* Estates; Land tenure relations; Peasant uprisings; Serfs; Servitude

Serfs, 5, 6, 9–12, 13, 27, 296n4. *See also* Serfdom; Tenants

Servility: as a condition of tenancy, 13; customary conditions of, 13, 42–43; in early Qing times, 41–42. *See also* Estates; Serfdom; Serfs; Tenancy

Servitude: bonds of, 7, 8, 13, 16–17; causes of, 7–8; increase in, 9. *See also* Estates; Land tenure relations; Peasant uprisings; Serfs; Servility; Tenancy

Shantou, 101, 104, 206

Shanwei, 47, 50, 51; exports from, 53; described, 53–54; hospital in, 99; troops in, 145; boycott organized in, 159; landlords flee to, 247; lepers in, 258

Sharecropping, 91–92, 111. *See also* Land tenure relations

Shinjinkai (New Man Society), 159–62

Skinner, G. William, xii, 56

Skocpol, Theda, 282

Social banditry, 29

Society for the Study of Socialism, 162, 164, 179

Soviet: urged by Stalin for China, 251

Steamships, 101, 119

Students, 133, 155–62 *passim*

Subsoil-topsoil rights. *See* Land tenure relations, permanent tenure

Su Cheng, 28

337

DESIGNED BY BRUCE GORE
COMPOSED BY IMPRESSIONS, INC., MADISON, WISCONSIN
MANUFACTURED BY CUSHING-MALLOY, INC.
ANN ARBOR, MICHIGAN
TEXT AND DISPLAY LINES ARE SET IN PALATINO

Library of Congress Cataloging in Publication Data
Marks, Robert B., 1949–
Rural revolution in South China.
Includes bibliographical references and index.
1. Hai-feng hsien (China)—Rural conditions.
2. Peasantry—China—Hai-feng hsien. 3. Hai-feng hsien
(China)—History. I. Title.
HN740.H34M37 1984   305.5′63′095127   83-16980
ISBN 0-299-09530-4